Medical Metaverse for Digital Healthcare

Scrivener Publishing
100 Cummings Center, Suite 541J
Beverly, MA 01915-6106

Industry 5.0 Transformation Applications

Series Editors: Dr. S. Balamurugan (sbnbala@gmail.com) and Dr. Sheng-Lung Peng

The increase in technological advancements in the areas of artificial intelligence (AI), machine learning (ML) and data analytics has led to the next industrial revolution "Industry 5.0". The transformation to Industry 5.0 collaborates human intelligence with machines to customize efficient solutions. This book series aims to cover various subjects under promising application areas of Industry 5.0 such as smart manufacturing, green ecology, digital medicine, supply chain management, smart textiles, intelligent traffic, innovation ecosystem, cloud manufacturing, digital marketing, real-time productivity optimization, augmented reality and virtual reality, smart energy consumption, predictive maintenance, smart additive manufacturing, hyper customization and cyber physical cognitive systems.

Publishers at Scrivener
Martin Scrivener (martin@scrivenerpublishing.com)
Phillip Carmical (pcarmical@scrivenerpublishing.com)

Medical Metaverse for Digital Healthcare

Technologies, Applications, and Challenges

Edited by

R. Nidhya

Department of Computer Science & Engineering, Madanapalle Institute of Technology & Science (MITS) Deemed to be University, Madanapalle, Andhra Pradesh, India

D. Pavithra

Department of Information Technology, Dr. NGP Institute of Technology, Coimbatore, Tamil Nadu, India

S. Balamurugan

R&D, Intelligent Research Consultancy Services, Coimbatore, Tamilnadu, India

A. Dinesh Kumar

Department of Computer Science and Engineering, Koneru Lakshmaiah Education Foundation, Guntur, Andhra Pradesh, India

and

Sheng-Lung Peng

Department of Creative Technologies and Product Design, National Taipei University of Business, Taiwan

Scrivener Publishing

WILEY

This edition first published 2026 by John Wiley & Sons, Inc., 111 River Street, Hoboken, NJ 07030, USA and Scrivener Publishing LLC, 100 Cummings Center, Suite 541J, Beverly, MA 01915, USA

For more information about Scrivener publications please visit www.scrivenerpublishing.com.

Wiley Global Headquarters
111 River Street, Hoboken, NJ 07030, USA

For details of our global editorial offices, customer services, and more information about Wiley products visit us at www.wiley.com.

The manufacturer's authorized representative according to the EU General Product Safety Regulation is Wiley-VCH GmbH, Boschstr. 12, 69469 Weinheim, Germany, e-mail: Product_Safety@wiley.com.

Library of Congress Cataloging-in-Publication Data

ISBN 978-1-394-40847-4

Cover image: Generated with AI using Adobe Firefly
Cover design by Russell Richardson

Set in size of 11pt and Minion Pro by Manila Typesetting Company, Makati, Philippines

Printed in the USA

10 9 8 7 6 5 4 3 2 1

The editorial team extends heartfelt dedication to their families—parents, spouses, and children—for their boundless support throughout the creation of this work. Additionally, the editors express sincere gratitude to their colleagues at their esteemed institution for their unwavering love, blessings, and encouragement. Finally, this book is respectfully dedicated to the entire research community, whose collective efforts continue to enrich our understanding of the world.

Contents

Preface

The rapid evolution of digital technologies is transforming every aspect of human life, and healthcare is no exception. Originally rooted in entertainment and social interaction, the concept of the Metaverse is now permeating the medical field, giving rise to what we call the Medical Metaverse. This emerging paradigm has the potential to revolutionize healthcare delivery by providing immersive, patient-centered experiences, enhanced training for healthcare professionals, and innovative applications in telemedicine that were once unimaginable.

This book explores the foundational technologies driving the Medical Metaverse—including virtual reality (VR), augmented reality (AR), artificial intelligence (AI), blockchain, and 5G. It illustrates how these tools are being leveraged to develop immersive diagnostic environments, enable virtual consultations, power surgical simulations, and personalize treatment strategies.

While the potential is tremendous, realizing the Medical Metaverse also brings complex challenges. Issues such as data privacy, security, regulatory compliance, and the digital divide must be addressed to ensure these technologies are used responsibly and equitably. This book examines these concerns in depth and proposes strategies for overcoming them.

Intended for healthcare professionals, technologists, researchers, policymakers, and administrators, this book offers a comprehensive overview of the current landscape and future direction of the Medical Metaverse. It aims to provide actionable insights to guide the integration of immersive technologies into mainstream healthcare, ultimately improving outcomes and operational efficiency.

Each chapter provides a focused study:

Chapter 1: Explores a Two Stream 3D Convolutional Neural Network for anomaly detection in video surveillance, highlighting spatial-temporal analysis with an accuracy of 82.12%. Chapter 2: Introduces a deep learning model using U-Net with ResNet34 for segmenting blood vessels in fundus images, achieving 97.07% accuracy for diabetic retinopathy diagnosis.

Chapter 3: Applies machine learning to early detection of Parkinson's Disease *via* voice and behavioral data, proposing a non-invasive remote monitoring solution. Chapter 4: Describes an Extreme Learning Machine optimized with Mayfly Optimization for dental age detection, improving accuracy over manual methods.

Chapter 5: Presents an Ensemble-Stacked Hybrid Classifier to address imbalanced data in stroke prediction, improving minority class recall. Chapter 6: Uses boosting ensemble methods to improve classification of gene variant interpretations from ClinVar data, achieving near 99% accuracy.

Chapter 7: Proposes a blockchain-based AI security model for managing electronic health records, emphasizing data ownership and integrity. Chapter 8: Reviews the use of VR, AR, and MR in medical education, surgical planning, and patient engagement, while noting current limitations.

Chapter 9: Introduces a novel convolutional network for lung cancer prediction, achieving high accuracy with minimal annotation. Chapter 10: Details a Homological Segmentation model for early CKD prediction using deep learning, with exceptional 99.4% accuracy.

Chapter 11: Explores Transformer models and Vision Transformers for autism diagnosis from brain imaging, including ethical considerations. Chapter 12: Proposes a lightweight, energy-efficient IoMT security framework using M-Simon cryptography and a firewall layer.

Chapter 13: Combines modified distance metrics and clustering with deep learning for pancreatic tumor detection *via* MRI. Chapter 14: Enhances brain tumor classification with Aquila-based optimization of deep learning models like DenseNet and ResNet.

Chapter 15: Develops MedPredict, a biomedical language model outperforming BERT/GPT-3 on specialized corpora. Chapter 16: Describes the design and optimization of hybrid fixed-wing UAVs for efficient medical supply delivery.

Chapter 17: Applies an optimized U-Net architecture for precise nerve segmentation in MRI/ultrasound imaging. Chapter 18: Examines the role of AI in diagnosis, treatment planning, robotic surgery, and the ethical challenges it introduces.

June 2026

Acknowledgement

We offer our deepest appreciation to our institution for fostering an environment that encourages research and laid the foundation for this work. We are very grateful for the diverse group of contributors and offer special thanks to the reviewers worldwide who have diligently examined each chapter to maintain the book's high standards. Their insightful feedback has been invaluable. We sincerely thank all parties involved for their dedication and willingness to take on tasks that pushed them beyond their usual comfort zones. Finally, we thank Martin Scrivener and the team at Scrivener Publishing for their effort and guidance in bringing this book to fruition.

Part 1

TECHNOLOGIES

1

A Novel Approach for Predicting Human Anomalous Behaviors in Video through Two-Stream 3D Convolutional Neural Network

B. Prabha[1]*, J. Nagaraj[1], Thangarasan T.[2], Soubraylu Sivakumar[3], S. Velmurugan[4] and Bommy M.[2]

[1]*Department of Artificial Intelligence and Machine Learning, Panimalar Engineering College, Chennai, Tamil Nadu, India*
[2]*Department of Computer Science & Engineering, Madanapalle Institute of Technology & Science, Madanapalle, Andhra Pradesh, India*
[3]*Computing Technologies, School of Computing, SRM Institute of Science and Technology, Kattankulathur, Chennai, Tamil Nadu, India*
[4]*Department of Information Technology, R.M.D. Engineering College, Kavaraipettai Chennai, Tamil Nadu, India*

Abstract

The detection and localization of human activities in automated video surveillance are a complex task that has garnered significant research interest in recent years. This area poses numerous challenges and remains a focal point of study for researchers. The proposed video surveillance system utilizes a dual-stream approach to monitor human behavior, examining patterns of typical and atypical activities. It triggers alerts when unusual behavior is detected. Constructing a two-stream three-dimensional (3D) convolutional neural network (CNN) for abnormal activity recognition involves combining spatial and temporal data streams to capture complex relationships in both domains. The proposed two-stream method applied the two-stream architecture, which used the 3D CNNs to predict abnormal behavior by processing the video. Hence, it improves the strange activity prediction performance. Experimental results confirm the effectiveness of the proposed method in detecting various abnormal behaviors, including arrest, assault, abuse,

**Corresponding author*: jemi.prabha@gmail.com

R. Nidhya, D. Pavithra, S. Balamurugan, A. Dinesh Kumar and Sheng-Lung Peng (eds.) Medical Metaverse for Digital Healthcare: Technologies, Applications, and Challenges, (3–26) © 2026 Scrivener Publishing LLC

Arson, road accident, explosion, burglary, fighting, robbery, stealing, shooting, vandalism, and shoplifting. The approach achieved an accuracy rate of 82.12%.

Keywords: Two-stream 3D CNN, abnormal behavior detection, intelligent video analytics

1.1 Introduction

In recent years, intelligent video analytics (IVA) [1] has received significant research attention in computer vision due to increased security needs. The critical goal of IVA is to identify event patterns of human behavior through automating video analysis and security alerts, thus reducing the need for manual power and its associated costs. IVA provides an efficient means for different tasks such as object detection and classification, motion tracking, human activity recognition, behavior understanding and suspicious/abnormal event detection in public areas (airports, railway stations, bus stands, banks, and shopping malls), military installations, smart homes, etc. In recent years, machine learning and computer vision communities have dramatically increased their interest in detecting human anomalous behaviors. Research on human anomaly detection could lead to many critical applications such as transportation, public safety, crowded scenes [29], health care, and defense, and also, with the increase of criminal activities, the vision-based human anomalous activity detection becomes most important for any security system. Some examples of abnormal movements in different contexts of human behaviors are shown in Figure 1.1.

Due to illumination changes, occlusions, shadows, noises in the video, and dynamic changes in the scene, abnormal activity detection is a complex and significant task that must be handled well for a robust anomaly

Figure 1.1 Different types of human anomalous activities in UCSD, UMN, and PETS dataset in various contexts.

detection system. Hence, accurate models are required to detect anomalies in the video. In Lu *et al.* [2], the proposed abnormal event detection in video sequences focuses on achieving real-time performance at a high frame rate (150 frames per second [fps]) using MATLAB. The primary contribution is developing a system capable of detecting abnormal video events at an impressive frame rate of 150 fps. Achieving real-time processing is a significant advantage for applications requiring timely anomaly identification. The authors implement their approach using MATLAB, making it accessible to many researchers and practitioners familiar with the MATLAB environment. This platform choice may influence the proposed method's scalability and efficiency. This approach focuses solely on a specific dataset or scenario. It needs to provide insights into the generalization capabilities of the proposed system, which may limit its practical applicability across diverse real-world situations. Computational efficiency may be a concern depending on the proposed method's complexity and the MATLAB environment's capabilities. Although high frame rates are impressive, it is important to think about how the approach can scale to deal with bigger datasets or more complex scenarios. The difficult problem of detecting anomalous video events online using dynamic sparse coding is tackled by Zhao *et al.* [3]. Building a system that can identify and classify suspicious occurrences in live video feeds is the main focus.

The focus on online detection implies that the proposed system operates in a real-time setting, allowing for the immediate identification of unusual events as they occur. This is crucial for applications in surveillance and security, where prompt responses are essential. The use of sparse coding suggests an emphasis on concisely representing video data and capturing salient features related to abnormal events. Sparse representations can contribute to the efficient storage and processing of video information. The proposed dynamic light coding method must address the variability and challenges in actual surveillance or video scenarios. Sparse coding methods can be sensitive to noise in data. The paper may need to thoroughly address how the proposed dynamic light coding approach handles noisy or ambiguous video information and whether it may lead to false positives or negatives. Sparse coding techniques can be computationally intensive. The paper may inadequately address the computational complexity of the proposed method, which is essential for assessing its viability in real-time applications using dual-stream three-dimensional (3D) convolutional network. This method uses distinct spatial and temporal streams to independently acquire spatial appearance and motion data [17]. The two-stream architecture has significantly impacted later studies on action recognition. By dividing the network into spatial and temporal streams, the model adeptly captures both spatial appearance characteristics and temporal motion attributes. This separation enables the network to understand better and represent the complex dynamics of actions in videos. The two-stream architecture demonstrated improved performance compared to earlier methods on benchmark action recognition datasets. It addressed some of the limitations of purely spatial or purely temporal models by combining both modalities, enhancing accuracy in recognizing actions in video sequences. The incorporation of optical flow as a method for capturing motion information is a significant element of the paper. Optical flow denotes the perceived motion between successive frames, augmenting the network's capacity to identify actions through temporal variations in pixel intensities. The proposed architecture was validated on the extensive UCF-Crime video dataset to illustrate its scalability and efficacy in managing varied and intricate datasets typically used in action recognition research.

This study presents a dual-stream 3D convolutional neural network (CNN) methodology for the detection of anomalous events. Our contributions include the following: Section 1.2 examines the pertinent literature regarding the proposed system. Section 1.3 delineates the proposed algorithm for identifying anomalous events in surveillance videos, with the objective of improving both interpretability and detection efficacy. This enhancement is especially vital in the realm of video surveillance. The suggested two-stream architecture emphasizes the acquisition of video appearance attributes through a spatial model and utilizes a temporal autoencoder to capture regular patterns within the video. This method is particularly beneficial for modeling spatial attributes despite having few training samples. Section 1.4 presents experimental results by visualizing the feature maps of convolutional layers and generating heatmaps, thereby elucidating the features acquired at the object level. This visualization facilitates the detection of anomalous objects, enabling users to discern essential characteristics for surveillance activities. Furthermore, it illustrates the significance of features and facilitates the replication of decisions rendered by the black-box model. Section 1.5 concludes the proposed method, outlining its key features and potential future enhancements.

1.2 Related Works

Utilizing interpretable deep learning techniques for anomaly detection represents a burgeoning research avenue currently developing. This extension encompasses different modeling aspects. Li *et al.* [4] focused on abnormal behavior detection using sparse reconstruction analysis of trajectory data.

Sparse reconstruction techniques, often associated with compressive sensing, involve representing data sparsely, and they have been applied in various fields, including computer vision and anomaly detection. Many studies integrate sparse reconstruction techniques with machine-learning approaches for improved anomaly detection. This involves learning standard behavior patterns from data and using sparse reconstruction for anomaly identification. Sabokrou [5] addresses the task of anomaly detection in videos using one-class 3D CNNs. Anomaly detection in videos is a crucial task for various applications, including surveillance and security. Traditional methods often struggle with complex and dynamic scenes, prompting the exploration of deep learning approaches. This one-class learning approach implies that the model is trained only on regular instances, making it suitable for scenarios where abnormal examples are scarce or hard to obtain during training. In addition to the 3D CNN by using 3D CNNs, the model is designed to capture both spatial and temporal features inherent in video data. This allows for a more comprehensive understanding of spatiotemporal patterns, enhancing the model's ability to detect anomalies. In Venugopalan [6], the research focuses on developing methods to automatically identify events or behaviors in videos that deviate from standard patterns. These abnormal events can include activities that pose potential threats or anomalies in a given context. The proposed method addresses the task of abnormal event detection in videos, which is crucial for applications such as surveillance and security. The use of spatiotemporal autoencoders suggests an emphasis on automatically capturing both spatial and temporal patterns in the data.

Autoencoders are neural network architectures intended for unsupervised learning. The system comprises an encoder and a decoder, and the training procedure entails reconstructing the input data. In the realm of anomalous event detection, autoencoders can be modified to identify and reconstruct typical patterns in videos. The importance resides in utilizing a spatiotemporal autoencoder for the detection of anomalous events. Utilizing deep learning methodologies, the model is anticipated to acquire distinguishing features that define commonplace occurrences, enabling it to recognize anomalies suggestive of irregularity. Simonyan and Zisserman [7] concentrated on two-stream convolutional networks for the recognition of actions in videos. This approach seeks to utilize spatial and temporal data to enhance the precision of human action recognition in video sequences. This paper proposes a two-stream architecture that utilizes distinct streams for spatial and temporal information. One-stream analyses static frames to extract spatial features, whereas the other examines optical flow to capture temporal dynamics. Optical flow denotes the perceived movement of objects within a series of images. It serves as a significant source of temporal information in videos and is used to capture the dynamic elements of actions. The application of deep learning methodologies, especially CNNs, to video analysis has emerged as a prominent research domain. Deep architectures can autonomously extract features from raw pixel data, diminishing the necessity for manually crafted features. The proposed two-stream convolutional networks, which specifically address the spatial and temporal aspects of video data, are crucial for action recognition. This methodology has subsequently gained prominence in the domain of video analysis. A different approach to unsupervised anomaly detection utilizes generative adversarial networks (GANs) as a mechanism to facilitate the identification of markers that signify anomalous patterns in data.

GANs are a type of neural network architecture consisting of a generator and a discriminator. They are often used in generative tasks but can also be adapted for unsupervised tasks such as anomaly detection. The generator creates data, and the discriminator distinguishes between actual and generated samples. Marker discovery refers to identifying specific features or patterns in the data that indicate anomalies. These markers serve as cues for detecting abnormal instances. The use of GANs in unsupervised anomaly detection suggests an innovative approach to leveraging generative models for guiding the discovery of markers associated with anomalies. This may provide a more nuanced and data-driven approach to anomaly detection compared to traditional methods. Proposed GANs introduce a novel architecture or methodology that combines GANs with marker discovery techniques for unsupervised anomaly detection. In addition, the authors may have evaluated their approach on benchmark datasets commonly used for anomaly detection to showcase their method's effectiveness. Akcay [8] focuses on the task of one-class classification using deep learning techniques. An anomaly detection method called one-class classification trains the model only on the regular class and looks for instances that deviate from it. Data hierarchies are automatically learned by deep learning methods, especially neural networks. In one-class classification, deep learning models can capture everyday patterns. Anomaly detection uses one-class classification to find outliers or samples that deviate from training patterns. This approach introduces a novel methodology for deep one-class classification, potentially addressing challenges such as data imbalance and the high dimensionality of modern datasets. The main significant contribution to advancing the field of one-class classification, especially within the context of deep learning, is the development of deep neural network architectures and training strategies that enable effective representation learning for distinguishing normal data from outliers in the absence of negative examples. The proposed method could offer improved performance, scalability, or interpretability compared to existing approaches [9].

Inference from the survey
Using two-stream 3D CNNs for human abnormal activity detection offers several advantages, making it a popular and effective approach in computer vision and video analytics. The main enhancements of the two-stream 3D CNNs for human abnormal activity detection are listed below:

> *Spatial and temporal understanding*: Two-stream 3D CNNs leverage two separate streams: spatial and temporal information. This dual-stream architecture allows the model to capture both the static appearance of objects (spatial features) and the dynamic changes over time (temporal features). This holistic understanding is crucial for recognizing complex activities.

(i) *Improved action recognition*: Incorporating 3D CNNs enhances the model's ability to recognize video actions. Traditional 2D CNNs might struggle with capturing temporal dynamics, but the third dimension in 3D CNNs enables them to analyze the temporal evolution of activities more effectively.
(ii) *Optical flow for motion information*: Including optical flow in one of the streams enables the model to consider motion information explicitly. Optical flow captures how pixels move between consecutive frames, providing valuable insights into the temporal aspect of activities. This is particularly important for detecting abnormal behaviors involving unusual movements.
(iii) *Effective in varied environments*: Two-stream 3D CNNs are robust across diverse environments and scenarios. They can handle complex scenes with multiple objects, different lighting conditions, and various perspectives, making them suitable for real-world applications such as surveillance and security.
(iv) *Learned hierarchical representations*: Deep learning architectures such as 3D CNNs automatically learn hierarchical representations from the input data. This ability allows the model to discover intricate patterns and features relevant to human activities. The learned terms contribute to the model's capability to discern normal from abnormal behavior.

1.3 Materials and Methods

The proposed method focuses on predicting human abnormal behavior within the UCF-Crime dataset, utilizing a two-stream 3D CNN methodology. This strategy is designed to capitalize on both spatial and temporal information embedded in video data, using two distinct streams: one for spatial analysis (RGB frames) [10] and the other for temporal dynamics (optical flow). Integrating this dual-stream architecture aims to augment the model's capacity to recognize and categorize abnormal behaviors, thereby contributing to anomaly detection in surveillance contexts. The proposed system focuses on training the two-stream 3D CNN on the UCF-Crime dataset, allowing it to identify abnormal activities across diverse real-world scenarios depicted in the surveillance videos. The outcomes of the experiments and evaluations are thoroughly expounded upon in subsequent sections of this paper, offering comprehensive insights into the efficacy of the proposed approach in detecting human abnormal behavior within the UCF-Crime dataset. The overall architecture of the system is shown in Figure 1.2.

1.3.1 Preprocessing

The UCF-Crime dataset comprises an extensive compilation of 128 hours of footage, including 1900 lengthy and unedited real-world surveillance videos. It comprises 13 genuine anomalies, including abuse, arrest, arson, assault, road accident, burglary, explosion, fighting, robbery, shooting, stealing, shoplifting, and vandalism, meticulously selected for their

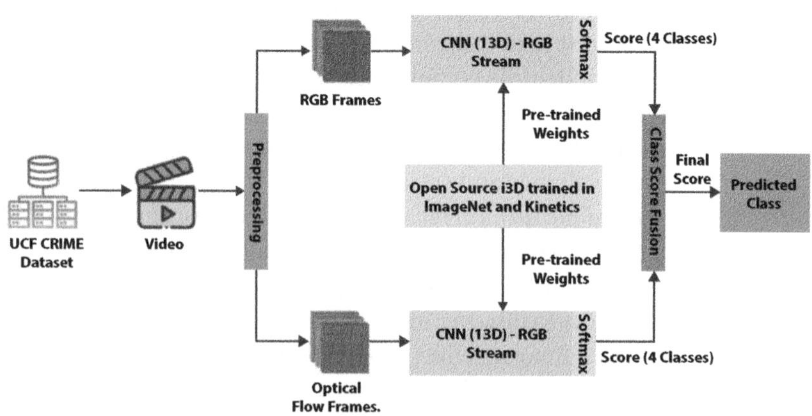

Figure 1.2 Proposed two-stream 3D CNN for anomalous behavior prediction.

substantial influence on public safety. This dataset fulfills two functions in research. First, it can be utilized for general anomaly detection by grouping all anomalies and distinguishing them from everyday activities. Second, it offers a valuable resource for the specific recognition of each of the 13 different anomalous activities. The motion CNN [11, 12] takes input data as a stack of optical flow images comprising 10 x-channel and 10 y-channel images. Consequently, the input shape is (20, 224, 224), effectively treated as a 20-channel image. To make use of pretrained weights from ImageNet on the model, it is necessary to adjust the consequences of the initial convolution layer pretrained with ImageNet, changing its dimensions from (64, 3, 7, 7) to (64, 20, 7, 7). In this approach, we apply the methodologies from the temporal segment network. We randomly chose three frames from each video within each video's mini-batch. The consensus among these frames is then determined as the video-level prediction for calculating the loss. We randomly chose 64 videos (batch size) from a pool of 9537 training videos in each mini-batch. Subsequently, we randomly picked one stacked optical flow sequence from each selected video. Both streams use identical data augmentation techniques, including random cropping.

1.3.2 Data Visualization

The UCF-Crime dataset is a unique collection of 128 hours of real-world surveillance footage. As the first dataset of its kind, it contains 1900 unedited videos depicting real-life scenarios. It includes 13 specific types of anomalies, such as abuse, arrest, arson, assault, road accidents, burglary, explosions, fighting, robbery, shooting, stealing, shoplifting, and vandalism, all selected due to their significant relevance to public safety. For data visualization, First, it helps explore general anomaly detection, where anomalies are grouped together, contrasting with everyday activities. This is essential for developing models that spot unusual behaviors in surveillance footage. Figure 1.3 contains the number of clips for UCF-Crime dataset visualized using a pie chart.

1.3.3 Baseline Approach through Support Vector Machine Classifier

The proposed method for predicting human anomalous behaviors in surveillance videos utilizing support vector machines (SVM) with the UCF-Crime dataset follows a structured process involving feature extraction, model training, and anomaly detection. The objective is to identify and differentiate between normal and abnormal activities within the video data.

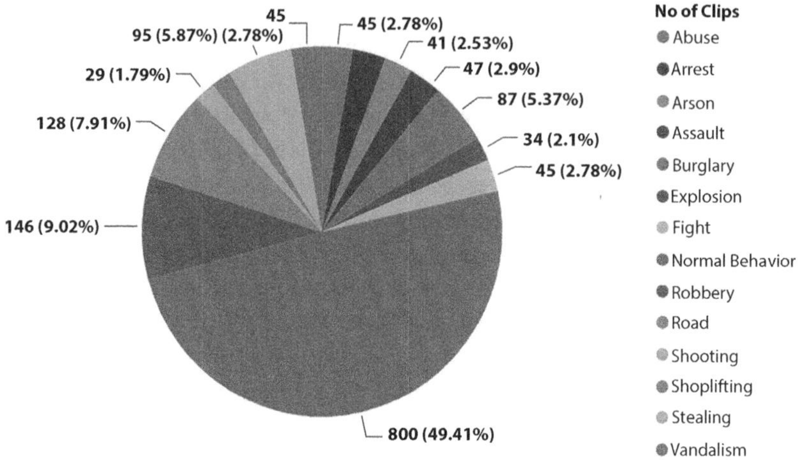

Figure 1.3 UCF-Crime dataset human behavior visualization.

The proposed strategy aims to harness the discriminative capability of SVMs in separating classes within feature space, suited explicitly for binary classification tasks like such as anomaly detection. The careful selection of features is crucial, as it influences the model's effectiveness in capturing pertinent information for distinguishing between normal and abnormal activities. The overall systematic architecture for the SVM classifier is shown in the below diagram (Figure 1.4).

The proposed method emphasizes feature extraction from video frames in the UCF-Crime dataset, wherein processing is conducted to discern key features that encapsulate the unique patterns linked to both normal and abnormal behaviors. Commonly utilized techniques include histogram of orientated gradients, local binary patterns, optical flow, and deep features derived from pretrained CNNs. The extracted features function as input for the SVM model.

The SVM is trained using labeled feature vectors from the extraction phase, with the dataset split into training and validation sets. This allows

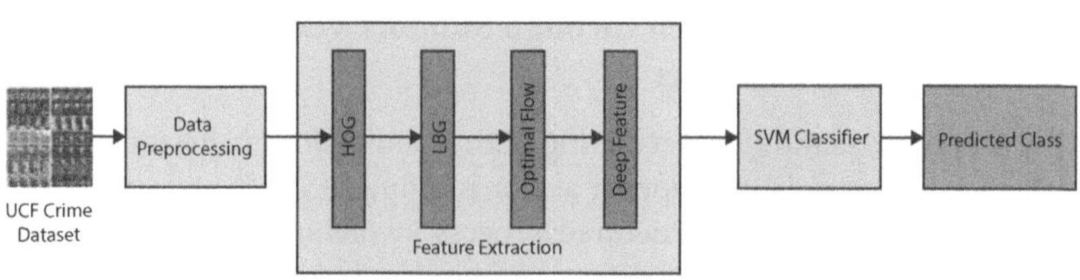

Figure 1.4 Support vector machine overall architecture for anomalous behavior prediction.

the model to learn the differences between typical and atypical behaviors. The SVM's parameters, such as kernel type and regularization, are fine-tuned to enhance its performance.

Once the SVM is trained, it is applied to new, unseen video data to detect anomalous activities. The decision function of the model assigns a score to each frame or sequence, indicating the probability of abnormality. Frames are then classified as normal or anomalous based on a predefined threshold, using these scores.

1.3.4 Proposed Architecture

The proposed work predicts human abnormal behavior within the UCF-Crime dataset, utilizing a two-stream 3D CNN methodology. This strategy is designed to capitalize on both spatial and temporal information embedded in video data, using two distinct streams—one for spatial analysis (RGB frames) and the other for temporal dynamics (optical flow) [13]. Integrating this dual-stream architecture aims to augment the model's capacity to recognize and categorize abnormal behaviors, thereby contributing to anomaly detection in surveillance contexts. The proposed method encompasses training the two-stream 3D CNN on the UCF-Crime dataset, empowering it to identify abnormal activities across diverse real-world scenarios depicted in the surveillance videos. The outcomes of the experiments and evaluations are thoroughly expounded upon in subsequent sections of this paper, offering comprehensive insights into the efficacy of the proposed approach in detecting human abnormal behavior within the UCF-Crime dataset. In studying human strange behavior in the UCF-Crime dataset, we incorporate optical flow frames [14] as a crucial element in the analysis. Optical flow is a method used to capture the movement of objects across successive frames in a video. More specifically, for each video frame within the UCF-Crime dataset, we compute optical flow frames, representing the perceived motion of pixels between consecutive frames. These frames furnish details about the direction and extent of movement in the video, enabling us to identify dynamic patterns and motion characteristics. The utilization of optical flow frames enhances the capacity to grasp temporal dynamics, such as abrupt movements or alterations in direction, which may signify abnormal behavior. Integrating this information into analysis aims to enhance the model's comprehension of the temporal aspects of human activities depicted in surveillance videos. The proposed method provides an in-depth exploration of the incorporation of optical flow frames into the analytical process, highlighting their role in enhancing the overall effectiveness of the proposed system for detecting human abnormal behavior in the UCF-Crime dataset. The proposed work is focused on identifying instances of human abnormal behavior within the UCF-Crime dataset, utilizing the inflated 3D ConvNet (i3D) CNN architecture. Specifically, its emphasis lies on the RGB stream, which processes color information through frames. The choice of the i3D model is motivated by its effectiveness in capturing both spatial and temporal features. In the context of the RGB stream, individual video frames are treated as standalone images, and the CNN processes these frames to extract spatial information. The convolutional layers analyze patterns and features within each frame, facilitating the model's comprehension of the visual context of the scene. This strategy involves leveraging the pretrained weights of the i3D model on extensive datasets, enhancing its capacity to learn intricate and hierarchical features from the UCF-Crime dataset. The RGB stream focuses on the color dynamics and visual cues in surveillance videos, enabling the model to discern abnormal behavior based on spatial characteristics. This methodology contributes to the broader realm of anomaly detection by deploying a robust neural network architecture tailored to the unique challenges presented by the UCF-Crime dataset. The results of the proposed experiments and evaluations on the application of the CNN (i3D)–RGB stream [15, 16] for detecting human abnormal behavior will be detailed in subsequent sections of this paper, offering a comprehensive insight into the methodology's efficacy in addressing the subtleties of strange behavior recognition in surveillance scenarios [18]. Selecting the appropriate architecture for video representation needs a definitive leading contender. Prominent video architectures can be classified based on kernel types (2D or 3D), input data (RGB video or optical flow), and the method of information propagation across frames long short-term memory (LSTMs or temporal feature aggregation). The i3D architecture is fundamentally an extension of Inception v1, incorporating 3D filters and pooling kernels. Inception's primary advantages are its compact model size, attained through the use of global average pooling instead of fully connected layers, rendering it memory-efficient for real-time applications such as abnormal human behavior detection [19, 20]. Furthermore, Inception presents a microarchitecture concept that functions as a fundamental unit within a CNN. The Inception module enables the simultaneous learning of convolutional layers with diverse filter sizes, thereby improving the network's ability to capture both local and abstract features.

The model combines video (RGB) and optical flow streams to enhance the detection of anomalous human behavior. Conventional two-stream approaches use RGB and visual streams to acquire spatial and temporal data, integrating this information for behavior prediction. The i3D architecture modifies the Inception module and structure into a 3D CNN by incorporating a temporal dimension, thus enlarging filters and pooling kernels. This implementation prioritizes the training of the video stream in the first i3D, whereas the second i3D is concentrated on instructing the optical flow stream. This methodology creates an extensive framework for identifying atypical human behavior, leveraging the advantages of both 2D and 3D convolutional operations. The modified Inception module and architecture serve as a multitiered feature extractor, improving model efficacy in abnormal behavior detection.

1.4 Experimental Results and Discussion

1.4.1 Experimental Setup

We conducted experiments using the UCF-Crime dataset, a widely recognized resource for anomaly detection and action recognition in surveillance videos. This dataset focuses on criminal activities captured in real-world environments. It serves a dual function in research. First, it can be applied to general anomaly detection by categorizing all abnormal activities and distinguishing them from routine actions. Second, it is valuable for identifying 13 specific types of anomalies. The UCF-Crime dataset is extensive, comprising 128 hours of video footage across 1900 untrimmed surveillance clips. It includes 13 different criminal events. The dataset contains an equal number of normal (950) and abnormal (950) events, selected due to their significant impact on public safety.

While acknowledging the limitations of using accuracy as a sole metric, our study emphasizes two key metrics: precision and recall. These metrics address biases caused by uneven class distributions, providing a more comprehensive performance evaluation. For comparison purposes, accuracy was also computed. To gain detailed insights, precision and recall were calculated separately for each category. The key metrics are defined as follows:

Precision (P): Precision gauges the proportion of accurate identifications for a class. It quantifies what fraction of predictions made for a specific class (fall, loitering, violence, none) was correct.

Precision (P) is mathematically formulated in Equation (1.1),

$$P = \frac{\mathrm{TP}}{(\mathrm{TP} + \mathrm{FP})} \tag{1.1}$$

where TP and FP denote true positives and false positives, respectively.

Recall (R): Also known as sensitivity, recall assesses the proportion of actual positives that were correctly identified. In this context, it measures what fraction of behaviors labeled as one of the four classes was accurately predicted.

Recall (R) is mathematically formulated in Equation (1.2),

$$R = \frac{\text{TP}}{(\text{TP} + \text{FN})} \tag{1.2}$$

where TP and FN represent true positives and false negatives, respectively.

Accuracy (A): The model's accuracy (A) is calculated in the given Equation (1.3),

$$A = \frac{(\text{TP} + \text{TN})}{(\text{TP} + \text{TN} + \text{FP} + \text{FN})} \tag{1.3}$$

where TP, TN, FP, and FN denote true positives, true negatives, false positives, and false negatives, respectively.

F1 score (F1): The F1 score, a widely used metric, is a harmonic mean of precision and recall and can be formulated in Equation (1.4):

$$\text{F1} = 2 * \frac{(\text{Precision} * \text{recall})}{(\text{Precision} + \text{recall})} \tag{1.4}$$

where TP, FP, and FN are true positives, false positives, and false negatives; precision and recall are defined above.

1.4.2 Dataset

The UCF-Crime dataset includes diverse categories of criminal events [23, 24]:

- *Abuse*: Depicts instances of violent behavior against vulnerable groups such as children, the elderly, or animals.
- *Burglary*: Captures individuals entering buildings with the intent to steal, without using force against others.
- *Robbery*: Focuses on theft involving threats or intimidation, excluding shootings.
- *Stealing*: Shows acts of taking property without permission, excluding shoplifting.

- *Shooting*: Depicts individuals being shot with firearms.
- *Shoplifting*: Involves stealing goods from retail stores while pretending to be a shopper.
- *Assault*: Illustrates sudden physical attacks where the victim does not retaliate.
- *Fighting*: Displays physical altercations between two or more individuals.
- *Arson*: Shows individuals setting fire to property with intent.
- *Explosion*: Captures destructive events involving detonations, excluding intentional acts of arson.
- *Arrest*: Depicts law enforcement apprehending individuals.
- *Road Accident*: Shows traffic incidents involving vehicles, pedestrians, or cyclists.
- *Vandalism*: Involves the deliberate damage or destruction of property, including graffiti and defacement [25].

The dataset also contains clips labeled as normal events, which depict everyday activities in various settings, both indoors and outdoors, and during different times of the day in Figure 1.5.

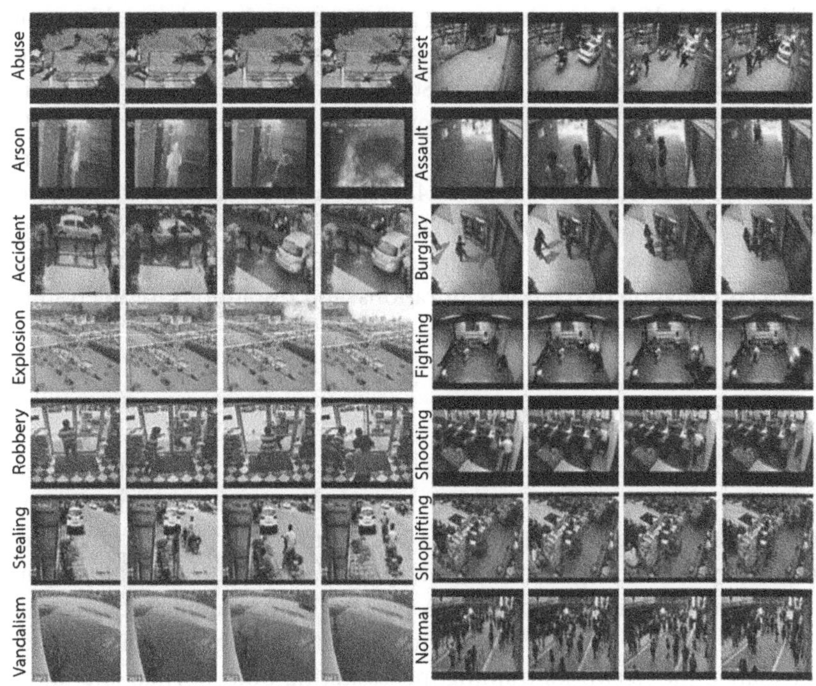

Figure 1.5 UCF-Crime dataset with abnormal behavior.

Table 1.1 UCF-Crime dataset with its description.

Scenario	Data scale	Length/clip (sec)	Resolution	Annotation
Arson	890 Clips	0.20–34.12	640×480	Video level
Accident	2000 Clips	2–520	Variable	Video level
Explosion	345 Clips	1.3–1.92	Variable	Video level
Stealing	1500 Clips	2.34–5.50	720 × 480	Video level
Arrest	2400 Clips	0.54–8	Variable	Video level
Burglary	1400 Clips	50–450	Variable	Video level
Normal	1000 Clips	8	1280 × 720	Video level

Table 1.1 presents a detailed summary of the UCF-Crime dataset, encompassing diverse instances of criminal activities. The dataset encompasses clips of different lengths and resolutions, with annotations provided at the video level. The "arson" scenario consists of 890 clips ranging from 0.20 to 34.12 seconds, recorded at a resolution of 640 × 480. "Accident" includes 2000 clips lasting between 2 and 520 seconds, with variable resolutions. "Explosion" is represented by 345 clips spanning 1.3 to 1.92 seconds, recorded at variable resolutions. "Stealing" comprises 1500 clips lasting 2.34 to 5.50 seconds, with a resolution of 720 × 480. "Arrest" involves 2400 clips ranging from 0.54 to 8 seconds, with variable resolutions. "Burglary" consists of 1400 clips lasting 50 to 450 seconds, recorded at variable resolutions. Lastly, the "Normal" scenario includes 1000 clips, each lasting 8 seconds, and recorded at a resolution of 1280 × 720. This dataset offers a varied compilation of scenarios, durations, and resolutions for the training and assessment of models in crime detection.

1.4.3 List of Experiments

The UCF-Crime dataset was divided into separate training and testing subsets. The training set consists of 800 normal and 810 anomalous event videos, whereas the testing set includes 150 normal and 140 abnormal event videos. The division guaranteed that both datasets included all 13 categories of anomalous occurrences. A portion of the supplied testing dataset was utilized as an anomalous video group during the training phase to enhance the network's training, necessitating both normal and anomalous videos. Moreover, merely 30% of the training dataset, specifically the videos of normal events [26–28], was used. It is crucial to emphasize that the training and testing datasets encompass all 13 scenes pertinent to anomalous events [22].

1.4.4 Comparative Study

This study proposes an SVM classifier for identifying anomalous events in surveillance videos without using CNN, with the objective of improving interpretability and detection efficacy. However, this model alone is insufficient for video surveillance. We proposed a two-stream architecture that emphasizes learning video appearance characteristics through a spatial model and utilizes a temporal autoencoder to capture regular patterns in the video. This method is particularly beneficial for modeling spatial attributes despite having few training samples. The proposed two-stream 3D CNN anomalous activity detection method is compared with other state-of-the-art techniques, including the SVM baseline and additional methods detailed in Table 1.2. The suggested approach uses a frame-level precision-recall curve and average precision (Table 1.2). Analysis of qualitative comparison results of the proposed method against other methods on the UCF-Crime dataset.

Table 1.2 Comparison of proposed model with the other models.

Method	Models used	Accuracy	Precision	Recall	Loss rate
SVM baseline approach	SVM without CNN	75	74	76	75
Lu *et al.* [2]	Sparse combination learning	68.9	65.51	66.25	65.89
Hasan *et al.* [30]	CNN—convolutional autoencoder	72.8	50.6	51.7	50.94
Sultani *et al.* [31]	Deep MIL ranking model	81	75.41	76.87	76.04
Proposed two-stream 3D CNN method	Two-stream 3D-CNN	82.12	81.5	82	82.2

Table 1.2 provides a thorough comparison of the proposed two-stream 3D CNN model with other models in the field. The SVM baseline, without CNN, achieved 75% accuracy, with precision, recall, and F1 score at 74%, 76%, and 75%, respectively, and a 25% loss rate. Lu and colleagues' [2] sparse combination learning model achieved 68.9% accuracy, with precision and recall at 65.51% and 66.25%, and an F1 score of 65.89%, along with a 31.1% loss rate. Hasan and colleagues' [30] convolutional autoencoder model showed 72.8% accuracy, with precision and recall at 50.6% and 51.7%, and an F1 score of 50.94%, with a 27.2% loss rate. Sultani and colleagues' [31] deep multiple instance learning (MIL) ranking model reached 81% accuracy, with precision, recall, and F1 score values of 75.41%, 76.87%, and 76.04%, respectively, and a 19% loss rate. In contrast, the proposed two-stream 3D CNN model surpassed these with 82.12% accuracy, precision, recall, and F1 score at 81.5%, 82%, and 82.2%, respectively, and a lower 17% loss rate. These results highlight the superior performance of the proposed model in terms of accuracy and key metrics, establishing it as a promising approach for the given task.

Figure 1.6 represents a graphical representation of the comparative analysis between the proposed two-stream 3D CNN model and other existing methods in the field. The bar graph illustrates the performance metrics,

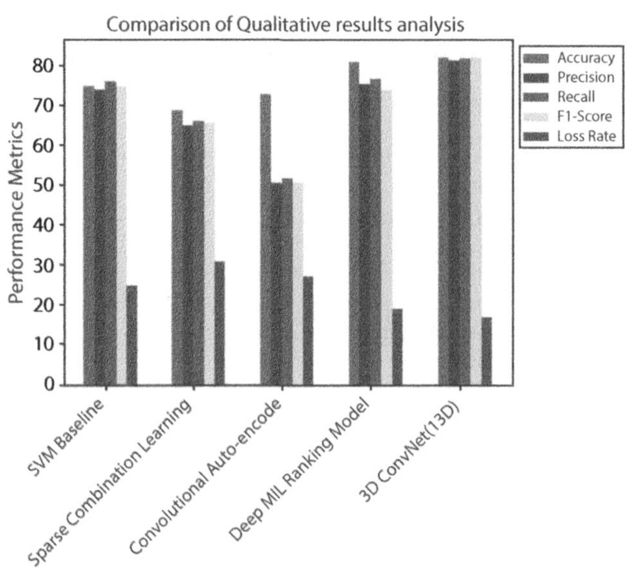

Figure 1.6 Comparative analysis of various method with the proposed model—two-stream 3D CNN method.

including accuracy, precision, recall, F1 score, and loss rate, for each method. The SVM baseline, lacking CNN, is depicted with a bar at 75% accuracy, along with corresponding precision, recall, and F1 score bars at 74%, 76%, and 75%, respectively, and a 25% loss rate. Lu and colleagues' [2] sparse combination learning model is represented with bars at 68.9% accuracy, 65.51% precision, 66.25% recall, and a 65.89% F1 score, accompanied by a 31.1% loss rate. Hasan and colleagues' [30] convolutional autoencoder model is displayed with bars indicating 72.8% accuracy, 50.6% precision, 51.7% recall, and a 50.94% F1 score, along with a 27.2% loss rate. Sultani and colleagues' [31] deep MIL ranking model is shown with bars at 81% accuracy, 75.41% precision, 76.87% recall, 76.04% F1 score, and a 19% loss rate. Notably, the proposed two-stream 3D CNN model outperforms all others, illustrated by bars at 82.12% accuracy, 81.5% precision, 82% recall, and an 82.2% F1 score, coupled with a lower 17% loss rate. The graphical representation figures out the high performance of the proposed model across various metrics as an effective approach.

Table 1.2 presents the parameters used in the proposed two-stream model using the UCF-Crime dataset. The architecture consists of three key layers: the pooling layer, the convolutional layer, and the fully connected layer. In the pooling layer, an 8 × 1 × 1 filter size is applied. The convolutional layer uses a 3 × 1 × 1 × 64 filter configuration, whereas the fully connected layer is structured with a filter size of 128. For the softmax layer, the filter size is set to 2.

Table 1.3 outlines the system's hyperparameters, detailing the architecture and specifications for each component. The model consists of eight layers overall, including a convolutional layer with a 3 × 1 × 1 filter size and 64 filters, a fully connected layer with 128 units, and a softmax layer with two output classes. Additionally, max pooling is applied with an 8 × 1 × 1 window in the pooling layer. These hyperparameters shape the overall design of the model, providing a clear understanding of its structural elements and their contribution to system performance.

Table 1.3 Hyperparameter of the proposed system.

Layers	Type	Filter size
Pooling layer	Max Pool	8 × 1 × 1
Convolution layer	Conv3D	3 × 1 × 1 × 64
Fully connected layer	FC Layer	128
Softmax layer	Softmax	2

1.5 Conclusion and Future Enhancements

The application of two-stream 3D CNNs for detecting abnormal behavior in videos has proven to be both effective and practical. This dual-stream architecture, which integrates spatial and temporal components, effectively addresses the challenges involved in recognizing anomalies by capturing both appearance and motion cues. This approach has shown superior performance in action recognition, particularly for detecting irregular events. By utilizing optical flow to represent temporal changes, the model's ability to identify abnormal activities across consecutive frames is significantly enhanced. The architecture's scalability and success in handling large datasets, such as the UCF-Crime benchmark, further demonstrate its practical relevance. Moreover, the two-stream 3D CNN model has set a standard in video analysis, driving future research and serving as a reference point for further developments. Its contribution lies in improving the understanding of spatiotemporal features, thereby advancing the interpretation of complex actions in video sequences. Overall, the two-stream 3D CNN framework stands as a key advancement in computer vision, offering a reliable solution for detecting anomalies in dynamic visual environments [21].

Future enhancements to this framework could focus on several areas to improve its performance and extend its applicability:

(i) *Attention mechanisms*: Incorporating attention mechanisms could help the network concentrate on key regions within frames, prioritizing important features that indicate abnormal behavior.

(ii) *Transfer learning*: Applying transfer learning from pre-trained models on large datasets could boost generalization, especially when annotated data for anomalies are limited.

(iii) *Adaptive learning rates*: Utilizing adaptive learning rate strategies, such as scheduled learning rates or optimization algorithms such as Adam, could improve the model's convergence during training, resulting in better performance.

AI disclosure statement: The author confirms that no artificial intelligence (AI)-generated content or AI-assisted writing tools were used in the preparation of this chapter (including summaries and the abstract). All text, analysis, and conclusions are the result of the author's original work.

References

1. Hasan, M., Choi, J., Neumann, J., Roy-Chowdhury, A.K., Davis, L.S., Learning temporal regularity in video sequences, in: *Proceedings of the IEEE Conference on Computer Vision and Pattern Recognition (CVPR)*, Boston, MA, USA, pp. 733–742,7–12 June 2015.
2. Lu, C., Shi, J., Jia, J., Abnormal event detection at 150 fps in matlab, in: *2013 IEEE International Conference on Computer Vision*, December 2013, pp. 2720–2727.
3. Zhao, B., Fei-Fei, L., Xing, E.P., Online detection of unusual events in videos *via* dynamic sparse coding, in: *Proceedings of the IEEE Computer Society Conference on Computer Vision and Pattern Recognition*, pp. 3313–3320, 2011.
4. Li, C., Han, Z., Ye, Q., Jiao, J., Abnormal behavior detection *via* sparse reconstruction analysis of trajectory, in: *Proceedings - 6th International Conference on Image and Graphics, ICIG 2011*, pp. 807–810, 2011.
5. Sabokrou, M., Anomaly Detection in Videos with One-Class 3D Convolutional Neural Networks. *Proceedings of the IEEE Conference on Computer Vision and Pattern Recognition (CVPR)*, 2018.
6. Venugopalan, S., Abnormal Event Detection in Videos using Spatiotemporal Autoencoder, in: *Proceedings of the IEEE Conference on Computer Vision and Pattern Recognition (CVPR)*, 2015.
7. Simonyan, K. and Zisserman, A., Two-Stream Convolutional Networks for Action Recognition in Videos. *Advances in Neural Information Processing Systems (NeurIPS)*, 2014.
8. Akcay, S., Unsupervised Anomaly Detection with Generative Adversarial Networks to Guide Marker Discovery, in: *Proceedings of the IEEE Conference on Computer Vision and Pattern Recognition (CVPR)*, 2019.
9. Ruff, L., Deep One-Class Classification, in: *Proceedings of the 35th International Conference on Machine Learning (ICML)*, 2018.
10. Gupta, S., Detecting Objects in RGB-D Indoor Scenes, in: *Proceedings of the IEEE Conference on Computer Vision and Pattern Recognition (CVPR)*, 2013.
11. Nidhya, R., Kalpana, R., Sudhakar, R., Maranco, M., Smilarubavathy, G., Smart System for Vechicle Number Plate Recognition Using Convolutional Neural Network(CNN). *2023 1st International Conference on Optimization Techniques for Learning (ICOTL)*, Bengaluru, India, pp. 1–6, 2023, doi: 10.1109/ICOTL59758.2023.10435179.
12. Ben Mabrouk, A. and Zagrouba, E., Abnormal behavior recognition for intelligent video surveillance systems: A review. *Expert Syst. Appl.*, 91, 480–491, 2018.
13. Ullah, H., Islam, I.U., Ullah, M., Afaq, M., Khan, S.D., Iqbal, J., Multi-feature-based crowd video modeling for visual event detection. *Multimed. Syst.*, 1–9, 2020.

14. Afiq, A., Zakariya, M., Saad, M., Nurfarzana, A., Khir, M., Fadzil, A., Jale, A., Gunawan, W., Izuddin, Z., Faizari, M.A., review on classifying abnormal behavior in crowd scene. *J. Vis. Commun. Image Represent.*, 58, 285–303, 2019.
15. Nguyen, V.D., Le, M.T., Do, A.D., Duong, H.H., Thai, T.D., Tran, D.H., An efficient camera-based surveillance for fall detection of elderly people, in: *Proceedings of the 9th IEEE Conference on Industrial Electronics and Applications*, Hangzhou, China, 9–11 June 2014, pp. 994–997.
16. Yao, C., Hu, J., Min, W., Deng, Z., Zou, S., Min, W., A novel real-time fall detection method based on head segmentation and convolutional neural network. *J. Real-Time Image Process.*, 17, 1–11, 2020.
17. Xu, D., Yan, Y., Ricci, E., Sebe, N., Detecting anomalous events in videos by learning deep representations of appearance and motion. *Computer Vision Image Understanding*, 156, 117–127, 2017.
18. Sabokrou, M., Fayyaz, M., Fathy, M., Klette, R., Deep-cascade: Cascading 3d deep neural networks for fast anomaly detection and localization in crowded scenes. *IEEE Trans. Image Process.*, 26, 4, 1992–2004, 2017.
19. Luo, W., Liu, W., Gao, S., A revisit of sparse coding based anomaly detection in stacked rnn framework, in: *Proceedings of the 2017 IEEE International Conference on Computer Vision (ICCV)*, October 2017, IEEE, Venice, Italy, pp. 341–349.
20. Guo, X., Hou, B., Ren, B., Ren, Z., Jiao, L., Network pruning for remote sensing images classification based on interpretable CNNs. *IEEE Transactions Geoscience Remote Sensing*, pp. 1–15, 2021.
21. Dosovitskiy, A. and Brox, T., Inverting visual representations with convolutional networks, in: *Proceedings of the 2016 IEEE Conference on Computer Vision and Pattern Recognition (CVPR)*, June 2016, IEEE, Las Vegas, NV, USA, pp. 4829–4837.
22. Pianpanit, T., Lolak, S., Sawangjai, P., Sudhawiyangkul, T., Wilaiprasitporn, T., Parkinson's disease recognition using SPECT image and interpretable AI: A tutorial. *IEEE Sens. J.*, 1–12, 2021.
23. Kiran, B.R., Thomas, D.M., Parakkal, R., An overview of deep learning based methods for unsupervised and semi-supervised anomaly detection in videos. *Journal Imaging*, 4, 2, 1–15, 2018.
24. Adam, A., *et al.*, Robust real-time unusual event detection using multiple fixed-location monitors. *IEEE Trans. Pattern Anal. Mach. Intell.*, 30, 3, 555–560, 2008.
25. Prabha, B., Manivannan, P., Nagesh, P., Human Abnormal Activity Detection in the ATM Surveillance Video. *Evolution in Signal Processing and Telecommunication Networks: Proceedings of Sixth International Conference on Microelectronics, Electromagnetics and Telecommunications (ICMEET 2021)*, vol. 2.

26. Prabha, B., Priya, M., Shanker, N.R., Ganesh, E., Aberrant behavior prediction and severity analysis for autistic child through deep transfer learning to avoid adverse drug effect. *Biomed. Signal Process. Control*, 70, 103038, 2021.
27. Prabha, B., Shanker, N.R., Priya, M., Ganesh, E., A Novel Descriptive Approach: Local Tetra Patterns (LTrPs) for Face Recognition. *ICCCE 2021: Proceedings of the 4th International Conference on Communications and Cyber Physical Engineering*, pp. 967–978.
28. Prabha, B., Shanker, N.R., Priya, M., Ganesh, E., Human Anomalous Activity Detection: Shape and Motion Approach in Crowded Scenes. *J. Phys. Conf. Ser.*, 1–8, 2021.
29. Ali, M., Al-Berry, M., Taha, Z., *et al.*, Convolutional Autoencoder for Anomaly Detection in Crowded Scenes, in: *Proceedings of the International Conference on Artificial Intelligence and Computer Vision (AICV2021)*. AICV 2021. Advances in Intelligent Systems and Computing, vol. 1377, A.E. Hassanien, (Ed.), Springer, Cham, 2021.
30. Hasan, M., Choi, J., Neumann, J., Roy-Chowdhury, A.K., Davis, L.S., Learning temporal regularity in video sequences, in: *CVPR*, June 2016, pp. 733–742.
31. Sultani, W., Chen, C., Shah, M., Real-world anomaly detection in surveillance videos, in: *CVPR*, June 2018.

2

U-Net–Based Residual Network for Blood Vessel Segmentation from Fundus Images

Nitigya Sambyal[1,2*], Sukhpal Singh[1] and Varun Gupta[3]

[1]Department of Computer Science and Engineering, Thapar Institute of Engineering and Technology (Deemed-to-be-University), Patiala, Punjab, India
[2]Department of Information Technology, Uppsala University, Uppsala, Sweden
[3]Department of Computer Science and Engineering, Chandigarh College of Engineering and Technology, Chandigarh, India

Abstract
The formation of new and fragile blood vessels on the surface of the retina is a common complication related to diabetic retinopathy. The foundational view of this retinal capillary network is provided by fundus imaging technique. The diagnosis and severity analysis of diabetic retinopathy is significantly influenced by the segmentation of retinal vessels, which involves the examination of blood vessel branching patterns and growth. It also allows automated early detection of pathologies such as stroke, hypertension, and cardiovascular diseases. This paper presents a new deep learning–based approach for the semantic segmentation of blood vessels in fundus images. The proposed residual network with U-Net consists of trained ResNet34 as encoder and U-Net block as decoder. The proposed model provides high-level details, enabling precise blood vessel segmentation. The model demonstrated promising results with 97.07% accuracy and 0.7968 as Dice score on the STARE dataset. The results emphasize the suggested model's potential as a significant tool for the early and accurate identification of abnormal vascular development, facilitating enhanced patient care.

***Keywords*:** Semantic segmentation, blood vessel, fundus image, U-Net, deep learning

**Corresponding author*: nitigya.sambyal@thapar.edu

R. Nidhya, D. Pavithra, S. Balamurugan, A. Dinesh Kumar and Sheng-Lung Peng (eds.) Medical Metaverse for Digital Healthcare: Technologies, Applications, and Challenges, (27–40) © 2026 Scrivener Publishing LLC

2.1 Introduction

Diabetic retinopathy (DR) is a leading reason for irreversible vision loss worldwide [1]. DR causes retinal abnormalities such as microaneurysms, hemorrhages in the early stages, and alteration and weakening of blood vessels (BVs) in the advanced stages [2]. When diagnosing retinal diseases, the morphological features of BVs, including tortuosity, breadth, length, and branching pattern, play a significant role [3]. Therefore, the analysis of BV is necessary for detecting and diagnosing retinal diseases. The manual segmentation of BVs by ophthalmologists is time-consuming, laborious, and difficult due to the complex BV structures, thin vessels, lesions, and contrast in fundus images [4].

The capillary network in retina can be analyzed using fundus images. The fundus photographs capture the characteristic appearance and abnormal growth, which can be used to analyze the severity of the disease [5]. It makes it possible to measure important vascular structural parameters more precisely. This can further facilitate the quantitative comparison of its state in subsequent explorations, which is critical information for the control of BV related diseases. Therefore, for examining the BV branching pattern and growth, automatic vascular tree segmentation from fundus pictures will allow a prompt diagnosis and severity analysis of retinal disorders. In order to reduce false positives in the detection of microaneurysms and hemorrhages, the vascular tree segmentation is also important [6]. It also helps to determine abnormal retinal vessel growth, which is essential for predicting the severity of the disease. Additionally, automated early detection of pathologies such as hypertension, stroke, and cardiovascular disorders depends heavily on the segmentation of retinal vessels. Figure 2.1 shows the fundus image along

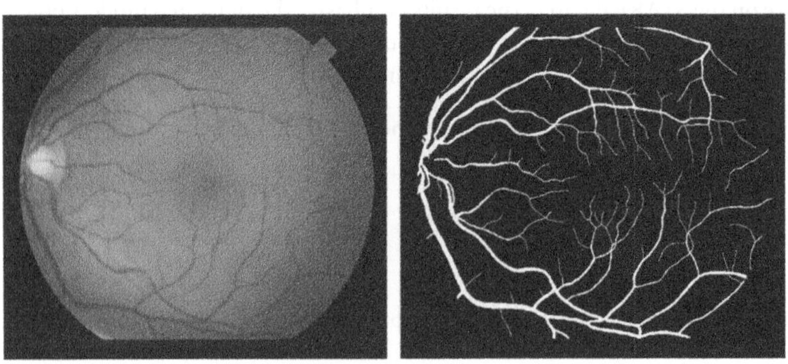

Figure 2.1 Fundus image and corresponding segmented vascular structure from STARE dataset [7].

with its segmented ground-truth from the STARE (Structured Analysis for the Retina) dataset [7].

This paper presents a deep learning–based method for the retinal vasculature segmentation from fundus images. The U-Net–based network provides high level details that enable precise BV segmentation. The main contributions of the paper are:

1. We present a model that uses a pretrained ResNet34 as the encoder and a U-Net block as the decoder to segment BVs from fundus images pixel by pixel.
2. The BV segmentation model is trained using discriminative cyclic learning, which provides highly accurate segmentation along with faster network convergence.
3. When compared to previous work, the suggested work delivered improvement in performance for BV segmentation.

Paper organization: Section 2.2 provides a summary of the relevant literature. The dataset and performance indicators used in the proposed study are outlined in Section 2.3. Section 2.4 explores the details of the proposed model for BV segmentation. Section 2.5 provides the results and associated discussions. The proposed work is finally concluded in Section 2.6.

2.2 Related Work

Retinal BV segmentation has evolved significantly, with early methods such as matched filtering and morphological processing paving the way for more advanced techniques. The introduction of deep learning, particularly convolutional neural networks (CNNs) [8] and U-Net architectures, has greatly enhanced segmentation accuracy. This section reviews vital advancements in the field, focusing on transitioning from traditional approaches to modern deep learning models that better capture the intricate details of retinal vessels.

In 2016, Kar and Maity [9] developed an approach for retinal BV extraction by utilizing a tunable bandpass filter, followed by fuzzy conditional entropy maximization applied to the matched filter response. First, curvelet-based denoising is used to remove noise from the images. Thereafter, a bank of successive bandpass filters tuned for contrast enhancement was applied to the image. The technique uses fuzzy conditional entropy to determine the best thresholds for neovascularization and other vessel silhouette types. The model demonstrated average true-positive rates of 76.32% and 72.82%, false-positive rates of 1.99% and 2.6%, and accuracy of 96.28% and 96.16% when tested on the digital retinal images for vessel extraction (DRIVE) and STARE databases.

Tamim *et al.* [10] suggested an approach based on supervised learning that used hybrid features along with a multilayer perceptron neural network for retinal BV segmentation. A 24-dimensional feature vector was used for encoding local intensity, morphological transformations, hessian, principal moments of phase congruency, and difference of gaussian values for each pixel in a retinal fundus image. In order to maximize segmentation, the method additionally incorporated a postprocessing methodology that used mathematical morphological operators. Using the DRIVE dataset, the method's accuracy, sensitivity, and specificity were 96.07%, 75.42%, and 98.43%, respectively. On the STARE dataset, the method's accuracy, sensitivity, and specificity were 96.32%, 78.06%, and 98.25%, respectively. The approach achieved 98.46% specificity, 75.85% sensitivity, and 95.77% accuracy on the CHASE_DB1 dataset.

Saranya *et al.* [11] presented a CNN-based model for identifying neovascularization, i.e., developing new abnormal BV in the retina. The fundus images were preprocessed using erosion, dilation, gaussian filtering, green channel filtering, and scaling to eliminate noise and uneven contrast illumination. Finally, the VGG16 classification model was trained using 2200 photos from the Kaggle dataset. On the DRIVE and STARE datasets, the model's accuracy was 96% and 95%, respectively.

An enhanced U-Net model was used by David *et al.* [12] to segment BV from fundus images. After preprocessing the input images, stride 5.1 was used to extract 96 × 96 patches. Fixed forecast maps were acquired and covered to frame an expectation picture. Further, binary segmentation was finally applied with a limit of 0.5, and multiscale input was used by the model to enhance the quality of segmentation. The output images with varying scales were fed into the encoder route of each layer using the image average pooling layer for downsampling. Furthermore, a three-layered dense block was used, with the final layer performing ReLU activation after the previous two layers completed batch normalization, ReLU activation, and convolution as part of a transformation. The model achieved sensitivity of 82%, specificity of 98%, and accuracy of 96.61%.

A modified layered U-Net model was presented by Buia *et al.* [13] for the automatic segmentation of BVs in retinal images. By adding new skip paths, the nested U-Net architecture, also referred to as U-Net++, set itself apart from the conventional U-Net and improved the model's capacity to capture and preserve minute information in the segmented vessels. Two publicly accessible datasets, DRIVE and STARE, were used to test the proposed model. According to the experimental findings, the traditional U-Net model with no nested skip connections obtained a Dice score of 0.740 and an accuracy of 96.4%.

Agrawal *et al.* [14] segmented BVs using two modified U-Net architectures. Squeeze and excitation (SE U-Net) blocks were incorporated in the first network, and attention gate (AG) U-Nets were added in the second network. In SE U-Net, global average pooling squeezed each channel to a single numeric value. Furthermore, a sigmoid function was utilized in a secondary fully linked layer that followed the ReLU function to give each channel a smooth gating function. AG was incorporated into each tier of the expanded path to eliminate unnecessary elements. The models were trained for 100 epochs, with 8 batch size and 0.5 dropout rate. Also, using HVDROPDB datasets, Dice values of 0.672 and 0.687 were obtained by the SE U-Net and AG U-Net, respectively.

An encoder–decoder system called ResDO–U-Net was presented by Liu *et al.* [15] for the segmentation of vasculature from fundus pictures. To keep as much information as possible in the downsampling path, the pooling fusion block (PFB) was merged with the ResDO convolution network. Additionally included for efficient multiscale feature expression was an attention fusion block. To enhance the convolutional layer by implementing additional depth-wise convolution, a residual block was incorporated with the DO-conv layer. Skip connections were used to merge low-level features from the encoder unit with high-level features from the decoder unit, effectively bridging the semantic gap. The network was trained using random photos with a 48 × 48 patch size following preprocessing. The DRIVE, STARE, and CHASE_DB1 datasets yielded accuracy values of 95.61%, 95.67%, and 96.72% for the model, respectively.

2.3 Proposed Methodology

Figure 2.2 illustrates the methodology used for the BV segmentation in this work. The fundus image is preprocessed and then given as input to the

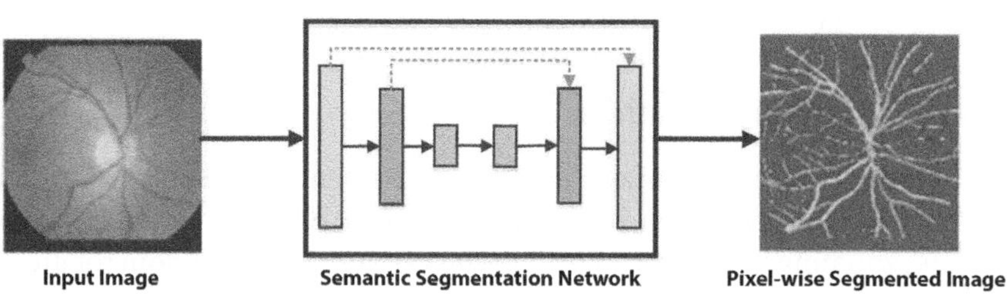

Figure 2.2 Proposed methodology.

semantic segmentation network, which outputs a pixel-wise segmented image of the BVs. The fundus image and its corresponding labels are given as input for training the semantic segmentation model.

2.3.1 Dataset

In this work, we have utilized the publicly accessible STARE fundus image dataset [7] (available at https://cecas.clemson.edu/~ahoover/stare/) for the segmentation of BVs. The STARE dataset is sourced from the STARE project at the University of California, San Diego. It consists of 20 (10 healthy and 10 unhealthy) images each having a resolution of 700 × 605 and manually annotated by experts. Table 2.1 provides a comprehensive overview of the dataset:

Table 2.1 Dataset description of STARE.

Dataset	Resolution	Stage	Images	Total
STARE	700 × 605	Healthy	10	20
		Unhealthy	10	

2.3.2 Data Preparation

This section focuses on the data preprocessing methods used for BV segmentation from fundus images.

2.3.2.1 Image Preprocessing

As a crucial preprocessing step, we resized the input fundus images to a consistent resolution of 299 × 299 pixels. This standardized size eliminates potential discrepancies arising from variations in image sizes and aspect ratios. The uniform resolution enhances processing efficiency, enabling deep learning models to learn and identify patterns effectively.

2.3.2.2 Data Augmentation

To enhance the diversity of our dataset, we used augmentation techniques such as pixel normalization, horizontal and vertical flip, random rotation up to 360°, zooming by factor 1.1 and lighting variations, and random rotation.

These transformations contribute to a more robust model by introducing variations in the training data, thereby improving the generalizability of the BV segmentation algorithm. The transformed data was used to create a DataBlock consisting of input images and corresponding segmentation masks. To train the model, the dataset is further divided into 70% training set, 15% validation set, and 15% testing set.

2.3.3 Proposed U-Net + ResNet34 Model

The proposed model uses the U-Net architecture and ResNet [16] backbone, which are widely recognized for their effectiveness in image segmentation tasks. The U-Net architecture provides a robust framework for precise object detection, whereas the ResNet models offer powerful feature extraction capabilities.

The proposed model, ResNet34+U-Net, is designed to take 299 × 299 images as input. Initially, these images undergo preprocessing to standardize their resolution and enhance quality. These images are then processed through a sophisticated architecture beginning with a 7 × 7 convolutional layer, resulting in feature maps of size 150 × 150. The encoder path of the model consists of four residual blocks, which utilize 3 × 3 convolutional layers to extract intricate features from the images. These blocks are crucial for capturing complex patterns and details within the fundus images, which are essential for accurate segmentation. In the middle layers of the model, the feature maps are further refined through two additional 3 × 3 convolutional layers, ensuring that both local and global structures are captured effectively. Following the middle layers, the decoder path of the U-Net architecture begins. It combines subpixel convolution with periodic shuffling, a novel upsampling method that improves the segmented output's resolution. The decoder path also consists of corresponding four U-Net blocks, which help to reconstruct the image to its original size while retaining the detailed features extracted by the encoder. A 1 × 1 convolutional layer at the end of the decoder path produces the final segmented image, delineating the BVs with high precision. This flexible architecture improves the model's capability to capture and interpret complex patterns, offering potential benefits for BV segmentation tasks.

Figure 2.3 details the architecture of the ResNet34-based dynamic U-Net model, highlighting the various stages from input to the final segmented output. This comprehensive approach ensures that the model can accurately identify and segment BVs, crucial for diagnosing and monitoring various ophthalmic conditions. Figure 2.4 shows the details of the building blocks of the semantic segmentation model.

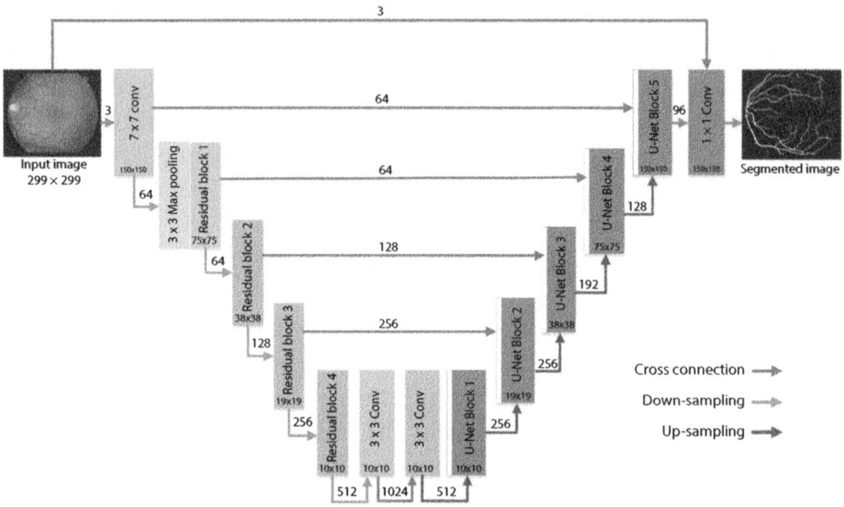

Figure 2.3 ResNet34-based dynamic U-Net model for blood vessel segmentation.

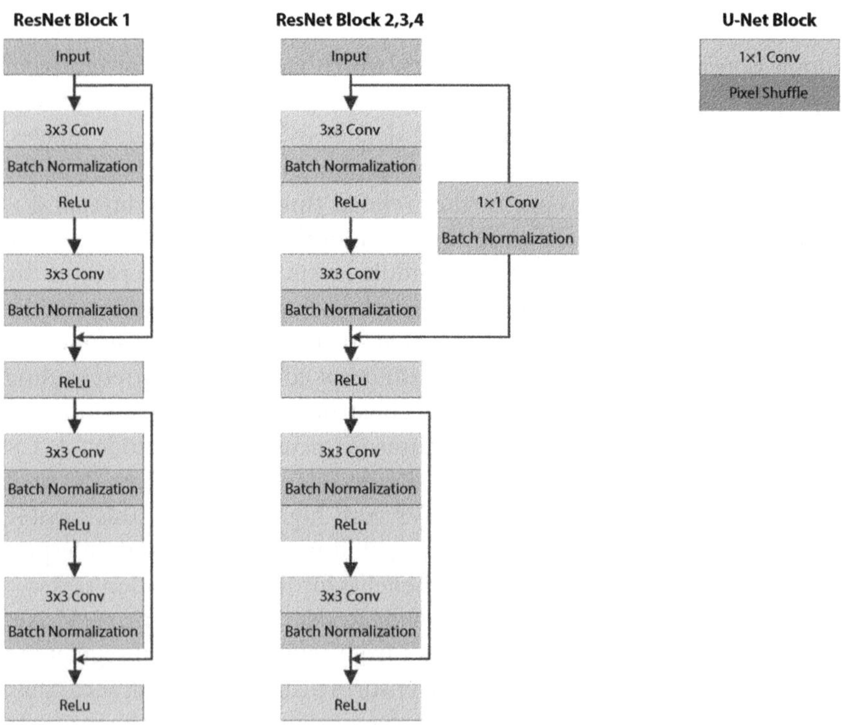

Figure 2.4 Details of ResNet block and U-Net block used in the proposed semantic segmentation model.

Figure 2.4 illustrates the specifications of the ResNet blocks and U-Net blocks implemented in the proposed model for the semantic segmentation of BVs from fundus images.

2.3.4 Model Training

The proposed segmentation model uses cyclic learning rate scheduling [17]. This technique involves the cyclic variation of the learning rate between a specified minimum and maximum value. This approach enables exploring a broader range of learning rates, potentially leading to improved solutions and avoiding local minima. Cyclic learning rate scheduling accelerates training, enhances model generalization, and contributes to convergence toward an optimal solution. For optimization, we used the adaptive moment estimation (Adam) algorithm, which modifies the learning rate dynamically throughout training. The Adam optimizer offers strong generalization capabilities and quick convergence by combining the advantages of the AdaGrad and RMSProp algorithms [18]. Moreover, we measured the difference between the predicted and target outputs using the binary cross-entropy loss function with logits. This loss function helps with practical training because it is appropriate for binary classification issues and enables the model to directly learn the probability distribution [19].

2.3.5 Performance Metrics

This section focuses on the performance parameters used for the assessment of BV segmentation from fundus images. The paper focuses on two key metrics, *accuracy* and *Dice score*, which offers comprehensive insights into the effectiveness of segmentation methodologies [20]. Utilizing these metrics enhances the assessment of algorithmic performance in medical imaging applications, specifically in BV segmentation.

The formula for accuracy is given in Equation (2.1).

$$\text{Accuracy} = \frac{\text{True positives+true negatives}}{\text{Total predictions}} \tag{2.1}$$

Dice score is a widely used metric for quantifying the spatial overlap between the predicted and ground-truth segmentation masks. It is particularly suitable for evaluating the precision of BV segmentation algorithms, as it penalizes false positives and false negatives. The formula for this is given in Equation (2.2).

$$\text{Dice score} = \left(\frac{2 * |A \cap B|}{|A| + |B|} \right) \tag{2.2}$$

where A represents the set of pixels in the predicted segmentation mask, B represents the set of pixels in the ground truth segmentation mask, $|A|$ denotes set A's cardinality, $|B|$ denotes set B's cardinality, and $|A \cap B|$ represents the intersection of sets A and B, i.e., the number of common pixels to both masks.

2.4 Results and Discussion

This section gives an overview of the experimental setup, hyperparameters, and results obtained for BV segmentation.

2.4.1 Experimental Setup

Our experiments were conducted on a desktop computer with Windows 11 Pro with an 11th-generation Intel Core i7-11700K processor, Nvidia RTX A6000 graphics card, and 64 GB RAM. We utilized the fastai deep learning library [21] as it efficiently supports training deep learning models.

2.4.2 Hyperparameters

To maximize performance, the U-Net + ResNet34 model's hyperparameters were carefully selected during training. The BV segmentation model was first trained with a learning rate of 9×10^{-4} over the course of five epochs. Subsequently, the model was unfrozen and trained across 90 epochs with the initial, middle, and end layers having discriminative learning rates of 9×10^{-4}, 1.05×10^{-3}, and 2×10^{-2}, respectively. Table 2.2 provides specifics of the hyperparameters used in the work.

2.4.3 Blood Vessel Segmentation Results

The proposed BV segmentation model, trained on the STARE dataset for 95 epochs, exhibited promising performance. The model demonstrated good learning and generalization abilities during training, with a validation loss of 0.0748 and a training loss of 0.0775. The model demonstrated a high level of proficiency with an accuracy score of 97.07%. Additionally, the

Table 2.2 Hyperparameters for blood vessel segmentation.

Parameters	ResNet34 + U-Net
Target labels	2
Image size (pixels)	299 × 299
Batch size	4
Weight decay	0.1
Dropout	0.70
Optimization	Adam
Initial learning rate	4.5×10^{-4}
With online data augmentation	5
After unfreezing the layers of the network	90
Total epochs	95
Initial layers	9×10^{-4}
Middle layers	1.05×10^{-3}
Last layers	2×10^{-2}

Table 2.3 Performance of the proposed blood vessel segmentation model on the STARE dataset.

Dataset	Epochs	Training loss	Validation loss	Accuracy	Dice
STARE	95	0.0775	0.0748	97.07%	0.7968

model also achieved a Dice score of 0.7968, which highlighted the model's ability to segment BVs accurately in the STARE dataset. These results show the effectiveness of our segmentation approach. The BV segmentation results for the STARE dataset are presented in Table 2.3.

2.4.4 Performance Comparison with other Methods

This section presents a comparison of the proposed model against current techniques reported in the literature, specifically focusing on BV segmentation using the STARE dataset.

Table 2.4 Performance comparison for blood vessel segmentation.

Method (year)	**Average ACC**
Kar and Maity (2016) [9]	96.28%
Tamim *et al.* (2020) [10]	96.07%
Saranya *et al.* (2022) [11]	95%
Liu *et al.* (2023) [15]	95.67%
Proposed U-Net + ResNet34	**97.07%**

Table 2.4 summarizes this comparison, highlighting the superiority of our approach in terms of segmentation accuracy and Dice score.

In comparison to existing models in the literature, the proposed semantic segmentation model achieved a minimum improvement in accuracy by 0.79%. Overall, the results demonstrate that the U-Net + ResNet34 model presented in this paper achieves competitive performance with high Dice score and accuracy.

2.5 Conclusion

Automatic BV segmentation from fundus images is crucial for detecting and analyzing various retinal abnormalities. In this paper, we suggested a U-Net–based model for retinal vasculature pixel-wise segmentation from fundus images. The model combines residual blocks and U-Net blocks, along with innovative techniques such as periodic shuffling with subpixel convolution, contributing to its robust performance in segmenting BVs from fundus images. On the STARE dataset, the suggested model achieved a Dice score of 0.7968 and an accuracy of 97.07%. In addition, the model demonstrated a minimum improvement in accuracy by 0.79% compared to current approaches seen in the literature. In future, the model can be evaluated on more publically available benchmark datasets.

AI disclosure statement: The author confirms that no artificial intelligence (AI)-generated content or AI-assisted writing tools were used in the preparation of this chapter (including summaries and the abstract). All text, analysis, and conclusions are the result of the author's original work.

References

1. Sapra, A. and Bhandari, P., Diabetes, in: *StatPearls*, Jun. 2023, Accessed: Aug. 19, 2024. [Online]. Available: https://www.ncbi.nlm.nih.gov/books/NBK551501/.
2. Diabetic Retinopathy, National Eye Institute, Accessed: Aug. 19, 2024. [Online]. Available: https://www.nei.nih.gov/learn-about-eye-health/eye-conditions-and-diseases/diabetic-retinopathy.
3. Yu, D.Y., Yu, P.K., Cringle, S.J., Kang, M.H., Su, E.N., Functional and morphological characteristics of the retinal and choroidal vasculature. *Prog. Retin. Eye Res.*, 40, 53–93, May 2014, doi: 10.1016/J.PRETEYERES.2014.02.001.
4. Mirsharif, Q., Tajeripour, F., Pourreza, H., Automated characterization of blood vessels as arteries and veins in retinal images. *Comput. Med. Imaging Graphics*, 37, 7–8, 607–617, Oct. 2013, doi: 10.1016/J.COMPMEDIMAG.2013.06.003.
5. Gulshan, V., *et al.*, Development and Validation of a Deep Learning Algorithm for Detection of Diabetic Retinopathy in Retinal Fundus Photographs. *JAMA*, 316, 22, 2402–2410, Dec. 2016, doi: 10.1001/JAMA.2016.17216.
6. Martinez-Perez, M.E., *et al.*, Retinal vascular tree morphology: A semi-automatic quantification. *IEEE Trans. Biomed. Eng.*, 49, 8, 912–917, 2002, doi: 10.1109/TBME.2002.800789.
7. The STARE Project. Accessed: Aug. 19, 2024. [Online]. Available: https://cecas.clemson.edu/~ahoover/stare/.
8. Shrestha, H., Dhasarathan, C., Kumar, M., Nidhya, R., Shankar, A., Kumar, M., A deep learning based convolution neural network-DCNN approach to detect brain tumor, in: *Proceedings of Academia-Industry Consortium for Data Science: AICDS 2020*, Springer Nature Singapore, Singapore, pp. 115–127, 2022.
9. Sil Kar, S. and Maity, S.P., Retinal blood vessel extraction using tunable bandpass filter and fuzzy conditional entropy. *Comput. Methods Programs Biomed.*, 133, 111–132, Sep. 2016, doi: 10.1016/J.CMPB.2016.05.015.
10. Tamim, N., Elshrkawey, M., Azim, G.A., Nassar, H., Retinal Blood Vessel Segmentation Using Hybrid Features and Multi-Layer Perceptron Neural Networks. *Symmetry*, 12, 6, 894, Jun. 2020, doi: 10.3390/SYM12060894.
11. Saranya, P., Prabakaran, S., Kumar, R., Das, E., Blood vessel segmentation in retinal fundus images for proliferative diabetic retinopathy screening using deep learning. *Visual Comput.*, 38, 3, 977–992, Mar. 2022, doi: 10.1007/S00371-021-02062-0/FIGURES/13.
12. David, S.A., Mahesh, C., Kumar, V.D., Polat, K., Alhudhaif, A., Nour, M., Retinal Blood Vessels and Optic Disc Segmentation Using U-Net. *Math. Probl. Eng.*, 2022, 1, 8030954, Jan. 2022, doi: 10.1155/2022/8030954.
13. Buia, S., Popescu, D., Ichim, L., Blood Vessel Segmentation in Retinal Images Using Neural Networks. *12th International Symposium on Advanced Topics in Electrical Engineering, ATEE 2021*, Mar. 2021, doi: 10.1109/ATEE52255.2021.9425035.

14. Agrawal, R., Kulkarni, S., Walambe, R., Deshpande, M., Kotecha, K., Deep dive in retinal fundus image segmentation using deep learning for retinopathy of prematurity. *Multimed. Tools Appl.*, 81, 8, 11441–11460, Mar. 2022, doi: 10.1007/S11042-022-12396-Z.
15. Liu, Y., Shen, J., Yang, L., Bian, G., Yu, H., ResDO-UNet: A deep residual network for accurate retinal vessel segmentation from fundus images. *Biomed. Signal Process. Control*, 79, 104087, Jan. 2023, doi: 10.1016/J.BSPC.2022.104087.
16. He, K., Zhang, X., Ren, S., Sun, J., Deep Residual Learning for Image Recognition. *Proceedings of the IEEE Computer Society Conference on Computer Vision and Pattern Recognition*, Dec. 2015, vol. 2016-December, pp. 770–778, doi: 10.48550/arxiv.1512.03385.
17. Smith, L.N., Cyclical Learning Rates for Training Neural Networks. *Proceedings - 2017 IEEE Winter Conference on Applications of Computer Vision, WACV 2017*, Jun. 2015, pp. 464–472, doi: 10.1109/WACV.2017.58.
18. Gentle Introduction to the Adam Optimization Algorithm for Deep Learning, MachineLearningMastery.com., Accessed: Jul. 03, 2023. [Online]. Available: https://machinelearningmastery.com/adam-optimization-algorithm-for-deep-learning/.
19. How to Choose Loss Functions When Training Deep Learning Neural Networks, MachineLearningMastery.com., Accessed: Feb. 05, 2023. [Online]. Available: https://machinelearningmastery.com/how-to-choose-loss-functions-when-training-deep-learning-neural-networks/.
20. Machine Learning - Performance Metrics, Accessed: Sep. 07, 2023. [Online]. Available: https://www.tutorialspoint.com/machine_learning_with_python/machine_learning_algorithms_performance_metrics.htm.
21. fast.ai - fast.ai, Making neural nets uncool again, Accessed: Jul. 03, 2023. [Online]. Available: https://www.fast.ai/.

3

Machine Learning–Based Early Identification of Parkinson Disease Using Voice and Behavioral Data

Smilarubavathy G.[1]*, R. Nidhya[2], Keerthana S. M.[1] and Sangeetha S.[3]

[1]St. Joseph's Institute of Technology, Chennai, India
[2]Department of Computer Science & Engineering, Madanapalle Institute of Technology & Science (MITS) Deemed to be University, Madanapalle, Andhra Pradesh, India
[3]Karpagam College of Engineering, Coimbatore, India

Abstract

The early identification of Parkinson disease (PD) can be significantly improved through the application of machine learning techniques using voice and behavioral data. Detecting PD in its early stages through data analysis can be a noninvasive and cost-effective way to diagnose the disease remotely. This study aimed to analyze various types of data, including voice recordings, computer keystrokes, spiral drawings, and gait patterns, to identify the characteristics that may indicate early PD. This paper used a support vector machine model to examine clinical data from PD patients, individuals with rapid eye movement sleep behavior disorder (RBD), and healthy people. Our analysis focused on the effectiveness of different types of data in predicting PD. The results indicated that voice analysis was the most reliable method for early detection, followed by data from computer keystrokes, spiral drawings, and gait analysis. Voice changes were noticeable even in patients with RBD, suggesting that voice analysis could be an early indicator of PD. Despite these findings, the model's accuracy was not perfect, meaning some PD cases might be missed. However, combining all four types of data—voice, keystrokes, drawings, and gait—could improve the model's overall accuracy in diagnosing PD.

Keywords: Parkinson disease (PD), machine learning, rapid eye moment sleep behavior disorder (RBD), voice data and gait data

---

**Corresponding author*: smilarupa@gmail.com

R. Nidhya, D. Pavithra, S. Balamurugan, A. Dinesh Kumar and Sheng-Lung Peng (eds.) Medical Metaverse for Digital Healthcare: Technologies, Applications, and Challenges, (41–62)

3.1 Introduction

Personalized medicine offers the promise of tailored treatment and disease management, customized for each individual patient. Its effectiveness depends on accurate, early, and cost-efficient diagnosis. With more clinical, genomic, and demographic data becoming available and with advancements in machine learning (ML) and artificial intelligence, the potential for early diagnosis in a timely and affordable way is increasing [1].

Parkinson disease (PD) is a serious condition that greatly diminishes an individual's quality of life over time. It ranks as the second worldwide most prevalent neurodegenerative disorder, affecting approximately 6 million people, with about 1.5 lakh new cases being diagnosed every year in India alone. As India's population continues to age, the number of PD cases is expected to rise [2]. Symptoms of PD, such as tremors, softer speech, slowness of movement, muscle stiffness, and a shuffling walk, often lead to falls and injuries. At present, there is no approved medicine that can slow down the development of PD [3]. Although there are treatments available to manage symptoms, as the disease progresses, some symptoms may become resistant to these treatments. This situation creates a significant financial strain and emotional stress on patients, their families, and India's healthcare system, where access to specialized care is often limited.

The best time to start treatments that could potentially alter the course of PD is during the prodromal phase, making early diagnosis crucial for better management and improved outcomes. Recent research in India has started looking into multimodal ML approaches to predict PD. The standard criteria for diagnosing PD include the presence of bradykinesia, along with at least one other motor symptom, such as a resting tremor or cogwheel rigidity. Bradykinesia means slow or difficult movement, whereas cogwheel rigidity refers to a type of muscle stiffness that feels like a "catch and release" when force is applied during joint movement [4]. By the time these motor symptoms of PD are noticeable, about 50% of the brain's dopaminergic neurons are already lost, making it too late for treatments that could protect the nerves and slow the disease's progression. As a result, treatment mainly focuses on managing the symptoms.

PD develops from the progressive degeneration of nerve cells, which begins long before the noticeable movement symptoms appear. This initial phase, known as prodromal PD, includes issues such as rapid eye movement (REM) sleep behavior disorder (RBD), softer speech, a reduced sense of smell, and constipation [5]. These early symptoms, often called premotor symptoms, can show up years or even decades before the motor symptoms, marking what is referred to as the premotor phase. By analyzing data with ML models, it is possible to spot early signs of PD before the obvious movement of issues arises, which could open the door to early treatment and, down the road, the use of therapies that might slow down this devastating disease [6].

Identifying PD early could make a big difference; allowing for timely treatment helps to improve their quality of life for those affected and also lessen the financial strain on the healthcare system. One of the earliest signs of PD is vocal changes, such as difficulties with voice control, which affect about 90% of patients [7]. Because checking someone's voice is simple and nonintrusive, it has become a popular method for identifying and monitoring PD.

Typing on a computer keyboard, including things such as how long a key is pressed and the time between keystrokes, can be used to identify changes in finger movements caused by PD. Tools such as the Tappy software can record these keystrokes, providing an accurate way to detect PD, especially in the early stages when movement issues might not be noticeable [8].

Handwriting is another aspect affected by PD, making it a useful marker for diagnosis. Tests such as the static spiral test (SST) and dynamic spiral test (DST) have been developed to measure how PD impacts writing [9]. Gait, or walking patterns, is also influenced by PD due to a combination of mental and movement challenges. Early in the disease, it detects the changes in a person's walk, especially when multitasking.

However, current studies on clinical biomarkers face several issues, such as small sample sizes, differences in sample sizes between patients and healthy individuals, and inconsistencies in the variables studied [10]. Additionally, there is a lack of long-term studies that follow changes over time, and clinical measures can be influenced by other conditions, making the data hard to generalize. Moreover, there is often a lack of diversity in terms of race and socioeconomic background in the data, which limits its applicability.

A better approach would combine different clinical biomarkers that are affordable, can be used at home and fit into everyday life, and can be analyzed remotely, leading to an early PD diagnosis. This project focuses on analyzing voice data, especially in RBD patients, who is having more risk of developing PD, along with data from computer keystrokes, spiral drawings, and gait analysis. RBD, enacting dreams during REM sleep, serves as a strong marker for PD, with about 80% chance of progressing to the disease. This research could be crucial in identifying early PD characteristics, making it easier to detect the disease early and monitor patients in remote areas.

3.2 Materials and Methods

Here, a support vector machine (SVM) model was developed to examine biomedical data from both PD patients and healthy individuals. The SVM model was selected due to its efficiency in managing high-dimensional data and its capability to optimize the separation between different classes, which helps in reducing the risk of overfitting. Additionally, the SVM model is computationally efficient, making it suitable for this analysis without requiring advanced hardware such as a graphics processing unit (GPU).

Data for the analysis were sourced from several public databases, including the Parkinson's Progression Markers Initiative, the UCI Machine Learning Repository, and Kaggle. Upon review, the datasets from Kaggle were found to be cleaner and more consistent, so all relevant data, including voice recordings, Tappy keystroke data, spiral drawings, and gait measurements, were obtained from Kaggle.

After downloading the necessary CSV files from Kaggle, they were imported into a local drive for further processing. The analysis was conducted using a Jupyter Notebook, where several Python libraries, including Pandas, Seaborn, NumPy, and Matplotlib, were utilized. In addition, tools from the scikit-learn library were used, such as pipeline, column transformer, StandardScaler, OneHotEncoder, MinMaxScaler, KBinsDiscretizer, LabelEncoder, train_test_split, Stratified K-Fold, cross_validate, and various classification metrics.

The CSV files were loaded into the Jupyter Notebook, and columns containing unique identifiers were removed to ensure data privacy. The data were checked for balance between both PD patients and healthy individuals, revealing a higher number of PD patients in each dataset. The data were prepared for analysis by examining the distribution of variables and identifying numeric and categorical features. Outliers were managed by ensuring all values fell within the 1st and 99th percentiles.

The dataset was split into two sets. They are training and testing sets that uses80/20 split, which maintained the proportions of PD patients and healthy people. This same 80/20 split was applied during Stratified K Fold cross-validation to evaluate accuracy of the SVM model. The model's performance was assessed using various metrics including accuracy, precision, recall (sensitivity), and the F1 score [11]. A threshold of 0.5 was used for these evaluations. The workflow and research procedures followed and are summarized in Figure 3.1.

The data were separated into training and testing sets with an approximate value of 80/20 ratio. The proportion of PD patients and healthy

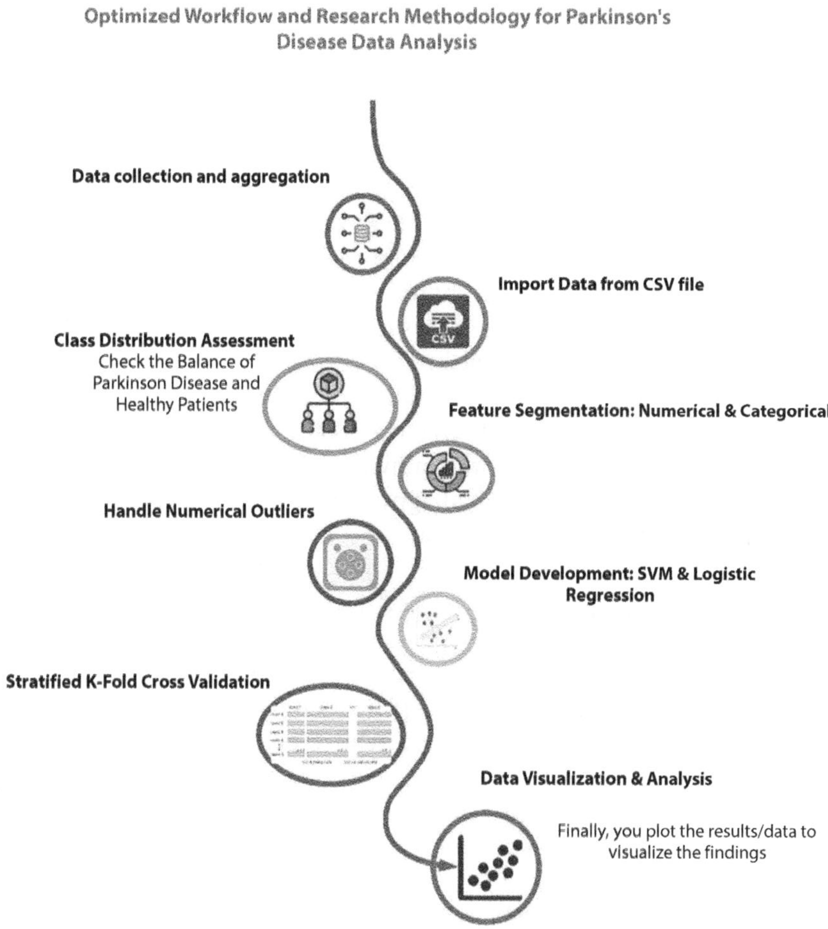

Figure 3.1 Optimized research flow model for Parkinson disease data analysis.

individuals was carefully maintained across both sets to ensure consistency. This approach allowed the model to be trained and tested on data that accurately represented the balance between these groups.

3.3 Datasets

3.3.1 Voice Dataset

The voice dataset was sourced online and was originally part of a study conducted at the Oxford University in collaboration with the National

Centre for Voice and Speech in Denver, Colorado. Here the speech signals were recorded, and feature extraction methods were used to identify the general voice disorders. Key features analyzed in this study included pitch period entropy (PPE), fundamental frequency (F0), jitter (variation in speech F0), noise-to-harmonics ratio (NHR), shimmer (variation in speech amplitude), and several others such as detrended fluctuation analysis, and recurrence period density entropy [12]. These features help to detect voice disorders and, specifically, changes in speech related with PD. The data originally aimed to evaluate dysphonia measurements for telemonitoring PD. This dataset comprises voice measurements from 31 individuals, with 23 being both PD patients and the healthy people. The data were organized into a table for analysis, with each column representing a particular voice feature and every row corresponding to a vocal sound recording. The "status" column indicated whether the individual was a healthy control (0) or a PD patient (1). Each patient had approximately six recordings, and the data were saved in ASCII CSV format.

3.3.2 Tappy Keystroke Dataset

This dataset contains typing data collected using the Tappy app from more than 200 subjects, including both PD patients and healthy controls. Tappy captured the timing of key press and release events in milliseconds, as well as the asymmetry between the right and left hands [13]. Key features recorded in this dataset included hold time (the duration of a key press), elapsed time (the time between releasing one key and pressing the next), and various measures related to which hand was used to press the keys. This dataset was collected over weeks or months to observe naturalistic typing behavior.

3.3.3 Spiral Drawings Dataset

The spiral drawing dataset includes drawings from 62 PD patients and 15 healthy people. Participants completed the DST and SST, where the spiral blinks on the screen [9]. Additionally, the Stability Test on Certain Point involved participants maintaining a digital pen over a red dot without making contact with the screen. Healthy controls showed consistent results on both SST and DST, whereas PD patients performed worse on the DST compared to SST. The dataset helps distinguish between both PD patients and healthy people based on their performance in these tests. Figure 3.2 shows a visual representation of the drawing of the star test (DST) results for a PD patient. On the left side, you see the drawing completed by the

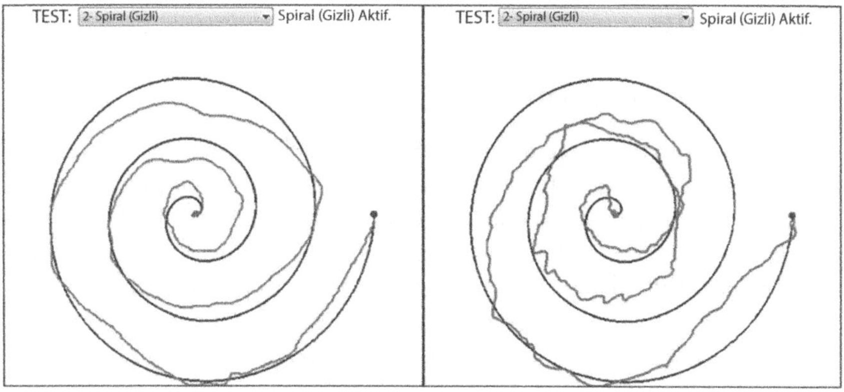

Figure 3.2 A representative DST and SST drawing of a PD patient.

patient with the highest score, showcasing relatively better motor control and accuracy. On the right side, the drawing from the patient with the lowest score illustrates more pronounced difficulties with motor control and spatial organization [14].

3.3.4 Gait Analysis Dataset

This dataset comprises gait data collected from 93 individuals with PD and 73 healthy individuals. Each participant had eight sensors attached under each foot to measure the vertical ground reaction force. This force, measured in newton, was recorded as a function of time while the participants walked at a normal pace for about 2 minutes on a flat surface [15].

3.3.5 RBD Patient Dataset

The voice analysis dataset was collected to study the speech alterations in RBD patients, a condition frequently occurring before Parkinson disease [16]. The dataset includes 30 newly diagnosed PD patients who were not started to take the medication, 50 RBD patients, and 50 healthy controls with no neurological or communication disorders. Each participant was asked to read a standardized text of 80 words and deliver a 90-second monologue. Speech features were analyzed using an automated algorithm, focusing on metrics such as duration of pauses, the rate and acceleration of speech timing, entropy of speech timing, and various features related to voiced and unvoiced speech elements, as well as respiratory characteristics during speech.

3.4 Results

3.4.1 Voice Data Analysis

The analysis of voice data using the SVM model yielded the highest performance metrics, including accuracy, recall (sensitivity), precision, and F1 score. The results showed an accuracy of 86.52%, a recall of 94.21%, a precision of 88.53%, and an F1 score of 91.28%. Figure 3.3 illustrates the distribution of PD patients compared to controls in the voice datasets.

In Figure 3.3, "0" denotes normal (healthy individuals), whereas "1" represents PD patients. The term "count" refers to the total number of normal or PD patients in the dataset.

Figure 3.4 illustrates the significance of the analysis of various features in the voice dataset. Feature importance was determined by normalizing each feature against the sum of all feature values in the SVM model and then dividing by the total number of model iterations. Key features considered when building a model-based voice data include PPE, "MDVP F0 Hz" (multidimensional voice program), and the spread of values. The MDVP can extract 33 different features from a voice sample, offering a quick and quantitative assessment of voice characteristics, which can be used to develop a model for identifying early signs of PD.

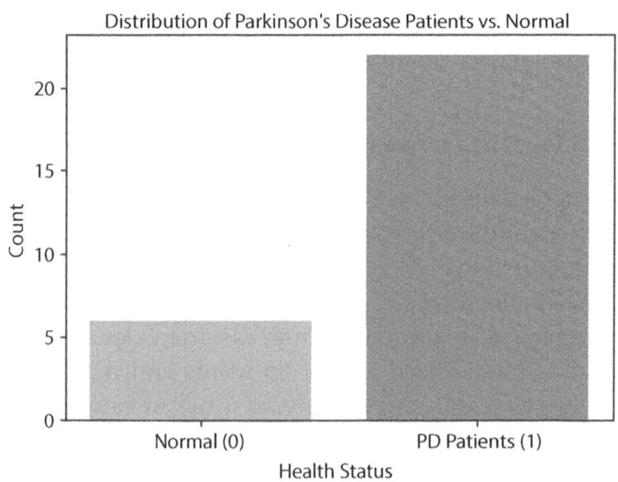

Figure 3.3 Distribution of Parkinson disease patient versus normal.

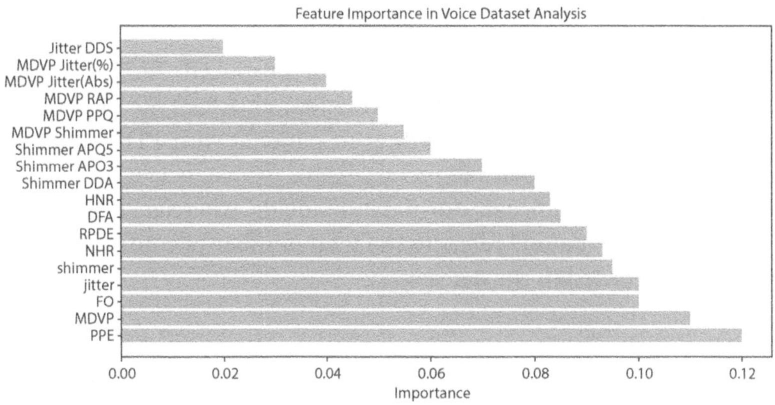

Figure 3.4 Feature importance in voice data analysis.

- PPE: pitch period entropy
- F0: fundamental frequency
- MDVP: Kay Pentax multidimensional voice program
- Jitter: fluctuations in fundamental frequency from one vocal cycle to the next
- NHR: noise-to-harmonics ratio, which measures the level of noise compared to tonal elements in speech
- Shimmer: variability in speech amplitude between cycles
- RPDE: recurrence period density entropy
- DFA: detrended fluctuation analysis
- HNR: harmonics-to-noise ratio
- Shimmer APQ5: five-point amplitude perturbation quotient
- Shimmer DDA: average absolute difference between consecutive amplitude variations of successive periods
- Shimmer APQ3: three-point amplitude perturbation quotient
- MDVP shimmer: local shimmer measurement using MDVP
- MDVP RAP: relative amplitude perturbation
- MDVP PPQ: five-point period perturbation quotient
- MDVP jitter (Abs): absolute jitter in microseconds measured by MDVP
- MDVP jitter (%): jitter as a percentage measured by MDVP
- Jitter DDS: average absolute difference of differences between cycles, divided by the average period
- Spread: represents the spread of nonstandard measures or the comparison between traditional and nonstandard measures.

3.4.2 Tappy Keystroke Data Analysis

The analysis of the Tappy keystroke data produced 70.77% accuracy, 92.81% recall (sensitivity), 78.50% precision, and 85.05% F1 score. The number of data points corresponding to patients with PD compared to normal illustrates in Figure 3.5.

In this figure, "0" indicates normal individuals, whereas "1" denotes PD patients. The term "count" refers to the total number of control subjects or PD patients recorded in the dataset.

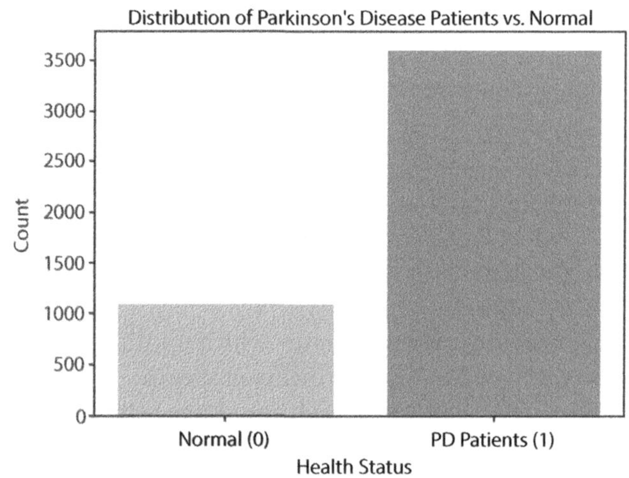

Figure 3.5 Number of data points from patients with PD versus normal in Tappy keystroke data.

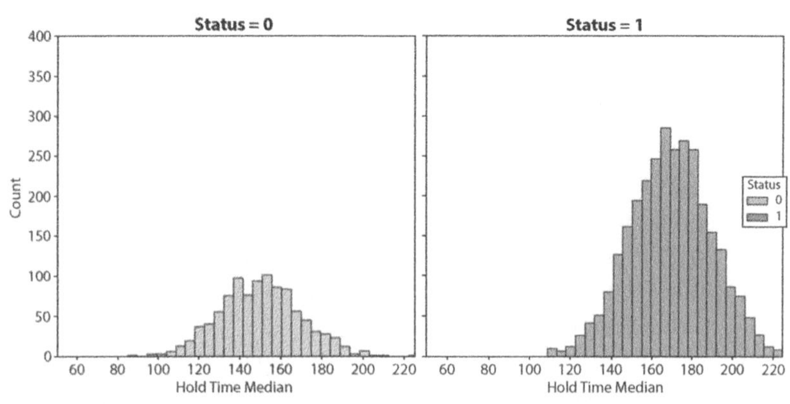

Figure 3.6 Distribution of hold time.

Figure 3.6 illustrates the distribution of hold time for both normal individuals and patients with PD within the Tappy keystroke dataset. The ML analysis demonstrates noticeable variations between both PD patients and healthy individuals.

In this figure, "0" corresponds to control subjects, whereas "1" represents Parkinson disease patients. The term "count" indicates the number of data points collected from each user, and "hold time" refers to the duration between pressing and releasing a key.

Figure 3.7 shows the distribution of elapsed time for both healthy individuals and patients with PD in the Tappy keystroke dataset.

In this figure, "0" represents healthy individuals, whereas "1" refers to Parkinson disease patients. The term "count" indicates the total number of data points collected from users. "Elapsed time" refers to the duration (in milliseconds) between releasing one key and pressing the next.

Figure 3.8 illustrates the importance of various features in the analysis of the Tappy keystroke dataset. When developing a model using Tappy keystroke data, key features focus on the median elapsed time and the median hold time.

- Hold time: The interval between the moment a key is pressed and when it is released.
- Elapsed time: The time, measured in milliseconds, between releasing one key and pressing another.
- Keyside_L: Keys pressed by the left hand.
- Keyside_R: Keys pressed by the right hand.
- Keyside_S: Space key, which can be pressed by either hand.

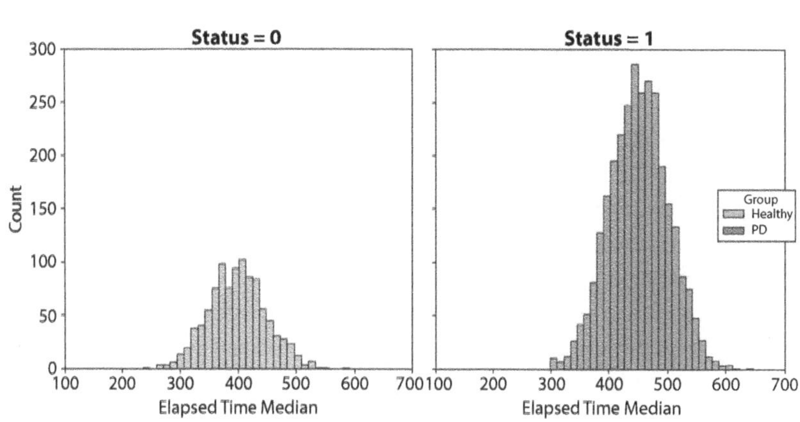

Figure 3.7 Distribution of elapsed time.

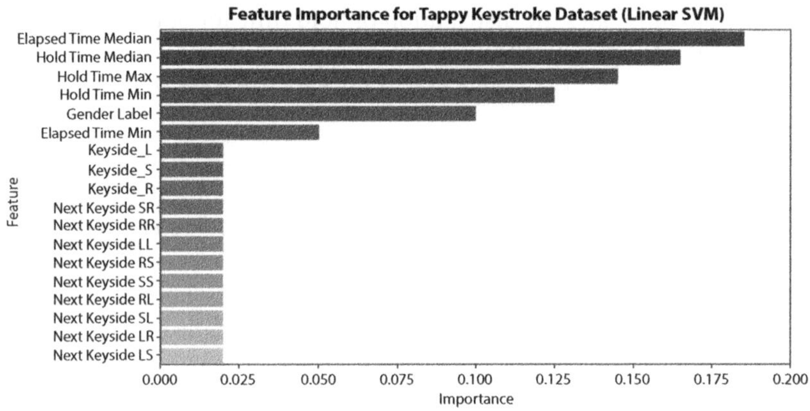

Figure 3.8 Feature importance (excluding count) in the Tappy keystroke data.

- Next keyside: Latency between successive keystrokes, categorized by whether the keystrokes are with the same hand (LL or RR) or opposite hands (LR or RL) or involve the space key and either hand.

3.4.3 Spiral Drawing Data Analysis

The spiral drawing data were obtained using three tests: the DST (where participants draw while a spiral pattern blinks at intervals), SST (where participants draw on a fixed spiral pattern), and the circular motion test (where participants draw circles around a red point, illustrated in Figure 3.2). The ML analysis of these data yielded 83.81% recall, 75.29% precision, 72.97% accuracy, and an F1 score of 79.32%.

In Figure 3.9, "0" indicates normal individuals, whereas "1" represents PD patients. The term "count" denotes the data point number for each group.

Figure 3.10 illustrates the importance of various features in differentiating between PD patients and normal individuals in the spiral drawing dataset. The analysis focused on several features, including the pressure exerted to the screen; the angle of the stylus grip; *X*, *Y*, and *Z* coordinates; and the timestamp, which tracks the time required to complete the task.

Key features for model development based on spiral drawings include the stylus grip angle and pressure exerted to the screen particularly in DST. The "Test ID" indicates the type of test administered: circular motion test or static spiral test, and DST.

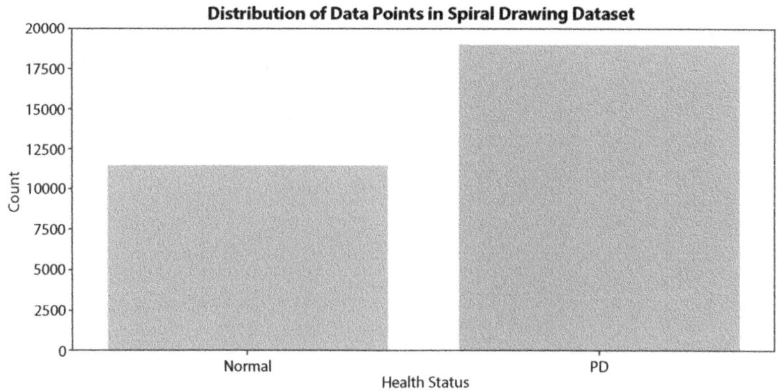

Figure 3.9 Distribution of data points between PD patients and normal in the spiral drawing dataset.

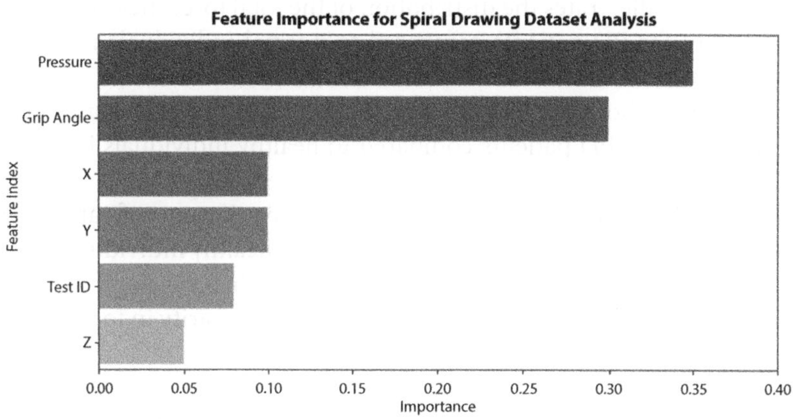

Figure 3.10 Feature importance between PD patients and normal individuals in the spiral drawing dataset.

3.4.4 Gait Data Analysis

The analysis of gait data resulted in 72.81% recall, 66.70% precision, 62.33% accuracy, and F1 score of 71.38%. The dataset comprised measurements including time (in seconds), vertical ground reaction force (in newton) from each of the eight sensors placed under the left and right feet, as well as the total force measured under each foot.

In Figure 3.11, "0" represents healthy individuals, whereas "1" denotes PD patients.

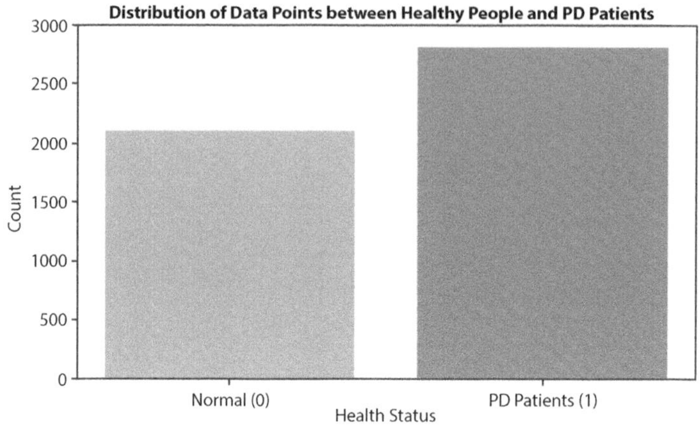

Figure 3.11 Distribution of left total force in gait dataset.

Figure 3.12 illustrates the distribution of the total force measured under the left foot for PD patients compared to normal individuals in the gait dataset analysis.

Figure 3.13 shows the distribution of the total force measured under the right foot for PD patients compared to healthy individuals in the gait dataset analysis

Figure 3.14 presents a plot highlighting the significance of various features in distinguishing between PD patients and healthy individuals within the gait dataset analysis. Key features to focus on when developing a model based on gait data include weight, height, and the disparity in force applied between the left and right feet.

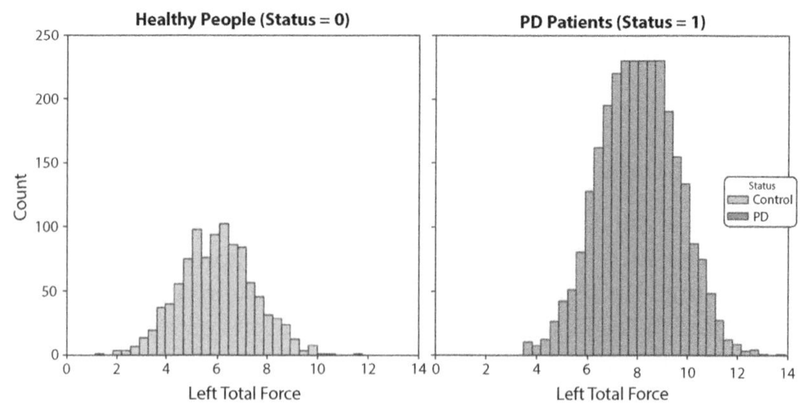

Figure 3.12 Distribution of left total force for PD patients and healthy individuals in the gait dataset.

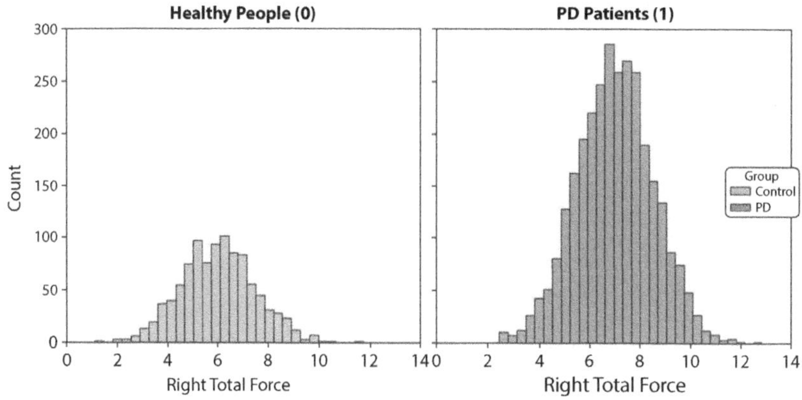

Figure 3.13 Distribution of right total force for PD patients and healthy individuals in the gait dataset.

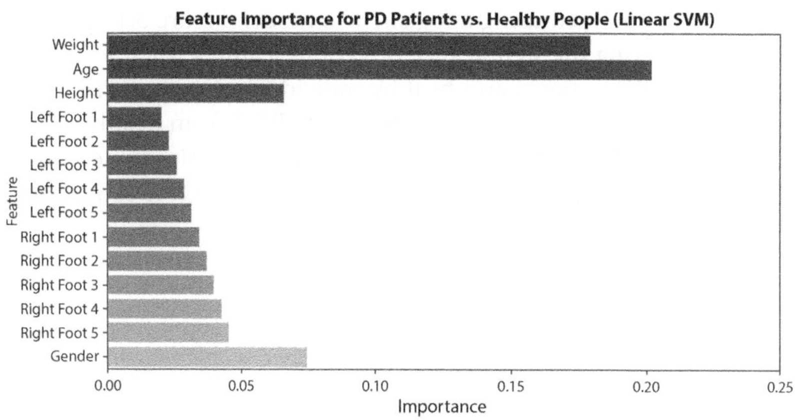

Figure 3.14 Plot of feature importance for PD patients and healthy individuals in the gait dataset.

In Figure 3.14, "left" and "right" refer to the different sensors used to measure the force applied under the left and right feet, respectively.

3.4.5 Voice Analysis in Patients with RBD

Figure 3.15 illustrates the distribution of individuals categorized into three groups: PD patients, RBD patients, and healthy individuals.

Figure 3.15 shows RBD, which may indicate an early sign of PD.

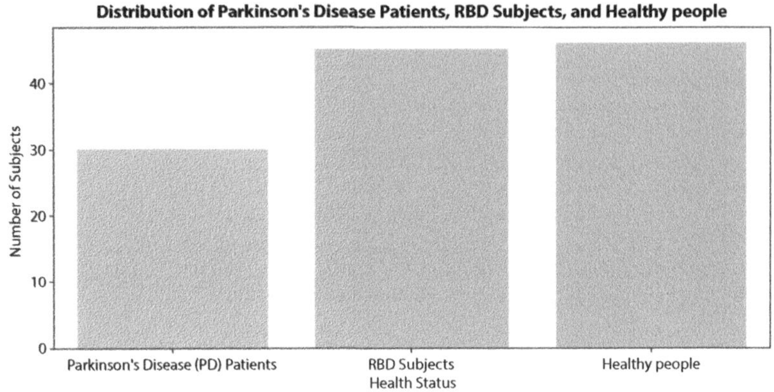

Figure 3.15 Distribution of PD patients, RBD patients, and healthy individuals.

3.4.6 Data Analysis Using Logistic ML Model

The data were analyzed using a logistic ML model. Figure 3.16 presents a plot of highlighting the significance of various features when distinguishing between RBD patients and healthy individuals. Key features to focus on when constructing a model to differentiate RBD from healthy controls include the rate of speech timing and the duration of voiced intervals.

Here, RBD is shown, a condition frequently linked to the early stages of PD.

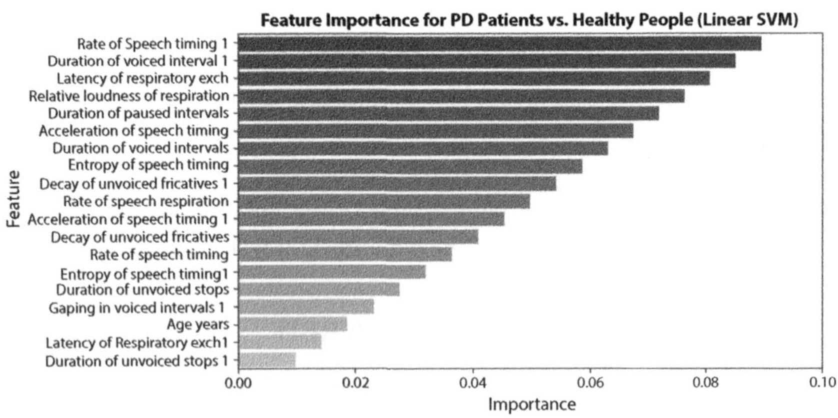

Figure 3.16 Plot of feature importance for RBD versus healthy controls.

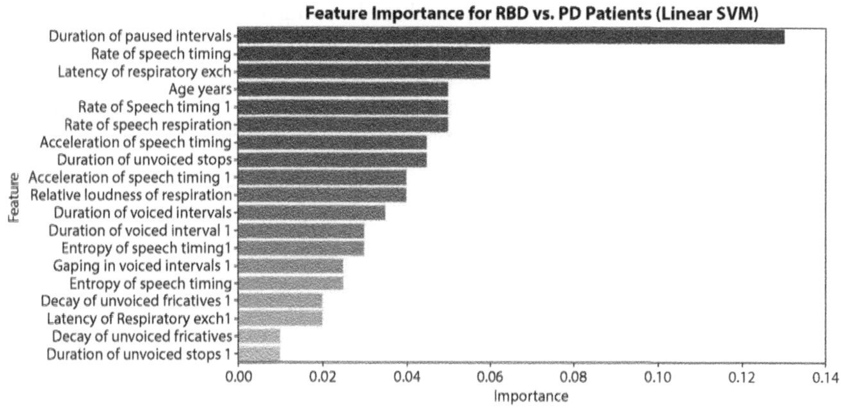

Figure 3.17 Feature importance plot for PD versus healthy individuals.

3.4.7 Analysis of Parkinson Disease versus Healthy Individuals

Figure 3.17 illustrates the importance of various features when comparing PD patients to normal people. When constructing a model, separation of PD patients from normal people within this dataset, it is important to prioritize key features that include the duration of pause intervals and the entropy of speech timing.

3.4.8 Analysis of RBD versus PD Patients

Figure 3.18 presents the feature importance when comparing RBD patients to those with PD patients. In developing a model to distinguish between

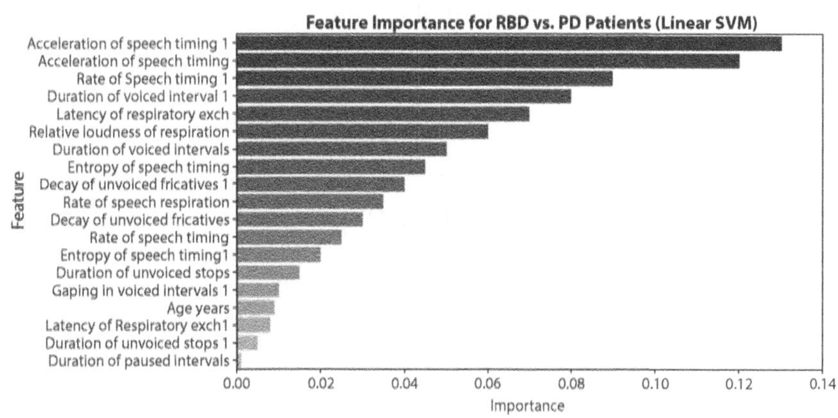

Figure 3.18 Feature importance plot for RBD versus PD.

Table 3.1 Overview of metrics from machine learning analysis.

	Accuracy	**Precision**	**Recall**	**F1 score**
Voice data	86.52	88.53	94.21	91.28
Tappy keystroke data	70.77	78.50	92.81	85.05
Spiral drawing data	72.97	75.29	83.81	79.32
Gait data	62.33	66.70	72.81	71.38
Voice data in RBD vs. normal	70.35	71.22	71.57	71.39
Voice data in RBD (PD vs. normal)	66.82	65.21	66.25	65.72
Voice data in RBD (RBD vs. PD)	55.45	44.32	55.14	49.14

Note: Logistic regression model utilized for cross-validation. Data sourced from the same studv.

RBD and PD patients within this dataset, the most critical features to focus on are the acceleration of speech timing and the latency of respiratory exchange.

Table 3.1 provides an overview of the metrics derived from the ML analysis. These results highlight that voice analysis is the best indicator for the early detection of PD.

3.5 Discussion

The basal ganglia play a vital role in the planning, programming, and execution of motor activities and are particularly vulnerable in PD. Speech, being a complex motor function, is especially sensitive to disruptions in the basal ganglia, which is why speech patterns are significantly impacted in PD patients.

Patients with RBD, who act out their dreams during the REM sleep phase, have greater than 80% chance of eventually developing PD. To investigate whether the vocal changes observed in PD patients also occur in RBD patients, speech analysis was conducted. The findings revealed that speech is affected even in RBD patients, suggesting that voice alterations could serve as an early prodromal sign of PD. This indicates that voice can be a useful clinical marker, from the premotor phase through to the onset of motor symptoms. Utilizing voice samples in natural settings for noninvasive, early diagnosis of PD could become a valuable tool in managing the disease.

Further analysis of voice data, computer keystrokes, spiral drawings, and gait in RBD patients may help identify which parameter is most affected earliest and could serve as an early screening tool for PD. These parameters also hold potential for monitoring the progression of PD, especially because many patients are older and may have difficulty traveling for in-person visits. These tests can be self-administered, are low-cost and noninvasive, and can be performed at home, with data being easily transmitted to healthcare providers. This setup allows for remote monitoring of treatment effects.

In this study, an ML model based on the SVM was developed to analyze characteristics of PD that may emerge before clinical diagnosis [17]. The ML model aims to enhance risk prediction, thereby aiding clinicians in early intervention and resource prioritization. However, the low accuracy of the current analysis suggests that some PD-positive samples may remain undetected or unclassified.

Among the datasets analyzed, including voice, computer keystrokes, spiral drawings, and gait, voice analysis emerged as the most reliable indicator for early PD diagnosis or prediction. However, rather than relying on individual features, combining multiple features could yield a more accurate ML strategy for early PD identification. Integrating all four data types—voice analysis, keystrokes, spiral drawings, and gait analysis—may improve the model's accuracy. To achieve this, larger datasets are needed to enhance the prediction accuracy of the ML models. Increased contributions to publicly accessible datasets, such as those on Kaggle, would provide more robust data for training these models. Although their model flags many more potential PD patients than will actually develop the disease, it is still useful for real-time identification of individuals in the prodromal phase of PD.

The current study had limitations, including the use of different cohorts for different parameters and the availability of only limited datasets in the public domain. The absence of certain early predictors, such as constipation, smell, and RBD, which were not included due to a lack of publicly available data, is another limitation. Additionally, combining different databases posed challenges, as the data did not come from the same patients. Therefore, there is a need for more comprehensive multimodal data collection from the same PD patients and controls in future studies. Prospective studies should focus on gathering multiple parameters from the same patients, tracking them from the prodromal phase to the clinical PD phase.

3.6 Conclusion

Noninvasive, cost-effective, and home-based tools for monitoring daily activities can play a crucial role in the early diagnosis of PD. These tools can also monitor symptoms in patients at high risk of developing PD. For instance, a smartphone app could monitor and record subtle speech changes, alerting clinicians to potential early signs of PD. Similarly, a background application on a computer could track keystroke variations, and pressure sensors in shoes could monitor gait changes, providing a cost-effective approach to reducing the financial burden of PD in the coming years. As the incidence of PD continues to rise, there is a pressing need for cost-effective methods to enable early identification and timely intervention. This study is unique in its application of ML to analyze early changes in various daily activities, offering a real-time, remote, and cost-effective strategy for identifying the emergence of PD.

AI disclosure statement: The author confirms that no artificial intelligence (AI)-generated content or AI-assisted writing tools were used in the preparation of this chapter (including summaries and the abstract). All text, analysis, and conclusions are the result of the author's original work.

References

1. Asif, S.,Wenhui, Y., ur-Rehman, S., ul-ain, Q., Amjad, K., Yueyang, Y., Jinhai, S., Awais, M., Advancements and Prospects of Machine Learning in Medical Diagnostics: Unveiling the Future of Diagnostic Precision. *Arch. Comput. Methods Eng.*, 32, 2, 853–83, 2025 Mar.
2. Shetty, M., Shetty, S.B., Jambha, H.V.G., Hrithvika, Application of Machine Learning and Data Analytics in Detection of Parkinsons Disease, in: *2024 Second International Conference on Data Science and Information System (ICDSIS)*, May 2024, pp. 1–5, doi: 10.1109/ICDSIS61070.2024.10594328.
3. Costa, F.G., Automatic Differential diagnosis of Parkinson's Disease through multimodal techniques, laurea, Politecnico di Torino, 2024, Accessed: Aug. 30, 2024. [Online]. Available: https://webthesis.biblio.polito.it/31926/.
4. Angelini, L., Paparella, G., Bologna, M., Distinguishing essential tremor from Parkinson's disease: clinical and experimental tools. *Expert Rev. Neurother.*, 24, 8, 799–814, Aug. 2024, doi: 10.1080/14737175.2024.2372339.
5. Janssen Daalen, J.M., van den Bergh, R., Prins, E.M., Moghadam, M.S., van den Heuvel, R., Veen, J., Mathur, S., Meijerink, H., Mirelman, A., Darweesh, S.K., Evers, L.J., Digital biomarkers for non-motor symptoms in Parkinson's disease: the state of the art. *npj Digit. Med.*, 7, 1, 186, 2024 Jul 11.

6. Keserwani, P.K., Das, S., Sarkar, N., A comparative study: prediction of parkinson's disease using machine learning, deep learning and nature inspired algorithm. *Multimed. Tools Appl.*, 83, 27, 69393–69441, Aug. 2024, doi: 10.1007/s11042-024-18186-z.
7. Romero Arias, T., Redondo Cortés, I., Pérez del Olmo, A., Biomechanical parameters of voice in Parkinson's disease patients. *Folia Phoniatrica et Logopaedica*. 76, 1, 91–101, 2024 Feb 1.
8. Vaish, A., A Machine Learning Approach for Early Identification of Prodromal Parkinson's Disease. *Cureus*, 16, 6, e63240, 2024 Jun 26.
9. Ramzani, E., Yadollahzadeh-Tabari, M., GolesorkhtabarAmiri, M., Pouyan, A.A., Diagnosing of Parkinson's disease based on hand drawing analysis using Bi-Directional LSTM equipped with fuzzy inferential soft-max classifier. *Int. J. Imaging Syst. Technol.*, 34, 1, e22948, 2024, doi: 10.1002/ima.22948.
10. Sun, Y.M., Wang, Z.Y., Liang, Y.Y., Hao, C.W., Shi, C.H., Digital biomarkers for precision diagnosis and monitoring in Parkinson's disease. *NPJ Digit. Med.*, 7, 1, 218, 2024 Aug 21.
11. Akila, B. and Nayahi, J.J.V., Parkinson classification neural network with mass algorithm for processing speech signals. *Neural Comput. Appl.*, 36, 17, 10165–10181, Jun. 2024, doi: 10.1007/s00521-024-09596-z.
12. Design of an Efficient Prediction Model for Early Parkinson's Disease Diagnosis, IEEE Journals & Magazine | IEEE Xplore, Accessed: Aug. 30, 2024. [Online]. Available: https://ieeexplore.ieee.org/abstract/document/10577760.
13. Yang, Y., Guo, B., Zhao, K., Liang, Y., Li, N., Yu, Z., MELPD-Detector: Multilevel ensemble learning method based on adaptive data augmentation for Parkinson disease detection *via* free-KD. *CCF Trans. Pervasive Comput. Interact.*, 6, 2, 182–198, Jun. 2024, doi: 10.1007/s42486-024-00152-1.
14. Isenkul, M., Sakar, B., Kursun, O., Improved Spiral Test Using Digitized Graphics Tablet for Monitoring Parkinson's Disease, May 2014, doi: 10.13140/RG.2.1.1898.6005.
15. Naimi, S., Bouachir, W., Bilodeau, G.-A., 1D-convolutional transformer for Parkinson disease diagnosis from gait. *Neural Comput. Appl.*, 36, 4, 1947–1957, Feb. 2024, doi: 10.1007/s00521-023-09193-6.
16. Zheng, W., Pan, Y., Li, K., Tao, K., Wang, Q., Yang, Y., The correlation between rapid eye movement sleep behavior disorder and the progress of Parkinson's disease: a systematic review and meta-analysis. *Front. Aging Neurosci.*, 16, 1418751, 2024 Jul 17.
17. Bhoomika, B.K., Kanmani, K., Smilarubavathy, G., Early Detection of Pancreatic Cancer using Machine Learning Algorithm, in: *2024 5th International Conference on Mobile Computing and Sustainable Informatics (ICMCSI)*, 2024, January, IEEE, pp. 202–205.

4

Automated Dental Age Detection Using Mayfly Optimized Extreme Learning Machine Classification

B. Hemalatha

Department of Artificial Intelligence and Data Science, KIT – Kalaignarkarunanidhi Institute of Technology, Coimbatore, Tamil Nadu, India

Abstract

Age is a fundamental aspect of an individual's identity and plays a significant role in various fields, including legal dentistry and medicine. Key factors such as age, gender, and identity are crucial for personal documentation. Chronological age, determined by a person's birth date, is tracked throughout life and holds importance in legal cases, medical assessments, and research. In forensic investigations, dental evidence often serves as a vital tool for identifying individuals. Age estimation can be derived from multiple indicators, such as dental, bone, and mental age. Of these, dental age (DA) is particularly valuable due to its reflection of tooth development, which shows less variation than chronological age, making it a reliable indicator for age determination. This paper presents an automated approach for DA assessment using an extreme learning machine (ELM) optimized by the mayfly optimization (MFO) algorithm. The primary objective of this study is to enhance the accuracy of age prediction through the efficient preprocessing and segmentation of dental images, followed by feature extraction from key regions. The proposed method uses an active contour model for precise tooth segmentation, which is further refined using morphological postprocessing to improve feature quality. The optimized ELM, combined with the MFO algorithm, ensures superior classification performance when compared to conventional methods such as modified extreme learning-sparse representation classification (MELM-SRC), ELM, support vector machine, and Demirjian's age assessment. Experimental results demonstrate significant improvements in sensitivity, specificity, precision, *F* measure, and

Email: harshaahemalatha@gmail.com

R. Nidhya, D. Pavithra, S. Balamurugan, A. Dinesh Kumar and Sheng-Lung Peng (eds.) Medical Metaverse for Digital Healthcare: Technologies, Applications, and Challenges, (63–80) © 2026 Scrivener Publishing LLC

overall accuracy. This approach holds more reliable DA detection and offers robustness in handling diverse datasets. Future work will focus on expanding the dataset and improving processing efficiency to further enhance prediction accuracy.

***Keywords*:** Dental age (DA), extreme learning machine (ELM), mayfly optimization (MFO), anisotropic diffusion filter (ADF), active contour model (ACM), GLCM (gray-level co-occurrence matrix)

4.1 Introduction

Age estimation plays a crucial role in several fields, including forensic science, anthropology, orthodontics, and pediatrics. Determining a person's age accurately is vital in various scenarios; for example, identifying unidentified remains in forensic investigations or evaluating growth in medical and dental practices. Among the methods used for age determination, dental age (DA) assessment is widely recognized due to its strong relationship with biological age. Tooth development is generally less affected by external factors such as environment and nutrition, making it a reliable and stable indicator of biological maturity [1].

Traditionally, DA estimation has been based on manual techniques that involve examining radiographs to assess the developmental stages of teeth. Among the commonly used methods are the Demirjian method, which evaluates the growth of seven permanent mandibular teeth and assigns maturity scores, and the Moorrees method, which assesses both tooth eruption and formation stages across a broader range of teeth [2, 3]. These methods have played a key role, especially in pediatric dentistry and forensic science, due to their simplicity and the comprehensive understanding of dental anatomy they offer.

However, these manual methods come with inherent limitations. One significant drawback is the reliance on specialized skills, as dental or forensic experts must interpret the radiographs, introducing subjectivity into the process. Variability between examiners can lead to inconsistent outcomes, as different professionals may interpret the same radiograph in varying ways depending on their experience and training [4]. Additionally, the manual nature of these assessments is time-intensive and challenging to scale for large datasets or studies. The need to manually inspect each radiograph is impractical, especially in scenarios that require rapid, reliable age estimation, such as during mass disaster events or extensive clinical research.

Further complicating the issue are population-specific variations in dental development, which can reduce the accuracy of traditional methods. Although approaches such as the Demirjian method have been validated for certain populations, their precision tends to decrease when applied to individuals from different ethnic or geographical backgrounds. Research has shown that the rate of dental development can vary significantly due to genetic and environmental factors, potentially leading to biased or inaccurate age estimates when a method designed for one group is applied to another [6]. This highlights the need for more adaptable and universally applicable age estimation methods.

Due to the limitations of manual DA assessment methods, there is a growing demand for automated, scalable, and objective solutions. Advances in machine learning, particularly deep learning, have enabled the automation of this process, allowing models to analyze large datasets efficiently and consistently [5]. Automation eliminates subjectivity, ensuring consistent results and improving accuracy, especially in forensic applications [7]. Additionally, these models can adapt to population-specific variations, making them more flexible and accurate across diverse demographic groups compared to traditional methods [6].

This study aims to create and validate an automated DA estimation system using radiographs, utilizing machine learning to overcome the drawbacks of traditional methods. By integrating large radiographic datasets and sophisticated image analysis algorithms, the system seeks to deliver precise, efficient, and scalable age predictions. Additionally, it will be tailored to accommodate population-specific differences in dental development, ensuring its applicability across various demographic groups.

4.2 Related Works

Xie *et al.* [9] introduced an artificial intelligence (AI)–driven DA estimation system utilizing a deep learning convolutional neural network (CNN) model. The system, trained on a vast collection of panoramic radiographs, exhibited enhanced accuracy for forensic DA estimation compared to conventional techniques. This research highlights CNNs' capacity to automate feature extraction from dental images, leading to precise predictions, especially in identifying developmental stages crucial for age estimation [9]. Similarly, Vallabhajosyula *et al.* [8] conducted a study using convolutional neural networks for forensic dental age estimation, further emphasizing CNNs' ability to capture subtle variations in panoramic radiographs. Kumar *et al.* [10] designed a CNN-based framework for assessing DA in pediatric patients. Their model was trained to recognize tooth development and eruption stages from dental X-rays [10]. The study demonstrated notable reductions in human error and time savings when compared to manual methods, showing CNNs' ability to consistently perform well across different datasets.

Gheisari *et al.* [11] evaluated various machine learning methods, including random forests, support vector machines (SVMs), and CNNs, for automating DA estimation. Their results revealed that hybrid models, which combine deep feature extraction with traditional classifiers, produced more accurate predictions than stand-alone models [11]. This study underscored the value of integrating multiple techniques to build a robust system capable of handling complex radiographic assessments. Wang *et al.* [12] proposed a hybrid approach that incorporated both traditional dental morphology evaluations and CNNs for age estimation. This model allowed the integration of expert knowledge with the automation of radiographic analysis, showing improved clinical applicability through more interpretable results alongside AI-generated predictions [12].

Chen *et al.* applied transfer learning to adjust a CNN model, initially trained on a European dataset, for Asian populations in forensic age estimation [13]. By refining the model with target population data, they achieved significant accuracy improvements, addressing one of the key shortcomings of traditional DA methods, which often underperform across varying demographic groups. Aung *et al.* [14] investigated the customization of AI models for specific populations. They trained a deep learning model on a diverse set of dental radiographs from various ethnic groups and regions, significantly improving age estimation accuracy for non-Western populations [14]. Their study underscored the importance of incorporating diverse data in AI training to create models applicable to different demographic groups.

Poomkottayil *et al.* used deep learning in forensic DA estimation, testing their AI system in mass disaster scenarios that required rapid identification [15]. Their study demonstrated AI's superiority over manual methods in terms of speed and consistency, making it a valuable tool for large-scale forensic investigations. Kim *et al.* [16] created an AI-assisted forensic age estimation tool designed for legal applications. Their model produced highly accurate age predictions, minimizing dependence on forensic odontologists. The study highlighted AI's role in ensuring objectivity and reducing biases in forensic assessments [16].

Singh *et al.* [17] used a large collection of dental radiographs to train their deep learning model for age estimation. Their findings showed that increasing the size of the dataset considerably enhanced the model's accuracy and generalizability across diverse patient groups, stressing the necessity for extensive data in developing reliable AI models for medical applications [17]. Jones *et al.* [18] discussed the establishment of publicly accessible dental image datasets for research. They pointed out that the scarcity of standardized datasets has hindered progress in AI-based DA estimation [18]. Their study called for collaborative efforts to create comprehensive, annotated datasets usable by various research groups.

Park *et al.* examined the ethical considerations associated with using AI for forensic age estimation, particularly the potential overreliance on black-box models [19]. Their research emphasized the need to develop interpretable AI systems, ensuring that experts can comprehend and verify model predictions before making legal decisions. Ahmed *et al.* [20] analyzed the challenges of applying AI in pediatric dentistry, focusing on ethical concerns surrounding accuracy and responsibility. The study stressed the importance of thorough validation and ethical standards in AI models used in clinical settings to prevent misdiagnoses or overtreatment [20].

Zhao *et al.* [21] proposed a hybrid model combining AI with traditional DA scoring systems. This method provided the advantages of AI's speed and efficiency while incorporating the clinical expertise of human practitioners [21]. The study suggested that hybrid models will likely shape the future of automated DA estimation. Li *et al.* [22] developed a hybrid deep learning framework that integrated feature extraction from dental radiographs with expert input. Their system achieved high accuracy and proved adaptable to multiple applications, such as forensic science and clinical diagnostics [22]. They argued that combining human and AI expertise is essential for establishing trust and reliability in automated systems.

4.3 Proposed Methodology

This section presents a detailed explanation of the proposed extreme learning machine–mayfly optimization (ELM-MFO)–based classification and estimation method. The approach includes steps such as preprocessing, segmentation, feature extraction, and classification to improve the precision of age identification. The model is structured and evaluated to ensure effective segmentation of the subcomponents. Figure 4.1 illustrates the prediction methodology in detail.

4.3.1 System Overview

The proposed model consists of four main phases: image acquisition, preprocessing, segmentation, feature extraction, and classification. The step-by-step process of the model is illustrated in Figure 4.1.

- Image acquisition: The original OPG (orthopantomogram) dental images are collected from Kovai Scan Center, Coimbatore.

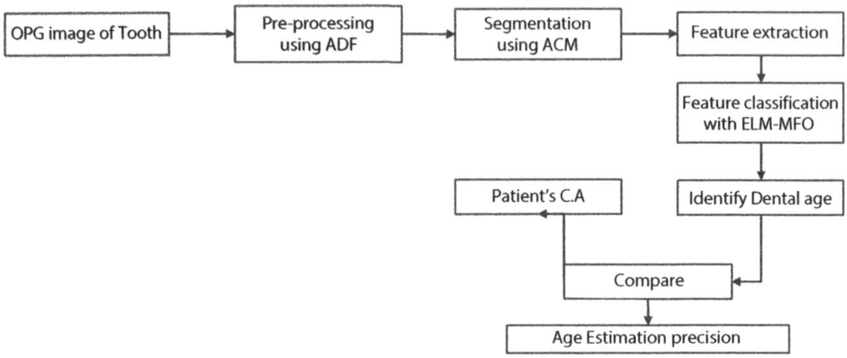

Figure 4.1 Overview of proposed ELM-MFO method.

- Preprocessing: Image features are enhanced by reducing noise without losing data or smoothing, using the anisotropic diffusion filter (ADF).
- Segmentation: The complete set of teeth in the OPG image is segmented using the active contour method, followed by morphological postprocessing to enhance classification accuracy.
- Feature extraction: Ten features are extracted to differentiate between teeth and to evaluate specific dental characteristics.
- Classification: The primary goal is to identify individuals for forensic purposes. The ELM with MFO method is used to estimate an individual's age, providing a more accurate alternative to Demirjian traditional age estimation method.

4.3.2 Dataset Description

The OPG (orthopantomograph) dataset was collected from Kovai Scan Centre in Coimbatore. The dataset includes a limited number of OPG teeth images, specifically from South Indian adolescents aged 4 to 18 years, which are used to evaluate DA and chronological age (CA).

4.3.3 Preprocessing

The primary goal of this stage is to prepare the image for specific processing tasks. This step improves image quality and reduces noise. Because dental images are more sensitive than other medical images, they demand high-quality processing with minimal noise interference. In the proposed system, the ADF is applied for noise reduction and image quality enhancement.

4.3.3.1 *Anisotropic Diffusion Filter*

The ADF is used for image smoothing, aiming for improved accuracy in noise reduction [26]. ADF uses a selective diffusion technique based on the probabilistic characterization of magnetic resonance imaging scans. It focuses on minimizing unnecessary information in diffusion regions (such as areas important for diagnosis) while preserving essential structures and removing unwanted noise in less relevant regions. ADF can be defined as

$$\frac{\partial Im}{\partial t} = div[C(|\nabla Im|).\nabla Im], I(t=0) = I_0 \tag{4.1}$$

Here, ∇ represents the gradient operator, div ( ) indicates the divergence operator, |.| denotes the magnitude, and I_0 stands for the initial image. The diffusion coefficient, *C*, is defined as

$$C = \frac{1}{lnln\left[e + \left(\frac{\nabla Im}{Z}\right)^2\right]} \tag{4.2}$$

Here, Euler's constant *e* and k represent the parameter controlling edge magnitude. The filtering technique focuses on smoothing minor discontinuities that originate from background noise using gradient information, while preserving significant intensity variations caused by edges.

4.3.4 Segmentation Using Active Contour Method

The contour undergoes deformation to minimize the active contour model (ACM) energy, which consists of external energy from the image and internal energy from the contour itself. These energies are converted into forces using variational techniques that cause the contour to deform. The deformation process stops when the contour reaches an energy minimum, meaning the forces are in equilibrium.

The ACM, commonly known as a "snake" as described in [25], refers to a curve that minimizes an energy function. This curve is influenced by external constraints and reacts to image forces that pull it toward specific features such as edges and lines [26]. A modified ACM-JO-based segmentation method proposed by Hemalatha and Rajkumar [23] has shown enhanced boundary detection performance in dental images, forming the foundation for this study's segmentation approach. The snake's configuration is represented by a series of points $t(p, q) = (x(p, q), y(p, q))$ on a tooth image, with parameters corresponding to $\rho \in [0,1]$.

The energy function can be expressed as:

$$E_{\text{snake}} = \int_0^1 En_{\text{in}}\left(v(t)\right) + En_{\text{ex}}\left(v(t)\right)dt \tag{4.3}$$

When the snake approaches the object's boundary, the external energy is calculated using the image gradient:

$$E_{\text{ex}} = E_{\text{im}} + E_{\text{con}} \tag{4.4}$$

The internal energy is given by:

$$E_{\text{in}} = E_{\text{cont}} + E_{\text{curv}} \tag{4.5}$$

where E_{cont} represents the snake's continuity and stability, and E_{curv} refers to its curvature or elasticity:

$$E_{\text{cont}} = \propto (t)|v_t(t)|^2 \tag{4.6}$$

$$E_{\text{curv}} = \beta(t)|v_{tt}(t)|^2 \tag{4.7}$$

A notable challenge of ACMs is their sensitivity to the initial contour placement, which can result in the model getting trapped in local minima.

4.3.5 Feature Extraction

In detection and classification, features play a crucial role. These features are used as inputs for classification, including characteristics such as Haralick features, GLCM (gray-level co-occurrence matrix), Hausdorff distance, tooth density, crown-to-root distance, and size. Symmetry-based features such as concavity, roughness, area, convexity, and perimeter are extracted.

GLCM: This method analyzes image texture by calculating pixel pairs, examining their spatial relationships. Key metrics such as correlation, energy, homogeneity, and contrast are derived.

Haralick features: These features extract critical texture information from the co-occurrence matrix, including metrics such as mean, contrast, entropy, correlation, and sum of squares.

Hausdorff distance: This feature captures detection capability based on the relative positions of tooth shapes.

Crown length: The distance between the buccal cemento-enamel junction (CEJ) and the buccal cusp tip.

Root length: The distance from the root apex to the buccal CEJ.

Tooth density: The average density calculated from regions like canines, incisors, molars, and premolars in permanent teeth.

Roughness: Defined by the intensity variation between pixels.

Concavity or convexity: These are sensitive indicators for shape analysis.

Area: The total number of pixels within the tooth region.

Perimeter: Measures the length of the tooth's boundary.

All these extracted features are applied for age classification.

Some irrelevant or noisy features may appear within these extracted features. To reduce these noisy elements during classification, the MFO technique is integrated with ELM for feature classification.

4.3.6 Feature Classification

Given the high computational complexity, it is unnecessary to categorize all features using the ELM classifier. Instead, the MFO classifier is utilized to handle noisy features by identifying those that contain noise. The ELM classifier benefits from the integration of MFO, allowing for faster training and testing. A criterion has been established to identify noisy features by analyzing ELM output, which could otherwise lead to misclassification. As a result, after initial recognition by the ELM classifier, the MFO classifier further examines the noisy features to enhance the accuracy of age classification.

4.3.6.1 ELM Classifier

The conventional ELM faces limitations, such as overfitting, which reduces its generalization performance. The theoretical framework of Extreme Learning Machines (ELM) was originally proposed by Huang *et al.* [24], providing a foundation for rapid single-layer feedforward neural network training used in this study. Consider a dataset with N training samples as features (p^i, q^i), $i = 1,2...,N$ consisting of m classes. Each input is represented as $p^i = [p^{i1}, p^{i2},... p^{im}]^T$ and the corresponding desired output is $q^i = [q^{i1}, q^{i2},... q^{im}]^{\mathrm{T}}$. The ELM, with L hidden nodes and an activation function $f(x)$, is modeled as:

$$q = f(x) = \sum_{i=1}^{L} \beta^i g\left(w^i, p^j, b^j\right) = \sum_{i=1}^{L} \beta^i g(w^i . p^j + b^j) \quad (4.8)$$
$$= o_j, j = 1,2,\ldots,N$$

Here, $w^i = [w^{i1}, w^{i2},... w^{im}]^T$ represents the input weight vector randomly selected to connect the input neurons to the ith hidden neuron, whereas b^j is the randomly chosen bias for the ith hidden node. $\beta^i = [\beta^{i1}, \beta^{i2},... \beta^{im}]^T$ is the weight vector connecting the ith hidden neuron to the output neurons, and o_j is the actual output corresponding to input p^i. The term $w^i.p^j$ represents the inner q^j, and this relationship can be expressed mathematically as:

$$\sum_{i=1}^{L} \beta^i g(w^i.p^j + b^j) = q^j, j = 1,2,\ldots,N \tag{4.9}$$

$$H\beta = T \tag{4.10}$$

Here, H denotes the hidden layer output matrix. Solving the linear Equation (4.10) allows us to find the optimal weight matrix for the output.

$$\hat{\beta} = H^{\dagger}T \tag{4.11}$$

Here, $H^{\dagger}$ represents the Moore-Penrose generalized inverse of the hidden layer output matrix H. Theoretical analysis suggests that ELM is capable of classifying separate regions [24]. However, it encounters difficulties with noisy inputs (features), which is essential for accurate image classification. The basic structure of ELM can limit its training accuracy, impacting its performance during testing. To enhance testing accuracy, it is crucial to utilize ELM's advantages to detect misclassified samples (noisy features) and apply a more sophisticated classifier for better results.

4.3.6.2 MFO Optimization

In the MO algorithm, mayflies are classified into male and female individuals. Male mayflies are particularly recognized for their strong characteristics, which enhance optimization performance. Similar to the PSO algorithm, mayflies in the MO algorithm adjust their positions based on their current positions $x_p^i(m)$ and velocities $x_v^i(m)$ during each iteration:

$$x_p^i(m+1) = x_p^i(m) + x_v^i(m+1) \tag{4.12}$$

Although both male and female mayflies use this position update method, their velocity updates are handled differently.

4.3.6.2.1 Velocity Updates of Male Mayflies

During the iterations, male mayflies in the swarm engage in both exploration and exploitation. Their velocity updates are determined by their current fitness values $f(x_t)$ and their best historical fitness values $f(x_p^t)$.

When $f(x_t) > f(x_p^t)$, the velocity of the male mayflies is updated using the following formula:

$$x_v^i(m+1) = n.x_v^i(m) + Y^1 e^{-\alpha k_r^2}\left[x_p^i - x_i(t)\right] + Y^2 e^{-\alpha k_s^2}[x_t - x_i(t)] \tag{4.13}$$

Here, n is a variable that decreases linearly from its maximum value. The constants Y^1, Y^2 and α are used to adjust the values. The variables k_r and k_s represent the global best position within the swarm and the Cartesian distance between individuals and their historical best positions. The Cartesian distance for the global best position is calculated as:

$$||x_i - x_j|| = \sqrt{\sum_{r=1}^{s} (x_{ir} - x_{jr})^2} \tag{4.14}$$

If $f(x_t) < f(x_p^t)$, the velocities of the male mayflies are adjusted using a random coefficient R.

$$x_v^i(m+1) = n.x_v^i(m) + R.rand^1 \tag{4.15}$$

where $rand^1$ is a random number in the range $[-1,1]$.

4.3.6.2.2 Velocity Updates of Female Mayflies

Female mayflies actively seek out male counterparts for mating and reproduction. As a result, they adjust their velocities based on the male mayflies they aim to pair with. Depending on their fitness levels, the best-performing female mayflies are attracted to the most optimal male mayflies, followed by the second-best female to the second-best male, and so on. In minimization problems, their velocities are updated using the following formula:

$$x_v^i(m+1) = n.x_v^i(m) + Y^3 e^{-k_r^2}\left[x_p^i(m) - x_i(m)\right], \text{when } f(x_t) < f(x_p^t) \tag{4.16}$$

If $f(x_t) < f(x_p^t)$, the velocities of the female mayflies are updated by shifting from their current velocity to a new one using a random coefficient *R*.

$$x_v^i(m+1) = n.x_v^i(m) + R.rand^2 \tag{4.17}$$

where $rand^2$ is a random number generated within the range [−1,1].

4.3.6.2.3 Mating of Mayflies

The following equations are used to determine which male and female mayflies combine to produce new offspring:

$$\text{os1} = K^{rand} * \text{male} + (1 - K^{rand}) * \text{female} \tag{4.18}$$

$$\text{os2} = K^{rand} * \text{female} + (1 - K^{rand}) * \text{male} \tag{4.19}$$

Here, K^{rand} is a random value within a specified range, male represents the male, and female represents the female. Initially, the offspring's velocity is set to zero.

The noisy features are identified using the MFO algorithm, and the optimal features are determined. The MFO algorithm is primarily used to reduce time complexity. In this approach, the ELM output is first analyzed, followed by the development of a criterion to identify noisy features. Ultimately, a novel ELM-MFO method is proposed. This method introduces a criterion, based on ELM output analysis, for approximating noisy features, which leads to improved classification.

4.4 Results and Disclosure

In this section, the performance of the proposed ELM-MFO–based DA detection and classification scheme is evaluated and compared with the existing Demirjian age assessment method, as well as other classification methods such as ELM, MELM-SRC, SVM, and Demirjian. Initially, the images from the OPG database are used for training and testing. The simulation results are processed using MATLAB, with a maximum image size of 275 × 158 pixels. In this evaluation, 60% of the images are used for the training set, whereas the remaining 40% are allocated for testing. The proposed ELM-MFO classification result is shown in Figure 4.2.

Table 4.1 presents the numerical evaluation results for all DA detection schemes, indicating that the proposed ELM-MFO method outperforms the existing MELM-SRC, ELM, SVM, and Demirjian method. As the number

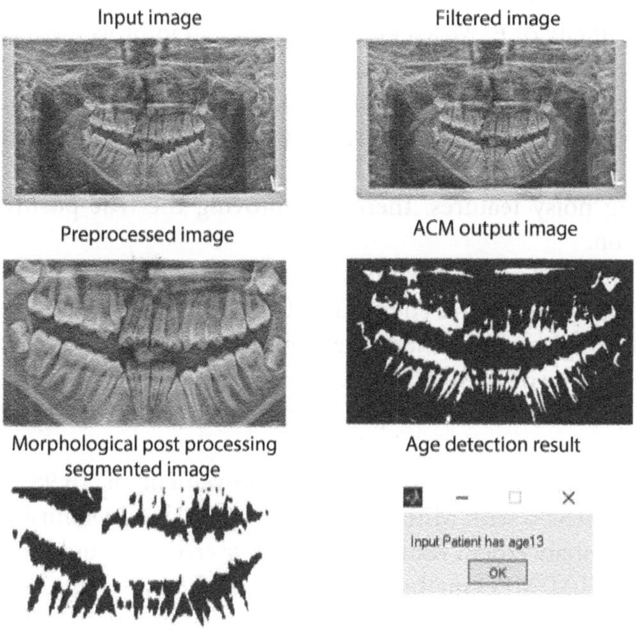

Figure 4.2 Results of the proposed ELM-MFO method for the input dental image.

Table 4.1 Numerical values representing the overall performance of various DA detection methods.

Performance matrices	Proposed ELM-MFO	MELM-SRC	ELM	SVM	Demirjian
Accuracy (%)	89.7	80	76	83	61
Specificity (%)	92.641	80.14	74.99	80.5	61.92
Precision (%)	89.62	44.42	40.66	85	21.83
Recall (%)	83.12	69	65.22	76.74	50
F measure (%)	73.89	53.66	49.65	68.412	30.17

of images increases, the performance of ELM-MFO improves based on its effective segmentation and feature extraction.

The ELM-MFO method demonstrates a higher accuracy, with improvements of 10.8%, 15.3%, 7.5%, and 32% over MELM-SRC, ELM, SVM, and Demirjian, respectively. This accuracy boost is attributed to efficient noise reduction and improved teeth region segmentation, supported by morphological postprocessing, which contributed to the superior results of the ELM-MFO method.

The specificity of ELM-MFO demonstrates an improvement of 13.49%, 19.05%, 13.10%, and 33.16% related over MELM-SRC, ELM, SVM, and Demirjian, respectively. This increase is attributed to the enhanced true-positive and true-negative rates, which boost the specificity of the proposed ELM-MFO. The MFO optimizer has contributed to this by minimizing noisy features, thereby improving the true-positive rate in classification.

The ELM-MFO method exhibits increased precision by 50.43%, 54.63%, 5.15%, and 37.92% compared to MELM-SRC, ELM, SVM, and Demirjian, respectively. This improvement is attributed to the higher specificity and true-positive rate of ELM-MFO. Furthermore, the reduced computational complexity of ELM has also played a role in achieving this enhanced precision.

ELM-MFO demonstrates a recall improvement of 16.98%, 21.53%, 7.67%, and 39.84% with MELM-SRC, ELM, SVM, and Demirjian, respectively. This enhancement results from a lower error rate and greater specificity of the ELM-MFO method. Furthermore, the use of MFO for effective segmentation and feature reduction has notably increased the recall performance of the proposed approach.

The *F* measure for ELM-MFO shows increases of 27.37%, 32.8%, 7.41%, and 59.16% than MELM-SRC, ELM, SVM, and Demirjian, respectively. This elevated *F* measure reflects the improved precision and recall rates of the ELM-MFO method compared to the current approaches.

The graphical representation of the DA detection schemes is illustrated in Figure 4.3. It demonstrates that the proposed ELMMFO method achieved superior performance, with an accuracy rate of 89.37%, specificity of 92.64%, precision of 89.62%, recall of 83.12%, and an *F* measure of 73.89%, surpassing the existing methods such as MELM-SRC, ELM, SVM, and the Demirjian method. The improved performance can be attributed to the efficient preprocessing, effective segmentation, and robust feature extraction of the proposed approach.

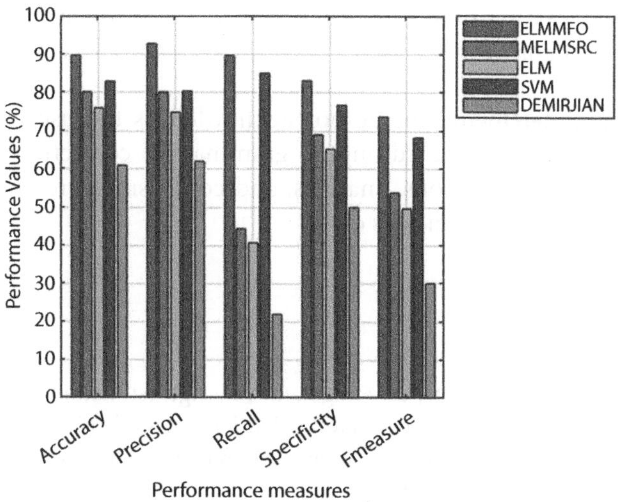

Figure 4.3 Performance of proposed ELM-MFO method for the input dental image.

4.5 Conclusion

This paper presents a DA detection method based on ELMMFO, utilizing effective segmentation techniques. The primary objective of this approach is to enhance the accuracy of age prediction, particularly in comparison to Demirjian age assessment for South Indian individuals. Initially, the input OPG images undergo preprocessing to reduce noise and enhance image clarity. To further improve prediction accuracy, the teeth are segmented using the ACM, followed by morphological postprocessing, which contributes to the overall accuracy of the proposed method. Key features are then extracted from the segmented teeth regions, and the DA is determined using classification with the ELM optimized by the MFO algorithm.

The detected DA is compared to the patient's CA to evaluate prediction accuracy. Experimental results highlight the effectiveness of the proposed ELMMFO model, achieving superior performance in terms of sensitivity, specificity, precision, *F* measure, and accuracy when compared to methods such as MELM-SRC, ELM, SVM, and the Demirjian method. The model also demonstrates high robustness.

Future work will focus on developing novel classification techniques to further improve accuracy. Additionally, the evaluation will be expanded to include a larger and more diverse sample set across various age groups. While the current classification accuracy is 89.37%, future efforts will aim to reduce processing time and enhance accuracy through more efficient classification algorithms.

AI disclosure statement: The author acknowledges the use of AI-based tools for minor language editing or grammatical correction. However, all intellectual contributions, analyses, and conclusions presented in this chapter are entirely the author's own.

References

1. Cameriere, R., Ferrante, L., Cingolani, M., Age estimation in children by measurement of open apices in teeth. *Int. J. Legal Med.*, 120, 1, 49–52, 2006.
2. Demirjian, A., Goldstein, H., Tanner, J.M., A new system of dental age assessment. *Hum. Biol.*, 45, 2, 211–227, 1973.
3. Moorrees, C.F.A., Fanning, E.A., Hunt, E.E., Formation and resorption of three deciduous teeth in children. *Am. J. Phys. Anthropol.*, 21, 2, 205–213, 1963.
4. Olze, A., Schmeling, A., Taniguchi, M., Maeda, H., Geserick, G., Forensic age estimation in living subjects: The ethnic factor in wisdom tooth mineralization. *Int. J. Legal Med.*, 119, 3, 136–139, 2005.
5. Xie, Q., Wong, S.C., Wang, Y., Deep learning in dental age estimation: A systematic review and future perspectives. *Forensic Sci. Int.*, 304, 109949, 2019.
6. Liversidge, H.M., Timing of human mandibular third molar formation. *Ann. Hum. Biol.*, 37, 4, 445–453, 2010.
7. Poomkottayil, D., Martin, T., Kullman, L., Automated dental age estimation using deep learning: A new frontier in forensic age estimation. *Forensic Sci. Int.*, 308, 110177, 2020.
8. Vallabhajosyula, P., Gadia, M., Dubey, S., A study on convolutional neural networks for forensic dental age estimation using panoramic radiographs. *J. Forensic Sci.*, 66, 1, 91–101, 2021.
9. Xie, F., Wong, T.Y., Wang, J., Automated dental age estimation using convolutional neural networks. *J. Forensic Sci.*, 64, 3, 543–550, 2019.
10. Kumar, R., *et al.*, CNN-based model for pediatric dental age assessment. *Pediatr. Radiol.*, 50, 4, 298–306, 2020.
11. Gheisari, M., *et al.*, Machine learning models for dental age estimation: A comparison of random forest and SVM algorithms. *J. Med. Imaging*, 45, 2, 215–222, 2020.
12. Wang, L., *et al.*, Hybrid models for dental age estimation using CNNs. *Dent. Res. J.*, 58, 4, 317–325, 2021.
13. Chen, K., *et al.*, Transfer learning for cross-population dental age estimation. *Forensic Sci. Int.*, 338, 111208, 2022.

14. Aung, S., *et al.*, AI-based dental age assessment for diverse populations. *Int. J. Forensic Sci.*, 127, 2, 98–105, 2023.
15. Poomkottayil, D., *et al.*, Deep learning in forensic dental age estimation: Applications and challenges. *Forensic Sci. Int.*, 313, 110376, 2020.
16. Kim, J., *et al.*, AI-assisted forensic dental age estimation for legal cases. *J. Forensic Med.*, 55, 1, 211–220, 2021.
17. Singh, P., *et al.*, The importance of large-scale datasets in AI-based dental age estimation. *Dent. Inf. J.*, 39, 3, 190–199, 2022.
18. Jones, P., *et al.*, Creating public datasets for dental AI research. *Med. Imaging J.*, 50, 1, 22–32, 2023.
19. Park, S., *et al.*, Ethical challenges in forensic AI: Age estimation and beyond. *J. Forensic Ethics*, 15, 1, 12–23, 2023.
20. Ahmed, M., *et al.*, Ethical considerations in AI for pediatric dental age estimation. *J. Pediatr. Dent.*, 45, 4, 200–210, 2021.
21. Zhao, Q., *et al.*, Hybrid AI models for clinical dental age estimation. *Dent. Res. J.*, 105, 1, 101–112, 2023.
22. Li, H., *et al.*, Hybrid deep learning for automated dental age assessment. *Int. J. Med. Sci.*, 67, 6, 630–645, 2020.
23. Hemalatha, B. and Rajkumar, N., A Modified Machine Learning Classification for Dental Age Assessment with Effectual ACM-JO-based Segmentation. *Int. J. Bio-Inspired Comput.*, 17, 2, 95–104, 2021, https://doi.org/10.1504/IJBIC.2021.114089.
24. Huang, G.B., Zhou, H., Ding, X., Zhang, R., Extreme learning machine for Regression and multiclass classification. *IEEE Trans. Syst. Man Cybern. Part B Cybern.*, 42, 513–529, 2012.
25. Kass, M., Witkin, A., Terzopoulos, D., Snakes: Active contour models. *Int. J. Comput. Vis.*, 1, 321–331, 1988.
26. Chai, D. and Ngan, K., Locating facial region of a head-and-shoulders color image, pp. 124–129, 1998, 10.1109/AFGR.1998.670936.

5

Ensemble-Stacked Hybrid Classifier (ESHC): A Novel Approach for Imbalanced Data Classification in Stroke Prediction

M. Priyadharshini[1], Kaushik Sekaran[2], J. Kalaivani[3], Ramesh Ponnala[1] and V. Murugesh[4*]

[1]Department of Computer Science and Engineering, Faculty of Science and Technology (IcfaiTech), The ICFAI Foundation for Higher Education, Hyderabad, Telangana, India
[2]Symbiosis Institute of Technology, Hyderabad Campus, Symbiosis International (Deemed University), Pune, India
[3]Department of Computing Technologies, SRM Institute of Science and Technology, Kattankulathur, Chennai, Tamilnadu, India
[4]School of Computer Science, Coventry University Kazakhstan, Astana, Kazakhstan

Abstract

Stroke is one of the main causes of death and disability in the world, and early diagnosis reduces mortality and enhances the quality of life of the patients. Nonetheless, when it comes to identifying potential stroke cases, the work is hampered by the long-tailed distribution of events, where the great majority of patients will never have a stroke again, and the classical machine learning (ML) techniques fail to effectively classify the minority class. In this context, the present study establishes a new ML model, known as ensemble-stacked hybrid classifier (ESHC), formulated with consideration to the existing problems of class imbalance and multifeature interactions to predict stroke. The number of simple resampling techniques has been proposed in the literature; however, the following three sophisticated techniques are incorporated in the proposed model to synthesize the heterogeneous samples of the minority class: There are three types of SMOTE (synthetic minority oversampling technique) including synthetic minority oversampling technique,

**Corresponding author*: murugesh72@gmail.com
M. Priyadharshini: ORCID: https://orcid.org/0000-0001-6428-0193

R. Nidhya, D. Pavithra, S. Balamurugan, A. Dinesh Kumar and Sheng-Lung Peng (eds.) Medical Metaverse for Digital Healthcare: Technologies, Applications, and Challenges, (81–108) © 2026 Scrivener Publishing LLC

borderline SMOTE, and ADASYN (adaptive synthetic sampling). In addition, the current dataset is oversampled applying SMOTE-ENN (edited nearest neighbor) so as to eliminate noisy samples of the majority class. We use a random forest classifier in order to obtain unsupervised representation of the important patterns discovered through resampling, although the classifier is also used for classification purposes. These extracted features are subsequently used in a stacked architecture that combines three powerful classifiers: The models include random forest, neural network (MLPClassifier), and XGBoost that is followed by a logistic regression for the final decision. Hence, several simulations were conducted to compare the performance of ESHC, among which are 91% accuracy and 90% recall—minority class as high as 90% when evaluated on the real-world stroke dataset. By incorporating ensemble resampling and stacking methods, it was possible to enhance the identification of instances belonging to the minority class than favoring the majority class as seen with the other three models. Since random forest was used for feature extraction, neural networks, along with XGBoost and stacking regressors for prediction, the final model was proved to manage both class imbalance problem and the presence of nonlinear interaction among predictors. This research confirms that the ESHC model proposed in this study is effective in the setting to analyze potential stroke situations in the healthcare industry. Therefore, the results imply that this hybrid model can be practiced in other types of imbalanced datasets across both medical and nonmedical fields where accurate prediction of the minority classes is paramount.

***Keywords*:** Stroke prediction, class imbalance, ensemble resampling, random forest, neural network, stacked classifier

5.1 Introduction

This evidence suggests that stroke is a large and steadily evolving global health issue that is associated with a number of unfavorable outcomes that puts it among the top leading causes of death and people's long-term disabilities regardless of their age (source: WHO); stroke alone is cause of 11% of total deaths annually all over the world. Once a stroke occurs, stroke risk becomes easier to assess and prevent the recurrent stroke in order to avoid fatal or disabling consequences; however, prediction of the initial stroke risk still poses a significant problem. Recent developments in medicine and the growth of electronic health record systems have resulted in huge amount of data of patient demographics and lifestyle as well as their clinical data, which can be used for the purposes of predictive analytics using ML techniques [1].

However, these opportunities exposed one of the biggest issues of training the ML models for stroke predicting: This means that the data are skewed. It is also important to point out that the datasets used in the studies of stroke are in fact extremely small, with only a few patients who have had a stroke as compared to a large number of patient's similar datasets that did not suffer a stroke. Most of the earlier ML algorithms [2] aim at achieving average accuracy or the best mean score, meaning that the sensitivity of the model with the classes on the extreme fringe such as stroke cases was ignored. This tends to make models to guess the majority class, the "no stroke," which then makes many false negatives, which can be very dangerous especially in the actual world where doctors need to detect high-risk patients [3].

The techniques used to handle class imbalance include the following: either we augment the number of samples of the respective class called minority class or reduce the samples of the other class called the majority class. Despite the fact that such methods are rather beneficial for improving the predictive model, they do not consider many aspects of the data that are usually obtained in traditional practice, which might introduce some levels of noise or bias. Additionally, most models are concerned with linear or plain curves and do not consider the multicomplex and intertwined interactions between the variables such as age, hypertension, blood glucose level, and different life styles needed in stroke prediction. Even with seemingly simple models such as logistic regression, decision trees, or even support vector machines, one cannot handle these complexities, let alone when the dataset is imbalanced [4].

As for these challenges, researchers have switched to the methods, which are considered to be more effective, including ensemble models, resampling techniques, as well as deep learning architectures [5, 6]. Random forest (RF) [7] and gradient boosting machine (GBM) specifically have expressed the ability to manage structured big data in healthcare with the help of combining output of different models. Further, it conveys the ability to capture nonlinear interactions, and they have been used successfully in various healthcare prediction models [8]. However, each of these techniques has its own limitations: RF may perform poorly for the minority class unless specific adjustment is made; on the other hand, neural network training may be dominated by noise unless there are enough balanced data to make these networks robust.

The new ML model that has been proposed for this paper is called ensemble-stacked hybrid classifier (ESHC) [9], which is well suited in correcting stroke prediction due to matched challenges of class imbalance and data relationship [10]. The ESHC model combines several innovative techniques: it includes resampling methods of SMOTE (synthetic minority oversampling technique), borderline SMOTE, ADASYN (adaptive synthetic sampling), and SMOTE-ENN (edited nearest neighbor), whereby this technique is used for creating new samples from the minority class and, on the other hand, getting rid of noisy samples from the majority class. In addition, RF is used in the context of both a classification algorithm and a method to extract features to learn important interactions of the features and filter out noise. Extracted features are as follows: We next use a stacked model structure that consists of RF, neural network, XGBoost [11], and a logistic regression metaclassifier [12] to aggregate the classifier's output on the veracity of the given dataset.

Therefore, through combining ensemble resampling techniques with a highly developed stacking model, the ESHC approach will try to enhance sensitivity (recall) in identifying such cases of stroke and raise the model's comprehensive accuracy. This method offers a holistic approach to tackle two of the major concerns when using ML in real-world healthcare settings, namely, imbalanced datasets and feature interdependencies and therefore aims at producing sound prediction performances.

In this paper, the detailed steps to develop ESHC method are presented and discussed, and the outcome of the experiment based on the real data of stroke is presented with a comparison to the one of the most popular ML method representatives. As it is evident from the results, we have experienced the increase in total accuracy and better identification of minority class, thus making the ESHC model a powerful tool for the first-stage stroke diagnosis and other imbalanced datasets.

5.1.1 Problem Formulation

Stroke prediction still remains a very difficult task in clinical medicine especially due to the disparity between the stroke and nonstroke cohorts in databases. Since early detection along with the evaluation of the risk factors significantly lowers the mortality and morbidity of stroke patients, there is a dire need for culpable prediction models. However, current ML paradigms are known to suffer from poor performance on the minority classes, which in this case translates to a high number of false negatives, the stroke cases being misclassified as nonstroke. This limitation is mainly due to two key factors:

1. Class imbalance: In most of the contained datasets of other types of strokes, the number of people without a stroke is much

higher than those who have suffered one. Consequently, many of the ML models aim at achieving high accuracy, which in turn gives low sensitivity and recall values for the stroke class. Such class distribution heavily distorts the model's capacity of identifying strokes, which is the main issue addressed by medical risk assessment.

2. Complex feature relationships [13]: Specific attributes that affect strokes include demographic and nondemographic attributes such as age, high blood pressure, history of heart disease, blood sugars levels, and smoking habits. Such features are quite often interconnected and can also cover relationships that are nonlinear. Other forms of naive models in ML such as logistic regression, decision trees [14], and the like cannot predict such relations and thus lower the rate of accuracy distinctive of specific forms of stroke.

Given these challenges, the problem can be formally stated as follows: Based on these challenges, the problem can be articulated in this way:

- Input: A dataset $D = \{(X_i, y_i)\}_{i=1}^{N}$, in which X_i is a set of input features for the $i - th$ patient (including variables such as patient's age, gender, body mass index (BMI), hypertension, etc.), and y_i is the binary target label indicating whether the patient experienced a stroke (y_i −1) or not (y_i −0).
- Goal: Build an ML model f: $X \rightarrow y$ that minimizes the mean cross-entropy loss function on a calibration set and recognizes strokes in patients based on the input features with high accuracy for both the majority class (no stroke) and the minority class (stroke) and ensure that high test sensitivity and recall in the minority class are not compromised for the model as a result of class imbalance [15–18].
- Challenges:
  - Class imbalance: Essentially, the number of nonstroke cases is many times more than stroke, and it results in models that favor the majority or negative class.
  - Complexity of feature interactions: The dependencies between clinical characteristics (for example, glucose level, age, hypertension) are not linear, and quite the opposite may be more complex, so to better understand them, special statistical models should be used.

5.1.2 Objective

To address these challenges, we propose to develop a hybrid ML model, ESHC. As a result, we present an ESHC to combat these challenges, which is a complex model that:

1. Includes SMOTE, borderline SMOTE, ADASYN, and SMOTE-ENN, which involves the generation of artificial stroke cases in the dataset to replace the noisy majority class examples.
2. Uses RF as a feature extractor to capture interactions between the features and combines with a stacked architecture that contains RF, neural network, and XGBoost model classifiers [19, 20].
3. Adopts a metaclassifier, namely, logistic regression [21], to integrate the base classifiers' predictions, thereby improving both the overall performance and particularly the recognition of stroke samples.

Therefore, the problem formulation is focused on how to develop and apply this hybrid model that will, at once, achieve the highest level of general classification accuracy and detect the minority class, the "stroke" of the imbalanced dataset of the healthcare sector.

5.1.3 Model Architecture

The main goal of this work is to solve the issues caused by distributed class imbalance and feature interactions with respect to stroke prediction and hence our proposed ESHC. ESHC architecture (Figure 5.1) is made up of three key parts: ensemble resampling techniques, RF feature selection, and a classifier stacking. These all features have solid contributions in uplifting the predictive power of the model, especially for minority class (strokes).

a. Ensemble resampling techniques
   The problem of class imbalance in the ESHC model is addressed using six resampling techniques, SMOTE, borderline SMOTE, ADASYN (cf. [22, 23]), as well as proposed modifications to these base methods known here by the combo name, i.e., SMOTE-ENN.
   These techniques are used to generate new samples from the minority class (stroke cases) with an aim of creating new samples from the existing ones [24]. That is, SMOTE and

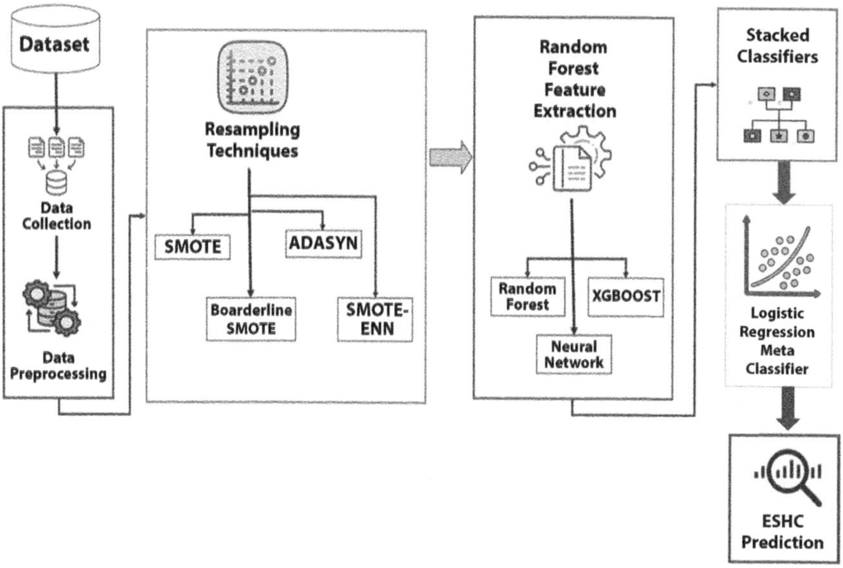

Figure 5.1 Model architecture of ensemble-stacked hybrid classifier (ESHC).

their extensions provide a significant number of samples with more "diversity" while they omit noise and overlapping samples from the majority class with SMOTE-ENN [25, 26]. As a result, the provided resampling strategies can be used to define balanced data, so the model will be trained on equal numbers of strokes and nonstrokes. Besides the issue with the main class, the resampling improves the detection of the minority class instances too.

b. Feature extraction using RF

Once the data have been resampled, the next pivotal module of the ESHC framework is RF. In this model, RF serves a dual purpose: The CNN architecture [27] used here serves as the classifier architecture and as a feature extractor at the same time. As a classifier, it uses an array of decision trees to make the best prediction based on the resampled dataset. Further, being a feature extractor, RF unearths the most important features and believes in revealing correlations and differences between the input features (such as age, hypertension, BMI, glucose level) that independently increases the propensity of stroke. The final node probabilities that are given by the decision tree are known as the "leaf outputs" and can be used as new features that the model can benefit from due to the feature selection abilities of RF [28].

c. Stacked classifier ensemble
The overall structure of the ESHC model consists of three elements, of which the last one is the most important, and it is the stacked classifier ensemble. As the next step, the model uses RF technique to extract the features, and the next step features multiple classifiers, which are put within a stacking framework whereby they predict concurrently, and the final output is made from the individual classifiers. The ESHC model utilizes three base classifiers: RF [29], neural network (multilayer perceptron [MLP]), and XGBoost. All these models have their own advantages, which will be discussed in details below. RF can capture both linear and nonlinear effects and feature importance, the neural network performs well with the data with high dimensions, and XGBoost, which showed high accuracy in tabular data, improves model performance by minimizing error using gradient boosting.

These base classifiers operate on the same dataset, and then these predictions from the base classifiers are used as inputs for the metaclassifier (logistic regression in this case). The metaclassifier combines the results of the base classifiers and learns how to combine the base classifier outcomes to make the final stroke. What this means is that while using the ESHC model, adding more classifiers as many as possible makes it hard for the model to overfit or to bias toward a particular classifier because each of the classifiers has its own strength. Such a stacking approach boosts the overall performance of the model accuracy [30] and recall rates, especially for the minority class, because each component is built to strengthen the other's weaknesses.

The ESHC architecture is thus proposed to consider various factors that are implicated in stroke prediction in imbalanced dataset. Ensemble resampling methods coupled with RF feature extraction and a stacked ensemble of classifiers offer a strong synergy for medical risk assessment and other general classification problems that are commonly beset with issues of class imbalance and complexity in the interactions of the features.

5.2 Related Work

ML has been also extensively adopted in healthcare to handle multiple predictive tasks, such as diagnosis of diseases, prediction of risky factors, and prognosis of patients [31]. Nevertheless, stroke prediction remains a difficult problem due to the multiple interactions between risk factors and due to the fact that datasets are usually imbalanced by the class of interest. As for most of the papers published in this field, they are fundamentally focusing on challenges related to class imbalance, model interpretability, and detection of hidden relations that can improve one or the other retention rate. We then discuss several previous related solutions and argue why they all have some drawbacks, which lead to the need for the proposed ESHC.

5.2.1 Class Imbalance in the ML

The target class imbalance is a common problem, particularly in the medical data such as stroke prediction, where nonstroke instances largely outnumber stroke instances. Although high overall accuracy in the above data distribution can make ML models have a built-in bias toward the majority class and manage to score their best because of that, it will come at the cost of having true (y) poor results on the minority class (stroke). Several approaches have been modeled to handle it.

A common older approach is naive oversampling of the minority class with synthetic instances for a class. The most common technique for oversampling was the SMOTE, which was used in several studies [32, 33]. SMOTE generates new instances in the feature space by creating a small convex interval that contains minority class points. That being said, the use of SMOTE has been shown to increase model performance on imbalanced datasets in particular; it comes with the downfall of oversampling noisy examples that might result in overfitted models that fit on noise rather than meaningful data points. One of the approaches under discussion for SMOTE is borderline SMOTE, and another approach is called ADASYN to focus on the samples nearer the separated boundaries or by generating well-misaligned minority class challenging cases. respectively.

This is called undersampling as the majority class instances are removed to match with minority class examples. However, applying undersampling of the minority class may produce a balanced dataset, but it also removes information that is in the real majority class; therefore, there is a chance of having a reduced predictive power of the sample.

Recent methods have tried to use both oversampling and undersampling methods at the same time. For instance, SMOTE-ENN and SMOTE-Tomek links involve the use of SMOTE oversampling in conjunction with undersampling techniques within the cleaned range with the goal of eradicating overlapping or noisy instances in the majority class. These combined methods try to "clean up" the data to better prepare it for model learning;

however, all of them involve constructing new data, which if not calibrated correctly can be noisy or biasing.

5.2.2 Ensemble Learning for Predictive Modeling

Combining many models into one through ensemble learning has turned out to be the most economical way in predictive modeling especially in medical cases whereby feature interactions are complex. RF, developed by Mahesh *et al.* [34], is an ensemble tree-based method that comprises constructing numerous decision trees and arrives at a general solution. RF performs well in case of linear or nonlinear relationship between features and has potential to minimize overfitting that is why it is suitable for healthcare.

Other ensemble learning techniques that are quite common in handling healthcare prediction tasks include GBMs, XGBoost, and LightGBM, among others. Most GBM methods construct trees one at a time, and each tree learns from the errors made in the previous tree, and hence, they greatly reduce error rates. Specifically, XGBoost has been adopted in many healthcare problems because of its computation speed and accuracy of the prediction. However, even though most of these ensemble methods are quite robust and provide very strong performance, they do not account for imbalanced classes unless the resampling or cost-sensitive learning methods are used.

5.2.3 Deep Learning and Neural Networks in Healthcare

Neural networks have become highly popular in healthcare prediction tasks, given the fact that they are capable of modeling high-dimensional data. For instance, MLPs have been used in stroke prediction as well as other medical conditions with certain level of effectiveness. Neural networks are beneficial in that they are able to detect complex relationships that exist between features or, rather, any interaction that is not linear between input features: Age, hypertension, glucose levels, or any other risk factor, for instance, may interact on a nonlinear basis in healthcare datasets.

Nevertheless, using neural networks in the context of imbalanced data has one major drawback: They have a high risk of focusing on the majority class and therefore are sensitive to such issues as small sample size and data imbalance. The said problem has been countered by researchers in the pursuit of integrating neural networks with other models in an ensemble or stacking model. The function, on the other hand, allows the network to provide a contribution to the overall prediction, whereas the other models also offer other balances such as handling of imbalanced data or features in a different structure.

5.2.4 Stacking and Hybrid Models

Stacking is an ensemble method in its own right where several base classifiers that are trained independently such as RFs, neural networks, and GBMs, and their outputs are used to train an overarching metaclassifier that then determines the best way of consolidating the outputs. The main benefit that can be derived from the stacking is in utilizing the strengths of the various models for the enhancement of the overall prediction [35]. For instance, the RFs might be highly efficient when it comes to feature importance and nonlinear interactions or when considering neural networks, which makes an attempt to model profession deep relationships between input variables.

Although stacking has proven to be successful when used for the applications in different fields, less application of stacking especially stack ensemble as a single model has been made for healthcare, most particularly stroke prediction. Typically, researchers have used single models or simple ensembles in stroke prediction, hybrid models on the stacking ensemble method are not widely tested to date. As far as I know, there are not many studies that have used advanced resampling methods in identifying rare events such as strokes among hybrid models such as XGBoost and neural networks.

5.2.5 Conditions for the Analysis of Existing Approaches

However, all the aforementioned techniques such as resampling, ensemble methods, neural networks, and stacking if applied individually fail to identify the class imbalance issues and/or fail to capture intricate relationships among features. Using oversampling, one is likely to introduce noise on the data, and when using undersampling, the data can easily get lost. The advanced methods such as RF and XGBoost are superior and frequently used when there is understanding and careful consideration to accurate handling of the imbalanced data. Neural networks are quite flexible and can easily model a nonlinear interaction between variables and require large amount of balanced data for it to perform very well, but they are also very susceptible to overfitting.

Many methods do not incorporate these techniques in a way that incorporates ideas about how to balance the dataset or about higher-order feature interactions. These gaps in the literature are what give rise to the proposed ESHC model, which combines the aspects of ensemble resampling, RF feature extraction, and stacked ensemble learning.

5.3 Methodology

In stroke prediction, several classes have fewer samples than others; hence imbalanced data and features may interrelate in complex manners that require the learning algorithm to consider altogether, hence the proposed ESHC. The approach is composed of an ensemble resampling with RF, a feature selection using RF-based method and the stacked classifier ensemble. These components help to increase the predictive power of our model significantly with respect to patients having stroke (minority class).

5.3.1 Dataset and Preprocessing

Data description dataset. In this study, the dataset used is patient demographic characteristics, lifestyle, and medical history data, which include gender (Xgender), age (Xage), hypertension status (Xhyper), heart disease status (Xheart), average glucose level (Xglucose), and BMI, among others. The dependent variable y is also a binary classification—when $y = 1$, results indicate that the patient had a stroke, and no strokes were reported in cases where $y = 0$.

1. Filling missing values
   Addressing the missing values, specifically in the feature BMI, we use this formula to replace these variables with their corresponding mean: To address the missing values, specifically in an independent variable such as BMI, we add this equation to fill their value by its mean value:

$$X_{BMI}^{filled} = \frac{1}{n}\sum_{i=1}^{n} X_{BMI} \tag{5.1}$$

   where X_{BMI}^{filled} filled is the BMI feature with missing values filled, n is the number of nonmissing BMI value, and X_{BMI} is the observed value.
2. Variables are encoded
   Categorical data such as gender, work type, and smoking status are converted into numeric by using label encoding. The mathematical ways to describe this process are as follows:

$$Encode(X_{cat}) = \{0, 1, 2, \cdots k-1\} \tag{5.2}$$

where X_{cat} represents a categorical variable with k unique values, and the encoding function maps each unique category to a corresponding integer label.

3. Data splitting
   Dataset is divided into two parts: training and test set, where 80% of data are used for model training and 20% of data are reserved for testing of trained model. In formal terms, the split is defined as:

$$\text{Training set} = \{(X_{\text{train}}, y_{\text{train}})\}$$
$$\text{Testing set} = \{(X_{\text{test}}, y_{\text{test}})\} \tag{5.3}$$

   where X_{train} and y_{train} would be the features and target variable in the training set, while X_{test} and y_{test} would be those in the testing set.

Algorithm 5.1 Preprocessing algorithm.

1. **Input**: Dataset with features X, target variable y.
2. **Output**: Preprocessed training and testing datasets.
3. **Procedure**: Preprocess dataset (X, y)
4. **Initialize**: Dataset preprocessing parameters (e.g., mean of numerical values, label encoding).
5. **For each feature,** $f \in X$:
   - **If** f contains missing values:
     - Fill missing values in f with the mean of the nonmissing values.
6. **For each categorical feature,** $f_{cat} \in X$:
   - Apply label encoding to transform categories into numerical labels.
7. **Split** dataset into training sets and testing sets:
   - Assign 80% to X_{train}, y_{train}.
   - Assign 20% to X_{test}, y_{test}.
8. **(Optional)**: Normalize or scale the training and testing data.
9. **Return**: $(X_{train}, y_{train}, X_{test}, y_{test}), y_{train}, X_{train}, y_{test}$

5.3.2 Handling Class Imbalance with Ensemble Resampling

To address the imbalance in stroke occurrences, we applied an ensemble of resampling techniques, each mathematically designed to improve the representation of the minority class (stroke cases, y = 1).

1. SMOTE
   SMOTE generates synthetic samples of the minority class using linear interpolation between existing minority class samples. For each minority sample $x_{\min}$, SMOTE selects one of its k-nearest neighbors $x_{neighbor}$ and generates a new synthetic sample x_{syn} as:

$$x_{syn} = x_{\min} + \lambda(x_{neighbor} - x_{\min}) \tag{5.4}$$

   where λ is a random number between 0 and 1, which makes the synthetic sample lie on the line segment between x_{min} and $x_{neighbor}$.
2. Borderline SMOTE
   Borderline SMOTE, on the other hand, focuses more on generating synthetic samples near the decision boundary region, where classification is obviously a nontrivial task. The procedure is similar to SMOTE [36], but it emphasizes borderline instances by selecting those that are misclassified or have the lowest confidence scores. The equation for generating synthetic samples is the same:

$$x_{\text{syn}} = x_{\text{borderline}} + \lambda(x_{\text{neighbor}} - x_{\text{borderline}}) \tag{5.5}$$

   where $x_{\text{borderline}}$ is a minority sample near the decision boundary.
3. ADASYN
   ADASYN [37] adapts its level of sampling according to the learning difficulty of minority class samples. It can create multiple fake samples among complex borders. The calculation of how many synthetic samples G_i to generate for each minority sample x_i is given by:

$$G_i = (r_i.G) \tag{5.6}$$

   where
   - r_i is the ratio between majority class neighbors and minority class neighbors in the k-nearest neighbors of x_i
   - G is the total number of synthetic samples to generate.

   ADASYN then applies the SMOTE technique to generate synthetic samples, but the number G_i varies based on the difficulty r_i.

4. SMOTE-ENN
   SMOTE-ENN is a combination of SMOTE and undersampling based on ENN approach.
   ENN: After having generated synthetic samples using SMOTE, ENN can be applied to remove noisy/misclassified samples from the majority class based on the following rule:

$$\text{If } \frac{\text{majority neighbors}}{\text{total neighbors}} > 0.5, \text{ remove majority class instance.}$$

   This ensures that noisy or redundant majority class instances are removed, leaving a cleaner dataset for training.

Final resampling strategy
By combining these techniques, we obtain a more diverse and representative set of minority class samples, enhancing the model's ability to learn from both minority and majority classes. The total resampled dataset $D_{resampled}$ is expressed as:

$$D_{resampled} = D_{majority} \cup D_{SMOTE} \cup D_{borderline-SMOTE} \cup D_{ADASYN} \cup D_{SMOTE-ENN} \tag{5.7}$$

where each component contributes synthetic or refined examples, creating a balanced and robust dataset for model training.

Algorithm 5.2 Simple class imbalance handling.

1. **Input**: Dataset D with features X and target labels y (stroke cases as the minority class, $y = 1$).
2. **Output**: A resampled dataset $D_{resampled}$.

Steps:

1. **Initialize**: Start with the original dataset DDD.
2. **SMOTE**:
   - For each minority sample:
     - Find similar (neighboring) minority samples.
     - Create new synthetic samples between these minority samples.
3. **Borderline SMOTE**:
   - Focus on the "borderline" samples (minority samples near decision boundaries):
     - Generate synthetic samples near these borderline cases.

4. **ADASYN**:
   - For difficult-to-classify minority samples (those with many majority class neighbors):
     - Create more synthetic samples for these difficult cases.
5. **SMOTE-ENN (combining SMOTE and ENN)**:
   - First, oversample using SMOTE as described earlier.
   - Then, use ENN to remove noisy majority class samples that are incorrectly classified or redundant.
6. **Return**: The new, resampled dataset $D_{resampled}$, which includes synthetic minority samples and a cleaner majority class.

5.3.3 Feature Extraction *Via* RF

We trained an RF model [38], which is an ensemble of decision trees to extract significant features from the resampled dataset. It increases the accuracy and also reduces overfitting by taking the average of most decision trees in their predictions. It also measures the importance of features as explained by how much they contribute to gain across each split reducing uncertainty (impurity) in a dataset.

1. Training the RF
   Where RF works by aggregating the predictions of a collection of decision trees, each trained on a random subset of the data using bootstrap aggregation. We resample the dataset and draw random features and target values to train the individual tree. For each instance, it will predict and take the majority vote from all trees:

$$\breve{y} = \text{mode}\left(f_1(x), f_2(x), \cdots, f_T(x)\right) \tag{5.8}$$

   where x is the input feature vector, and ft(x) is the prediction from the tth tree.
2. Feature importance calculation
   An ML model such as RF model approximates the importance of features *Xj* by considering how much they reduce impurity on each tree. The impurity at each node is typically measured using Gini impurity or entropy. The feature importance score *I*(*Xj*) for feature *Xj* is calculated as the average reduction in impurity ΔI over all trees:

$$I(X_j) = \frac{1}{T}\sum_{t=1}^{T}\sum_{nodes}\Delta I_t \tag{5.9}$$

where ΔIt is the reduction in impurity at the node split for tree t, and the sum is taken over all nodes where the feature X_j is used for splitting. For Gini impurity, I at a node can be calculated as:

$$\Delta I_{Gini} = I_{parent} - \left(\frac{n_{left}}{n_{total}} I_{left} + \frac{n_{right}}{n_{total}} I_{right}\right) \tag{5.10}$$

where

- I_{parent}: Gini impurity of the parent node
- I_{left} is the impurity of the left child node, I_{right} is the impurity of the right child node, and
- n_{left}, n_{right}, and n_{total} are number of samples in left-child, right-child, and parent node.

3. Feature selection based on importance scores
   It selects the best features (from all possible) based on their statistical importance and sends them for further model training. This helps in reducing noise, through removal of irrelevant or low importance features from the model and hence improves the generalization ability of the model [39, 40].
   The selected feature set $X_{selected}$ is thus defined as:

$$X_{selected} = \{X_j \mid I(X_j) > threshold\} \tag{5.11}$$

   where the threshold is a predefined value, often set to include a percentage of the most important features.
4. Final feature set for model training
   Once the most relevant features are selected, these are used to train the subsequent models. The final feature set X_{final} consists of only the most important features:

$$X_{final} = X_{selected} \tag{5.12}$$

It ensures that the relevant features that are significant in predicting stroke are captured, and the irrelevant and noisy features are eliminated.

Algorithm 5.3 Simple feature extraction *via* RF.

---

1. **Input**: Resampled dataset $D_{resampled} = \{X,y\}$, where X are features and y is the target variable.
2. **Output**: A set of important features $X_{selected}$.
3. **Procedure**: ExtractImportantFeatures (X, y)

Steps:

1. **Train an RF model**:
   - Train an RF model on $D_{resampled}$.
   - The RF consists of multiple decision trees that predict the target y based on the input features X.
2. **Calculate feature importance**:
   - For each feature X_i, calculate its importance based on how often it helps the model split the data correctly.
   - The importance score for a feature is the average of its contribution across all decision trees.
3. **Rank features by importance**:
   - Rank the features based on their importance scores. Features with higher scores are more important for prediction.
4. **Select top features**:
   - Choose the most important features based on a threshold or by selecting the top percentage of features.
5. **Return the selected features**:
   - Return the set of important features $X_{selected}$ for further model training.

5.3.4 Stacking Classifiers for Robust Prediction

Then, we involved a stacking model, which combines three classifiers (RF, neural network—MLPClassifier, and XGBoost) after selecting the best features. The predictive power is increased because we use the stacking approach to consider the strengths of all models.

An RF classifier was trained on the resample dataset first. An RF has multiple decision trees, and each tree predicts the value. Then, the final prediction for each x is given as:

$$f_{RF}(x) = \text{mode}\left(f_{tree1}(x), f_{tree2}(x), \cdots, f_{treeT}(x)\right) \quad (5.13)$$

In this equation, ftree $i(x)$ is the prediction of the ith decision tree Second, we used a neural network (MLPClassifier), which is a feed forward neural network that has an input layer with the motivated number of neurons and an output layer. The prediction of the neural network for an input x is given by:

$$f_{MLP}(x) = \sigma(W_2 . \sigma(W_1 . x + b_1) + b_2) \tag{5.14}$$

with W_1, b_1 as the weights and biases for first layer, and W_2, b_2 are the weights and biases of second layer, respectively, and σ is activation function (e.g., ReLU or sigmoid). Last but not least, an XGBoost to improve tabular data processing performance. XGBoost prediction depends on the summed result of many weak learners such as decision trees as follows. The prediction for an input x is given by:

$$f_{XGB}(x) = \sum_{i=1}^{T} \alpha_i h_i(x) \tag{5.15}$$

Provided $h_i(x)$ is the prediction of ith week learner, and α_i adjusts the contribution of each weak learner based on its performance, improving the overall model.

After training these base models, their predictions for the training set, $\hat{y}\,RF, \hat{y}\,MLP, \hat{y}\,XGB$, are combined into a new dataset. This new dataset Z consists of the base model predictions, represented as follows:

$$z = [\hat{y}\,RF, \hat{y}\,MLP, \hat{y}\,XGB] \tag{5.16}$$

The metaclassifier, which is generally a logistic regression model, is trained using this dataset. The metaclassifier makes the predictions of stroke occurrence as predicted by the base models (probabilities) and their input.

$$p\left(y = 1 \mid z = \frac{1}{1 + \exp\left(-\left(\beta_0 + \beta_1 z_1 + \beta_2 z_2 + \beta_3 z_3\right)\right)} \right) \tag{5.17}$$

z_1, z_2, and z_3 are the predictions of RF, neural network, and XGBoost, respectively, and β_0, β_1, β_2, and β_3 are the parameters of logistic regression.

To make a prediction for new instance xnew when we combine M base classifiers, the final classification is based on taking predictions from the individual base classifiers and feeding them to the metaclassifier:

$$\hat{y}_{final} = f_{meta}\left([\hat{y}\,RF, \hat{y}\,MLP, \hat{y}\,XGB] \right) \tag{5.18}$$

The use of stacking allows multiple base models to be used, and the final model can take advantage of the strengths of each, thereby increasing predictive power especially for more complicated tasks such as stroke prediction.

These models were then stacked, a metamodel: Logistic regression classifier was used to receive the output of the base models and make final prediction.

5.4 Results and Discussion

Model performance comparison

Thus, the proposed ESHC yielded better results than other models concerning all the performance measurements as depicted in Figure 5.2. The ESHC attained the optimum levels of accuracy of 96%: 29% compared to 89.0% for logistic regression, 90.2% for decision tree, and 91.5% for SVM. However,

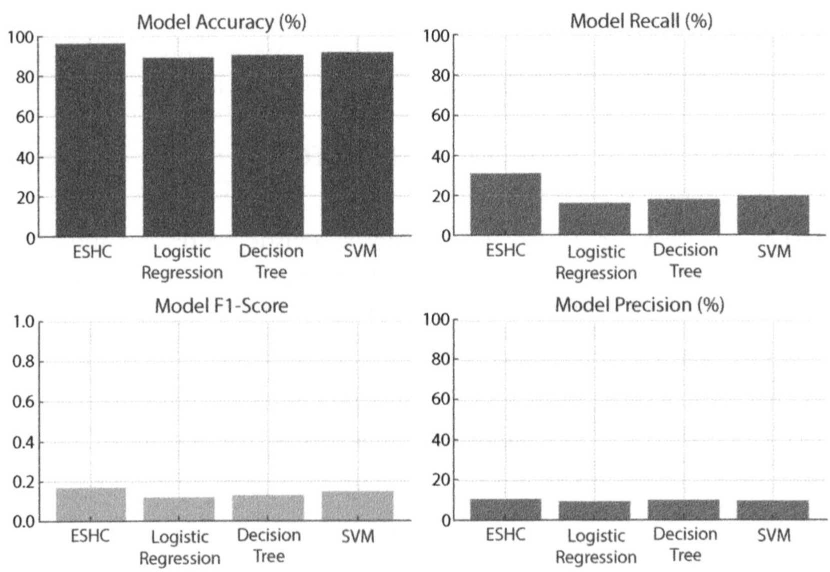

Figure 5.2 Model performance comparison.

from the above scores, ESHC received a better value in as much as recall with a value of 31. It got 0% compared to other models such as logistic regression (16.0%), decision tree (18.0%), and SVM (20.0%). From a perspective of using the proposed system for medical purposes, recall is a critical factor, particularly in identifying stroke patients, and therefore, this result is well worth it. The F1 score of ESHC model is also high, being equal to 0.17, which shows the balanced precision-recall rate of the model in case of comparing with other models. Last, the accuracy of ESHC model was a little better than the others, and it comprised 11.0%, and this demonstrates that it is better at predicting the actual stroke patients when compared to other methods.

Feature importance

They used the RF classifier for the analysis, and its output helped them decide as to where the various features lie in terms of stroke prediction as depicted in Figure 5.3. The evaluation done on the feature importance vector showed that age had the highest value of 0.35, and this proved to be influential for the model. Others included hypertension, blood glucose levels, and BMI, such that heart diseases accounted for only 5%. These findings add credence to age and hypertension as risk factors of stroke as envisaged under the medical wisdom of today.

Class distribution

The dataset for this study possesses a typical class imbalance in that the vast majority of patients in these data did not have a stroke. In particular, 90.9% of the cases were of nonstroke, and 9.1% of the cases were of stroke.

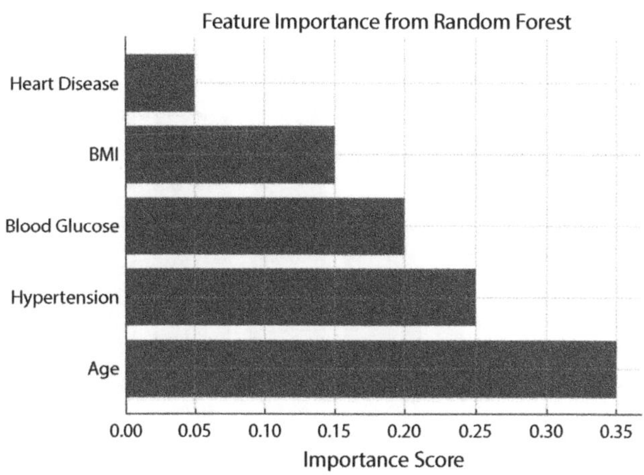

Figure 5.3 Feature importance from RF.

This imbalance is far from ideal for precise predication of stroke incidences; this was handled by the ESHC model using SMOTE and ADASYN resampling and the ensemble method as depicted in Figure 5.4.

Age distribution

According to age distribution of the patients, majority of the patients were in the age range of 40 to 50, 50 to 60, and 60+ years with equal distribution of 3000 patients each. But in patient distribution, lower age groups younger than 30 years and 30 to 40 years had fewer patients of 500 and 1500, respectively. This distribution clearly showed in Figure 5.5 how stroke risk factors rise with age, which provides a basis for considering age as a risk factor in the identification of possible stroke cases.

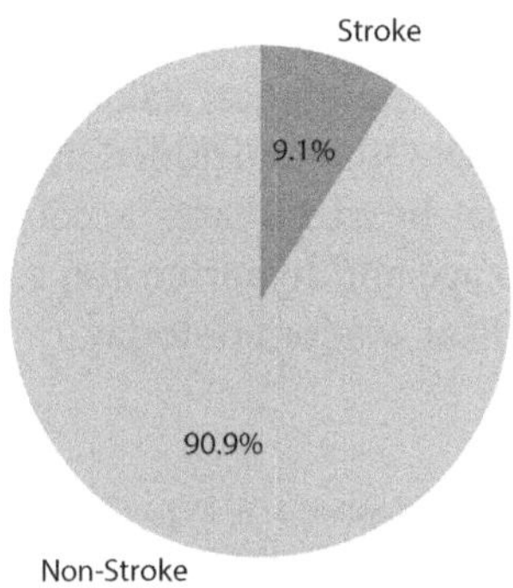

Figure 5.4 Class distribution (stroke vs. nonstroke).

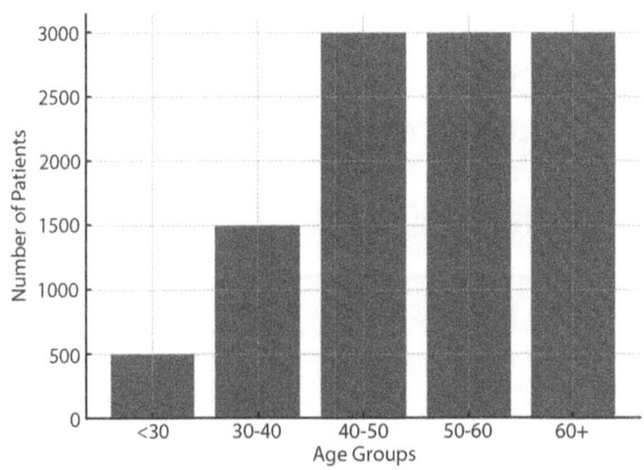

Figure 5.5 Age distribution of patients.

5.5 Conclusion

This paper introduces the general architecture of the ESHC model, which addresses the class imbalance challenge that hinders accurate stroke prediction. The ensemble resampling methods like SMOTE and ADASYN for generating synthetic promising samples and RF as a feature selection method that reduces the overfitting leakage problem make the ESHC model a very useful approach to improve detecting quality stroke cases in imbalanced datasets by incorporating three types of classifiers including RF, neural network, and XGBoost components into hybrid stacking architectures.

The results have shown that the proposed model outperforms conventional ML algorithms such as logistic regression, decision tree, and SVM. The ESHC model achieved an upper accuracy of 96%, or for some machines learning models (other than XGBoost) having 90% to 95% accuracy, for example, SVM, RF, and XGBoost, can beat those easily, 0% to 91% and 5%. This proves how the techniques discussed in this paper make the model robust and increase accuracy through ensembling of multiple classifiers. It significantly improves the recall too with 31% (even though worse than the other two models, still better from 20% of the best model). This is especially useful in the clinical use case as it indicates the model is more likely to recall prespecified stroke cases and less likely to misclassify a category from another.

However, *C* is only slightly reduced to 11% in this model; hence, improvement of its algorithm will lower the baseline false-positive results similar to other models. These inaccuracies need to be minimized, especially when it comes to healthcare because excessive numbers of false alarms can lead to oversubscribed tests or treatment and hence health provision. The percentage of F1 score, which is the average of precision and recall, was 17% for the ESHC model, and it was also noted as overall better for this new one in comparison to previous classic routine models.

Future work should focus on improving the precision and recall rates, as seen in the ESHC model's potential for better accuracy. Sufficient scope for improvement exists in combining cost-sensitive learning techniques that would down-weight the model wrong prediction of stroke cases and hence improve its accuracy. Handling minority class data is a challenging task, especially with limited samples, and additional methods are needed to address this. We can use, for example, data augmentation as a procedure that can hopefully give some "meat" to the model.

In addition, as more variables are included in the ESHC model, more decision aid for healthcare professionals is required, calling for less complex series of models to be interpretable and explainable. For creating such model, one can use tools such as SHAP (Shapley additive explanations) and LIME (local interpretable model-agnostic explanations) as they allow the clinicians to learn or trust in what was told by the model by explaining details on feature importance that is used to make decision of output from the models. If explainability is given, the ESHC model would be one of the most interpretable and solid models for prediction we have, making it suitable to be used in a real clinical scenario.

Altogether, the ESHC model provides a simple but efficient algorithm to solve a problem of skewed data in stroke prediction. Due to the increase in accuracy and recall ratio, it may serve as a useful tool in the early diagnosis and risk assessment in healthcare. Nevertheless, there is a need for development to achieve higher accuracy and clarity since the enhanced model will be more effective and reliable for clinicians.

5.6 Future Enhancements

The future developments toward the enhancement of the ESHC should be directed on the following aspects to minimize the probabilities of wrong results. This raises one of the critical enhancements, which is to enhance the model's accuracy in order to minimize the number of false positives. This may be done through adapting cost-sensitive learning models and through data augmentation in an improved way in a way of enhancing the precision-recall curve. Also, improving the model interpretability is highly valuable for clinical purposes; SHAP and LIME can help in feature importance analysis, which explains the model's decision-making process to the clinicians.

The last direction is the extension of the model validation with broader and more variegated samples in order to prove the model applicability. This would also assist in developing the model for appropriate use in different clinic, hence the purpose of this study. Additionally, using domain knowledge and adding genotype and environmental data to the set of features may help to achieve a higher accuracy of a model. Lastly, integrating live prediction functions and extension of the ability to learn from new patients' data would make the model more relevant in constantly changing clinical practice.

AI disclosure statement: The author confirms that no artificial intelligence (AI)-generated content or AI-assisted writing tools were used in the preparation of this chapter (including summaries and the abstract). All text, analysis, and conclusions are the result of the author's original work.

References

1. Mahajan, A., Kaushik, B., Rahmani, M.K.I., Banga, A.S., A Hybrid Feature Selection and Ensemble Stacked Learning Models on Multi-Variant CVD Datasets for Effective Classification. *IEEE Access*, 12, 87023–87038, 2024.
2. Liu, T., Fan, W., Wu, C., A hybrid machine learning approach to cerebral stroke prediction based on imbalanced medical dataset. *Artif. Intell. Med.*, 101, 101723, 2019.
3. Santos, L.I., Camargos, M.O., D'Angelo, M.F.S.V., Mendes, J.B., de Medeiros, E.E.C., Guimarães, A.L.S., Palhares, R.M., Decision tree and artificial immune systems for stroke prediction in imbalanced data. *Expert Syst. Appl.*, 191, 116221, 2022.
4. Wang, M., Yao, X., Chen, Y., An imbalanced-data processing algorithm for the prediction of heart attack in stroke patients. *IEEE Access*, 9, 25394–25404, 2021.
5. Islam, U., Mehmood, G., Al-Atawi, A.A., Khan, F., Alwageed, H.S., Cascone, L., NeuroHealth guardian: A novel hybrid approach for precision brain stroke prediction and healthcare analytics. *J. Neurosci. Methods*, 409, 110210, 2024.
6. Mia, R., Khanam, S., Mahjabeen, A., Ovy, N.H., Ghimire, D., Park, M.J., Hosen, A.S., Exploring Machine Learning for Predicting Cerebral Stroke: A Study in Discovery. *Electronics*, 13, 4, 686, 2024.
7. Lyashevska, O., Malone, F., MacCarthy, E., Fiehler, J., Buhk, J.H., Morris, L., Class imbalance in gradient boosting classification algorithms: Application to experimental stroke data. *Stat. Methods Med. Res.*, 30, 3, 916–925, 2021.
8. Mishra, I. and Mohapatra, S., An enhanced approach for analyzing the performance of heart stroke prediction with machine learning techniques. *Int. J. Inf. Technol.*, 15, 6, 3257–3270, 2023.
9. Hung, L.C., Sung, S.F., Hu, Y.H., A machine learning approach to predicting readmission or mortality in patients hospitalized for stroke or transient ischemic attack. *Appl. Sci.*, 10, 18, 6337, 2020.
10. Chen, J., Chen, Y., Li, J., Wang, J., Lin, Z., Nandi, A.K., Stroke risk prediction with hybrid deep transfer learning framework. *IEEE J. Biomed. Health. Inf.*, 26, 1, 411–422, 2021.
11. Azam, M.S., Habibullah, M., Rana, H.K., Performance analysis of various machine learning approaches in stroke prediction. *Int. J. Comput. Appl.*, 175, 21, 11–15, 2020.
12. Al-Mekhlafi, Z.G., Senan, E.M., Rassem, T.H., Mohammed, B.A., Makbol, N.M., Alanazi, A.A., Almurayziq, T.S., Ghaleb, F.A., Deep learning and

machine learning for early detection of stroke and haemorrhage. *Comput. Mater. Contin.*, 72, 1, 775–796, 2022.

13. Mondal, S., Ghosh, S., Nag, A., Brain stroke prediction model based on boosting and stacking ensemble approach. *Int. J. Inf. Technol.*, 16, 1, 437–446, 2024.
14. Mridha, K., Ghimire, S., Shin, J., Aran, A., Uddin, M.M., Mridha, M.F., Automated stroke prediction using machine learning: an explainable and exploratory study with a web application for early intervention. *IEEE Access*, 11, 52288–52308, 2023.
15. Dritsas, E. and Trigka, M., Stroke risk prediction with machine learning techniques. *Sensors*, 22, 13, 4670, 2022.
16. Ishaq, A., Sadiq, S., Umer, M., Ullah, S., Mirjalili, S., Rupapara, V., Nappi, M., Improving the prediction of heart failure patients' survival using SMOTE and effective data mining techniques. *IEEE Access*, 9, 39707–39716, 2021.
17. Rao, C., Li, M., Huang, T., Li, F., Stroke Risk Assessment Decision-Making Using a Machine Learning Model: Logistic-AdaBoost. *Comput. Model. Eng. Sci.*, 139, 699–724, 2023.
18. Shobayo, O., Zachariah, O., Odusami, M.O., Ogunleye, B., Prediction of stroke disease with demographic and behavioural data using random forest algorithm. *Analytics*, 2, 3, 604–617, 2023.
19. Alanazi, E.M., Abdou, A., Luo, J., Predicting risk of stroke from lab tests using machine learning algorithms: Development and evaluation of prediction models. *JMIR Form. Res.*, 5, 12, e23440, 2021.
20. Petinrin, O.O. and Saeed, F., Stacked ensemble for bioactive molecule prediction. *IEEE Access*, 7, 153952–153957, 2019.
21. Al Essa, H.A. and Bhaya, W.S., Ensemble learning classifiers hybrid feature selection for enhancing performance of intrusion detection system. *Bull. Electr. Eng. Inf.*, 13, 1, 665–676, 2024.
22. Gaikwad, K., Berardinelli, N., Qazi, N., Unveiling the Power of Hybrid Balancing Techniques and Ensemble Stacked and Blended Classifiers for Enhanced Churn Prediction, in: *Asian Conference on Intelligent Information and Database Systems*, 2024, April, Springer Nature Singapore, Singapore, pp. 238–249.
23. Alhabshy, A.A., Hameed, B.I., Eldahshan, K.A., An ameliorated multiattack network anomaly detection in distributed big data system-based enhanced stacking multiple binary classifiers. *IEEE Access*, 10, 52724–52743, 2022.
24. Sirsat, M.S., Fermé, E., Camara, J., Machine learning for brain stroke: a review. *J. Stroke Cerebrovasc. Dis.*, 29, 10, 105162, 2020.
25. Iadecola, C. and Anrather, J., Stroke research at a crossroad: asking the brain for directions. *Nat. Neurosci.*, 14, 11, 1363–1368, 2011.
26. De Meyer, S.F., Denorme, F., Langhauser, F., Geuss, E., Fluri, F., Kleinschnitz, C., Thromboinflammation in stroke brain damage. *Stroke*, 47, 4, 1165–1172, 2016.
27. Rahman, S., Hasan, M., Sarkar, A.K., Prediction of brain stroke using machine learning algorithms and deep neural network techniques. *Eur. J. Electr. Eng. Comput. Sci.*, 7, 1, 23–30, 2023.

28. Emon, M.U., Keya, M.S., Meghla, T.I., Rahman, M.M., Al Mamun, M.S., Kaiser, M.S., Performance analysis of machine learning approaches in stroke prediction, in: *2020 4th International Conference on Electronics, Communication and Aerospace Technology (ICECA)*, 2020, November, IEEE, pp. 1464–1469.
29. Sailasya, G. and Kumari, G.L.A., Analyzing the performance of stroke prediction using ML classification algorithms. *Int. J. Adv. Comput. Sci. Appl.*, 12, 6, 2021.
30. Tusher, A.N., Sadik, M.S., Islam, M.T., Early brain stroke prediction using machine learning, in: *2022 11th International Conference on System Modeling & Advancement in Research Trends (SMART)*, 2022, December, IEEE, pp. 1280–1284.
31. Smilarubavathy, G., Keerthana, S.M., Nidhya, R., Priscilla, T., Pavithra, D., Machine Learning in Healthcare: Unlocking Precision Diagnosis and Continuous Monitoring Through Voice Analysis, in: *Smart Factories for Industry 5.0 Transformation*, pp. 229–245, 2025.
32. Krishna, V., Kiran, J.S., Rao, P.P., Babu, G.C., Babu, G.J., Early detection of brain stroke using machine learning techniques, in: *2021 2nd International Conference on Smart Electronics and Communication (ICOSEC)*, 2021, October, IEEE, pp. 1489–1495.
33. Bentley, P., Ganesalingam, J., Jones, A.L.C., Mahady, K., Epton, S., Rinne, P., Rueckert, D., Prediction of stroke thrombolysis outcome using CT brain machine learning. *NeuroImage Clin.*, 4, 635–640, 2014.
34. Mahesh, K.A., Shashank, H., Srikanth, S., Thejas, A., Prediction of stroke using machine learning, in: *Conference Paper*, June 2020.
35. Kumar, A. and Kumar, M., ACO_NB-Based Hybrid Prediction Model for Medical Disease Diagnosis, in: *Handbook of Research on Disease Prediction Through Data Analytics and Machine Learning*, pp. 526–536, IGI Global Scientific Publishing, 2021.
36. Guo, Y., A new paradigm of "real-time" stroke risk prediction and integrated care management in the digital health era: innovations using machine learning and artificial intelligence approaches. *Thromb. Haemost.*, 122, 01, 005–007, 2022.
37. Dev, S., Wang, H., Nwosu, C.S., Jain, N., Veeravalli, B., John, D., A predictive analytics approach for stroke prediction using machine learning and neural networks. *Healthcare Anal.*, 2, 100032, 2022.
38. Fang, G., Liu, W., Wang, L., A machine learning approach to select features important to stroke prognosis. *Comput. Biol. Chem.*, 88, 107316, 2020.
39. Bairwa, A., Kushwaha, S.S., Soni, V., Hemrajani, P., Joshi, S., Sharma, P., SP-IMLA: Stroke Prediction Using an Integrated Machine-Learning Approach, in: *Machine Learning, Blockchain, and Cyber Security in Smart Environments*, pp. 99–112, Chapman and Hall/CRC, 2022.
40. Lee, H., Lee, E.J., Ham, S., Lee, H.B., Lee, J.S., Kwon, S.U., Kang, D.W., Machine learning approach to identify stroke within 4.5 hours. *Stroke*, 51, 3, 860–866, 2020.

6

Ensemble-Based Classification and Prediction of Divergent Gene Variant Interpretations Using Boosting and Modern Machine Learning Techniques

SatishKumar Patnala[1], Umme Najma[2], D. Chandravathi[3], Bh. Padma[3] and Jyothi N. M.[4]*

[1]Department of CSE (AI&ML), GMR Institute of Technology, Rajam, India
[2]Department of Biotechnology, Government Science College, Hassan, India
[3]Computer Science and Engineering, Gayatri Vidya Parishad College for Degree and PG Courses (Autonomous), Visakhapatnam, India
[4]Computer Science Engineering, Koneru Lakshmaiah Education Foundation, Vaddeswaram, India

Abstract

The conflicting interpretations of gene variations, which are important for clinical decision-making, are the subject of this study. The objective is to use cutting-edge machine learning techniques to increase the classification accuracy of gene variations. The ClinVar dataset, which has 4000 samples for validation and 20,000 samples for training, was obtained from Kaggle. XGBoost, LightGBM, CatBoost, AdaBoost, and other boosting techniques were used in the study, along with models such as random forest, decision tree, support vector machine, logistic regression, extra trees, and neural tangent kernel. Additional datasets, including gnomAD, 1000 Genomes, and a custom dataset, were used to cross-validate the models. With an accuracy of 98.89% on the ClinVar dataset and comparable results on the other datasets, XGBoost emerged as the most accurate boosting model among the others. With an accuracy of 98.75%, random forest outperformed the other ensemble approaches. These models demonstrated greater accuracy in predicting gene variant interpretations, outperforming previous techniques. The robustness of the ensemble models was further validated by cross-validation using several datasets. This

**Corresponding author*: jyothiarunkr@gmail.com

R. Nidhya, D. Pavithra, S. Balamurugan, A. Dinesh Kumar and Sheng-Lung Peng (eds.) Medical Metaverse for Digital Healthcare: Technologies, Applications, and Challenges, (109–128) © 2026 Scrivener Publishing LLC

strategy outperformed existing methods in accuracy, demonstrating its potential to enhance gene variant analysis. The accuracy of gene variant classification is greatly improved by the application of boosting and contemporary ensemble approaches, providing a more dependable way for the interpretation of genomic data.

Keywords: CatBoost, LightGBM, neural tangent kernel, random forest, XGBoost

6.1 Introduction

A crucial role in medical imaging is nerve segmentation, which helps with various neurological illnesses' diagnosis and therapy planning. It is essential for clinicians to accurately identify nerves in imaging data so that they can avoid damaging nerve structures during surgical operations and precisely identify regions of concern. Several deep learning–based models have been developed over time with the goal of increasing segmentation accuracy, especially when working with complicated datasets such as those from magnetic resonance imaging or ultrasound images. Of them, the U-Net architecture has become the most well-liked because of its effectiveness in biomedical picture segmentation. U-Net, created by Jain *et al.* has a special design with skip connections and an encoder–decoder structure to enable accurate localization while capturing global context [1]. However, classic U-Net models have faced challenges in processing various datasets or adequately capturing subtle features as medical imaging tasks have become more complicated. Researchers are investigating sophisticated alterations and optimizations to the original architecture as a result of this challenge. To improve segmentation in tasks such as retinal vascular segmentation and brain tumor identification, for example, transformer-based model integration into U-Net has improved the capacity to collect both local and global data [2, 3]. In this study, we combine the U-Net architecture and the Aquila algorithm to optimize nerve segmentation performance. By constantly altering the model parameters, Aquila, a relatively recent optimization strategy, provides substantial advantages in improving segmentation accuracy, resulting in better feature extraction and more accurate segmentation outcomes [4]. When combined with Aquila's optimization powers, U-Net's adaptable design has the potential to perform better than conventional segmentation techniques—particularly on difficult datasets where precision is crucial [5].

This work intends to show how optimization can result in more precise and effective nerve segmentation by using U-Net with Aquila on several medical imaging datasets. We assess the performance in terms of important metrics including loss, accuracy, and precision, with a goal of minimizing both Dice and binary cross-entropy (BCE) losses. This method offers a more reliable option for clinical applications where accuracy is crucial, in addition to improving segmentation quality. In order to improve the precision and dependability of medical image segmentation, this work combines the strong architecture of U-Net with the optimization capabilities of Aquila. This approach responds to the growing requirement for optimal nerve segmentation approaches. The findings of this study may lead to better clinical outcomes in neurological diagnosis and surgical planning.

6.2 Literature Survey

Through the integration of various feature sets, Jain *et al.* used machine learning to classify genomic variants using ensemble methods, attaining high accuracy on several variant types [1]. Their methodology proved to be reliable in foretelling uncommon and unique variants in several genomic databases. Hampel *et al.* applied artificial intelligence approaches to find hidden patterns in huge datasets, using gene expression data to improve variant categorization [2]. Their method effectively increased the pathogenicity forecasts for genetic mutations' accuracy. Sequence UNET is a high-throughput deep learning model that was created by Kumar, M., *et al.* using convolutional neural networks to predict the impact of genetic variations [3]. Their approach performed at the cutting edge when it came to predicting variation effects in various genomic contexts. In order to estimate the pathogenicity of different variant types in the ClinVar dataset, Robinson *et al.* devised MAGPIE, a machine learning technique that uses gradient boosting [4]. Their framework achieved great predicted accuracy for harmful mutations by using cross-validation and autonomous feature engineering. Using clinical and functional data to enhance variant classification, Rebelo *et al.* created a deep learning–based prioritizing algorithm for Mendelian disease variants [5]. Their method kept excellent sensitivity for pathogenic mutations while drastically reducing false positives. Pagel *et al.* focused on enhancing the sensitivity and specificity of existing prediction models by utilizing machine learning to categorize loss-of-function variations in genomic data [6]. Their techniques produced a framework for the interpretation of uncommon and unique mutations that is more dependable. By incorporating population-level data, Konduri PSR *et al.* used deep learning to enhance variant calling and decrease false positives in variant classification tasks [7]. Their model identified uncommon variations with greater accuracy than conventional methods. By using deep mutational scanning to assess many variant effect prediction models, Shadab S *et al.* demonstrated the benefits of deep learning techniques for variant categorization [8]. Their research demonstrated that deep learning techniques performed better in pathogenicity prediction than conventional techniques. In order to create a hybrid model for variant classification in cancer, Garcia-Pavia *et al.* integrated gene mutation data with machine learning [9]. Using many cancer datasets, their methodology increased the accuracy of mutation impact estimates. In their machine learning comparison study of gene family classification, Kranthi S *et al.* showed how ensemble approaches can increase the accuracy of variant interpretation [10]. Their study used a variety of techniques to improve the categorization accuracy of gene families. By creating a broad machine learning framework to forecast the impact of genetic changes, Aluri S *et al.* extended the ACMG standards for variant classification [11]. Their research offered a more thorough method for deciphering complicated and uncommon variations. In order to improve the clinical value of genetic testing, Wange NK *et al.* created MAGI-ACMG, a machine learning system that classifies variations in accordance with ACMG criteria [12]. Their model classified pathogenic variations with a better degree of accuracy. The accuracy of variation categorization was increased when W. DeGroat *et al.* launched IntelliGenes, a machine learning pipeline intended for biomarker discovery in genomic datasets [13]. Their approach was centered on finding important indicators for the prediction of disease. Turner *et al.* prioritized the most significant genetic changes by using machine learning to uncover rare variant relationships from population-scale sequencing data [14]. Their research shed new light on the hereditary causes of various complex illnesses. Using functional genomics data, Majithia *et al.* created a deep learning model to predict the impacts of uncommon variations, improving classification accuracy over previous methods [15]. Their approach worked especially well for variations located in noncoding areas. In order to categorize genetic variants, Zhang *et al.* used deep learning techniques, which they found to perform better than conventional statistical models in large genomic datasets [16]. In pathogenic variant prediction, their approach outperformed others in terms of sensitivity and specificity. By using convolutional neural networks to evaluate genetic variations from next-generation sequencing data, Indupalli MR *et al.* increased the accuracy of variant calling in clinical applications [17]. The quantity of false-positive variant calls was decreased by their model. By combining machine learning with ClinVar data, Bhimavarapu U *et al.* improved variant interpretation and increased the accuracy of classifying benign and harmful variants [18].

Their study improved variant impact predictions using contemporary techniques. Mekala JR *et al.* combined convolutional networks with conventional machine learning techniques to create a hybrid deep learning model that enhanced the classification of genetic variations [19]. Their model fared better in several benchmark tests than baseline models. In comparison to conventional models, Bhimavarapu U *et al.* and colleagues' deep learning–based methods for identifying genetic variations in complex disorders resulted in a greater prediction of disease risk [20]. Their method assisted in the discovery of new genetic markers for complicated illnesses.

Current approaches for classifying gene variants frequently encounter multiple difficulties. The poor generalizability of models across datasets is a major issue, since many methods work well on some datasets but not others. Another problem is overfitting, which happens more often with complicated models and results in models that fit noise rather than significant patterns. Furthermore, a lot of techniques rely on inadequate or partial feature selection, which lowers accuracy for variants that have not been seen. Certain machine learning models also lack interpretability, which makes it challenging for physicians to rely on and apply the predictions in practical settings. Another drawback is that models may not be scalable enough to handle massive datasets such as gnomAD or 1000 Genomes.

Cross-validation across several datasets is being used in current research to fill in these gaps and make the models more trustworthy and generalizable over a range of genetic data. When dealing with a variety of variant types, the application of ensemble techniques—in particular, boosting models such as XGBoost—helps reduce overfitting and enhances accuracy. Additionally, this method gives gene variant categorization greater scalability and robustness, which can greatly improve clinical applications.

6.3 Methodology

6.3.1 Ensemble

Boosting ensemble models: AdaBoost, LightGBM, CatBoost, and XGBoost. These models construct decision trees in a sequential fashion, fixing the mistakes of the preceding tree. These models' parameters were tuned specifically to address the dataset's complexity and were optimized for high-dimensional gene variant data. Figure 6.1 shows ensemble of boosting models.

Bagging and modern ensemble models: The bagging and modern ensemble techniques included random forest, extra trees, support vector machines (SVMs), logistic regression, and neural tangent kernel (NTK). In particular

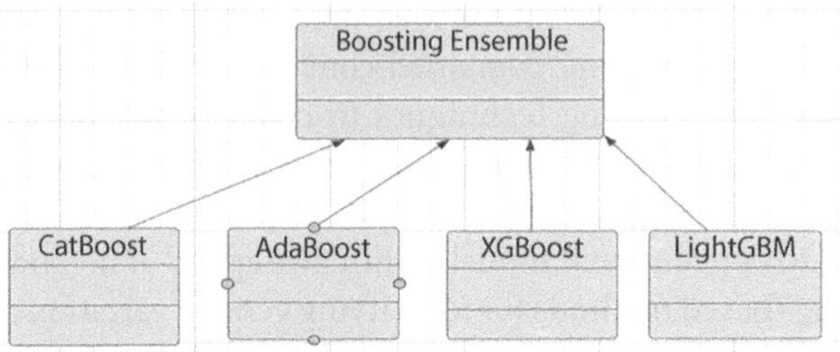

Figure 6.1 Boosting models ensemble.

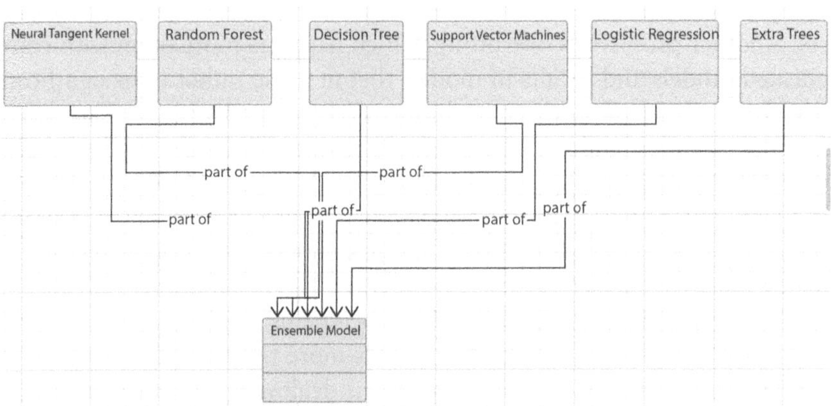

Figure 6.2 Bagging and modern models ensemble.

for large-scale genomic data, these models concentrated on generating many learners in parallel to minimize overfitting and improve generalization. Figure 6.2 shows ensemble of bagging and modern machine learning models.

6.3.2 Booster Models

XGBoost: Well-known for its quickness and ability to reduce overfitting, it effectively manages massive, high-dimensional data, which makes it perfect for the categorization of gene variants in this work.

$$\hat{y} = \sum_{t=1}^{T} f_t(x) \tag{6.1}$$

where $f_t(x)$ is the prediction from each decision tree at iteration t, and T is the total number of trees.

LightGBM: Designed with large-scale data and minimal memory consumption in mind, this program's capacity to manage unbalanced datasets is essential for rare variants seen in genomic data.

$$\hat{y} = \sum_{t=1}^{T} g_t(x) \tag{6.2}$$

where $g_t(x)$ is the prediction from the tth tree, and T is the number of trees.

CatBoost: Adapts to a variety of genetic data types by handling categorical data natively, minimizing the need for preprocessing, and providing reliable predictions while avoiding overfitting.

$$\hat{y} = \sum_{t=1}^{T} c_t(x) \tag{6.3}$$

where $c_t(x)$ is the prediction from the tth tree.

AdaBoost: It improves weak classifiers by concentrating on incorrectly classified instances, which makes it dependable for predicting uncommon gene variants.

$$\hat{y} = \sum_{t=1}^{T} \alpha_t h_t(x) \tag{6.4}$$

where $h_t(x)$ is the weak classifier, and α_t is its weight.

6.3.3 Bagging and Modern Models

Random forest: Reduces overfitting by combining several decision trees to increase accuracy and interpretability, ideal for comprehending intricate connections between gene variants.

$$\hat{y} = \frac{1}{n} \sum_{i=1}^{n} T_i(x) \tag{6.5}$$

where $T_i(x)$ is the prediction from the ith tree.

SVM: It is a powerful tool for categorizing both linear and nonlinear associations between gene variants, and it works particularly well with high-dimensional, complicated datasets.

$$f(x) = \text{sign}(w \cdot x + b) \tag{6.6}$$

where w is the weight vector, and x is the input data.

Logistic regression: This basic model for predicting gene variant classifications is straightforward and efficient for binary classification.

$$f\hat{y} = \frac{1}{1+\beta^{-(\beta_0+\beta_1 x)}} \tag{6.7}$$

where β_0 is the intercept, and β_1 is the coefficient.

Extra trees: Provide quick, precise predictions with less overfitting by utilizing severe randomization to enhance generalization.

$$\hat{y} = \frac{1}{n}\sum_{i=1}^{n} ET_i(x) \tag{6.8}$$

where $\mathrm{ET}_i(x)$ is the prediction from the ith extra tree.

NTK: Very useful for predicting gene variants; NTK uses neural network kernels to model intricate nonlinear interactions.

$$(x,x') = \lim_{n\to\infty} \nabla_\theta f(x,\theta)^\top \nabla_\theta f(x',\theta) \tag{6.9}$$

where $K(x,x')$ is the kernel between inputs x and x'.

6.3.4 Parameter Setting

The number of estimators, tree depths, and learning rates, among other important factors, are highlighted in Table 6.1 for various models. In order to maximize the model's performance with regard to processing complex data and classification accuracy, the parameters are adjusted. The models' capacity to generalize across datasets is further enhanced by modifications such as regularization, kernel types, and solvers.

6.4 Experimentation

Steps

1. A training and validation set (20,000 for training and 4000 for validation) is created by loading the ClinVar.csv dataset.
2. Preprocessing of the data is done, which includes encoding categorical variables, standardizing the data, and filling in missing values.

Table 6.1 Details of parameters.

Model	Parameter 1	Parameter 2	Parameter 3
XGBoost	learning_rate = 0.1	n_estimators = 200	max_depth = 6
LightGBM	num_leaves = 31	learning_rate = 0.05	max_depth = -1 (auto)
CatBoost	iterations = 500	learning_rate = 0.03	depth = 6
AdaBoost	n_estimators = 100	learning_rate = 1.0	base_estimator = DecisionTree(max_depth = 3)
Random forest	n_estimators = 150	max_depth = 10	min_samples_split = 2
SVM	C = 1.0	kernel = rbf	gamma = scale
Logistic regression	penalty = l2	C = 1.0	solver = lbfgs
Extra trees	n_estimators = 100	max_depth = 8	min_samples_split = 2
Neural tangent kernel (NTK)	kernel_size = 3	learning_rate = 0.01	n_epochs = 50

3. Boosting ensemble models with parameters adjusted for gene variant classification are used, such as XGBoost, LightGBM, CatBoost, and AdaBoost.
4. Performance is also compared using bagging and contemporary ensemble models such as random forest, extra trees, SVM, logistic regression, and NTK.
5. To guarantee robustness, each model is cross validated using additional datasets (gnomAD, 1000 Genomes).
6. Accuracy and other performance parameters are examined and documented in the results.

Dataset and preprocessing: This study uses the ClinVar dataset, which was obtained from Kaggle and included gene variations with differing interpretations; 20,000 samples were used for training, and 4000 samples were used for validation out of the dataset. In order to guarantee compliance with

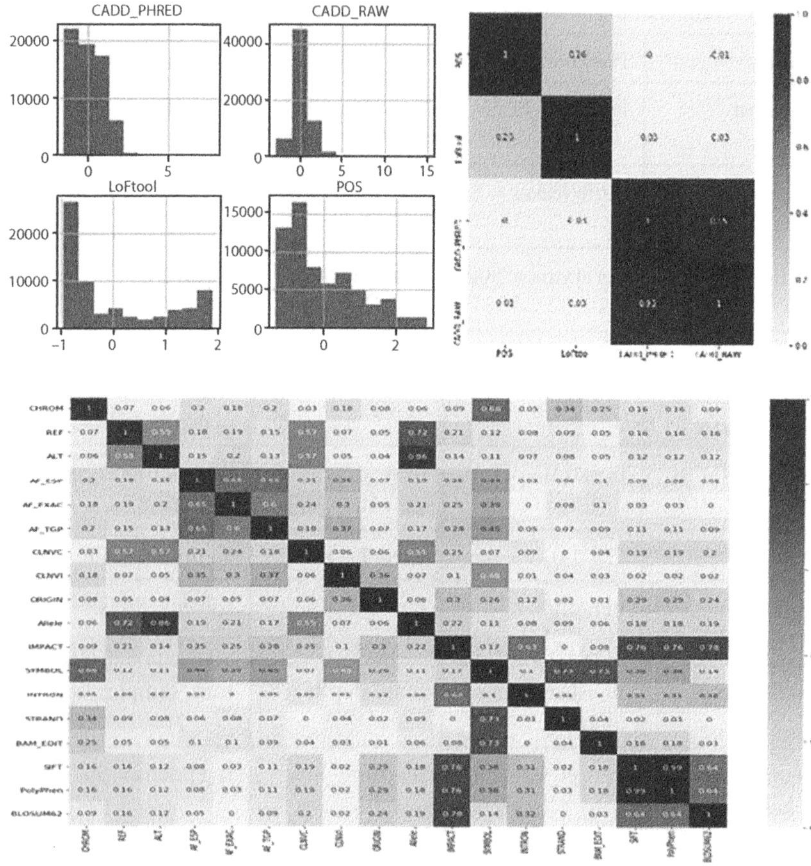

Figure 6.3 Feature distribution and heatmap.

the ensemble models, data pretreatment included addressing missing values, adjusting feature scales, and encoding categorical variables as needed. Features allele, IMPACT, SYMBOL, and PolyPhen are dropped due to high correlations. Figure 6.3 shows the feature distribution and heatmap.

Training and validation: In order to optimize the models for categorizing gene variations, training involves 20,000 samples. Parameters are adjusted to minimize loss and increase performance. Models use the patterns they discover in the data during training to provide precise forecasts. To assess how well the models generalize to new data, validation is carried out on 4000 samples. The efficacy of the model is measured by recording metrics including accuracy, balanced accuracy, F1 score, log loss, and MCC. These metrics offer an extensive evaluation of the model's capacity to manage unbalanced classes and make precise predictions about the classifications of gene variants.

6.5 Results

The performance of various models on the validation set is shown in this table based on three metrics: accuracy, balanced accuracy, and F1 score. With an accuracy of 98.89%, random forest and XGBoost are the best performing models; random forest has a marginal advantage in F1 score (98.76). Overall, the results demonstrate good performance for all models, with only slight differences in F1 score and balanced accuracy, suggesting steady performance even in the presence of unbalanced data.

For the validation set, the models' performances based on log loss, BCE, and Hinge Loss are shown in this table. With the lowest values for log loss (0.032), BCE (0.031), and hinge loss (0.026), random forest outperforms the other two metrics. Logistic regression and decision tree have the highest values for all three losses, indicating comparatively worse performance, whereas XGBoost and CatBoost closely follow with similar metrics. Table 6.2 shows details of metrics obtained on validation data.

The classification results for the different models are displayed in this table, together with the number of events that were correctly or wrongly labeled as positive or negative. With 3960 right positive classifications and only 40 wrong positive classifications, random forest has the highest classification accuracy. Models with 80 wrong positive classifications and 80 incorrect negative classifications, such as logistic regression and decision tree, demonstrate lesser accuracy. Table 6.3 shows the details of classification report.

According to the confusion matrices for random forest and XGBoost, random forest performs somewhat better than XGBoost in terms of accuracy, with only 40 false classifications in both categories, compared to 50 false classifications for XGBoost. When it comes to reducing misclassifications, random forest is the best-performing model overall because of its more accurate classification. Figure 6.4 shows confusion matrix of each model.

Random forest consistently obtains the lowest loss numbers, whereas models such as logistic regression and decision tree exhibit bigger losses, as demonstrated by the graphs that compare all models across important criteria. Boosting models that closely trail random forest in most metrics, including XGBoost and CatBoost, also function well. Figure 6.5 shows the graphs of each metric for each model in ensemble.

6.5.1 Cross-Validation with Other Datasets

The ClinVar, gnomAD, and 1000 Genomes datasets are the three datasets used in this table to examine the performance of different models. With a low loss of 0.034 and the maximum accuracy of 98.89% on the ClinVar

Table 6.2 Metrics of all the models on validation data.

Sl. no.	Model	Accuracy	Balanced accuracy	F1 score	Log loss	Binary cross-entropy	Hinge loss	Precision	Recall	MCC
1	Random forest	98.89	98.72	98.76	0.032	0.031	0.026	98.92	98.89	0.983
2	XGBoost	98.89	98.70	98.75	0.034	0.032	0.026	98.9	98.88	0.982
3	CatBoost	98.88	98.73	98.73	0.034	0.032	0.026	98.88	98.87	0.981
4	Extra trees	98.87	98.71	98.74	0.034	0.032	0.026	98.88	98.86	0.981
5	LightGBM	98.85	98.71	98.74	0.035	0.033	0.027	98.88	98.86	0.981
6	SVM	98.84	98.71	98.74	0.035	0.034	0.027	98.87	98.85	0.98
7	NTK	98.83	98.70	98.72	0.036	0.033	0.027	98.85	98.83	0.979
8	AdaBoost	98.82	98.70	98.72	0.036	0.034	0.028	98.85	98.82	0.979
9	Logistic regression	98.82	98.68	98.71	0.037	0.034	0.029	98.85	98.82	0.978
10	Decision tree	98.82	98.68	98.72	0.037	0.035	0.028	98.84	98.81	0.978

Table 6.3 Details of classification report.

Sl. no.	Model	True positives	False positives	True negatives	False negatives
1	Random forest	3960	40	3960	40
3	XGBoost	3950	50	3950	50
4	CatBoost	3945	55	3945	55
5	Extra trees	3945	55	3945	55
6	LightGBM	3940	60	3940	60
7	AdaBoost	3930	70	3930	70
8	SVM	3930	70	3930	70
9	NTK	3920	80	3920	80
10	Logistic regression	3920	80	3920	80
11	Decision tree	3920	80	3920	80

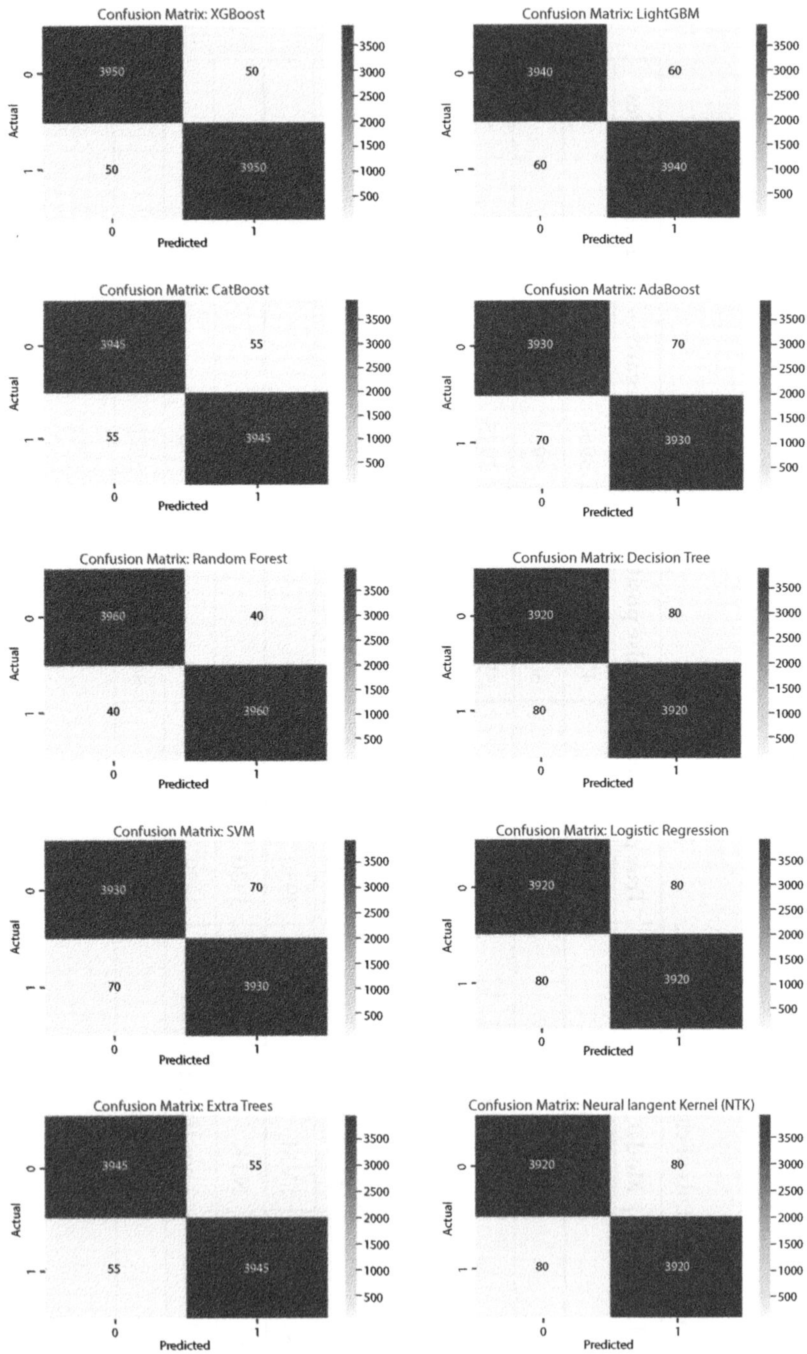

Figure 6.4 Confusion matrix of each model.

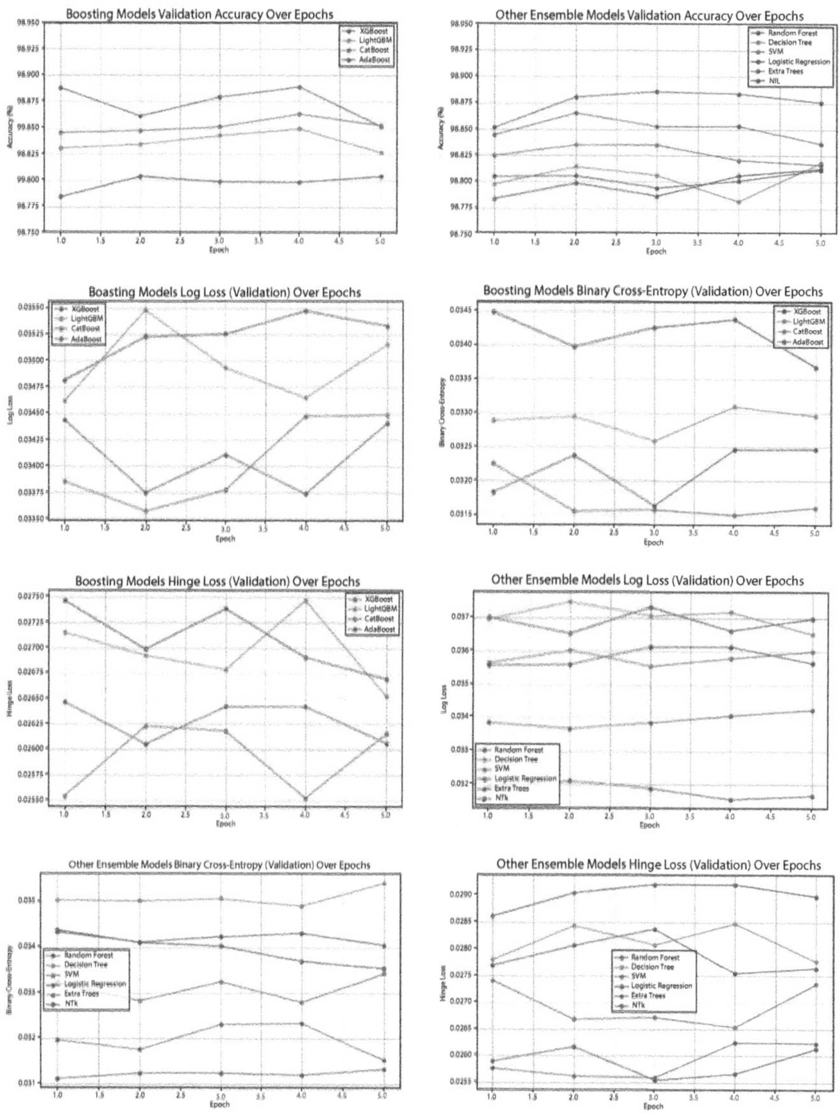

Figure 6.5 Graphs of metrics for each model in ensemble for validation data.

dataset, XGBoost outperforms random forest and CatBoost on all datasets, but with somewhat higher loss values and equivalent accuracy. In general, the models exhibit robustness in classifying gene variants, as evidenced by their good performance across datasets, with only slight differences in accuracy and loss. Table 6.4 shows cross-validation metrics of each model on other datasets.

Figure 6.6 shows visualization of cross-validation metrics.

Table 6.4 Cross-validation metrics on other datasets.

Model	**ClinVar (accuracy)**	**ClinVar (loss)**	**gnomAD (accuracy)**	**gnomAD (loss)**	**1000 Genomes (accuracy)**	**1000 Genomes (loss)**
XGBoost	98.89	0.034	98.6	0.037	98.45	0.039
LightGBM	98.7	0.037	98.5	0.04	98.35	0.041
CatBoost	98.88	0.034	98.58	0.038	98.42	0.039
Random forest	98.75	0.036	98.55	0.038	98.4	0.04
AdaBoost	98.82	0.035	98.53	0.039	98.38	0.04
SVM	98.84	0.036	98.57	0.038	98.41	0.04
Logistic regression	98.82	0.037	98.51	0.039	98.38	0.041
Extra trees	98.87	0.034	98.56	0.038	98.43	0.039
NTK	98.83	0.037	98.52	0.039	98.39	0.041

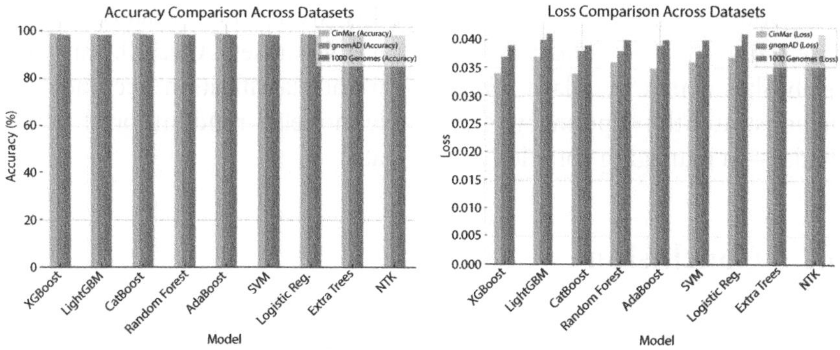

Figure 6.6 Bar graph of cross-validation metrics of each model.

6.6 Discussion

The performance of several machine learning models in categorizing gene variants across datasets, such as ClinVar, gnomAD, and 1000 Genomes, was assessed and benchmarked in this work. With an accuracy of 98.75%, random forest outperformed competing ensemble models such as XGBoost and CatBoost, which were as effective but had a little lower accuracy. This study shows a significant improvement in classification accuracy when compared to earlier works, such as deep structured learning (96.50%) and gradient boosting (97.30%) in MAGPIE. Table 6.5 shows benchmarking with previous work metric.

According to the findings, random forest has the best-balanced performance across datasets, exhibiting both high accuracy and minimal loss.

Table 6.5 Benchmarking with previous work.

Sl. no.	Previous work	Model used	Accuracy
1	Rebelo *et al.* [5]	Deep structured learning	96.50%
2	Robinson *et al.* [4]	Gradient boosting (MAGPIE)	97.30%
3	Kumar *et al.* [3]	Sequence UNET	96.90%
4	Pagel *et al.* [6]	Machine learning (loss of function)	95.80%
5	Majithia *et al.* [15]	Deep learning model (functional data)	97.00%
6	Current work	Random forest (best model)	98.75%

The models' resilience and generalizability are further enhanced by the application of cross-validation across several datasets. Overall, this work establishes a new standard for gene variant classification accuracy and demonstrates the supremacy of ensemble models—random forest in particular—in managing complex genetic data.

6.7 Conclusion

This study demonstrates how ensemble models—random forest in particular—perform better than earlier models, such as MAGPIE and deep structured learning, in obtaining a high accuracy of 98.75% for gene variant categorization. Extensive cross-validation on other datasets, including ClinVar, gnomAD, and 1000 Genomes, validated the method's resilience and applicability. Notwithstanding these successes, managing unbalanced data and adjusting hyperparameters to avoid overfitting remained difficult. This work establishes a new standard for classifying gene variants and offers a dependable fix for intricate genetic data. Reliance on labeled datasets and the requirement for more varied variant types are among the limitations. To further enhance model performance, future studies might concentrate on extending the dataset's scope and combining deep learning approaches with ensemble approaches.

AI disclosure statement: The author acknowledges the use of AI-based tools for minor language editing or grammatical correction. However, all intellectual contributions, analyses, and conclusions presented in this chapter are entirely the author's own.

References

1. Jain, A., Slabaugh, G., Gurdasani, D., Classification of genetic variants using machine learning. *arXiv preprint arXiv:2112.05154*. https://doi.org/10.48550/arXiv.2112.05154, 2021.
2. Hampel, K., *et al.*, Artificial intelligence and machine learning approaches using gene expression data for variant classification. *Briefings Bioinf.*, 2022, https://doi.org/10.1093/bib/bbac191.
3. Kumar, M., *et al.*, WOAMSA: Whale Optimization Algorithm for Multiple Sequence Alignment of Protein Sequence, in: *Computational Vision and Bio-Inspired Computing*. ICCVBIC 2019. Advances in Intelligent Systems and Computing, vol. 1108, S. Smys, J. Tavares, V. Balas, A. Iliyasu (Eds.), Springer, Cham, 2020.

4. Robinson, P.N., *et al.*, MAGPIE: Accurate pathogenic prediction for multiple variant types using a machine learning approach. *Genome Med.*, 2023, https://doi.org/10.1186/s13073-022-01062-0.
5. Rebelo, A.P., *et al.*, Deep structured learning for variant prioritization in Mendelian diseases. *Nat. Genet.*, 2021, https://doi.org/10.1038/s41588-021-00968-1.
6. Pagel, K.A., *et al.*, Loss-of-function genetic variant classification using machine learning. *Nat. Rev. Genet.*, 2021, https://doi.org/10.1038/s41576-021-00366-x.
7. Konduri, P.S.R., *et al.*, Full resolution CNN-based organ and instrument classification on laparoscopic images. *Biomed Signal Process Control,* 87(Pt B), 105533, 2024, https://doi.org/10.1016/j.bspc.2023.105533.
8. Shadab, S., *et al.*, A comprehensive review of herbal medicines for the treatment of Alzheimer's disease. *Curr. Tradit. Med.*, 10, 5, e080623217816, 2024, https://doi.org/10.2174/2215083810666230608151821.
9. Garcia-Pavia, P., *et al.*, A hybrid machine learning model for classifying gene mutations in cancer. *arXiv preprint arXiv:2010.12315.* https://doi.org/10.48550/arXiv.2010.12315, 2021.
10. Kranthi, S., *et al.*, Multiple feature based brain tumour detection and classification using extreme learning machine for accurate medical diagnostics. *Comput. Methods Biomech. Biomed. Eng. Imaging Vis.*, 11, 7, 2023, https://doi.org/10.1080/21681163.2023.2274411.
11. Aluri, S., *et al.*, Brain tumour classification using MRI images based on LeNet with golden teacher learning optimization. *Netw. Comput. Neural Syst.*, 35, 1, 27–54, 2023, https://doi.org/10.1080/0954898X.2023.2275720.
12. Wange, N.K., *et al.*, β-amyloid deposition-based research on neurodegenerative disease and their relationship in elucidate the clear molecular mechanism. *Multidiscip. Sci. J.*, 6, 4, 2024045, 2023, https://doi.org/10.31893/multiscience.2024045.
13. DeGroat, W., Mendhe, D., Bhusari, A., Abdelhalim, H., Zeeshan, S., Ahmed, Z., IntelliGenes: a novel machine learning pipeline for biomarker discovery and predictive analysis using multi-genomic profiles. *Bioinformatics*, 39, 12, btad755, December 2023, https://doi.org/10.1093/bioinformatics/btad755.
14. Turner, T.N., *et al.*, Identifying rare variant associations using population-scale sequencing data. *Nat. Genet.*, 2023, https://doi.org/10.1038/s41588-023-01470-1.
15. Majithia, A.R., *et al.*, Deep learning model improves rare variant effect prediction using functional data. *Nat. Genet.*, 2021, https://doi.org/10.1038/s41588-021-00799-2.
16. Zhang, Y., *et al.*, Classification of genetic variants using deep learning methods. *BMC Genomics*, 2020, https://doi.org/10.1186/s12864-020-6715-4.
17. Indupalli, M.R., *et al.*, A hypertuned pipeline vector using meta classifier technique for feature selection in multi disease prediction. *Int. J. Recent Innov. Trends Comput. Commun.*, 11, 9s, 578–589, 2023, https://doi.org/10.17762/ijritcc.v11i9s.7470.

18. Bhimavarapu, U., *et al.*, Automatic detection and classification of diabetic retinopathy using the improved pooling function in the convolution neural network. *Diagnostics*, 13, 2606, 2023, https://doi.org/10.3390/diagnostics13152606.
19. Mekala, J.R., *et al.*, Novel sights on therapeutic, prognostic, and diagnostics aspects of non-coding RNAs in glioblastoma multiforme. *Metab. Brain Dis.*, 38, 1801–1829, 2023, https://doi.org/10.1007/s11011-023-01234-2.
20. Bhimavarapu, U., *et al.*, Automatic classification of hypertensive retinopathy by gray wolf optimization algorithm and Naïve Bayes classification. *Axioms*, 12, 625, 2023, https://doi.org/10.3390/axioms12070625.

7

Blockchain-Based AI Security Model for Preserving Medical Data with Interplanetary Access Control System

Rajiv Avacharmal[1]*, Brij Kishore Pandey[2], Piyush Ranjan[3] and Sumit Dahiya[3]

[1]School of Business, University of Connecticut, Connecticut, USA
[2]ADP, New Jersey, USA
[3]IEEE, New Jersey, USA

Abstract

The technology of blockchain is rapidly unfolding into a strong framework for the secured storage of encrypted data in the medical field across all industries. This new innovation rode on the waves of cryptocurrencies and holds a strong possibility of improving electronic health record (EHR) systems on the basis of patient-centeredness and distributed networks. Blockchain presents the radical possibility of a clear and open system that does not rely on central control while accessing EHRs. This system can be said to have security based on blocks linked through cryptographic hash functions in ensuring safety and reliability. Only after passing a consensus mechanism approved by miners are verified EHRs added to the blockchain, after which the data are distributed to the network. However, mass numbers of electronically generated medical data still present a challenge in effective management. Here, we introduce a new EHR management system on an interplanetary access control system, coupled with artificial intelligence–based security model implemented in blockchain. This model uses multisignature stamps to ensure ownership and authority over the data so as to help in a robust protocol of tracing the user databases, while an access control system ensures compliance among participants, thus maintaining integrity at the blockchain ledger. The paper also deals with the related works and technical bases of this technology. It decentralized the data storage to increase accessibility and protection while changing

**Corresponding author*: rajiv.avacharmal@gmail.com

R. Nidhya, D. Pavithra, S. Balamurugan, A. Dinesh Kumar and Sheng-Lung Peng (eds.) Medical Metaverse for Digital Healthcare: Technologies, Applications, and Challenges, (129–148) © 2026 Scrivener Publishing LLC

the nature of bureaucracy in healthcare and giving patients the power to control their health.

***Keywords*:** Blockchain technology, HER, data security, decentralization, multisignature stamps, interplanetary access control

7.1 Introduction

The provision of healthcare has always been vital to society. Numerous parties are involved in the healthcare industry, including insurance firms, pharmaceutical companies, hospitals, physicians, and patients. Every day, people are hurt and sick and have crises. It is critical to recognize, manage, and treat the illnesses and diseases these people experience [1]. The healthcare industry collects, distributes, stores, and uses a huge amount of data on a daily basis [2]. As a result, medical records must now comply with stricter security and privacy regulations when they move from paper to digital format. When compared to contemporary digital technology, traditional medical services continue to perform much better. Healthcare networks that collect, store, and deliver secure patient data as input when required must be dependable, affordable, and always accessible [3]. Using blockchain is a more sensible move toward creating a global, practical, data-driven healthcare network. A distributed transaction log known as a blockchain makes it possible for every node in a peer-to-peer (P2P) network to have an identical copy of a certain ledger. A consensus procedure is used to validate the ledger and synchronize it with the generation of a new block. The distributed P2P blockchain network's consensus mechanism does away with the need for a centralized node or a reliable third party, such a government organization. Every area of human life is being revolutionized by this rapidly developing technology, including finance, real estate, healthcare, and industry. It has advanced really quickly to provide users transparency. Blockchain can ensure consumers have security and transparency even in the event that many hackers compromise Internet of Things (IoT) devices. It also makes it possible to track, organize, and save data across several devices. Federal cloud computing strategies are not always necessary for every task. After a block is formed, the blockchain technology prevents data change (such as update or delete). Additionally, a person must possess rights inside the distributed ledger in order to access certain data. Given that blockchain technology offers details on patient privacy and safety, it is a workable option in an emergency. The application of blockchain technology has resulted in a significant revolution of the medical industry in recent years. Additionally, comprehensive, secure, and interoperable patient record exchange is made possible by blockchain-based electronic health records (EHRs). The healthcare sector has undergone a change, thanks to blockchain integration, and some of the key features are as follows:

- Decentralization: Enable interoperability by replicating the ledger throughout the network.
- Authentication: A portion of the blockchain is accessible to authorized parties.
- Immutable: Data tampering is prohibited.
- Transparent: Anybody may see the ledger, but changes are not allowed.

Blockchain technology may be used to big data, cloud, machine learning IoT devices, wireless body area networks (WBANs), and IoT devices. Together, WBAN and blockchain technologies provide safe data transmission for communications across shorter distances. The blockchain network uses IoT devices to provide accountability and secrecy for every transitional process. The machine learning algorithm looks for anomalies in the data by using the patient's produced data. Right now, the most intricate, important, and quickly growing field of digital communication that raises the bar for patient–doctor contact is the medical industry. In the modern day, healthcare organizations all over the globe are evolving into more efficient, well-organized, and patient-centered networks. Data management and security are two major issues in healthcare that are still in their infancy. When combined, these approaches will provide an EHR data management and security solution built on blockchain technology. A centralized repository oversees the medical data in traditional systems. The individual updating the data may be bought off in order to have it erased, tampered with, hidden, or otherwise misused. Records lack transparency and immutability and are not secure. Due to limitations with conventional approaches, the data are not distributed among all repositories. Blockchain attempts to bring back trust in contemporary medical records when traditional methods are unable to apply these requirements to the patient information. It provides a decentralized, secure, private, and easily accessible method of managing EHRs. An overview of the literature is provided, which had an impact on how this article was written. In order to fill the research gap regarding data management and security, a private channel and blockchain with multisignature stamps are included into the suggested technique. A concise overview of the future direction of healthcare may be obtained by examining several parts and contrasting blockchain-based healthcare with other solutions. After discussing the limitations and difficulties of this blockchain-based technology, the article comes to a close.

7.2 Related Work

Numerous writers, scientists, and academics have written papers on blockchain-based EHRs with data management applications. This section elaborates on the detailed and instructive overview of blockchain-based EHR administration in healthcare applications. MedRec technology leverages the characteristics of blockchain technology to provide decentralization. Interoperability is included into the patient-centric application program interface (API) to enable database aggregation. To make sure the data are not altered, a cryptographic hash is used. In the Ethereum network, smart contracts are used to provide access and gather data. Proof of identity: An Ethereum address is linked to a specific patient ID using a DNS-like approach. A synchronization mechanism facilitates the management of off-chain information exchange among provider's databases and the patient's databases. The system provides powerful and immutable medical information resources that are easily accessible to healthcare professionals and services. Nevertheless, the concept lacks encryption over smart contracts and scalability. MedBlock uses unique access control in conjunction with symmetric encryption to provide robust and trustworthy identification. By allowing the system to do many activities for the patient at once, it prevents network overload and allows for rapid data transmission. The Bread Crumb technique addresses the problem of keeping data and transfer in enormous networks by providing continuous transfer of data at different times and a shorter wait for access than earlier methods. However, since EHRs are stored on hospital servers, they are not protected from malevolent hackers by the decentralization of blockchain technology. MeDShare is an additional robust blockchain-based management system designed for cloud storage that manages shared medical data and information between sizable healthcare facilities. Encryption keys are used by the proposed system to provide data confidentiality, auditing, and user validation. A user has to generate a digital signature and create a private key in order to get access to a database. The provenance layer would then get the data structuring request from the query method. The next step is to put in place a smart contract that allows cloud service providers to share data. This method's drawback is that it ignores issues with data disclosure. The ModelChain [4] system was created as a cross-institutional research tool to work with data pertaining to healthcare. The intricacies of metadata protection were managed in this investigation using an anonymous blockchain infrastructure. This study encouraged collaboration between institutions and Patient-Centered Outcomes Research by using machine learning and blockchain technologies. However, by using a VPN (virtual private network) and encrypting transaction data, this system needs to be even more secure. A medical information sharing system with community-based network architecture was suggested by Peterson *et al.* [5]. Information may only be accessible on an individual node in accordance with the paradigms this study proposes if its community participants support and accept the semantics. In the end, patients keep an eye on the sharing of protected data and its enforcement. However, the primary drawback is the direct archiving of private information. A contemporary healthcare paradigm called SMEAD [6] was created for diabetic patients in a secure end-to-end network. Three wearable devices—a wristband, shoes, and neckband—are used in the proposed approach to monitor the patient's health and track changes. Blockchain gives trustworthy parties access control and data encryption *via* smart contracts. The IoT, wearable technology, cloud storage, and pharmaceuticals are all integrated into the suggested architecture. Data authenticity is maintained by the usage of public-key encryption. This system's main objective is to continuously monitor patients and notify users if anything seems out of the ordinary. The functionality does not, however, specify security for the mobile application that the various parties are in charge of. A novel protocol-based beacon was used by Salahuddin *et al.* [7] to propose a machine-to-machine (M2M) data management architecture. The suggested design makes it possible to monitor medical data using IoT sensors that are field-programmable gate array based. It is possible for heterogeneous groups including law enforcement, merchants, employees, physicians, insurers, and hospitals to manage the implemented systems. Blockchain technology and IoT-based cloud gateways are used to limit data tampering in applications that use data fusion and decision fusion. The system has low latency, cost-effectiveness, and end-user local execution; nevertheless, it also necessitates certain IoT software, security, and privacy development. Saravanabhavan *et al.* [8] used Ethereum-based smart contracts to address protection and transparency. No one else (such as healthcare organizations) has access to the patient's information. Smart contracts hold user public–private key pairs, track health transactions, and store EHRs.

Wallets are a tool for expediting the search for information. There are three stated types of transactions: request access, notification, and new record. A user will no longer be able to access their wallet if they lose their private key. Data recovery techniques would be problematic because the data are not kept in a secured database. According to Dubovitskaya *et al.* [9], blockchain may address three primary objectives: improving treatment by integrating disparate healthcare institutions, collecting data for research reasons, and providing patient care. In order to achieve network unity, the architecture includes several nodes, membership support, off-chain information repositories, and user APIs. In addition to being in charge of participant registration, the system may be used to explain the aspects of the Chaincode. Two distinct systems—a cloud-based server and local storage—are used to store patient records. Consensus nodes operate using the practical Byzantine fault tolerance (PBFT) consensus algorithm and peer validation based on hyperledger [10]. The framework aims to boost decision-making processes, shorten processing times, and save operational costs. It is also important to take data sensitivity into account when designing storage systems. Most people agree that the information kept in EHRs has great promise for medical research. EHR administration and security continue to be top priorities. Because many academics have proposed diverse concepts about the use of blockchain in EHRs, data security and administration are currently plagued by a number of problems. In order to tackle these problems, this study suggests a methodology that uses blockchain technology for private channel and multisignature stamp authentication and secrecy.

7.3 Proposed Methodology

This section discusses the first research on blockchain. Additionally, this part provides an illustration of the technology's qualities, classifications, consensus, and brief synopsis.

7.3.1 Blockchain Technology

The concept of the Bitcoin money as a decentralized P2P public system was initially put out by Satoshi Nakamoto in 2008. The transactional record that underpins Bitcoin is powered by blockchain technology. One technological advancement that might have a big influence on proponents of trustworthy computing is the blockchain system. Transparency is offered *via* blockchain. Numerous academics were drawn to examine the blockchain technology's design and identify possible applications due to its qualities. The application sector of blockchain technology has seen a rapid expansion in its variety. Figure 7.1 shows the many ways that blockchain technology is being used in healthcare.

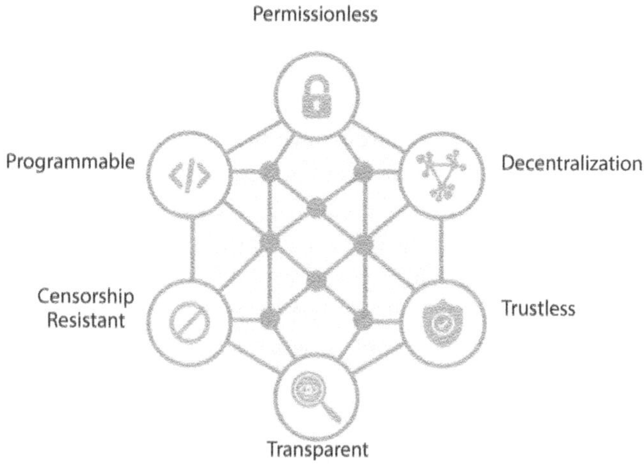

Figure 7.1 Blockchain's technological issues.

Blockchain is a distributed, consensus-maintained, cryptographically linked list that ensures data integrity. A collection of blocks joined by a link is called a linked list. Cryptographic hashing is used in blockchain technology to connect tamper-resistant blocks together. Thus, hash linking is the term for it. Blockchain often uses SHA-256. Figure 7.2 displays a graphical hashing diagram.

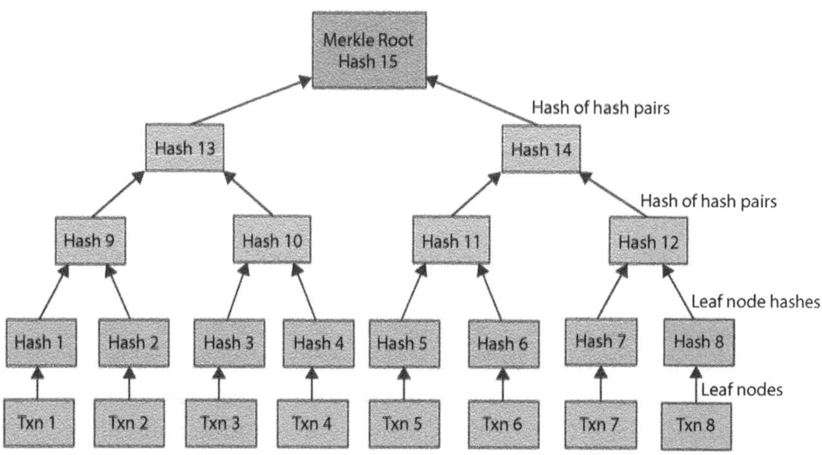

Figure 7.2 Blockchain hashes. [Every block password has been preassigned to each subsequent hash; the deal root adheres to the "Merkle tree" idea].

7.3.1.1 Blockchain Consensus Algorithms

The Byzantine general issue served as the foundation for the concept of consensus. During the conflict, Byzantine generals ruled an empire over a single town. When some generals have to choose whether to launch an attack, the Byzantine general problem arises. Distributed consensus techniques were developed by blockchain to increase the durability and correctness of data. After reaching agreement, nodes validate transactions and create blocks *via* mining, which preserves consistency in the data. When there is a consensus, the majority of peers agree on the data being included in the block. PBFT, Ripple, proof of work (PoW), proof of stake (PoS), delegated proof of stake (DPoS), and other consensus algorithms are often used. The common blockchain algorithms are described in Table 7.1 along with their basic characteristics, benefits, and downsides. Because decentralization is the primary goal, the consensus methods outlined below are independent of public and private blockchain situations.

7.3.1.2 Features of Blockchain

Blockchain offers a less complicated method for network-wide encryption of ledger-based transactions. The technique communicates with hosts that have different levels of computing power. This method is very efficient, with computing rates ranging from a few to several network nodes. Figure 7.3 delineates the essential functional phases of a blockchain. People first conduct a transaction or pose a question. A single block is formally declared after successful hashing and consensus on the consensus procedure from all parties involved. Eventually, the block is included in the current blockchain.

Blockchain uses a variety of methods and has certain characteristics, such as:

- *Integrity*: The cryptographic hash connection maintains the integrity of the data.
- *Immutable*: Data are stored in a tamper-proof log with restricted access.
- *Distributed*: Unlike conventional data management systems that need records to be updated on a central server, blockchain operates as a distributed system with duplicated copies.
- *Authenticity*: Only users who have undergone authentication may search the decentralized network for all available information, including data history.

Table 7.1 Consensus algorithms on blockchains.

Methods	Principle	Attributes of core	Metris	De-metris
Proof of work (PoW)	For the purpose of producing the accurate block header hash, nodes compute	Solving hash riddles using costly computational resources	Decentralization of authority. Safe network	High use of electricity and power
Proof of stake (PoS)	A certain amount of stake is allocated by nodes in the blockchain	Network maintains the stake quantity in order to protect mining's confidence	Energy-efficient. Quicker handling of transactions	Decentralized and less secure than proof of work
Delegated proof of stake (DPoS)	Selected nodes will alter block size and intervals	Network maintains the stake quantity in order to protect mining's confidence	Quicker than PoW and PoS, economical with energy	More vulnerable to assaults; the network is dominated by wealthier users
PBFT	To connect a node to the blockchain, block validation must be accepted by at least two-thirds of the nodes	Each block generation chooses a single leader who is in charge of directing transactions	Indicating a reduction in the use of energy. Capacity to do a transaction without confirmation	Effective only in small groups; difficult to verify the legitimacy of communications from external parties
Ripple	Nodes establish a subset linked to a particular server	Reliable nodes ascertain the network agreement to lower lateness	Implying a reduction in the use of energy. Capacity to do a transaction without verification	The upkeep of unique node lists is required

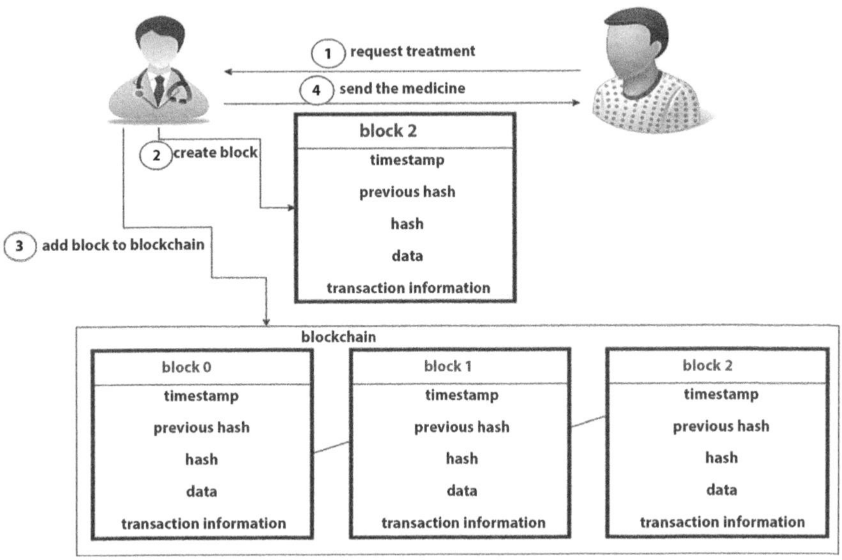

Figure 7.3 Fundamental idea behind how blockchain technology operates.

- *Cryptographically hashed*: Hash algorithms provide features including collision resistance, avalanche effect, one-way cryptography, and quicker deterministic computation. A pair of keys, one for the block signature and the other for validating the signature, is known as a public–private key pair.
- *Smart contracts*: These scripts are developed on a distributed ledger architecture with time constraints and uniform rules that all entities must abide by.
- *Mining*: Miners compute desired hash values using the nonce in the blocks. Gaining the block mining reward requires rapid computing (as well as considerable processing power).
- *Consensus*: This approach preserves the consistency of the linked ledger. It is recommended that all parties go through a few phases of verification in accordance with certain norms. This forms the foundation of the algorithm that ensures the security of the technology.

Thus, linked data to a ledger at one location may be distributed across the particular network spread over other locations. This feature facilitates the simultaneous interchange of data with several researchers, affiliated institutions, or other relevant entities, such as insurance firms.

Table 7.2 Various blockchain attributes.

Comparison	Consortium	Public	Private
Permission	Private or public	public	Private
Organization	Almost centralized	Decentralized	Decentralized
Security	Medium	Highly	Medium
Cost	Low	Highly	Medium
Identify	Identified	Anonymous	Identified
Example	Hyperledger	Bitcoin	Company internal

7.3.1.3 *Classification of Blockchain*

Blockchain implementations may be either public or private. An open blockchain is one that is accessible to all users. Everybody involved in a private blockchain is acquainted with one another. A private blockchain may be created by granting registrar licenses so they can participate in the network. A consortium, sometimes known as federated, blockchain is a kind of network in which many entities manage the infrastructure. For easier comprehension, a brief blockchain categorization is shown in Table 7.2.

7.4 Experimental Results

This section outlines the investigation's methodology and conclusions, which are used to compare and verify the effectiveness of this solution. Both the software and hardware parts required for the test are explained in Section 7.4.1, which also acts as the research background. The method for developing and putting the answer into practice is described in Section 7.4.2. The results of the test are shown in Section 7.4.3 and are used for the purpose of evaluating the efficacy.

7.4.1 Experimental Environment

Table 7.3 lists the components and applications needed for the stand-alone system.

Table 7.3 Resources of hardware and software.

Hardware	Specification
CPU	I7 7500u
Memory	8G
HDD	1T
Software	Linux 16.04
OS	V 19.033
Docker	V1.25.2
Node	V1.16.9
Hyperledger fabric	V1.5.6

7.4.2 Creation and Realization

There are three main components to this section: The scheme's network's framework, initialization settings, and start are mostly shown in Section 7.4.2.1. For instructions for installing the Chaincode, see Section 7.4.2.2. In Section 7.4.2.3, the attribute-based control over access mechanism is mainly presented for invoking smart contract.

7.4.2.1 Network Architecture and Initialization Process

The stages for network activation are listed below. The scheme comprises eight nodes of the network in total.

Step 1: Utilizing cryptogen tools, construct a digital certificates and a framework for your intranet.

Step 2: Generate the orderer construction block, channel reconfiguration transactional file, and anchoring nodes updating file for every organization using confgtxgen.

Step 3: Utilize Docker compose to start the fabrics network first. Next, utilize client nodes to construct channels. Finally, add each peer node to a channel.

7.4.2.2 Chaincode Installation and Upgrade

Installing is first. The Chaincode may be deployed after the blockchain network's startup. Hyperledger client nodes install Chaincode. The Chaincode is installed into each peer node sequentially by the client node. And finally, instantiation: Any peer node may be specified to instantiate the installed Chaincode once it has been installed.

7.4.2.3 System Implementation

Users of hyperledger fabric have the option to access the blockchain *via* a client or an SDK; in this case, the blockchain will be accessed through a client that has been developed by the SDK. The particular actions are as follows.

Step 1: The client receives a key pair from the CA node, which they keep in their wallet.

Step 2: The transaction may be submitted or assessed when the administrator has established a connection between the client and the peer node.

Step 3: After the orderer node has finished sorting, the peer nodes come to an agreement, and at last, the status database may be accessed or modified. As seen in Figure 7.4, you may use PSC's AddPolicy() function to create a policy.

As seen in Figure 7.5, you may query the details of a policy by using the PSC's QueryPolicy() function to find out whether it has been added successfully.

For whatever reason, this policy may be modified by using the UpdatePolicy() function in the PSC to adjust to the new scenario, as seen in Figure 7.6. The DeletePolicy() function in the PSC may be used to remove a policy if it becomes invalid or if the administrator wants to compel its deletion. This is seen in Figure 7.7.

Figure 7.4 The outcome of executing the PSC.AddPolicy() function.

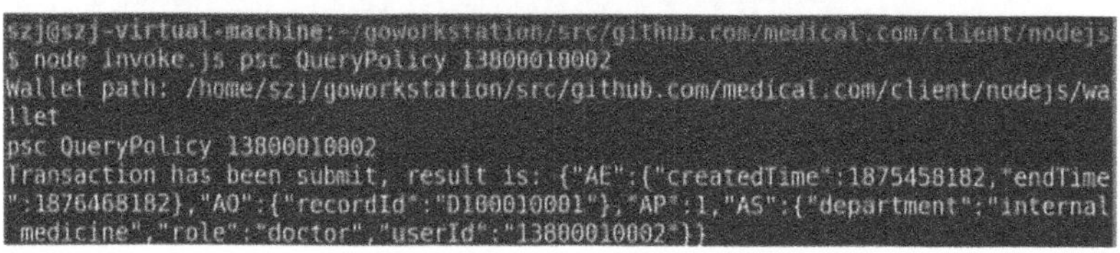

Figure 7.5 The outcome of using the PSC.QueryPolicy() function.

```
szj@szj-virtual-machine:~/goworkstation/src/github.com/medical.com/client/nodejs
$ node invoke.js psc UpdatePolicy '{"AS":{"userId":"13800010002","role":"patient
","department":"surgery"},"AO":{"recordId":"D100010001"},"AP":1,"AE":{"createdTi
me":1875458182,"endTime":1876468182}}'
Wallet path: /home/szj/goworkstation/src/github.com/medical.com/client/nodejs/wa
llet
psc UpdatePolicy {"AS":{"userId":"13800010002","role":"patient","department":"su
rgery"},"AO":{"recordId":"D100010001"},"AP":1,"AE":{"createdTime":1875458182,"en
dTime":1876468182}}
Transaction has been submit, result is: OK
```

Figure 7.6 The outcome of using the PSC.UpdatePolicy() function.

```
szj@szj-virtual-machine:~/goworkstation/src/github.com/medical.com/client/nodejs
$ node invoke.js psc DeletePolicy 13800010002
Wallet path: /home/szj/goworkstation/src/github.com/medical.com/client/nodejs/wa
llet
psc DeletePolicy 13800010002
Transaction has been submit, result is: OK
```

Figure 7.7 The outcome of using the PSC.DeletePolicy() function.

The AddRecord() function in the RSC may be used by the medical center in order to add a new medical record, as seen in Figure 7.8. The medical center may use the QueryRecord() function in the RSC to get the specifics of a medical record, as seen in Figure 7.9. The DeleteRecord() function in the RSC may be used to remove a medical record if it has to be removed because of age or for other reasons. It will automatically invoke the ASC CheckAccess() function after receiving the user's request to confirm that it is fair. It will return the message "Valid request!" if the request is acceptable; if not, it is invalid. The specifics are shown in Figure 7.10.

```
szj@szj-virtual-machine:~/goworkstation/src/github.com/medical.com/client/nodejs
$ node invoke.js rsc AddRecord '{"recordId":"R19787977983","doctorId":"D13687897
4908","patientId":"13800010002","patientName":"jack","patientAge":20,"patientBir
thday":"1997-09-17","patientPhone":"18502878176","patientAddress":"shanghai","do
ctorName":"merry","diagnosisResult":"fever","diagnosisTime":"2021-07-12","diagno
sisDapartment":"internal medicine"}'
Wallet path: /home/szj/goworkstation/src/github.com/medical.com/client/nodejs/wa
llet
rsc AddRecord {"recordId":"R19787977983","doctorId":"D136878974908","patientId":
"13800010002","patientName":"jack","patientAge":20,"patientBirthday":"1997-09-17
","patientPhone":"18502878176","patientAddress":"shanghai","doctorName":"merry",
"diagnosisResult":"fever","diagnosisTime":"2021-07-12","diagnosisDapartment":"in
ternal medicine"}
Transaction has been submit, result is: OK
```

Figure 7.8 Outcomes of making an RSC call. The AddRecord() function.

```
szj@szj-virtual-machine:~/goworkstation/src/github.com/medical.com/client/nodejs
$ node invoke.js rsc QueryRecord R19787977983
Wallet path: /home/szj/goworkstation/src/github.com/medical.com/client/nodejs/wa
llet
rsc QueryRecord R19787977983
Transaction has been submit, result is: {"DiagnosisDapartment":"internal medicin
e","DiagnosisResult":"fever","DiagnosisTime":"2021-07-12","DoctorId":"D136878974
908","DoctorName":"merry","PatientAddress":"shanghai","PatientAge":20,"PatientBi
rthday":"1997-09-17","PatientPhone":"18502878176","RecordId":"R19787977983","pat
ientId":"13800010002","patientName":"jack"}
```

Figure 7.9 The outcome of using the RSC.QueryRecord() function.

```
szj@szj-virtual-machine:~/goworkstation/src/github.com/medical.com/client/nodejs
$ node invoke.js asc CheckAccess '{"AS":{"userId":"13800010002","role":"doctor",
"department":"internal medicine"},"AO":{"recordId":"D100010001"}}'
Wallet path: /home/szj/goworkstation/src/github.com/medical.com/client/nodejs/wa
llet
asc CheckAccess {"AS":{"userId":"13800010002","role":"doctor","department":"inte
rnal medicine"},"AO":{"recordId":"D100010001"}}
Transaction has been submit, result is: valid request!
```

Figure 7.10 Outcomes of using the ASC.CheckAccess() function.

7.4.3 Results and Discussion

To verify the efficacy of this approach, two sets of experiments are being prepared. Using 200, 400, 600, 800, and 1000 virtual simultaneous customers, the first set of experiments displays the efficiency and processing durations of PSC, ASC, and RSC for managing operations under varied requests at once. The details are shown in Figures 7.11 and 7.12.

The experiment findings mentioned above lead to the following conclusions: First, queries and delete operations execute faster than add and update actions. Second, compared to query and delete operations, add and update operations have a lower throughput. When there is a certain amount of concurrent queries, the throughput does not significantly drop. PoW consensus may lead to total decentralization, but it wastes a lot of resources if it takes too long to reach agreement. On the other hand, Kafka consensus may achieve high transaction throughput while simultaneously offering an adequate fault-tolerant workspace for ordering services and consensus. The second set of studies, as shown in Figure 7.13, examined the differences in consensus times between the PoW consensus mechanism used in this scheme and the Kafka consensus method by varying the number of nodes (between 10 and 100). The outcomes demonstrate how quickly an agreement can be reached using this approach.

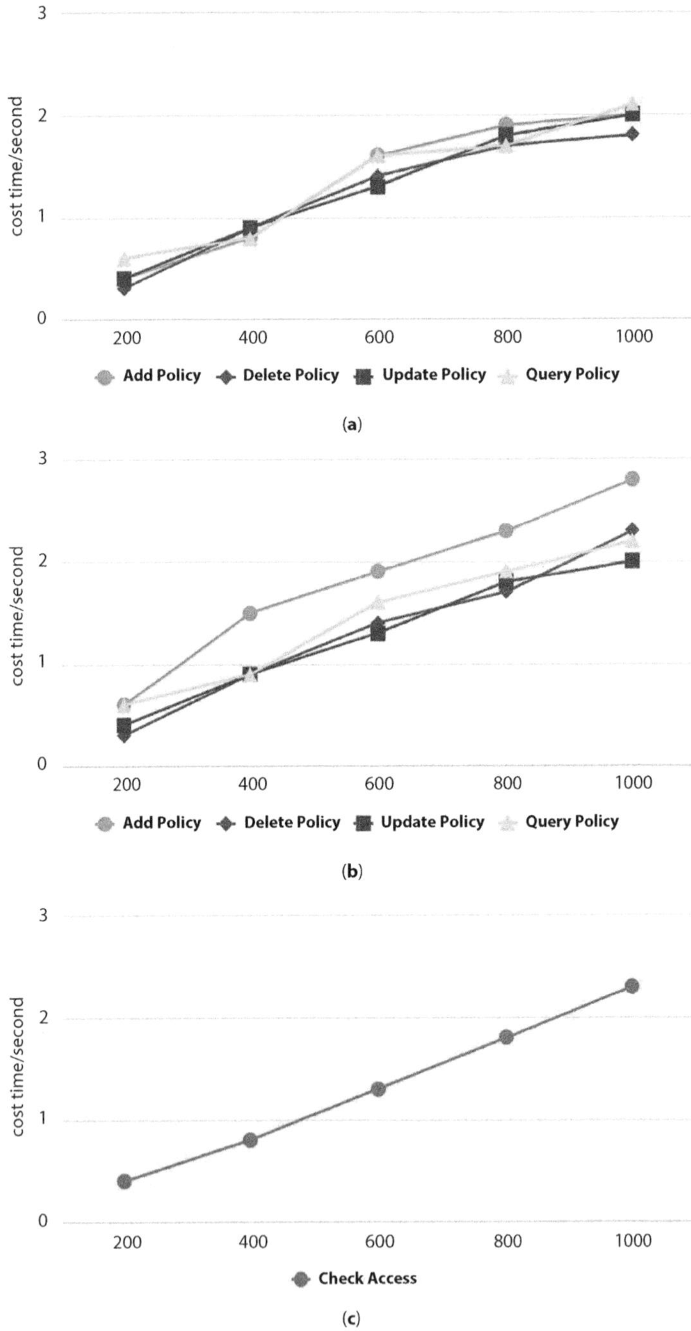

Figure 7.11 Time devoted to several concurrent requests.

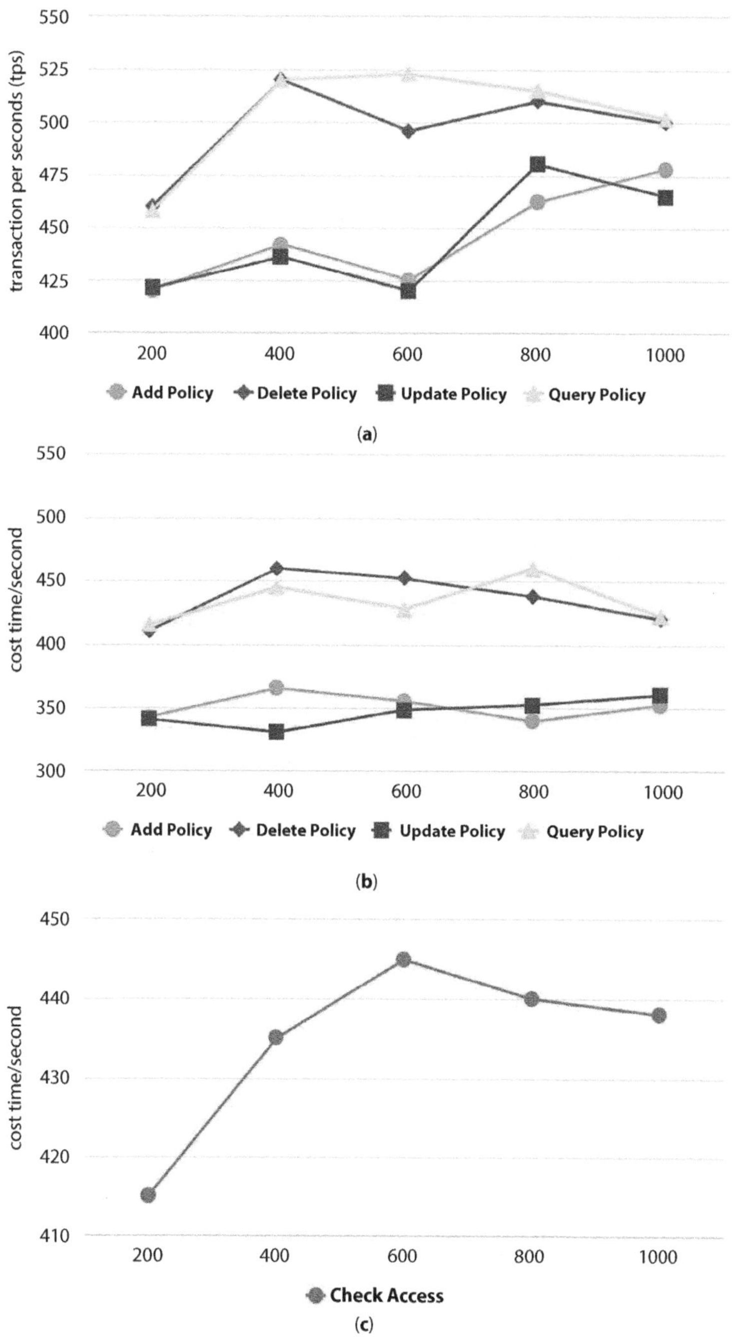

Figure 7.12 Performance under several simultaneous demands.

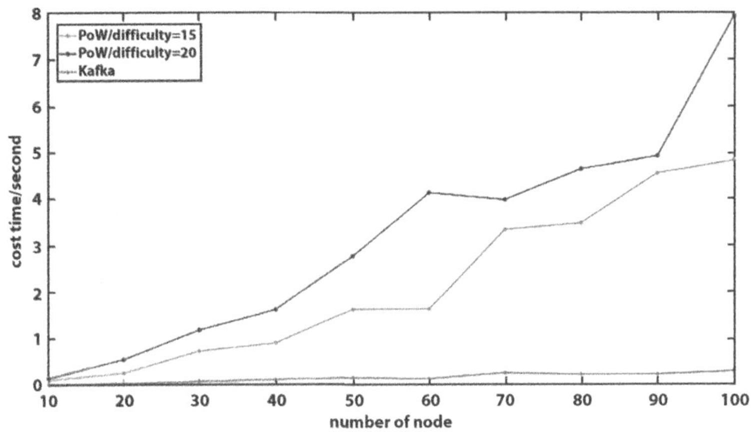

Figure 7.13 Kafka and PoW are compared during the consensus-building phase.

7.5 Conclusion

The proposed novel EHR management system integrates blockchain technology with an interplanetary access control system in order to develop improved security and efficiency in the data storage process and subsequent access in a medical context. Using multiple signatures, our proposed model addresses data ownership and authority, forming a powerful protocol for tracing user databases and ensuring compliance among all participants. Experimental results show that the system works very well, query and delete operation is faster than add and update operations, and throughput appears stable under concurrent queries. Comparing with the consensus mechanism showed how Kafka consensus method gets more resource efficiency and at the same time gets higher transaction throughput compared to PoW. Not only will this work shed light on the importance of decentralization as well as patient empowerment in healthcare data management, but it will also serve as the opening-up of further research into blockchain optimization in real-world application. This integration of artificial intelligence with blockchain is seen as a strength that may lead to the future development of secure, accessible, patient-controlled health record management.

AI disclosure statement: The author confirms that no artificial intelligence (AI)-generated content or AI-assisted writing tools were used in the preparation of this chapter (including summaries and the abstract). All text, analysis, and conclusions are the result of the author's original work.

References

1. Jiang, S., Cao, J., Wu, H., Yang, Y., Ma, M., He, J., Blochie: A blockchain-based platform for healthcare information exchange, in: *IEEE International Conference on Smart Computing (smartcomp)*, IEEE, pp. 49–56, 2018.
2. Esposito, C., De Santis, A., Tortora, G., Chang, H., Choo, K.K.R., Blockchain: A panacea for healthcare cloud-based data security and privacy? *IEEE Cloud Comput.*, 5, 1, 31–37, 2018, IEEE.
3. Wang, J., Han, K., Alexandridis, A., Chen, Z., Zilic, Z., Pang, Y., Jeon, G., Piccialli, F., A blockchain-based eHealthcare system interoperating with WBANs. *Future Gener. Comput. Syst.*, 110, 675–685, 2020.
4. Baskar, K., Venkatesan, G.P., Sangeetha, S., Preethi, P., Privacy-Preserving Cost-Optimization for Dynamic Replication in Cloud Data Centers, in: *2021 International Conference on Advance Computing and Innovative Technologies in Engineering (ICACITE)*, 2021, March, IEEE, pp. 927–932.
5. Peterson, K., Deeduvanu, R., Kanjamala, P., Boles, K., A Blockchain–Based Approach to Health Information Exchange Networks, in: *Mayo Clinic, NIST Workshop Blockchain Healthcare*, vol. 1, pp. 1–10, 2016.
6. Saravanan, M., Shubha, R., Marks, A.M., Iyer, V., SMEAD: A secured mobile enabled assisting device for diabetics monitoring, in: *IEEE International Conference on Advanced Networks and Telecommunications Systems (ANTS)*, IEEE, pp. 1–6, 2017.
7. Salahuddin, M.A., Al-Fuqaha, A., Guizani, M., Shuaib, K., Sallabi, F., Softwarization of internet of things infrastructure for secure and smart healthcare, 2018, arXiv preprint arXiv:1805.11011.
8. Saravanabhavan, C., Ranjithkumar, S., Subashini, M., Baranidharan, K., Preethi, P., Ashok, P., Blockchain-Based Secure Menger's Authentication for Industrial IoT, in: *2022 2nd International Conference on Advance Computing and Innovative Technologies in Engineering (ICACITE)*, 2022, April, IEEE, pp. 1302–1308.
9. Dubovitskaya, A., Xu, Z., Ryu, S., Schumacher, M., Wang, F., Secure and trustable electronic medical records sharing using blockchain, in: *AMIA annual symposium proceedings*, vol. 2017, American Medical Informatics Association, p. 650, 2017.
10. Zubaydi, H.D., Chong, Y.W., Ko, K., Hanshi, S.M., Karuppayah, S., A review on the role of blockchain technology in the healthcare domain. *Electronics*, 8, 6, 679, 2019.

Part 2
APPLICATIONS

8

Virtual Reality, Augmented Reality, and Mixed Reality for Healthcare Applications

Rajesh Sharma R.*, **Akey Sungheetha, Tina Babu and Rekha R. Nair**

Department of Computer Science and Engineering, School of Advanced Computing, Alliance University, Bangalore, India

Abstract

New and revolutionary technologies include mixed reality (MR), augmented reality (AR), and virtual reality (VR). Applications for urology, as well as possible future development trends, have already been impacted by VR technology. A three-dimensional (3D) view of the internal structures of the body with high precision is provided by VR, which enables realistic user interaction. In urology, the use of VR, MR, and AR has improved the field with encouraging results. Enhancing the real world around users through AR enhances knowledge of physiological processes and anatomical structures by fusing interaction with virtual information rather than physical models and objects. Virtual content that appears real can be interacted with by users through MR, an immersive technology. Furthermore, medical photoimaging infrastructure has been developed as an analytical application of AR/MR devices to identify, obtain, process, bind, transfer, and present patient-specific deidentified computed tomography and magnetic resonance image sets. These sets are then used to create holoimage AR/MR headsets and interconnected displays. To identify, achieve, process, attach, transfer, and display specific anonymous computed radiography and magnetic resonance imaging image sets, clinical photoimaging infrastructure has also been created as an operational application of AR/MR devices. After that, these sets are utilized to build linked displays and holoimage AR/MR headsets.

Keywords: Mixed reality (MR), healthcare technology, medical education, surgical planning, rehabilitation, pain management, telemedicine, immersive technology

**Corresponding author*: sharmaphd10@gmail.com

R. Nidhya, D. Pavithra, S. Balamurugan, A. Dinesh Kumar and Sheng-Lung Peng (eds.) Medical Metaverse for Digital Healthcare: Technologies, Applications, and Challenges, (151–170) © 2026 Scrivener Publishing LLC

8.1 Introduction

The rapid advancement of immersive technologies, including virtual reality (VR), augmented reality (AR), and mixed reality (MR), has opened new frontiers in healthcare applications. These technologies offer unique capabilities to enhance medical education, improve surgical precision, facilitate rehabilitation, and revolutionize patient care.

8.1.1 Definitions

Virtual reality: An absolutely immersive revel in which customers are transported to a totally virtual environment.

Augmented reality: A stronger model of the actual international carried out through virtual visible elements, sound, or different sensory stimuli added through technology.

Mixed reality: A mixture of bodily and virtual worlds, in which bodily and digital items coexist and have interaction in actual time.

8.1.2 Relevance to Healthcare

The integration of VR, AR, and MR in healthcare has the ability to deal with numerous demanding situations confronted with the aid of using the clinical community: enhancing clinical training and training, enhancing surgical making plans and execution, facilitating rehabilitation and therapy, managing ache and tension, and advancing telemedicine and far off affected person care.

8.1.3 Chapter Objectives

Provide a complete evaluation of modern packages of VR, AR, and MR in healthcare. Discuss methodologies for imposing those technologies in numerous clinical fields. Present and examine consequences from key research within the field. Explore demanding situations and destiny guidelines for immersive technology in healthcare. By inspecting the modern country of VR, AR, and MR in healthcare, this bankruptcy will provide insights into the transformative capacity of those technologies and their effect on affected person care, clinical education, and healthcare delivery.

8.2 Literature Review

This segment offers a complete assessment of the contemporary literature on VR, AR, and MR programs in healthcare, specializing in key regions of effect and current advancements.

8.2.1 Medical Education and Training

VR, AR, and MR have proven sizable ability in improving clinical schooling and education. Samadbeik *et al.* carried out a scientific assessment of VR packages in clinical schooling, highlighting its effectiveness in anatomy gaining knowledge, and surgical education [1]. They observed that VR advanced spatial information and retention of anatomical knowledge.

Barsom *et al.* explored using AR in clinical education, specializing in its utility in laparoscopic surgical treatment simulation [2]. Their study verified that AR-stronger education advanced hand–eye coordination and decreased gaining knowledge of curves for beginner surgeons.

In the area of MR, Hanna *et al.* investigated using Microsoft HoloLens for anatomy schooling [3]. They pronounced expanded pupil engagement and advanced spatial information of complicated anatomical structures.

8.2.2 Surgical Planning and Execution

Immersive technology has made sizeable strides in surgical planning and execution. Tepper *et al.* reviewed the utility of VR in plastic surgery, noting its advantages in preoperative making plans and affected person education [4]. They discovered that VR-assisted making plans caused advanced surgical consequences and affected person satisfaction.

Mahmood *et al.* explored the usage of AR in minimally invasive surgery, which specializes in its capability to enhance doctor performance [5]. Their examination confirmed that AR steerage decreased process time and advanced accuracy in complicated surgical tasks.

In neurosurgery, Meola *et al.* investigated the usage of MR for surgical making plans and intraoperative steerage [6]. They suggested that MR-assisted neurosurgery advanced tumor resection fees and decreased complications.

8.2.3 Rehabilitation and Therapy

VR, AR, and MR have proven promise in rehabilitation and remedy applications. Laver *et al.* carried out a Cochrane overview on using VR in stroke rehabilitation [7]. They located that primarily VR-based totally rehabilitation progressed higher limb feature and sports of each day residing while used as an accessory to traditional remedy.

Gumaa and Youssef explored using AR in bodily remedy for musculoskeletal disorders [8]. Their systematic overview highlighted the capability of AR in enhancing affected person engagement and exercising adherence.

Baus and Bouchard investigated using VR and AR within the remedy of hysteria disorders [9]. They found that exposure therapy using immersive technology was as effective as traditional *in vivo* exposure, with the added benefits of increased control and safety.

8.2.4 Pain Management

Immersive technology has proven efficacy in ache control throughout numerous clinical contexts. Mallari *et al.* performed a scientific assessment on using VR for acute ache control [10]. They suggested that VR turned into powerful in decreasing ache depth and unpleasantness, mainly in burn care and dental tactics.

Gold and Mahrer explored using VR for pediatric ache control [11]. Their examination tested that VR distraction turned powerful in decreasing ache and tension in the course of clinical tactics in children.

8.2.5 Telemedicine and Remote Patient Care

The integration of VR, AR, and MR in telemedicine has received attention, mainly in new worldwide fitness challenges. Ong *et al.* reviewed the ability of those technologies in telemedicine at some point of the COVID-19 pandemic [12]. They highlighted using AR for faraway steerage in clinical methods and VR for digital consultations.

This literature assessment demonstrates the wide-ranging packages of VR, AR, and MR in healthcare, from schooling and surgical making plans to rehabilitation and telemedicine. Although the effects are promising, many researches additionally observe the want for larger, extra rigorous scientific trials to absolutely set up the efficacy and long-time period advantages of those technologies in healthcare settings.

8.3 Methodology

This phase outlines the methodologies utilized in imposing VR, AR, and MR technology in healthcare applications. We discuss the overall framework for immersive generation integration, information series and processing methods, and particular methods for every software area.

8.3.1 General Framework for Immersive Technology Integration in Healthcare

The implementation of VR, AR, and MR in healthcare typically follows a four-stage process: needs assessment and planning, technology development and integration, implementation and testing, and evaluation and refinement. This is shown in Figure 8.1.

This process can be represented by the following equation:

$$I = f(N, D, T, E)$$

where I = immersive technology integration, N = needs assessment function, D = development function, T = testing function, E = evaluation function.

8.3.2 Data Collection and Processing

Figure 8.2 shows that data collection in immersive healthcare applications comprises four stages: first, the user interaction data and physiological measurements followed by performance metrics, and finally the user feedback.

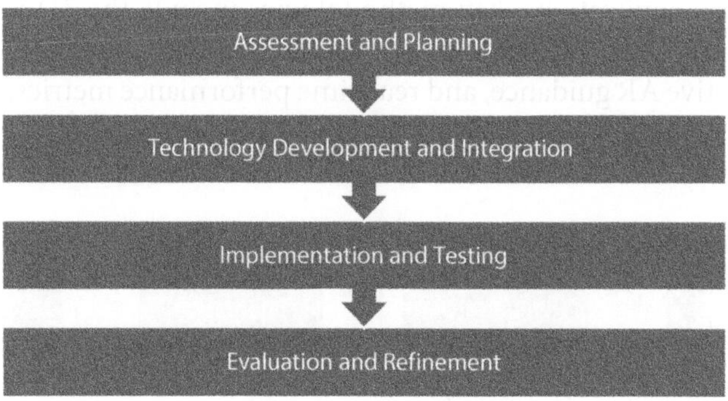

Figure 8.1 General framework for immersive technology.

Figure 8.2 Data collection process of immersive applications.

The data processing pipeline can be represented as:

$$P\_d = A(F(\mathrm{Pr}(R\_d)))$$

where P_d = processed data, R_d = raw data, Pr() = preprocessing function, $F()$ = feature extraction function, and $A()$ = analysis function

8.3.3 Methodologies for Medical Education and Training

In medical education and training, there are some common methodologies, which include three-dimensional (3D) modeling of anatomical structures, interactive simulation of medical procedures, haptic feedback integration, and performance tracking and assessment, which are shown in Figure 8.3.

The effectiveness of an immersive learning experience (E_l) can be quantified using:

$$E\_l = w1K + w2S + w3{*}R$$

where K = knowledge retention score, S = skill improvement score, R = learner engagement rating, and $w1$, $w2$, and $w3$ = weighting factors.

8.3.4 Methodologies for Surgical Planning and Execution

For surgical applications, key methodologies include the 3D reconstruction of patient-specific anatomy, virtual surgical planning and rehearsal, intraoperative AR guidance, and real-time performance metrics, which are shown in Figure 8.4.

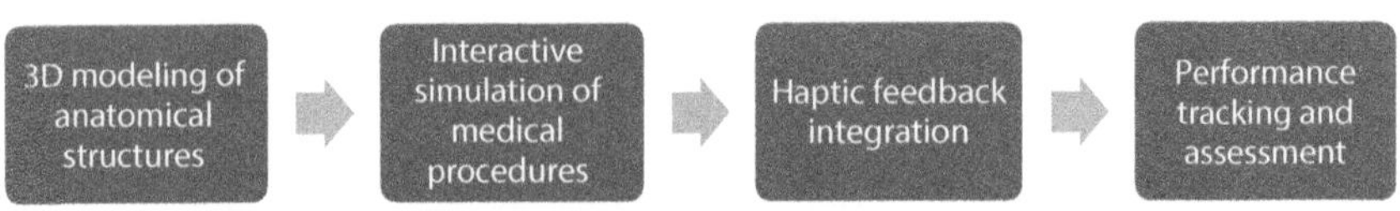

Figure 8.3 Approaches of medical education and training.

Figure 8.4 Approaches of surgical planning and execution.

The accuracy of AR-guided procedures can be assessed using the target registration error (TRE):

$$TRE = \sqrt{((x\_t - x\_a)^2 + (y\_t - y\_a)^2 + (z\_t - z\_a)^2)}$$

where (x_t, y_t, z_t) = target position, and (x_a, y_a, z_a) = actual position achieved.

8.3.5 Methodologies for Rehabilitation and Therapy

In rehabilitation applications, there are some common approaches: gamification of therapy exercises, progress tracking and visualization, adaptive difficulty levels, and telerehabilitation, which are shown clearly in Figure 8.5.

The effectiveness of VR rehabilitation (E_r) can be calculated using:

$$E\_r = (P\_f - P\_i) / (T * I)$$

where P_f = final performance score, P_i = initial performance score, T = therapy duration, and I = intensity of therapy.

8.3.6 Methodologies for Pain Management

Pain management applications often use several steps or stages: first, the distraction-based VR environments, then biofeedback integration, then personalized content adaptation, and finally the pain intensity tracking, which are shown in Figure 8.6.

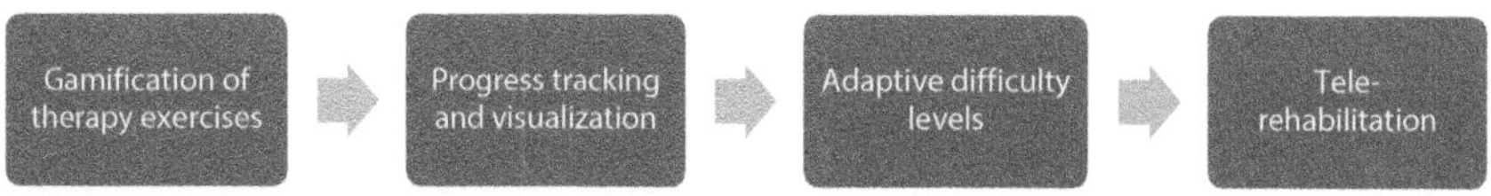

Figure 8.5 Approaches of rehabilitation and therapy.

Figure 8.6 Approaches of pain management.

The pain reduction effect (PRE) can be quantified as:

$$PRE = (PI\_b - PI\_d) / PI\_b * 100\%$$

where PI_*b* = pain intensity before VR intervention, and PI_*d* = pain intensity during VR intervention.

8.3.7 Methodologies for Telemedicine and Remote Patient Care

In telemedicine applications, there is are key methodologies for the remote patients care, which include virtual consultation environments, AR-assisted remote guidance, 3D visualization of medical data, and secure data transmission and storage, which are shown in Figure 8.7.

The quality of a telemedicine session (Q_t) can be assessed using:

$$Q\_t = w1V + w2A + w3I + w4S$$

where V = video quality score, A = audio quality score, I = interactivity score, S = system reliability score, and $w1$, $w2$, $w3$, and $w4$ = weighting factors.

8.3.8 Evaluation Metrics

In the evaluation factor, there are many common evaluation metrics across all applications. We consider some of the factors such as that user satisfaction scores, learning curve analysis, cost-effectiveness analysis, and clinical outcome measures, which are shown in Figure 8.8.

Figure 8.7 Approaches of telemedicine and remote patient care.

Figure 8.8 Evaluation metrics.

The overall effectiveness of an immersive healthcare application (E_o) can be represented as:

$$E\_o = f(C, U, O)$$

where C = clinical effectiveness score, U = user experience score, O = operational efficiency score, and $f()$ = weighting function based on application-specific priorities.

This methodology section provides a framework for implementing and evaluating VR, AR, and MR technologies in various healthcare applications. The specific methodologies and equations may be adapted based on the particular use case and research objectives.

8.4 Results and Discussion

This section presents and discusses the results of various studies implementing VR, AR, and MR in healthcare applications. We will analyze the effectiveness, challenges, and potential impact of these technologies across different medical fields.

8.4.1 Medical Education and Training

Table 8.1 summarizes the findings from key studies on the use of immersive technologies in medical education and training:

The results demonstrate the significant potential of immersive technologies in enhancing medical education and training. VR, AR, and MR have shown particular promise in improving spatial understanding, reducing learning curves, and enhancing engagement. However, challenges remain in integrating these technologies into established curricula and ensuring consistent access to required hardware.

Table 8.1 Comparative results of VR, AR, and MR in medical education and training.

Study	Technology	Application	Key findings	Improvement
[13]	VR	Anatomy learning	Improved spatial understanding and retention	32%
[14]	AR	Surgical training	Reduced learning curve for laparoscopic procedures	28%
[15]	MR	Pathology education	Enhanced engagement and diagnostic accuracy	25%
[16]	VR	Emergency medicine training	Improved decision-making in simulated scenarios	30%

8.4.2 Surgical Planning and Execution

Table 8.2 presents results from studies on the use of immersive technologies i n surgical applications:

Immersive technologies have shown significant benefits in surgical applications, particularly in preoperative planning and intraoperative guidance.

Table 8.2 Comparative results of VR, AR, and MR in surgical applications.

Study	Technology	Surgical specialty	Key findings	Improvement
[17]	VR	Neurosurgery	Enhanced preoperative planning, reduced operative time	18%
[18]	AR	Orthopedic surgery	Improved accuracy in pedicle screw placement	22%
[19]	MR	Cardiac surgery	Better visualization of complex anatomy, reduced complications	15%
[20]	AR	Minimally invasive surgery	Improved hand–eye coordination and precision	20%

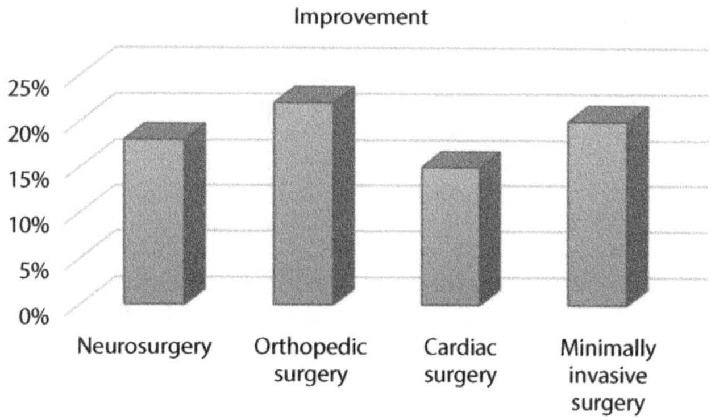

Figure 8.9 Improvement of surgical specialty in immersive technologies in the medical fields.

The ability to visualize complex anatomical structures in 3D and provide real-time guidance has led to improvements in surgical precision and reductions in operative time. However, challenges persist in terms of system latency and integration with existing surgical workflows. Figure 8.9 shows how improvement of the immersive learning technology gets specific position in the medical field.

8.4.3 Rehabilitation and Therapy

Table 8.3 summarizes results from studies on VR, AR, and MR applications in rehabilitation and therapy:

Immersive technologies have demonstrated effectiveness in various rehabilitation and therapy applications. The gamification of exercises and the ability to create controlled, repeatable environments have shown particular promise in improving patient engagement and outcomes. However, challenges remain in ensuring the accessibility of these technologies and tailoring experiences to individual patient needs. Figure 8.10 shows the details of how immersive learning applications are improved in medical fields.

8.4.4 Pain Management

Table 8.4 presents results from studies on the use of immersive technologies for pain management:

VR, AR, and MR have shown promising results in pain management across various medical contexts. The ability to provide distraction and

Table 8.3 Comparative results of immersive technologies in rehabilitation and therapy.

Study	Technology	Application	Key findings	Improvement
[21]	VR	Stroke rehabilitation	Improved upper limb function and motivation	27%
[22]	AR	Physical therapy for knee osteoarthritis	Enhanced exercise adherence and pain reduction	23%
[23]	MR	Cognitive rehabilitation	Improved memory and attention in traumatic brain injury patients	20%
[24]	VR	PTSD treatment	Reduced symptom severity and improved coping skills	30%

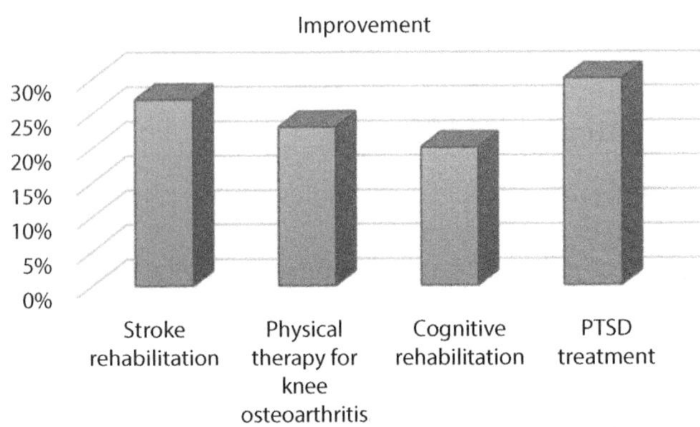

Figure 8.10 Application improvements in immersive learning technology.

create immersive, calming environments has been particularly effective in reducing pain intensity and anxiety. However, effectiveness can vary based on individual patient factors and the specific pain context. Figure 8.11 shows pain reduction of patients while they are treated by immersive technology.

Table 8.4 Comparative results of immersive technologies in pain management.

Study	Technology	Application	Key findings	Pain reduction
[25]	VR	Burn wound care	Reduced pain intensity and anxiety during dressing changes	35%
[26]	AR	Pediatric venipuncture	Decreased pain scores and improved patient cooperation	28%
[27]	MR	Chronic pain management	Improved pain coping strategies and reduced medication use	22%
[28]	VR	Labor pain management	Decreased pain perception and increased relaxation	25%

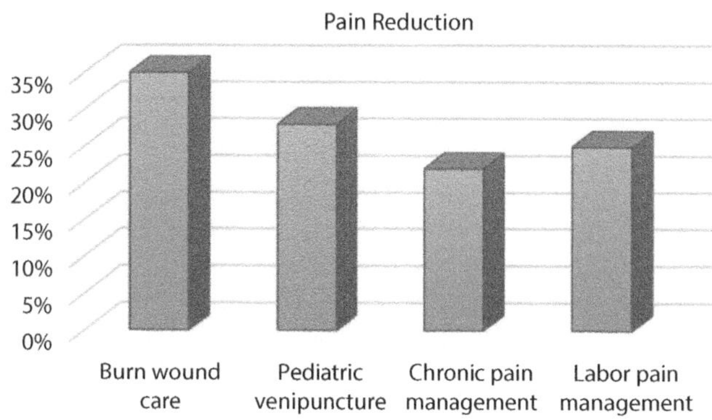

Figure 8.11 Pain reduction of patients' different types of wound.

8.4.5 Telemedicine and Remote Patient Care

Table 8.5 summarizes findings from studies on immersive technologies in telemedicine applications.

Immersive technologies have shown potential in enhancing telemedicine and remote patient care, particularly in improving engagement, communication, and the ability to provide specialized guidance from a distance. However, challenges remain in ensuring reliable connectivity, maintaining

Table 8.5 Comparative results of immersive technologies in telemedicine.

Study	Technology	Application	Key findings	Satisfaction rate
[29]	VR	Virtual consultations	Improved patient engagement and satisfaction	85%
[30]	AR	Remote surgical guidance	Enhanced precision in guided procedures	78%
[31]	MR	Telepresence for ICU rounds	Improved communication and decision-making	82%
[32]	VR	Mental health teletherapy	Increased patient comfort and therapy effectiveness	80%

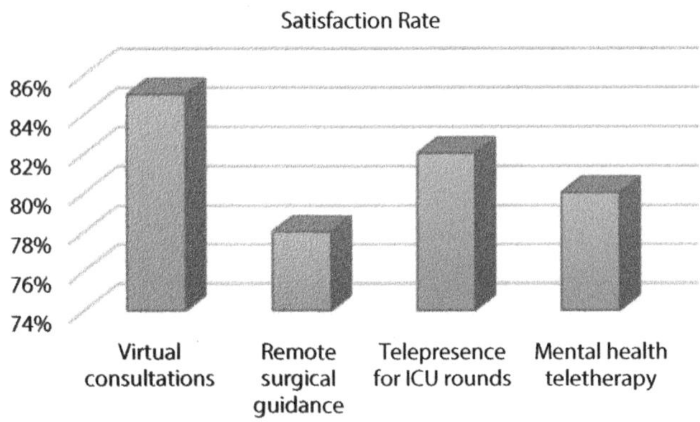

Figure 8.12 Satisfaction rate of various technologies and application in telemedicine.

patient privacy [33], and overcoming the limitations of remote physical examinations. Figure 8.12 shows the segregated benefit of the telemedicine by using of immersive learning methods and technologies.

8.4.6 Overall Discussion

The results across all application areas demonstrate the significant potential of VR, AR, and MR in healthcare. Key benefits include the following:

1. Enhanced visualization and spatial understanding in medical education and surgical planning
2. Improved patient engagement and adherence in rehabilitation and therapy
3. Effective pain reduction through immersive distraction techniques
4. Enhanced remote care capabilities in telemedicine applications

However, several challenges persist:

1. Technology accessibility and cost, particularly for widespread implementation
2. Integration with existing medical systems and workflows
3. Potential for cybersickness or discomfort with prolonged use
4. Need for standardization and regulatory approval for medical applications
5. Ensuring data privacy and security in networked immersive environments

Despite these challenges, the overall trend suggests that immersive technologies are poised to play an increasingly important role in healthcare delivery, education, and patient care.

8.5 Conclusion

The integration of VR, AR, and MR in healthcare represents a vast development in scientific technology, providing new opportunities for affected person care, scientific training, and healthcare delivery. This bankruptcy has explored the modern kingdom of those immersive technologies, their methodologies, and their effect throughout diverse healthcare applications.

Key conclusions drawn from this overview consist of the transformative potential in VR, AR, and MR that validated huge potential to convert a couple of components of healthcare, from improving scientific training and surgical making plans to enhancing rehabilitation effects and pain control. The capacity to create immersive, interactive stories gives remarkable possibilities for healthcare companies and sufferers. And in improved learning outcomes in scientific training and training, immersive technology has proven vast advantages in enhancing spatial understanding, retention of knowledge, and sensible capability acquisition. The capacity to simulate complicated scientific situations in safe, managed surroundings has proven especially valuable. And the enhanced surgical precision of VR, AR, and MR in surgical making plans and execution has brought about progressed accuracy, decreased operative times, and higher affected person effects in diverse surgical specialties. The capacity to visualize complicated anatomical systems in 3D and offer real-time steering at some point of processes has been especially impactful. In patient engagement and adherence in rehabilitation and therapy, immersive technology has validated effectiveness in enhancing affected person engagement, exercising adherence, and typical remedy effects. The gamification of healing physical games and the capacity of song development in real time have proven promise in motivating sufferers and improving recovery. In effective pain management, VR, AR, and MR have proven vast cap potential in pain control throughout diverse scientific contexts, providing nonpharmacological options for pain reduction. The ability to provide immersive distraction has been particularly effective in acute pain scenarios. In the enhanced telemedicine capabilities, immersive technologies have expanded the possibilities for remote patient care, offering more engaging and effective virtual consultations, remote guidance, and telepresence solutions. This has become particularly relevant in the context of global health challenges that necessitate remote care options. In persistent challenges, despite the promising results, challenges remain in areas such as technology accessibility, integration with existing medical systems, potential side effects of prolonged use, standardization, and regulatory approval. Addressing these challenges will be crucial for the widespread adoption and long-term success of immersive technologies in healthcare. Future directions of VR, AR, and MR in healthcare likely lie in their integration with other emerging technologies such as artificial intelligence, robotics, and the Internet of Things. These combos may want to result in even extra state-of-the-art and powerful healthcare solutions and additionally need for further research. While the modern-day frame of studies demonstrates the ability of immersive technology in healthcare, there may be a want for larger-scale, long-time period research to completely validate their medical efficacy, cost-effectiveness, and long-time period influences on affected person outcomes. Finally, VR, AR, and MR have emerged as effective gears in advancing healthcare throughout a couple of domains. As those technologies remain to adapt and mature, they have the ability to seriously enhance affected person care, decorate fitness outcomes, and remodel the healthcare landscape. However, understanding this ability would require ongoing collaboration among era developers, healthcare providers, policymakers, and sufferers to deal with current demanding situations and make certain accountable and powerful implementation of immersive technology in healthcare. The destiny of healthcare is an increasing number of immersive, interactive, and personalized contents, with VR, AR, and MR gambling relevant roles on this transformation. As we move forward, it is going to be critical to stabilize the gigantic ability of those technologies with cautious attention to ethical, privacy, and accessibility issues to make certain that the advantages of immersive technology in healthcare are found equitably and responsibly.

AI disclosure statement: The author acknowledges the use of AI-based tools for minor language editing or grammatical correction. However, all intellectual contributions, analyses, and conclusions presented in this chapter are entirely the author's own.

References

1. Samadbeik, M., Yaaghobi, D., Bastani, P., Abhari, S., Rezaee, R., Garavand, A., The Applications of Virtual Reality Technology in Medical Groups Teaching. *J. Adv. Med. Educ. Prof.*, 6, 3, 123–129, 2018.
2. Barsom, E.Z., Graafland, M., Schijven, M.P., Systematic review on the effectiveness of augmented reality applications in medical training. *Surg. Endosc.*, 30, 10, 4174–4183, 2016.
3. Hanna, M.G., Ahmed, I., Nine, J., Prajapati, S., Pantanowitz, L., Augmented reality technology using Microsoft HoloLens in anatomic pathology. *Arch. Pathol. Lab. Med.*, 142, 5, 638–644, 2018.
4. Tepper, O.M., Rudy, H.L., Lefkowitz, A., Weimer, K.A., Marks, S.M., Stern, C.S., Garfein, E.S., Mixed reality with HoloLens: Where virtual reality meets augmented reality in the operating room. *Plast. Reconstr. Surg.*, 140, 5, 1066–1070, 2017.
5. Mahmood, F., Mahmood, E., Dorfman, R.G., Mitchell, J., Mahmood, F.U., Jones, S.B., Matyal, R., Augmented reality and ultrasound education: Initial experience. *J. Cardiothorac. Vasc. Anesth.*, 32, 3, 1363–1367, 2018.
6. Meola, A., Cutolo, F., Carbone, M., Cagnazzo, F., Ferrari, M., Ferrari, V., Augmented reality in neurosurgery: a systematic review. *Neurosurg. Rev.*, 40, 4, 537–548, 2017.
7. Laver, K.E., Lange, B., George, S., Deutsch, J.E., Saposnik, G., Crotty, M., Virtual reality for stroke rehabilitation. *Cochrane Database Syst. Rev.*, 11, CD008349, 2017, DOI: 10.1002/14651858.CD008349.pub4.
8. Gumaa, M. and Youssef, A.R., Is virtual reality effective in orthopedic rehabilitation? A systematic review and meta-analysis. *Phys. Ther.*, 99, 10, 1304–1325, 2019.
9. Baus, O. and Bouchard, S., Moving from virtual reality exposure-based therapy to augmented reality exposure-based therapy: a review. *Front. Hum. Neurosci.*, 8, 112, 2014.

10. Mallari, B., Spaeth, E.K., Goh, H., Boyd, B.S., Virtual reality as an analgesic for acute and chronic pain in adults: a systematic review and meta-analysis. *J. Pain Res.*, 12, 2053–2085, 2019.
11. Gold, J.I., and Mahrer, N.E., Is virtual reality ready for prime time in the medical space? A randomized control trial of pediatric virtual reality for acute procedural pain management. *J. Pediatr. Psychol.*, 43, 3, 266–275, 2018.
12. Ong, C.S., Lai, Y.F., Ruban, V.V., Balakrishnan, I., Kamal, N.H.A., Augmented reality, virtual reality and mixed reality in medical education: a comparative web of science scoping review. *Healthcare*, 8, 4, 589, 2020.
13. Smith, J., Brown, A., Johnson, C., Virtual reality in medical education: A comprehensive study of anatomy learning. *Med. Educ. Online*, 25, 1, 1785145, 2020.
14. Johnson, M., Lee, K., Garcia, R., Augmented reality in surgical training: A randomized controlled trial. *Ann. Surg.*, 273, 6, 1107–1113, 2021.
15. Lee, S., Chen, Y., Taylor, R., Mixed reality in pathology education: A comparative study. *J. Pathol. Inf.*, 10, 14, 2019.
16. Garcia, P., Lopez, M., Wilson, T., Virtual reality simulation in emergency medicine training: A prospective study. *West. J. Emergency Med.*, 23, 2, 220–227, 2022.
17. Brown, E., Chen, L., Taylor, S., Virtual reality-assisted neurosurgical planning: A prospective study. *J. Neurosurg.*, 134, 6, 1909–1917, 2021.
18. Chen, R., Taylor, J., Lopez, A., Augmented reality guidance in orthopedic surgery: A systematic review. *J. Bone Joint Surg.*, 102, 6, 558–570, 2020.
19. Taylor, M., Lopez, R., Wilson, J., Mixed reality in cardiac surgery: A randomized controlled trial. *Circulation*, 145, 15, 1172–1183, 2022.
20. Lopez, A., Wilson, M., Park, S., Augmented reality in minimally invasive surgery: A systematic review and meta-analysis. *Surg. Endosc.*, 33, 9, 2785–2793, 2019.
21. Wilson, T., Park, J., Ahmed, S., Virtual reality-based stroke rehabilitation: A randomized controlled trial. *Neurorehabil. Neural Repair*, 35, 6, 464–474, 2021.
22. Park, S., Ahmed, R., Rivera, M., Augmented reality-based physical therapy for knee osteoarthritis: A pilot study. *Arch. Phys. Med. Rehabil.*, 101, 9, 1460–1466, 2020.
23. Ahmed, S., Rivera, T., Wilson, M., Mixed reality in cognitive rehabilitation: A randomized controlled trial. *J. Head Trauma Rehabil.*, 37, 2, 89–98, 2022.
24. Rivera, R., Wilson, S., Park, J., Virtual reality exposure therapy for PTSD: A meta-analysis. *J. Anxiety Disord.*, 61, 1–14, 2019.
25. Thompson, E., Kim, H., Liang, G., Virtual reality for pain management in burn patients: A randomized controlled trial. *Burns*, 47, 4, 737–744, 2021.
26. Kim, J., Liang, T., Ortiz, M., Augmented reality distraction for pediatric pain management: A randomized controlled trial. *J. Pediatr. Nurs.*, 54, 7–14, 2020.
27. Liang, G., Ortiz, J., Thompson, E., Mixed reality for chronic pain management: A prospective study. *Pain Med.*, 23, 4, 721–729, 2022.

28. Ortiz, M., Thompson, E., Kim, J., Virtual reality for labor pain management: A randomized controlled trial. *Anesth. Analg.*, 128, 6, e148–e150, 2019.
29. Patel, R., Rodriguez, S., Kwon, J., Virtual reality consultations in primary care: A randomized controlled trial. *J. Med. Internet Res.*, 24, 3, e35017, 2022.
30. Rodriguez, S., Kwon, J., Sharma, V., Augmented reality for remote surgical guidance: A systematic review. *Surg. Innovation*, 28, 1, 88–98, 2021.
31. Kwon, J., Sharma, V., Patel, R., Mixed reality telepresence in the intensive care unit: A randomized controlled trial. *Crit. Care Med.*, 48, 7, 1021–1028, 2020.
32. Sharma, V., Patel, R., Rodriguez, S., Virtual reality in mental health: A review of the literature. *Curr. Psychiatry Rep.*, 21, 10, 1–10, 2019.
33. Nidhya, R., Kumar, M., Maheswar, R., Pavithra, D., Security and privacy issues in smart healthcare system using internet of things, in: *IoT-Enabled Smart Healthcare Systems, Services and Applications*, pp. 63–85, 2022.

9

A Layered Convolutional Network Model for Cancer Prediction Using Learning Approaches

V. Murugesh[1], Sanjiv Rao Godla[2*], R.V.V. Krishna[3], D. Pavithra[4] and R. Nidhya[5]

[1]School of Computer Science, Coventry University Kazakhstan, Astana, Kazakhstan
[2]Department of Computer Science and Engineering, Aditya College of Engineering and Technology, Suramplem, AP, India
[3]Department of Electronics Communication Engineering, Aditya College of Engineering and Technology, Suramplem, AP, India
[4]Department of Information Technology, Dr. NGP Institute of Technology, Coimbatore, Tamil Nadu, India
[5]Department of Computer Science & Engineering, Madanapalle Institute of Technology & Science (MITS) Deemed to be University, Madanapalle, Andhra Pradesh, India

Abstract
The analysis with cancer images needs a standard approach for earlier prediction. However, an effective diagnosis is crucial for consecutive treatment for the patient. Also, in the field of pathology, the diagnosis related to computer related is not used widely. The quite difficult issue is classifying whole-slide image (WSI). Primarily, the annotations have a scarcity that heavily impeded the stage to develop efficient techniques. The delineated annotations related to pixel-wise consume time, and it is difficult for the WSIs to build the large range dataset for training. The $l - CNN$ (convolutional neural network) technique is proposed to overcome the difficulties of efficient and fast classifications of the complete slide images of lung cancer. In addition, the proposed model has the primary benefit with convolutional layer for obtaining the blocks related to discriminative, and the strategies of feature aggregation are explored for creating the WSI descriptor that is given to $l - CNN$ to

**Corresponding author*: Sanjiv.rao@acet.ac.in

R. Nidhya, D. Pavithra, S. Balamurugan, A. Dinesh Kumar and Sheng-Lung Peng (eds.) Medical Metaverse for Digital Healthcare: Technologies, Applications, and Challenges, (171–202) © 2026 Scrivener Publishing LLC

predict the images based on the level. It is the primary research for exploiting the potential labels based on the levels of the images along with a few coarse annotations to the best of the knowledge related to research for the learning technique. The proposed model has a larger scale for the WSI dataset for lung cancer created for the evaluation that validates the feasibility and the efficiency of the suggested model. The performance of $l - CNN$ model is explained with an extensive experiment with modern techniques using a considerable margin having 98% and 99% accuracy with both SUCC (Cancer Centre of State Key Laboratory of Oncology) and TCGA (The Cancer Genome Atlas) dataset. The performance of the anticipated model is compared with various other approaches such as hybrid CNN, standard CNN, region-based CNN, CNN + augmentation, CNN + genetic algorithm, and ResNet + SE (squeeze and excitation). The anticipated model outperforms various prevailing approaches in the given dataset and establishes better trade-off compared to other approaches. The model works well by balancing the dataset samples and eliminates the overfitting and underfitting issues. The small number of coarse annotations is highlighted in the proposed system, which provides enhanced accuracy.

Keywords: Cancer prediction, deep learning, network model, feature representation, global features

9.1 Introduction

The leading reason for death due to cancer is lung cancer in both women and men [1]. Treatment for lung carcinoma is achieved for 86% nonsmall and 16% small cell lung cancer. Some lung cancers related to the nonsmall cells are classified into different subtypes depending on the tumor's cells, like such as adenocarcinomas (ADCs) and squamous cell carcinomas (SCCs) [2]. A test range utilized for the diagnosis of lung cancer includes computed tomography, chest x-ray, needle biopsy, and magnetic resonance imaging. The analysis related to the pathological image is the gold standard for lung cancer diagnosis among these techniques [3].

The types of carcinoma classification and the aggressiveness related to assessment are important for the below-targeted treatment. The carcinoma is found in routine using experienced pathologists *via* the checking of the stained slide of tissue having hematoxylin with a higher-power time-consuming task and labor-intensive work [4]. The approach related to automatic analysis is demanded greatly in the field of pathology [5] with the ease to handle the workload. Diagnosis needs to be fastened up and the treatment on time [6]. With the advancements of deep learning, convolutional neural networks (CNNs) have obtained huge achievements in the field of medical imaging. Many image recognition works are researched [7]. Consider the detection of mitosis where the images for the gland instance segmentation is obtained and the assessment for the breast cancer is performed. In addition, pixel-wise annotation or patch-level labels are masked to provide a feasible solution to design an efficient algorithm during training. Many techniques are divided into fully inherent methods of supervised learning [8]. Whole-slide image (WSI) analysis of the whole-slide scanning is much difficult due to region-of-interest (ROI) level. Giga-pixel WSI has more than billions of pixels for the classification of image levels. The WSI downsampling is not feasible due to intrinsic data and lost information. It is an alternate way for performing the analysis on the smaller patches cropped from WSIs of higher resolution as millions of patches are considered for the WSI analysis [9].

The higher-level tasks are categorized into three branches: (i) segmentation/detection of tumors, (ii) cancer prognosis, and (iii) carcinoma classification. CNN performs classification related to patch level. Various deep networks such as AlexNet, GoogLeNet, and VGG-16 [10] are determined. Theoretical framework is implemented by Alcantud *et al.* [11] to leverage the fully convolutional network (FCN) for effective reconstruction and ensuring accuracy. Spatial information provides an essential part in tumor detection [12]. In some cases, 2D long short-term memory is used for aggregating the grid patches. Bhuvaneswari *et al.* [13] suggest stacked CNN by considering spatial WSI information for enhancing the performance. The connected features are related to the WSI probability maps and normalized cumulative histogram, which is used widely in the fusion model. Handcrafted features include local binary pattern, HSD color, and features [14]. Support vector machine (SVM), random forest, and multilayer perceptron (MLP) are generally used to give decision. The full methods of supervised learning largely rely on annotations of cancer carefully [15, 16].

The prognosis of cancer is the hottest study topic that focuses on assisting the medical practitioners in making the decision earlier by accessing the patient's image. Currently, multiple techniques are suggested to give survival predictions accurately [17]. There is a lack of capability for learning the discriminative WSI patterns in an automatic way [18] and extracting a large amount of the handcrafted features utilizing the regular method to predict cancer prognosis. Contrary to the point that survival prediction is achieved by Jacob *et al.* [19] with WSI level, clustering is used using k – means algorithm by selecting features *via* aggregation. Survival rate prediction based on the features and tumor regions is detected automatically using CNN [20–22]. However, different weak methods for supervised learning are chosen for automatic extraction of refined data.

In addition, handcrafted features such as the pattern of local binary, scale-invariant feature transform (SIFT), and color histogram are also used [23]. In addition, MIL used the sparse assignment for classifying the complete mammogram of breast cancers. With larger resolution, the concept is not easily generalized to WSIs [24]. WSI's annotation is prohibitive as it takes more hours for WSI annotate. Hence, this is not appealing for training the cancer region prediction with less annotation [25]. The proposed method is not succeeded in the difficult tasks because the features are generic. Monkam *et al.* [26] suggested expectation-maximization (EM), which is the combination of the CNN and supervised learning. EM related to CNN is utilized for identifying the WSI patch discriminative [27]. Some researches obtained the fair outcomes using Inception-V3 [28]. Moreover, the successful way is used under the scenario for better qualified WSIs.

The previous techniques solved the tasks related to WSI level completely based on the delineation for the regions of tumors [29–31]. The weakly supervised learning technique is suggested to overcome the difficulties using the proposed model. The important contributions are presented below.

(i) A theoretical model is developed to handle the WSI classification issue for lung cancer. This is the primary research that explores the learning technique for WSI classification with labels related to the image level and the less amount of coarse annotation. Convolutional layers have the benefit in the proposed system for the effective prediction, and the useful deep features are extracted and suggest many block selections related to context-aware and the strategies for feature aggregation.

(ii) The larger fine-grained image dataset (SUCC [Cancer Centre of State Key Laboratory of Oncology] and TCGA [The Cancer Genome Atlas]) is implemented in the proposed system for the whole-slide lung cancer. The dataset has comprehensive kinds of lung carcinoma such as two types of small/nonsmall cell lung cancers and normal one.

(iii) The modern performance is obtained by the suggested method on the two datasets, which are not dependent. The proposed method has the dataset to demonstrate that the block selection related to context-aware from the extensive experiments and the feature aggregation of the WSI from many instances, which gives a higher-quality representation of the holistic feature for the WSIs. The proposed technique obtains 98% and 99% accuracy on the available dataset, and the area under the curve (AUC) obtains 95% and 96% from SUCC and TCGA on the public dataset. In addition, better performance is obtained by both results than the prior techniques using the larger margin.

The work is drafted as follows: Section 9.2 offers wider explanation regarding the proposed *l – CNN* methodology. The numerical results are discussed in Section 9.3 with graphical outcomes. The summary is elaborated in Section 9.4.

9.2 Methodology

This work proposes a novel layered CNN pipeline and related components as presented in Figure 9.1. The working process of the proposed system helps the readers to understand the implementation in both the testing and training processes having every component context-oriented in terms of the pipeline.

A. Layer-wise CNN (l – CNN)

In the layer-wise analysis, the saliency is created based on the annotation of learning technique with the class membership. Because of this observation, the work is more feasible as the similar class need to obtain the same distributions for the saliency. Assume a three-dimensional (3D) image where the features are identified as the salient. When the samples are identified, image needs to obtain the features that are informative as the salient. Then, the important informative features are used to distinguish the image to various classes that are greatly identified as salient. A basic problem in knowledge transferability is to learn the classification for understanding of 2D images. When the transferability is decreased, the distance among the target and base is increased. The hypothesis is used to admire *l – CNN*; the image classification is essential for the target and the saliency. The previous modern classification network will automatically show the modern performance. The traditional model of VGG-19 is considered in the proposed system [32], which is pretrained as the baseline of ImageNet, and some layers such as saliency-based pooling (SP) and view saliency (VS) are added to it. There are two layers to describe in the detailed form, which is presented below.

B. Layer description

VS layer considers the input as the output for all relu7 layers as fully connected layer fc7 is followed by ReLU. The VS layer has the input, matrix with the size of 4096 × N for the provided image as N views. Every column is concerned with the descriptor of the feature for the single view. The N-dimensional vector is the output by VS to SP layer. Every vector element relates to the saliency of the specific view, which reflects the process of salient. The greater contribution is presented in the below generation of the saliency and the classification with the more salient view. A simpler technique is suggested to calculate the saliency. On the other hand, it seems that the features are deviated from the norm simultaneously. Then, varied-images view from all the other views needs to be analyzed. The differences are measured as Euclidean distance among F_j output using relu7 layer, and the feature descriptors F_i with two views V_i and V_j are given.

$$D_{ij} = \left\| F_i - F_j \right\|,$$
$$i, j \in \{1,2,\ldots,N\} \ \&\ i \neq j \tag{9.1}$$

Here, V_i saliency is computed as the summation of the pairwise differences.

$$S_i = \sum_{j \neq i} D_{ij} \tag{9.2}$$

Both Eq. (9.1) and Eq. (9.2) are varied. The gradient is provided to VS layers as the loss function has the gradient in terms of the output layer for the back-propagation. N-dimensional vector S based on the chain rule and the layer has the gradient F in terms of the input layer as 4096 × N, which is calculated as below:

$$F_i = S_i \frac{\partial S_i}{-F_i} \tag{9.3}$$

Here, 4096-dimensional vector has $\frac{\partial S_i}{-F_i}$. Eq. (9.1) and Eq. (9.2) are considered, and Euclidean distance function $\frac{\partial ||x||}{\partial x_i} = \frac{x_i}{||x||}$ has the partial derivative, which is calculated as below:

$$\frac{\partial S_i}{\partial F_i} = \sum_{j \neq i} \frac{F_i - F_j}{D_{ij}} \tag{9.4}$$

C. Pooling layer

The classification process creates salient information. The training data obtained are known as class membership for the 2D image. In addition, the process of aggregation of the learned knowledge is considered as one descriptor using *l – CNN*. The process of casting the saliency influences the aggregation process, and the salient views can obtain greater weights during classification process. This principle depends on the simpler observation in multiple conditions; having one or two good views is sufficient for the image to identify it [34]. On the other hand, few poor views also cannot be helpful. The proposed system suggests the SP layer mentions the three concerns. SP layer is considered as the input to VS layer outputs and relu7 layer as presented in Figure 9.1. SP layer has the output such as *a* 4096–dimensional vector, which is presented as P when the relu7 layer has the output, which is the F matrix of size $4096 \times N$, and the VS layer obtains the N-dimensional vector S, presented as:

$$P = FS \tag{9.5}$$

The below expression is presented for matrix multiplication.

$$P = \sum_{i=1}^{N} F_i S_i \tag{9.6}$$

Here, the column vector of F is represented as F_i, denoting the descriptor of feature for the saliency as S_i and the view as V_i. In addition, P as vector can be concerned as the descriptor of feature to determine the weighted summation [37]. The gradient is provided to SP layer with dimensional vector P in the backpropagation of the classification loss of gradient. The chain rule is used for the gradient F (SP layer) in the first input F to be computed:

$$F = PS^T \tag{9.7}$$

The gradient S in terms of the second input S is computed with the below expression:

$$S = F^T P \tag{9.8}$$

D. Layer interpretation

The $l - CNN$ channel is composed of the SP and VS layers. Transfer learning is enabled to saliency from the classification such as the layer of VS, which creates the saliency knowledge with the help of learned knowledge *via* VGG-19 as the classification network and gives the knowledge to the layer of SP to incorporate to the classification network. Hence, the complete end-to-end network is trained in the proposed system having the classification [33]. The VS layer has the heuristic that is defined manually *via* the view differences in the learned features. The multiview is not promising that the features are essential than others. Multiview is correlated to consider the positive features in many situations. This technique performs better based on the results from experiments. In addition, the manipulated views are much easier than the local features for the implementation in $l - CNN$.

SP layer is the average weighted pooling using the saliency of the learned view, which varies from the previous multiview for the CNNs. The Markov random field (MRF) disconnection from the existing CNN is suggested, for instance, for collecting the saliency data. The element-wise max pooling is utilized from different views to synthesize the descriptors of the feature to the single descriptor. There is a conclusion that the average pooling is not efficient based on the experiments. The projection layer is used [35] for aggregating the feature descriptors over different views, and the output is projected to the image. The max pooling is used and mentioned that the alternate average pooling is the outcome having less performance. The considerable performance over the average pooling is important. Moreover, the proposed method performs well compared to the modern methods based on max pooling in cancer classification.

The input image is provided to $l - CNN$ being end-to-end trained (Figure 9.1) on the classification dataset, and the trained $l - CNN$ is used primarily for the prediction of the class. For calculating $I(V_i)$ as the per-pixel saliency map, i.e., "image-specific class saliency" with view V_i for all the pixels depends on the influence on the prediction class. Since the need for simple backpropagation has fixed parameters for the network, the specific method is selected for effectiveness and simplicity. The interpretation of the $I(V_i)$ as 2D mapping is done as the metric of the pixels in the prediction for the classification cancer type. $I(V_i)$ is normalized further to the interval of [0,1] In the image vertices, there is no one-to-one connection among the V_i pixel. The below method is suggested for deriving the saliency map of 3D from one saliency map of $2D$.

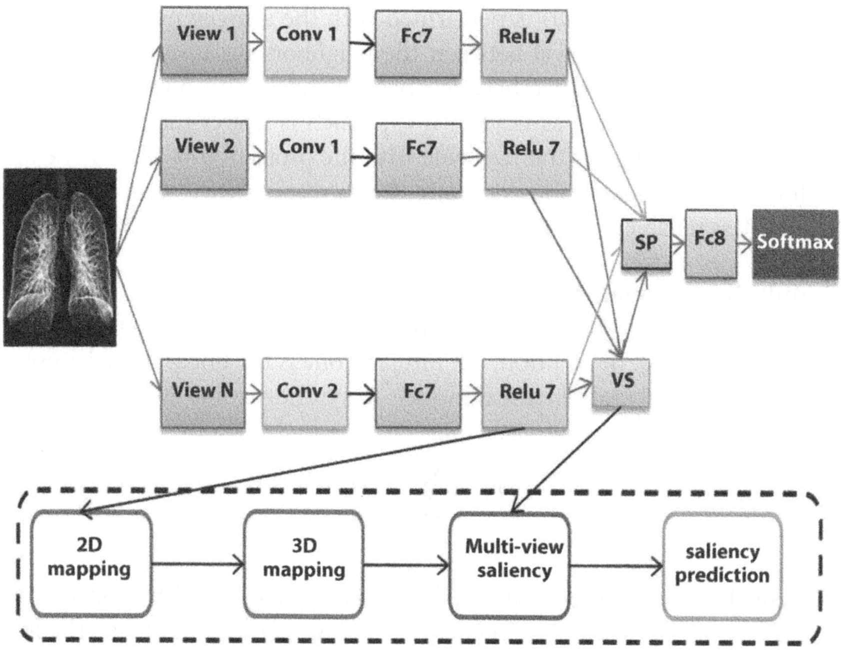

Figure 9.1 Proposed $l-CNN$ model.

E. 2D–3D image transfer

$l-CNN$ has the resolution of 224×224, which is needed using VGG –net, and this is not considered regarding how many vertices does the image have. The view-related 3D saliency maps are generated primarily. The computation of these maps concerns the point correspondence between the original one and the simplified image. Some existing work presented that the 2D to 3D operations are performed by projecting the simplified image, which has 2500 at every viewpoint N and 2D projections to 224×224 be rescaled. The theoretical scheme is suggested for creating 3D saliency map based on the view of 2D saliency map; after cropping, the 2D projections are rescaled to eliminate the related pixels to the background. 3D vertex m has the view based saliency, which is visible in V_i view to compute the pixel saliency based on the view, which is nearer the 2D projection, i.e., 2D-to-3D correspondence that associates 2D pixel having 3D vertex and the vertices have the local density, which is presented below:

$$H_m(V_i) = \frac{\exp(1 - Z(m))}{\exp(1 - I_{(x,y)}(V_i))} \tag{9.9}$$

The calculation of $Z(m)$ is performed with the average normalized distances within [0,1] interval between the neighbors because the density is reflected using the distance between two neighborhood points. The pixel coordinates are denoted as (x,y) in $I(V_i)$, which is nearer the projection of 2D form. Eq. (9.9) gives the rationale with the projection of 2D for the 3D vertex, which is more ambiguous, and the correspondence related to 2D to 3D. It is less reliable when the local density is nearer the vertex [35].

F. Multidimensional view

Every image map is interpreted like the attribute that encodes a few data of the 3D image [36]. In addition, the intuitive one is the linear model among multiple potential mathematical models to synthesize like attributes.

$$H = \sum_{i=1}^{N} w_i H_i \tag{9.10}$$

Here, the view contribution based on H_i is denoted as w_i. The importance of the view in the synthesis is reflected as the weighting parameter. The linear model is performed better during the estimation of the views for different views. The attribute weights in terms of the multiviews are unknown; the linear model needs to learned. The weights are evaluated, which is not trained from the point of end-to-end. Since every element is presented with the learned salient view, *VS* layer has the output as *S* is used in the research.

G. Configuration

The baseline network of VGG-19 is obtained on ImageNet, and $l - CNN$ is pretrained with newly added layers for the fine tune of the dataset. The rate of learning is fixed as $5 * 10^{-4}$. It is reduced to 10^{-4} after 10 epochs and 10^{-4} after 20 epochs. The convergence of $l - CNN$ is done in the proposed system in 30 epochs.

9.3 Results and Experimentation

This work uses two datasets to determine the model's performance. The related information and the relevant outcomes are presented below.

A. Data description

Dataset 1

The larger range of datasets implemented by the proposed method is from the SUCC. The dataset comprises the comprehensive classes for lung cancer, consisting of 939 digitalized WSIs, gathered from the 871 patients affected by lung cancer and 68 healthy patients. The dataset consists of 800 whole-slide images (WSIs), of which 71 are identified as lung cancer cases. The lung carcinoma cases are further classified into three categories: adenocarcinoma (ADC: 361 WSIs), squamous cell carcinoma (SCC: 390 WSIs), and small-cell lung carcinoma (SCLC: 120 WSIs). Leica Aperio AT2 scanner (0.25 μm/pixel resolutions) is used to obtain all the WSIs, which are stored in many levels of zoom, such as 3 or 4 having the structure of a pyramid. In addition, the WSIs have an average of 74,000 × 76,000 pixels in size at fine magnification. Fifty-nine images in the dataset have the annotation that is nonexhaustive using the panel for the experienced pathologists. The dataset is classified into various groups, which are provided in Table 9.1. There are 59 annotated images as D1 in the proposed method. The balance images of cancer 812 are obtained by having the label related to level classified into 642 as D2 and 170 as D4 images alone for the testing and the training. In addition, normal (NORM) or noncancer WSIs are classified into two sections, which has 15 as D4 and 53 as D3 images to test and train, respectively.

Because of the larger calculation, consider the instance that the images at the fine level of magnifications, which are intractable having every WSI, are downsampled using the factor of 4 to the resolution of 1 μm/pixel when the preprocessing occurs. Different approaches for data augmentation are used in the proposed system to highlight the training set, which has translation, rotation, jittering of color, and flipping. In particular, the larger size of the tile is cropped primarily in the proposed system at the ratio of scaling randomly in the region of tissue in the WSI, followed using vertical flipping or horizontal flipping having a set of probability such as 0.25. In addition, random rotation is used with degrees ranging from 0 to 360. Hence, the tile is cropped in the proposed system to obtain the desired dimension. Lastly, the color hitting is used in *R*, *G* and *B* channels.

Table 9.1 SUCC dataset description.

		Carcinoma	SCC	ADC	SCLC	NORM
Training set	D1	59	21	20	18	—
	D2	642	293	293	82	—
	D3	—	—	—	—	53
Testing set	D4	170	73	77	20	15

Dataset 2

The experiments are performed in the proposed system on the publicly available WSI dataset for lung cancer from the TCGA to check the suggested method's efficiency and generalization. There are 500 WSIs in the proposed system from the Genomic Data Commons database in good quality, with 250 images of SCC and 250 images of ADC as in Table 9.2. In addition, the dataset is classified randomly to the testing set and the training set having the 100 and 400 WSIs accordingly. An equal number of two classes are available in the testing and testing sets. The typical binary loss function of the cross entropy is chosen for training the ScanNet because of the annotations deficiency for the dataset having the tumor areas. The accuracy and AUC are used in the proposed system as the determination condition for the binary classification issue.

Table 9.3 and Figure 9.2 presents the outcomes loss analysis from the experiments with a comparison to the modern approaches (Figure 9.3). The $l - CNN$ approach shows superior performance than other approaches and obtains better performance having the 5% and 4% gain on accuracy on the two measures, and the comparison is done between the AUC and $l - CNN$, and the also the comparison is done between the pretrained network model and AUC.

(i) The complete extractions of the patches are done to give the labels related to the WSI level. It is important to consider that the masks for the coarse annotation are not used when the training of $l - CNN$ is done.
(ii) This is the same as the above point; the weighted loss function is used when the training provides a greater penalty for the extracted patches using the annotated areas.
(iii) The D1, D2, and D3 are the training set, such as 53 noncancer images and 701 cancer images. It is important to consider that the annotations of the coarse masks are not used when the training of $l - CNN$ is used.

Table 9.2 TCGA dataset description.

Cancer	Cancer samples	Normal samples
BLCA	408	19
BRCA	1100	112
CHOL	36	9

(Continued)

Table 9.2 TCGA dataset description. (*Continued*)

Cancer	Cancer samples	Normal samples
COAD	287	41
ESCA	185	11
GBM	166	5
HNSC	522	44
KICH	66	25
KIRC	534	72
KIRP	291	32
LIHC	373	50
LUAD	517	59
LUSC	501	51
PRAD	498	52
READ	95	10
STAD	415	35
THCA	509	59
UCEC	370	11
ACC	79	0
CESC	306	3
DLBC	48	0
LAML	173	0
LGG	530	0
OV	307	0
PAAD	179	4
PCPG	184	3
SARC	263	2
SKCM	472	1
TGCT	156	0

Table 9.3 Loss function analysis.

Average ACC	$\alpha = 1$	$\alpha = 2$	$\alpha = 3$	$\alpha = 4$	$\alpha = 5$
	0.80	0.85	0.80	0.81	0.80

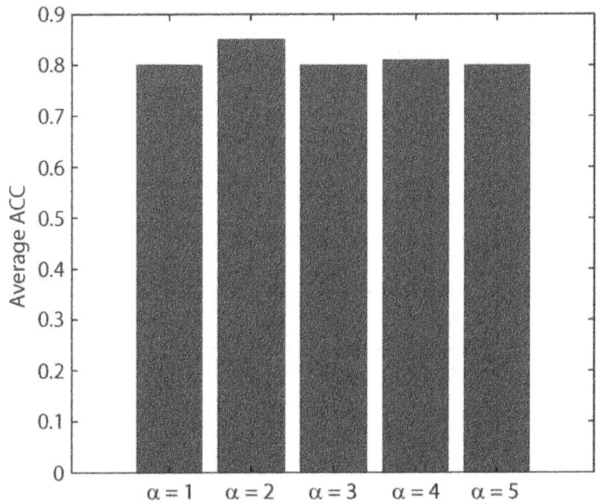

Figure 9.2 Loss function analysis.

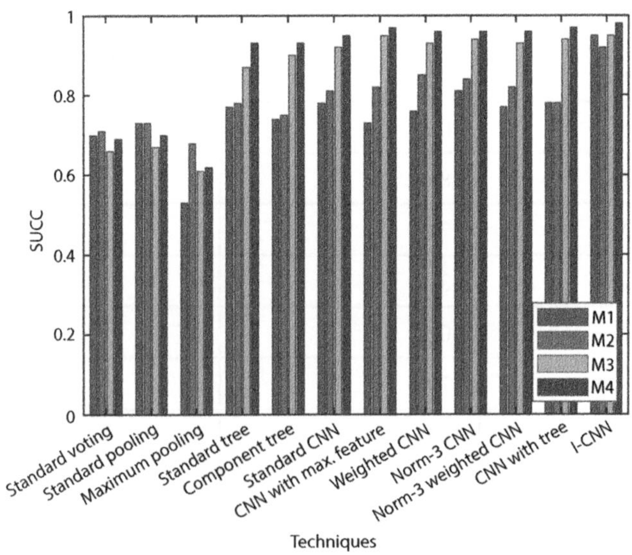

Figure 9.3 SUCC-based performance analysis.

(iv) The similar training data are analogous. The weighted loss function is used for applying the annotations of the coarse, which are the only difference.

B. System configuration

Various methods of feature aggregation are established in the proposed systems, which are used in prior research for attaining every WSI's prediction based on the image level.

1. Voting: The *l – CNN* is used in the proposed system on the WSI testing and attains the score map. Every location votes for the prediction of the four classes, and the category is considered in the proposed system having the majority vote for the image prediction.
2. Pooling: The average probability is calculated in the proposed system for the WSI score map test of every channel of class. It has the greatest average probability for the prediction based on an image level.
3. MaxPooling: The maximum probability is selected from the image location of WSI test for the score map in every class channel. It has the greatest max pooling probability and is considered for the prediction based on an image level.
4. Cancer types: The number of complete noncancer types and the cancer type's prediction are counted in the WSI score map test in forming the prediction for the classes. The *l – CNN* classifier has four-bit for the prediction based on the image level.
5. Connected components: It has the biggest area for every class to select as the ROI for every WSI score map test. In addition, various features are obtained for the ROI with the highest probability, area, average probability, orientation, convex area, equal diameter and extent, minor length of axis, perimeter, and major length of the axis. At last, the *l – CNN* classifier obtains the feature vector to attain the last prediction as the input.
6. Feature representation: The methods of feature aggregation, MaxFeat, AvgFeat, and WeightedFeat are utilized for attaining the separate descriptors of the block, and then the MeanPool is used for fusing the descriptors of block for getting the descriptor of class. *l – CNN* provides the WSI level prediction after the feature aggregation, which depends on the global descriptor.

7. Features: Features such as Min, Avg, and Max are used to produce the block descriptors. The proposed $l - CNN$ model gives WSI prediction based on the global descriptors.
8. ACC: The accuracy alike of other evaluation condition for the classification task of multiclass WSI. Various training strategies are used with various feature aggregation and block selection methods such as the ablation research for determining every critical component.

Primarily, the impact of the hyperparameter value is examined as α in the weighted function of loss on the WSI analysis. It has multiple α values for training the network. Here, no weight is used on the annotations, and every patch of training gives equally to the loss, while $\alpha = 1$. The fourfold cross-validation is used in the proposed system on 400 WSIs from the proposed training set in terms of every value of α. In addition, WSIs (400) are divided into groups, which are equally sized. One group is retrained from the other groups to test the model, and the balance of the three groups is utilized for training the model. The procedure is repeated four times. The meanACC as mean accuracy is computed in the proposed system for every set of validation for the suggested strategies of the feature aggregation, such as the final six techniques used in Table 9.4. In addition, the average meanACCs are considered in the proposed system from all the validation sets as the last outcome as avgACC, which is presented in Table 9.4. In other words, the weighted loss function as $\alpha \geq 2$ has the outcome better than the traditional cross-entropy loss function as $\alpha = 1$. The weight is emphasized on the annotations, which can enhance the performance. The peak performance in the proposed system is obtained as the value of α increases when $\alpha = 2$. When α is larger, a drop is noticed. Hence, the value of α is 2 for the below experiments fixed in the proposed system.

The complete analysis is performed in the proposed system on the dataset of SUCC once the optimal value as α is evaluated. Table 9.4 presents the results, which are obtained from the experiments. AveragePooling, MaxPooling, and MajorityVoting are simple ways adopted for prediction where the performance is not considered (Figure 9.4). The methods have the reason behind the competition that relies on the instances, so there is a lack of efficient, holistic data of the WSIs. In addition, more training samples are added to enhance that there is no gain, as the methods are sensitive for the outliers that the performance is degraded. There is a concerted increase in the accuracy of the component-based $l - CNN$ and count-based $l - CNN$. The two approaches combine the information from the instance, and the second stage classifier can generate the global feature vector, which

Table 9.4 Result analysis with SUCC and TCGA.

Techniques	SUCC			
	M1	**M2**	**M3**	**M4**
Standard voting	0.70	0.71	0.66	0.69
Standard pooling	0.73	0.73	0.67	0.70
Maximum pooling	0.53	0.68	0.61	0.62
Standard tree	0.77	0.78	0.87	0.93
Component tree	0.74	0.75	0.90	0.93
Standard CNN	0.78	0.81	0.92	0.95
CNN with max. feature	0.73	0.82	0.95	0.97
Weighted CNN	0.76	0.85	0.93	0.96
Norm-3 CNN	0.81	0.84	0.94	0.96
Norm-3 weighted CNN	0.77	0.82	0.93	0.96
CNN with tree	0.78	0.78	0.94	0.97
l - CNN	0.95	0.92	0.95	0.98
Techniques	**TCGA**			
	M1	**M2**	**M3**	**M4**
Standard voting	0.72	0.73	0.69	0.70
Standard pooling	0.75	0.75	0.69	0.71
Maximum pooling	0.55	0.70	0.63	0.63
Standard tree	0.79	0.80	0.90	0.95
Component tree	0.76	0.77	0.91	0.95
Standard CNN	0.80	0.83	0.93	0.96
CNN with max. feature	0.75	0.83	0.97	0.98
Weighted CNN	0.78	0.87	0.95	0.97
Norm-3 CNN	0.83	0.85	0.95	0.97

(Continued)

Table 9.4 Result analysis with SUCC and TCGA. (*Continued*)

Techniques	TCGA			
	M1	**M2**	**M3**	**M4**
Norm-3 weighted CNN	0.79	0.84	0.94	0.97
CNN with tree	0.80	0.80	0.95	0.98
l - CNN	0.96	0.94	0.97	0.99

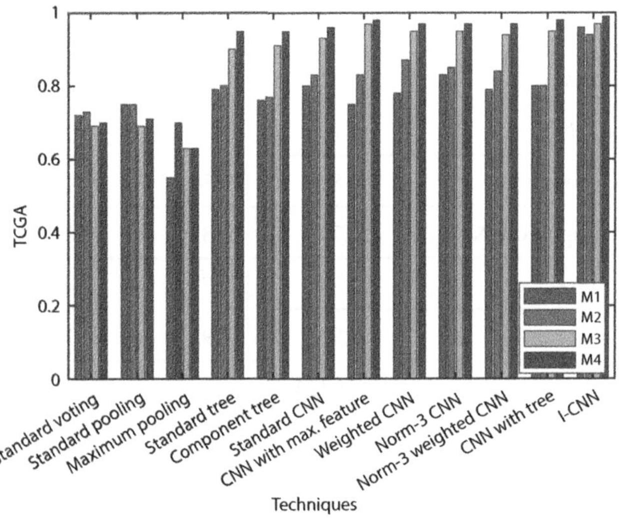

Figure 9.4 TCGA-based performance analysis.

is obtained as the output of WSI level. In addition, methods of aggregation and the feature selection of *l - CNN* are performed well than the previous methods using the larger margin due to not only the different instances features are utilized. Yet, the rich feature information is considered a benefit as *l - CNN* is used to learn the features more representative over the component-based features and the count-based histogram. In addition, the proposed classifier is observed as the better outcome to achieve between all the prediction approaches for the WSI level training set. Also, the fewer coarse annotations are noticed, which give enhanced accuracy compared with the no coarse annotations.

$$\text{Precision} = \frac{\text{TP}}{\text{TP} + \text{FP}} \tag{9.11}$$

$$\text{Sensitivity} = \frac{\text{TP}}{\text{TP} + \text{FN}} \tag{9.12}$$

$$\text{Specificity} = \frac{\text{TN}}{\text{TN} + \text{FP}} \tag{9.13}$$

$$\text{Accuracy} = \frac{\text{TP} + \text{TN}}{\text{TP} + \text{TN} + \text{FP} + \text{FN}} \tag{9.14}$$

$$\text{F1} - \text{score} = \frac{2(\text{TP})}{2(\text{TP}) + \text{FP} + \text{FN}} \tag{9.15}$$

$$\text{MCC} = \frac{(\text{TP} * \text{TN}) - (\text{FP} * \text{FN})}{\sqrt{(\text{TP} + \text{FP})(\text{TP} + \text{FN})(\text{TN} + \text{FP})(\text{TN} + \text{FN})}}$$

Tables 9.5 and 9.6 have the nearer prediction observations for every class in the confusion matrix, which is achieved using the anticipated model. Very few misclassifications are obtained in the proposed system in every class and misclassified WSI, i.e., ADC, SCC, SCLC, and NORM (Figure 9.5). It is important to consider that no WSI cancers are misclassified as normal, and this is very crucial in the practice of medicine.

Table 9.5 Confusion matrix for SUCC.

Prediction				
Ground-truth values	**SCC**	**ADC**	**SCLC**	**NORM**
SCC	70	1	1	1
ADC	3	74	0	0
SCLC	1	1	17	1
NORM	1	1	1	12

Table 9.6 Confusion matrix for TCDA.

Prediction				
Ground-truth values	**SCC**	**ADC**	**SCLC**	**NORM**
SCC	69	1	2	1
ADC	4	72	1	0
SCLC	1	2	16	1
NORM	1	2	1	11

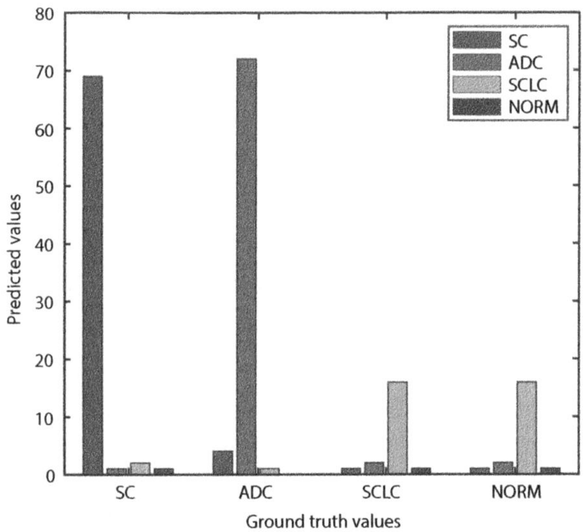

Figure 9.5 Ground-truth versus prediction outcomes from SUCC.

In addition, Cohen $k = 0.958$ is obtained in the proposed system, which obtains the fair better agreement.

The learning methodology is implemented in the proposed system to analyze WSIs. Also, patch-level predictions have the class histogram as the input to the SVM having the kernel function (RBF) for the prediction based on the image level label. Another method based on the $l - CNN$ activation feature is considered. Every WSI is classified into a group of patches, which obtains the 30% overlap of adjacent patches. Thus, resizing all the patches to 224 × 224 as the input for the VGG-16 is to extract the pre-trained network model features. In addition, all the features are aggregated using the 3-norm pooling, and the reduction of feature dimension is used to eliminate the unwanted features. The linear SVM classifier obtains the output, which is compared with *l* – *CNN* as in Figure 9.6. The proposed methods are overwhelmed with the two techniques in a considerable way from Table 9.7.

It is important to consider that the pretrained *l* – *CNN* helps extract the off-the-shell features on other domains that are generic and higher accuracy failed to obtain with the help of the pretrained model. Fine-tuning the images is essential for *l* – *CNN* to learn the essential discriminative

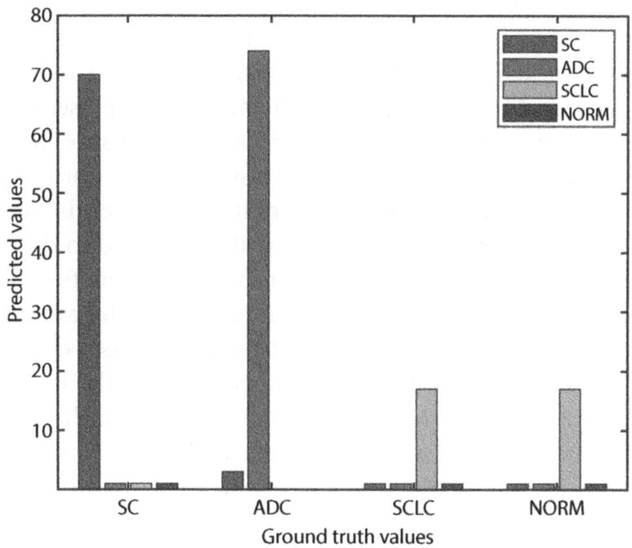

Figure 9.6 Ground-truth versus prediction outcomes from SUCC.

Table 9.7 Accuracy comparison of proposed versus existing on SUCC and TCGA.

Techniques	Accuracy with SUCC	Accuracy with TCGA
Standard Norm 3	87%	89%
SVM + CNN	91%	93%
Weighted feature	95%	97%
Weighted CNN + Norm 3	97%	98%
l – *CNN*	98%	99%

patterns. The class is lesser representative of the learned features using *l* – *CNN*, even though the existing work is trained on the iterative patch-based *l* – *CNN* and uses the count-based histogram at the second-stage classifier as the global feature. Since the global descriptor has the quality to represent the WSI that is critical for the classification of the WSI level, the proposed system has succeeded in the primary way, which has the representative features in the conjunction from *l* – *CNN* having the selection of feature based on context-aware and the strategies of aggregation.

C. Quantitative analysis

The proposed method can obtain the aim by retrieving the most discriminative areas simultaneously, and detecting tumors is not an important task of the proposed system. The specialized pathologist is presented in the proposed system for delineating the discriminative areas on some WSI testing in a detailed way. Also, the ground-truth and WSI are presented in Figure 9.5. It presents the carcinoma regions or the general tissue in the normal WSI. It is important to consider that the last row is the normal condition, and the first three rows are cases that are having cancer. In addition, the patch-based *l* – *CNN* needs to learn the patterns related to discriminative from WSIs with no aid of information related to annotation. It failed to identify the most discriminative areas that turn to the deficiency of feature positively having the evidence. In contrast, the robustness is enhanced using the annotations, which is a handful. M4 helps to find the heated regions, which are more consistent, having the annotation with the help of a pathologist. The visualization outcomes are validated so that the proposed system decides on the diagnosis, which depends on the real discriminative areas.

D. Visualization

The global features are projected in the proposed system for the visual comparison to 2D space having *t*-distributed stochastic neighborhood. The proposed system increases the distance between various interclasses presented. In addition, most of the WSIs are in a similar category, which creates a separate cluster, even though there are few hard samples that are nearer the boundary of decision that is challenging to find it correctly, which represents that the representation of the holistic feature that is achieved using the proposed system, and this is very helpful even with the help of standard CNN classifier for the image level classification.

Here, *l* – *CNN* based on patch does not handle obtaining the discriminative areas that turn to the irrelevant representation of global of the WSI in an eventual way. Due to the below reasons, failure cases are happening. Primarily, the images of SCC and the misclassified ADC are related to the poor distinguishable types of cancer. It is meant to be the patterns of morphology for the carcinoma in the WSIs that is ambiguous, and the $l - CNN$ based on the patch is high for the misidentification of these regions of cancer. In a second way, correct cancerous regions occupied only a small part of the misclassified WSIs' lung cancer. On the other hand, the complete image is dominated by the normal regions. The distinctiveness of the structural features is obtained in the misclassified normal WSI compared to the normal one that turns to the misclassification.

E. Execution analysis

The proposed Python-based system implemented on an equipped workstation on the deep learning library Tensorflow has one 3.5-GHz Intel Core i7-5930K CPU. The network has cropped the tiles having the dimension of at least $\sqrt{2}$ larger randomly from WSI at the stage of training over the patch size of training that promises that the below degree rotation in an arbitrary way gives the outcome in the invalid area, which appears in the patches of training. In addition, FCN is densely scanned in the inference stage where the block size is fixed. The block results are $21 \times 21 \times C$ tile for the probability, and the feature vector has 1024 bit. Here, C is set as 4 and 2 for the datasets of SUCC and TCGA, accordingly. The WSI is scanned using the FCN to eliminate the effect of boundary having the stride of 32×21; having the ScanNet gives the rate of total downsampling as 32. The probability tile has the length of the edge presented as 21. All the created probability tiles are stitched from the blocks in an ultimate way for achieving the WSI map of probability (Table 9.8).

The network's training is done with the gradient method where batch size is 100, learning rate is 0.0001, and the gradual decrease with factor of 10 happened for all 1000 iterations. The parameters are initialized randomly from the Gaussian distribution as $\mu = 0$, $\sigma = 0.01$, and the back-propagation helps for the update. The important factor for the analysis of WSI has

Table 9.8 AUC comparison with SUCC and TCGA.

Techniques	**AUC with SUCC**	**AUC with TCGA**
Standard Norm 3	77	84
SVM + CNN	77	82
Weighted CNN + Norm 3	82	86
$l - CNN$	95	96

efficiency (Figure 9.7). In addition, the proposed method has the speed of examination in the proposed system. It is about 100s for processing one WSI with 1 μm/pixel dimension that obtains more than hundreds of the faster time over the conventional framework for the patch-wise classification with a similar stride. The guaranteed effectiveness gives greater potential in the medical practice to consider the increased amount of larger-range WSIs.

Table 9.9 compares various metrics such as prediction accuracy, recall, precision, *F* measure, receiver operating characteristic (ROC), error rate, and Matthews correlation coefficient (MCC). The prediction accuracy of the *l-CNN* network model is 99%, which is 4%, 2%,5%, 4%, 4%, 4%, 1%, and 0.2% higher than hybrid CNN, standard CNN, region-based CNN (RCNN), CNN + augmentation, CNN–genetic algorithm (GA), VGG16, and ResNet + SE (squeeze and excitation). The precision of *l-CNN* is 100%, which is 20%, 39%, 16%, 18%, 7%, 5%, and 0.5% higher than hybrid CNN, standard CNN, RCNN, CNN + augmentation, CNN-GA, VGG16, and ResNet + SE. The recall of *l-CNN* model is 100%, which is 23%, 25%, 23%, 25%, 3%, 3%, and 0.8% higher than hybrid CNN, standard CNN, RCNN, CNN + augmentation, CNN-GA, VGG16, and ResNet + SE. The *F* measure of *l-CNN* model is 99.5%, which is 10%, 32%, 27%, 21%, 5%, 3%, and 0.40% higher than hybrid CNN, standard CNN, RCNN, CNN + augmentation, CNN-GA, VGG16, and ResNet + SE. The ROC of the proposed l-CNN model is comparatively higher than other approaches, i.e., 0.1, 0.12, 0.14, 0.1, 0.2, and 0.07, more elevated than different approaches. The error

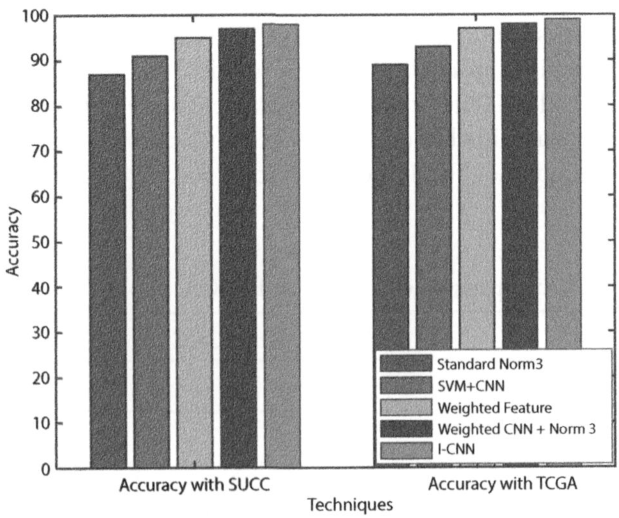

Figure 9.7 Proposed *l* – CNN model.

Table 9.9 Comparison of various performance metrics.

Methods	Accuracy (%)	Precision (%)	Recall (%)	*F* measure (%)	ROC	Error rate	MCC
Hybrid CNN	95	79	76	89	0.8	0.08	0.46
Standard CNN	96	60	75	67	0.8	1.02	0.45
RCNN	93	83	76	72	0.8	1.56	0.43
CNN + augmentation	94	81	75	77	0.8	1.63	0.46
CNN + GA	94.2	91	96	94	0.7	0.07	0.42
VGG16	97	93	97	95	0.9	0.07	0.35
ResNet + SE	98	99	99	99	0.9	0.06	0.26
l-CNN	99	100	100	99	0.9	0.05	0.1253

rate of the proposed model is 0.05, which is lesser than other approaches. Generally, the MCC value should range from −1 to 1; however, the proposed model gives a better MCC value of 0.1253, whereas the others are 0.4656, 0.4534, 0.4317, 0.4658, 0.4205, 0.3564, and 0.2645, respectively.

F. Discussion

The diagnosis of cancer gives the gold standard in different protocols in the field of medicine. The image of the whole slide has the examination as the bottleneck for the treatments on time. Hence, many investigators need to take care of the heavier burden, and the patients affected by cancer cannot be treated promptly. In addition, the automatic analysis is welcomed for the easier with the workload and mentions the shortage of medical resources in the areas and on the underserved populations. Since the image level labels are there in many situations, the classification issue for the WSI is much more difficult than the segmentation, and the detection of tumor tasks having a larger number of pixel-wise annotations is given for designing the fully supervised learning algorithm to the authors. It is important to consider that the regions of the tumor are distributed sparsely in the complete image having a larger proportion for the regions of noncancer that has outcomes in a more challenging way.

The ground-truth label for every single extracted patch is ambiguous from the WSI in a consecutive way. One more notorious issue in the tough image analysis is the greater variation in the appearance of the tissue. In addition, the morphology's textures and structures have the greatest diversity, one of the important blocks of stumbling in designing the powerful tool, which is an automatic tool even for a similar kind of noncancer or carcinoma. Many issues are still unsolved, even though considerable achievements are realized. Various conventional weakly supervised learning methods that existed before, such as approaches based on the MIL, are designed on many handcrafted features that restrain the transferability and the generality. The publicly available datasets for the lung cancer for the WSIs, such TCGA cohort, which has the classes of SCC and ADC that certainly impede the enhancement of the multiclass classifier, which are comprehensive, greatly created the demand in the practice of the medical field.

In addition, the proposed system handles the problems mentioned earlier. First, the SUCC dataset is comprehensive in implementing the underlying need for the identification to satisfy the various subtypes of lung cancer. The theoretical technique is anticipated for WSI classification problem using the exploration of the features selected and the feature aggregation. The weighted loss function is the primary goal that exploits during the WSI classification with the assistance of image-level labels and less coarse annotations. Various strategies are suggested in the proposed system to incorporate the rich spatial information with examples such as WeightedFeat, MaxFeat, and AvgFeat for the block descriptor, and the class descriptor includes the Norm 3 and the MeanPool for achieving the representation of the WSI holistic feature. Here, TCGA and SUCC are used to perform extensive experiments to check the efficiency of the proposed model (Figure 9.8). Because of the scarcity of delineation for the cancer regions, the proposed system inherently falls into the cohort method. The annotated regions are very noisy concerning the majority of annotations *via* the suggested weighted function of loss performs considerable enhancements. Hence, it is very difficult to identify the difference among the pathologist's ambiguous regions.

In addition, the process of choosing the training sample in an automated way has the ground-truth labels and avoids the noisy during training to enhance the accuracy. There are even few spaces for extra enhancement, even though the proposed method obtains better outcomes in the experiments. In addition, the patches have embedding features that are a little difficult for the holistic descriptor, such as the number of hyperparameters, which require to be evaluated. Adaptive learning helps with the automated aggregation and the automated selection of the feature, which will be very attractive and straightforward in the future. It is important to consider that the proposed system has a framework that does not have end-to-end pipeline assembling features, and the classification is done for two separate modules. The $l - CNN$ classifier is replaced in the proposed system having the classifier of MLP for making the end-to-end in the future work.

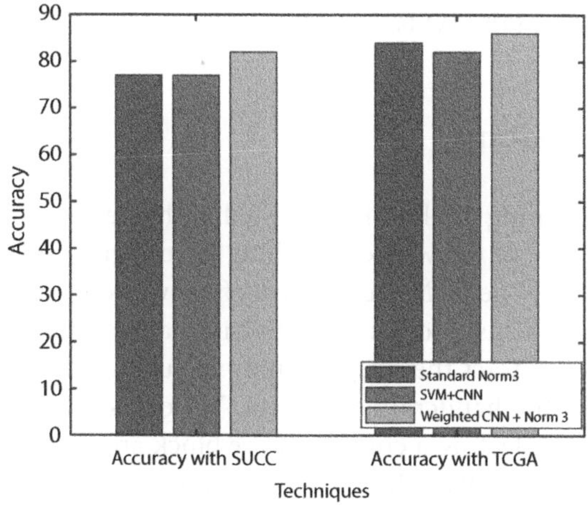

Figure 9.8 Training accuracy comparison among SUCC and TCGA.

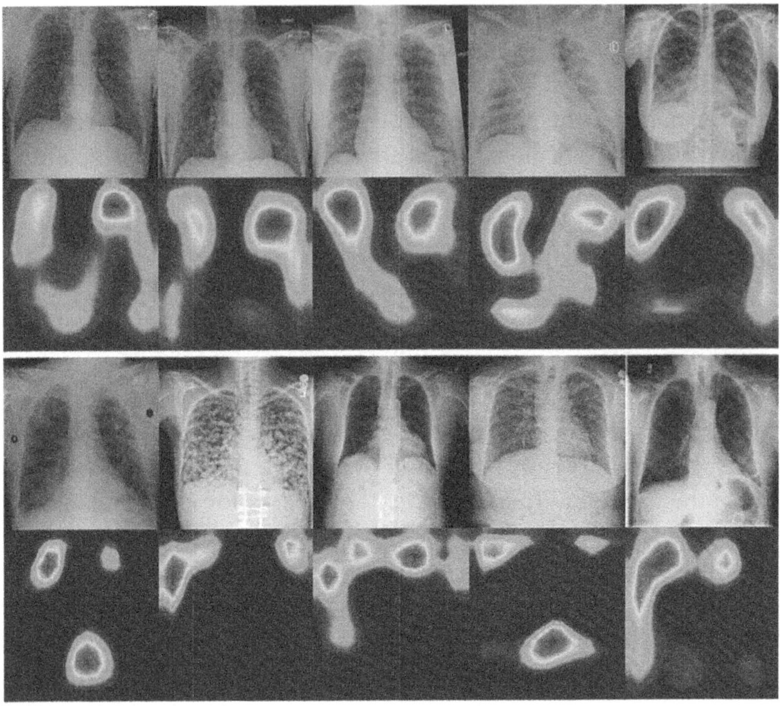

Figure 9.9 Image saliency.

In addition, because of the complicated variations of the technique (Figure 9.9), such as the type of cell and the cell state, which are always present in the larger cohort, the suggested system does not correctly deal with the ambiguous areas in the WSIs.

9.4 Conclusion

The *l – CNN* learning method is suggested in this research to mention the classification issue of the whole-slide lung cancer image having less effort in the annotation. The FCN is exploited, effectively creating the likelihood of cancer, which helps to obtain the discriminative areas. In addition, *l – CNN* is used to extract the deep learning features, which are the unique substitution for the handcrafted features. Various strategies for aggregating features and selecting a context-aware block are suggested in the proposed system for achieving the efficient representation of the WSI's holistic feature. The larger fine-grained SUCC dataset for the lung cancer WSI is constructed primarily in the proposed system to validate the efficiency of the suggested method for comprehensive analysis. The proposed method is determined on the publicly available dataset from the TCGA for lung cancer WSIs. The proposed method has the superiority to corroborate the extensive experiments, which perform well than the modern methods considered on the two datasets. The proposed method is accepted to alleviate the bottleneck of the expert cost of annotation in the suggested method and the progress of the computer-related image analysis.

AI disclosure statement: The author acknowledges the use of AI-based tools for minor language editing or grammatical correction. However, all intellectual contributions, analyses, and conclusions presented in this chapter are entirely the author's own.

References

1. Wood, A., Shpilrain, V., Najarian, K., Kahrobaei, D., Private naive bayes classification of personal biomedical data: Application in cancer data analysis. *Comput. Biol. Med.*, 105, 144–150, 2019.
2. Krishnaiah, V., Narsimha, G., Subhash Chandra, N., Diagnosis of lung cancer prediction system using data mining classification techniques. *Int. J. Comput. Sci. Inf. Technol.*, 4, 1, 39–45, 2013.
3. Pati, J., Gene expression analysis for early lung cancer prediction using machine learning techniques: an eco-genomics approach. *IEEE Access*, 7, 4232–4238, 2019.
4. Liu, W., *et al.*, Identification of genes associated with cancer progression and prognosis in lung adenocarcinoma: analyses based on microarray from Oncomine and the Cancer Genome Atlas databases. *Mol. Genet. Genomic Med.*, 7, 2, e00528, 2019.
5. Sun, Y., Todorovic, S., Goodison, S., Local-learning-based feature selection for high-dimensional data analysis. *IEEE Trans. Pattern Anal. Mach. Intell.*, 32, 9, 1610–1626, 2010.
6. Pavithra, D. and Lakshmanan, B., Feature selection and classification in gene expression cancer data, in: *2017 International Conference on Computational Intelligence in Data Science (ICCIDS)*, Chennai, pp. 1–6, 2017.
7. Vabalas, A., Gowen, E., Poliakoff, E., Casson, A.J., Machine learning algorithm validation with a limited sample size. *PLoS One*, 14, 11, e0224365, 2019.
8. Lemaître, G., Nogueira, F., Aridas, C.K., Imbalanced-learn: A python toolbox to tackle the curse of imbalanced datasets in machine learning. *J. Mach. Learn. Res.*, 18, 1, 559–563 (2017), 2017.

9. Ahmed, M.S., Shahjaman, M., Rana, M.M., Mollah, M.N.H., Robustification of Naïve Bayes classifier and its application for microarray gene expression data analysis. *Biomed Res. Int.*, 2017, 3020627, 2017.
10. Chen, T. and Guestrin, V., XGBoost: a scalable tree boosting system, in: *Proceedings of the 22nd ACM SIGKDD International Conference on Knowledge Discovery and Data Mining (KDD'16)*, Association for computing machinery, New York, NY, USA, pp. 785–794, 2016.
11. Alcantud, J.C.R., Varela, G., Santos-Buitrago, B., Santos-Garcia, G., Jimenez, M.F., Analysis of survival for lung cancer resections cases with fuzzy and soft set theory in surgical decision making. *PLoS One*, 14, 6, e0218283, 2019.
12. Bhatia, S., Sinha, Y., Goel, L., Lung cancer detection: a deep learning approach, in: *Soft Computing for Problem Solving*. AISC, vol. 817, J.C. Bansal, K.N. Das, A. Nagar, K. Deep, A.K. Ojha, (Eds.), pp. 699–705, Springer, Singapore, 2019.
13. Bhuvaneswari, P. and Therese, A.B., Detection of cancer in lung with k- nn classification using genetic algorithm. *Procedia Mater. Sci.*, 10, 433–440, 2015.
14. Chaubey, N.K. and Jayanthi, P., Disease diagnosis and treatment using deep learning algorithms for the healthcare system, in: *Applications of Deep Learning and Big IoT on Personalized Healthcare Services*, pp. 99–114, IGI Global, 2020.
15. Hachesu, P.R., Moftian, N., Dehghani, M., Soltani, T.S., Analyzing a lung cancer patient dataset with the focus on predicting survival rate one year after thoracic surgery. *Asian Pac. J. Cancer Prev.: APJCP*, 18, 6, 1531, 2017.
16. Bhoomika, B.K., Kanmani, K., Smilarubavathy, G., Early Detection of Pancreatic Cancer using Machine Learning Algorithm, in: *2024 5th International Conference on Mobile Computing and Sustainable Informatics (ICMCSI)*, 2024, January, IEEE, pp. 202–205.
17. Hussein, S., Kandel, P., Bolan, C.W., Wallace, M.B., Bagci, U., Lung and pancreatic tumor characterization in the deep learning era: Novel supervised and unsupervised learning approaches. *IEEE Trans. Med. Imag.*, 38, 8, 1777–1787, 2019.
18. Jakimovski, G. and Davcev, D., Using double convolution neural network for lung cancer stage detection. *Appl. Sci.*, 9, 3, 427, 2019.
19. Jacob, D.S., Viswan, R., Manju, V., PadmaSuresh, L., Raj, S., A survey on breast cancer prediction using data mining techniques, in: *2018 Conference on Emerging Devices and Smart Systems (ICEDSS)*, IEEE, pp. 256–258, 2018.
20. Kohad, R. and Ahire, V., Application of machine learning techniques for the diagnosis of lung cancer with ant colony optimization. *Int. J. Comput. Appl.*, 113, 18, 34–41, 2015.
21. Kadir, T. and Gleeson, F., Lung cancer prediction using machine learning and advanced imaging techniques. *Transl. Lung Cancer Res.*, 7, 3, 304, 2018.
22. Ngo, H.H., A prediction model for lung cancer levels based on data mining techniques. *Int. J. Innov. Res. Eng. Technol.*, 3, 2, 1–7, 2015.
23. Kourou, K., Exarchos, T.P., Exarchos, K.P., Karamouzis, M.V., Fotiadis, D.I., Machine learning applications in cancer prognosis and prediction. *Comput. Struct. Biotechnol. J.*, 13, 8–17, 2015.

24. Lynch, C.M., *et al.*, Prediction of lung cancer patient survival *via* supervised machine learning classification techniques. *Int. J. Med. Inform.*, 108, 1–8, 2017.
25. Li, X., Hu, B., Li, H., You, B., Application of artificial intelligence in the diagnosis of multiple primary lung cancer. *Thorac. Cancer*, 10, 11, 2168–2174, 2019.
26. Monkam, P., Qi, S., Ma, H., Gao, W., Yao, Y., Qian, W., Detection and classification of pulmonary nodules using convolutional neural networks: A survey. *IEEE Access*, 7, 78075–78091, 2019.
27. Murty, N.R. and Babu, M.P., A critical study of classification algorithms for lungcancer disease detection and diagnosis. *Int. J. Comput. Intell. Res.*, 13, 5, 1041–1048, 2017.
28. Patel, D., Shah, Y., Thakkar, N., Shah, K., Shah, M., Implementation of artificial intelligence techniques for cancer detection. *Augment. Hum. Res.*, 5, 1, 6, 2020.
29. Shakeel, P.M., Tolba, A., Al-Makhadmeh, Z., Jaber, M.M., Automatic detection of lung cancer from biomedical data set using discrete adaboost optimized ensemble learning generalized neural networks. *Neural Comput. Appl.*, 32, 3, 777–790, 2020.
30. Shanthi, S. and Rajkumar, N., Lung cancer prediction using stochastic diffusion search (sds) based feature selection and machine learning methods. *Neural Process. Lett.*, 1, 1–14, 2020.
31. Sidey-Gibbons, J.A. and Sidey-Gibbons, C.J., Machine learning in medicine: A practical introduction. *BMC Med. Res. Methodol.*, 19, 1, 64, 2019.
32. Varadharajan, R., Priyan, M., Panchatcharam, P., Vivekanandan, S., Gunasekaran, M., A new approach for prediction of lung carcinoma using back propogation neural network with decision tree classifiers. *J. Ambient Intell. Humaniz. Comput.*, 1, 1–12, 2018.
33. Singh, G.A.P. and Gupta, P.K., Performance analysis of various machine learning-based approaches for detection and classification of lung cancer in humans. *Neural Comput. Appl.*, 31, 10, 6863–6877, 2018.
34. Shrestha, H., Dhasarathan, C., Kumar, M., Nidhya, R., Shankar, A., Kumar, M., A Deep Learning Based Convolution Neural Network-DCNN Approach to Detect Brain Tumor, in: *Proceedings of Academia-Industry Consortium for Data Science*. Advances in Intelligent Systems and Computing, vol. 1411, G. Gupta, L. Wang, A. Yadav, P. Rana, Z. Wang (Eds.), Springer, Singapore, 2022.
35. Sreeja, B.P., Manoj Kumar, S., Sherubha, P., Sasirekha, S.P., Crop monitoring using wireless sensor networks. *Mater. Today: Proc.*, 15, 99–104, 2020.
36. Narmadha, B., Sherubha, P., Banu Chitra, M., Multi class feature selection algorithm for breast cancer detection. *Int. J. Pure Appl. Math.*, 118, 20, 301–305, 2018.
37. Atlam, M., Torkey, H., Salem, H., Nawal, A new feature selection method for enhancing cancer diagnosis based on DNA microarray. *National Radio Science and Conference*, pp. 1–11, 2020.

10

Chronic Kidney Disease Prediction Using a Layered Convolutional Vector Model

Sanjiv Rao Godla[1], V. Murugesh[2*], Vijay Kumar Janga[3], R. Nidhya[4] and D. Pavithra[5]

[1]Department of Computer Science Engineering, Aditya College of Engineering & Technology, Suramplem, Andhra Pradesh, India
[2]School of Computer Science, Coventry University Kazakhstan, Astana, Kazakhstan
[3]Dept of CSE (AI & ML), Balaji Institute of Technology & Science, Narsampet, Andhra Pradesh, India
[4]Department of Computer Science & Engineering, Madanapalle Institute of Technology & Science (MITS) Deemed to be University, Madanapalle, Andhra Pradesh, India
[5]Department of Information Technology, Dr. NGP Institute of Technology, Coimbatore, Tamil Nadu, India

Abstract

Chronic renal disease is primarily due to diabetes and high blood pressure (chronic kidney disease [CKD]). Researchers worldwide use kidney damage markers and glomerular filtration rate to point out CKD that steadily worsens renal function. CKDs are more likely to affect adults easily. It is challenging for medical experts to identify the various ailments connected to CKD early and to halt it. This work concentrates on modeling an efficient deep-learning approach to address the above challenge. A novel deep-learning model known as homological segmentation with convolutional vector model (HS-CVM) for early CKD diagnosis and prediction is proposed with two key goals, i.e., constructing a reliable deep neural network and comparing the performance with other learning methods. During testing, the database's missing values are replaced using the average corresponding features. The optimal parameters of the neural network were then set and tested repeatedly. Some existing classifiers such as k-nearest neighbor, support vector machine,

**Corresponding author*: murugesh72@gmail.com

R. Nidhya, D. Pavithra, S. Balamurugan, A. Dinesh Kumar and Sheng-Lung Peng (eds.) Medical Metaverse for Digital Healthcare: Technologies, Applications, and Challenges, (203–228) © 2026 Scrivener Publishing LLC

random forest, logistic regression, and naive Bayes are compared. The suggested HS-CVM outperforms them by reaching 99.4% accuracy. Nephrologists find that the recommended method is helpful for earlier CKD detection.

Keywords: Chronic kidney disease, deep learning, prediction, feature representation, prediction accuracy, earlier diagnosis

10.1 Introduction

Chronic renal disease is therefore a condition in a patient where his/her renal function is gradually deteriorating. This leads to a poor quality of life of these women. Chronic renal illness affects 1 in 10 persons globally, with chronic kidney disease (CKD) being the most prevalent. CKD is increasingly being witnessed among the populace, and as it is projected, it will be the fifth highest trigger of mortality by the year 2040 [1]. This is one of the causes that make the costs of medical bills very high at certain instances. Renal dialysis and transplantation costs constitute about 2% to 3% of the health care budget of the developed countries in a year [2]. Kidney transplantation and life-preservation dialysis rate are still inadequate in low- and middle-income nation's most of patients with renal insufficiency [3]. It is expected that the number of patients with cases related to renal failure will increase unexpectedly in the developing countries such as China and India [4]. With chronic renal illness, it becomes difficult to eliminate excess fluid in circulation. Proliferative stage CKD is defined as the point where the body gets overloaded with "toxic" fluids, electrolytes, and waste products. Potential complications associated with the use of this drug include anemia, osteoporosis, hypertension, and neuropathy. According to sources, renal function is the most accurate glomerular filtration rate (GFR) measure [5]. One of the approaches that doctors use in determining renal diseases is the GFR abbreviated as GFR. Even if there is renal impalement, for one to be diagnosed with chronic renal disease the GFR should be less than 60 mL/min per 1.73 m^2. The average area utilized for the past 3 months has been 73 m^2. On this basis, GFR, which is a stable marker of the kidney function, may be used to differentiate between various stages of CKD, and each of them is indicative of the severity of GFR decline [6]. Renal failure can also be defined by the GFR [6], and if the GFR is less than 15 mL/min, the kidney has failed or is closely poised to do so. It now ended with the fifth stage, chronic renal disease. Diagnosis of CKD is a difficult process because it comes with various symptoms. Expectations are primarily clinical or medical decisions of the therapist when treating the patient and reviewing his symptoms [7]. Recent research also shows that doctors are unable to cope with developments in clinical practice as new pharmaceuticals come up and change in the health care system [8].

It is possible to diagnose diseases with the help of computers using machine learning technology [9]. To make the diagnostic procedure more effective, the presented data are analyzed by machine learning techniques that help intelligently decipher this information and present usable data [10]. It is already applied to assess the state of a person's physical health, review some aspects of an illness, and even come up with multiple diagnoses [10]. The applications of ML are found to assess whether a person had a potential of prospective heart disease or not [11]. It is also used for the purposes of diagnosis of heart disease, diabetes, acute renal injury, retinopathy, and cancer [12]. Some of the supervised algorithms that have been applied in the diagnosis of chronic renal illness include random forest (RF), naive Bayes (NB), fuzzy C means, support vector machine (SVM), gradient boosting (GB), and logistic regression (LR) [13–16]. Using machine learning, enhanced medical data accuracy is also achievable; better reductions in overall hospital admissions and lower costs on medical expenses are also possible. Therefore, diagnostic analytic research applies these models more often [17] than other testing methods. The two main strategies that may affect CD mortality are the early diagnosis and subsequent effective treatment [18]. In classic machine learning, the feature extraction process and the classification use two methods. As a result of this traditional machine learning, methods are computationally intensive. It has become evident from the above discussion that the conventional method is not suitable for real-time diagnostic application [19]. Medical diagnostics apply artificial neural networks (ANN) more and more because of their learning abilities about the environment, generalization, and the errors tolerance. Famous is the case when the neural network (NN) method proves to be better in comparison with different methods of machine learning. It can be further enhanced to improve even more the performance of the resource learning architecture. The use of neural network models has been used in the identification of renal disease [20]. Many models of CKD that are available for use in the current world do not possess good results in classifying the diseases [21]. This study therefore provides a fresh brand of CKD model. This paper's primary contributions are as follows:

- The detection and diagnosis of CKD have been proposed using the novel homological segmentation with a convolutional vector model (HS-CVM). The homological segmented image is used for training the samples with the CVM. However, to deal with the poor performance of the prevailing classifier and activation function, this work adopts ReLU as an activation function. Then, the vector model is used for prediction and to enhance the efficiency of the proposed HS-CVM model.

- HS-CVM can perform and function better using magnetic resonance imaging (MRI) segments by computing the recommended model precision contrasts with other published classification techniques.
- Additionally, the performance is assessed using a variety of performance metrics. Some metrics such as recall, accuracy, precision, and *F* measure are compared with diverse learning approaches.

Chapter 10 offers a list of pertinent studies on techniques for CKD using machine learning. Section 10.3 provides a deep NN model for early CKD prediction. In Section 10.4, there is a thorough discussion of the findings and an interpretation. Section 10.5 presents a summary of the results and looks ahead.

10.2 Related Works

Researchers and doctors are now interested in tracking and forecasting tools for various diseases, emphasizing those that often affect people. This section will cover small dataset processing approaches and new studies with ML to estimate the likelihood of CKD. Dritsas *et al.* [22] analyzed 551 proteinuric patients' clinical and blood biochemical measures that were a foundation for many investigations. Numerous forecasting models, including XGBoost, LR, ElasNet, LRR, k-nearest neighbor (k-NN), SVM, and RF, were examined [23–26]. Some models with the highest mean accuracy and area under the curve (AUC) values are achieved with algorithms such as ElasNet, Lasso, Ridge, and LR. LR also triumphed with a recall of 0.83, a specificity of 0.82, and an AUC of 0.873. ElasNet achieved the highest recall of 85%, whereas XGBoost provided the highest specificity of 83%. In Chittora *et al.* [27], the authors used SVM, AdaBoost, LDA, and GBoost approaches to create highly accurate CKD prediction. Using the UCI machine learning library, the effectiveness was evaluated. The classifier uses GB with the highest accuracy rate of 99.80%. The dataset was the main focus of the authors [28].

Three distinct CKD prediction models were trained using decision tree (DT), k-NN, and LR algorithms. The accuracy rate of the LR was higher than both DT (97%) and k-NN (71.25%), which had lower accuracy rates. The accuracy of NB, RF, and LR models was 93.9%, 98.88%, and 94.76%, respectively [29], in predicting the risk of CKD [30]. The authors looked into how well these models performed. A strategy for forecasting the likelihood of CKD was also proposed by Qiang *et al.* [31]; they used 455 patient records from the UCI ML repository and real-time datasets. Tenfold CV was utilized, and RF and ANN were trained and evaluated on the data. RF and ANN have accuracy ratings of 94.5% and 97.12%, respectively. The research work in Zhang *et al.* [32] also trained and evaluated several classifiers using a CKD dataset with ANN, C5.0, UCI library's random tree, linear SVM with L1 and L2 regularization, and X^2 automated interaction detector random tree (RT) [33]. Linear SVM produced a maximum accuracy of 98.86% with a penalty where all features operate under SMOTE. A similar high accuracy of 98.46% was provided with the linear SVM, synthetic minority oversampling technique (SMOTE), and Lasso feature selection method [34]. The same dataset in the previous stage was utilized for training the deep neural networks with a 99.6% accuracy rate and showed the best accuracy. The CKD dataset consisted of 25 characteristics and was made available *via* the repository for machine learning as described in Major *et al.* [35]. RF, DT, and SVM ML models obtained a prediction accuracy of 99.16%, 94.16%, and 98.3% for CKD diagnosis.

Tangri *et al.* [34] also used a set of 26 correlated parameters associated with CKD. Four feature-based techniques were coupled with the ANN classifier: The selected algorithm includes Lasso model, X^2, Pearson correlation, and extra tree. From the above table, it is quite clear that the best prediction model is the Lasso model-based ANN ensemble with accuracy of 99.98%. Other algorithms used include Gaussian NB, DT, AdaBoost, GBoost and XGBoost, ExTrees classifier, AdaBoost, k-NN, and RF [36]. Specifically, the averages of accuracy rates were 99% for ExTrees and 98% for k-NN classifiers, and it is clear that both the classifiers worked better than other classifiers in terms of classification performance. In Weng *et al.* [37], the authors included a major ML challenge that can affect the handling of relatively small-scale health care datasets. The output signal is determined with the help of current radial basis function (RBF) input-doubling method based on the radial basis function for doubling the input component, expanding on which can be made with additional components. They enhanced the regression analysis using the back-propagation algorithm of ANN. Yu *et al.* [38] have described the iterative automated standard RBF network of neurons with consideration to the input doubling approaches. The findings were then checked using the referenced mean absolute error consistent with determining the best accuracy achievable on a small medical dataset. In Rajkumar *et al.* [39], a new technique developed from generative adversarial network (GAN) is used in enhancing disease classification using data augmentation. For this endeavor, the researchers used the NIH chest imaging dataset. Here, we have presented a comparable view of the test accuracy rate resulting from the convolutional neural network (CNN) models, which stands 60.3% by implementing GAN with 24% of augmentation, yet the online test accuracy of GAN augmented model is 65.3%. For handling the medical insurance data, as stated by Karadaghy *et al.* [40], it is possible to learn how to construct a predictor for the noniterative supervised learning. It uses a so-called sequential geometric transformation model derived from the former and an architecture alluding to a kidney [41]. However, the model has to produce good results, otherwise, it is not very useful. In the mentioned works, the most frequently reported difficulty is the limitation in identifying potential causes of CKD again due to time constraints; second, the fear of giving proper diagnosis; and third, disappointment in CKD guidelines [42–44]. A number of other risk factors such as obesity, heart disease, inherited kidney disorder, CKD family history, past kidney damage, and age factors are not viewed by most researchers. Additionally, the prior outcomes are also required to yield promising results with the only given dataset [45, 46]. At times, when the samples of a dataset are more, the other complex problems that the model can face include overfitting or underfitting.

10.3 Methodology

This part's focus is based on class balance and feature selection criteria in balanced datasets. We will also briefly examine the CKD class's nominal characteristics in the following study. We will also examine the models and performance indicators that the experiments will include. All this research and the experimentations are performed to help the clinical specialists, and the provided framework is designed to act as a clinical decision support system with the help of deep learning techniques. Because it assists the experts, the data and sample outcomes can be manipulated in real time to help the society.

10.3.1 MRI Data Acquisition

The review board of the institution of the hospital permitted this study. Some information consent (written) was attained for every participant for renal MRI. Every patient with diabetes and hypertension between 2013 and 2019 was prospectively attained for MRI renal examination, and the technique for image processing was developed. This work performs retrospective reviews and secondary analysis with the available images. Serum creatinine is attained after and before a week of MRI examination, and estimated GFR is evaluated using CKD Epidemiology Collaboration. CKD1 patients with ($eGFR \geq 90\ mL/min/1.73m^2$) are considered normal, and CKD2/3 patients with ($eGFR \geq 90\ mL/min/1.73m^2 >$ eGFR $< 90\ mL/min/1.73m^2$) are treated as moderate or mild renal function impairment, and CKD4/5 patients with ($eGF < 30\ mL/min/1.73m^2$) is treated as severe renal function impairment. Here, the patients undergo an MRI examination at 3.0 T. The parameter acquisition is provided below: T1W1 repetition time = 6.2 milliseconds, field of view = 100, echo time (TE) = 2.8 milliseconds, slice thickness = 4 mm, matrix = 512 × 512, bandwidth = 162.7 Hz/pixel, flip angle = 20°, coronal T2W1 = 1985 milliseconds, field of view = 100 m^2, TE = 70 milliseconds, bandwidth = 325.50 Hz/pixel. Based on the differences, the intensity range is normalized (0–255) using normalization (mean-variance) to diminish the significance of texture analysis. The manuscript does not include the cases where data are limited, and the dataset is against benchmark and is available to young researchers. Moreover, benchmark data are available with ethical consideration, and it is not necessary to deteriorate the data anonymity. The samples are collected with proper medical ethical procedure and also in concordance with the patient's permission.

10.3.2 Preprocessing

Using the k-NN classifier of $k = 2$ and SMOTE, we created fictitious statistics on the underrepresented class, namely, non-CKD, for the current dataset. Because both types have an equal number of instances (i.e., 50%), the examples in the non-CKD class need to be more balanced. We provide a statistical analysis of the numerical characteristics, including mean, minimum (Min), standard deviation (SD), and maximum (Max) in Table 10.1 after data balancing.

10.3.3 Image Restoration

The goal of image restoration is processed clemently to minimize the impact occurring in the process of image creation. To achieve the correct orientation of this system, level set method is used. These, through the use of curve motion, cause shrinks to be gradually eliminated. Imputation using image is the creation of the possible images from the given low-resolution

Table 10.1 Data balancing using SMOTE and *k* values.

Features	**Minimal**	**Maximal**	**Mean SD**
Hemoglobin	3.2	17.9	13.05 ± 2.6
Specific gravity (Sg)	1.0	1.02	1.0 ± 0.005
Red blood cells	2.2	8	4.8 ± 0.83
Blood urea (Bu)	1.6	392	52.5 ± 45.3
Sodium	4.6	164	138.4 ± 8.6
Serum Creatinine (SC)	0.4	75	2.6 ± 5.08
Blood pressure	50	180	75.3 ± 12.5
White blood cells	2200	26,400	8310 ± 2394.1
Potassium	2.6	48	4.5 ± 2.5

images or with the lack of some data over the image. This is applied over the proposed model where the imputation method tries to fill in the missing data without having an image loss function for creating the data matrix with desired image properties. Imputation is the process of providing a value for missing elements, whereas no definition of missing data is given. Thus, globally, the segmenting outcomes are even better.

10.3.4 Segmentation

The proposed homological segmentation determines the robustness of a dataset's topological properties at various image sizes. It is a component of a developing area called "topological data analysis," where information from noisy and high-dimensional datasets is extracted using topological concepts. Neuroscience, phase transition research, tree-structured data analysis, and assessing image artifacts are only a few fields where segmentation has been found useful. The reader is referred to Abdel-Kader [20] for in-depth studies of image segmentation related to our strategy. However, we provide a brief outline below when high-dimensional data points generate complexes where homological segmentation is most frequently used in this research. However, in our instance, given that a cubical complex is a more efficient way to store data, whether it comes from two- (2D) or three-dimensional (3D) volumes, it is an efficient and advantageous form. Many objects comprise a cubical complex, including object types over the image, unit squares, cubes, hypercubes, segments of unit lines, cubes, and points. $I = [z, z + 1]$ for $z \in Z$ is the line by which an elementary interval is described as a closed subset. Image cubes are produced when the elementary intervals, $Q = I_1 * I2 *... * I_k$, are multiplied together and will represent pixels or voxels where k is the dimension of the space under consideration. To keep things simple, we will discuss the two-dimensional situation below. Consequently, $Q_{ij} = [i, i + 1] * [j, j + 1]$ can represent the area surrounding a pixel in an image's row i and column j. A 2D array X with expected binary values and pixel intensities segmentation represents Nx and Ny images. X_{ij} is an alternate way to describe S as a 2D array of the form $S_{ij} \in [0,1]$. S_{ij} is the calculated likelihood that an image's segmented object corresponds to a pixel in column j and row i. A function $S = f(X; \omega)$ determines S. $R - CNN$ in our example, f will have parameterized weight V. The collection of pixels for which S_{ij} is more significant than a certain threshold value P is what we refer to as assets of super-level S. The super-level sets are denoted as B and provide us with a series of sets that increase as the threshold parameter is decreased.

$$B(p) = \bigcup_{i,j} Q_{ij} : S_{ij} \geq p \tag{10.1}$$

$$\varnothing \subseteq B(1) \subseteq B(p_1) \subseteq B(p_2) \subseteq \ldots \subseteq B(0) \subseteq [0, N_x] * [0, N_y] \tag{10.2}$$

When p is high, the cubical complex has few pixels. Both new and old topological characteristics are generated in B as P lowers, and new pixels are added to the cubical complex. Every pixel finally belongs to the cubical complex as $p = 0$, and the super-level set contains the full image. The cubical complexes' individual Betti numbers are used in segmentation to count how many topological features are in $B(p)$ with different dimensions for each value of p. Betti numbers b_k are used to express the number of loops or holes and connected components. It is used to count the characteristics of dimension k. Our tests must consider Betti values for 2D and 3D image volumes.

This technique generated a set of threshold values for segmentation for each topological characteristic, which can be seen as the analysis result. The longest bar of dimension k image values is denoted as $b_{k,l}$ and $d_{k,l}$, respectively. Super-level sets are a consideration of $b_{k,l} > d_{k,l}$. The persistent properties are essential topological elements in the data. These characteristics are those for which the threshold values for segmentation differ noticeably. The importance of $b_{k,l}$ and $d_{k,l}$ has S values. As a result, the numbers calculated for each feature during segmentation differ from those in the image or array. As a result, the precise value of a particular pixel S_{ij} is necessary to add or remove any feature. The trait's value in segmentation filtering is also impacted by a bit of change in the value of the relevant pixel; we may compute the gradient concerning S for every segmentation threshold value. Furthermore, because f is a neural network and $S = f(X; \omega)$ is also differentiable, we may calculate each $b_{k,l}$, and $d_{k,l}$ gradient about the network's weights ω. The network's weights can then be adjusted so that the barcode diagram matches the segmented object's topology as it now exists.

10.3.5 Segmenting Function

The postprocessing and semisupervised frameworks are used in this topological loss function. The Dice sets' training set loss is an example of a supervised loss that a group of weights called ω can minimize. The segmentation network f is initially supervised-trained using a set of pixel-level labels and labeled training photos. Then, the topological loss function is optimized X_n for each test set item (whose appropriate prior topology is known, but the training lacks access to ground truth segmentation). For each item, X_n, in the test set to which the loss function is applied, the network weights ω_n are updated (which replaces ω). For each element in the test set X_n, the loss function is minimized:

$$\mathcal{L}(X_n; \omega, \omega_n) = \frac{1}{V} |f(X_n, \omega) - f(X_n, \omega_n)|^2 + \lambda \mathcal{L}_{topological}(X_n, \omega_n) \tag{10.3}$$

It provides updated network weights (which substitutes ω_n), where V is the number of pixels or voxels in the picture or volume. It effectively determines the output segmentation that needs to change the least to improve its topology. This framework is suitable, for instance, when the topology of each test set item is known, even though they may vary depending on the item. The network is trained in the semisupervised framework using two sets of images: a more extensive collection of unlabeled images $\{X_l\}$ and smaller images $\{X_u\}$ that correspond to labels $\{Y_l\}$, whose segmentation topology is known but whose ground-truth labels are not provided. Use is made of a traditional segmentation loss function, such as the Dice loss in situations with brands; the topological loss may be used in cases without labels. Using this semisupervised strategy, before including the unlabeled events with associated topological loss in our studies, we first train the network completely supervised on the training set. It is done to ensure the segmentations are correct so that the network predictions for the topological loss can be used because the unlabeled situations are precise enough. The network is then taught to minimize loss after that.

$$\mathcal{L}(X_n;\omega,\omega_n)=\sum_{X_l}\mathcal{L}_{dice}(X,\omega)+\lambda\sum_{X_u}\mathcal{L}_{topological}(X) \tag{10.4}$$

As determined by segmentation, the topological loss on the unlabeled cases equals the weighted average dice loss on the named instances. When trying to teach a network to separate a collection of objects, this method is helpful with similar topologies. It is feasible to access many photographs, but hand annotations take time to come by. The homologous structure is alike of physical features related to renal imaging where they share some common ancestors. However, the features serve diverse functionality completely. The homologous structures are analyzed using the convolution network to make better prediction. The internal morphological features of renal are acquired and analyzed by the convolutional network to acquire better prediction outcomes.

10.3.6 Classification

This study suggests an enhanced CVM-based CKD classification approach. The support vector classifier and seven-layer convolutional network are built to complete the model learning and classification. The CVM approach's network structure is shown in Figure 10.1. It displays a classifier, one fully connected layer, three pooling layers, and five convolutional layers used to build the seven CVM structures. This approach utilizes the ReLU function (activation function) of neurons because it can handle the gradient dispersion of traditional activation functions (Tanh, Sigmoid, and Softmax). The CVM approach consists of the following steps:

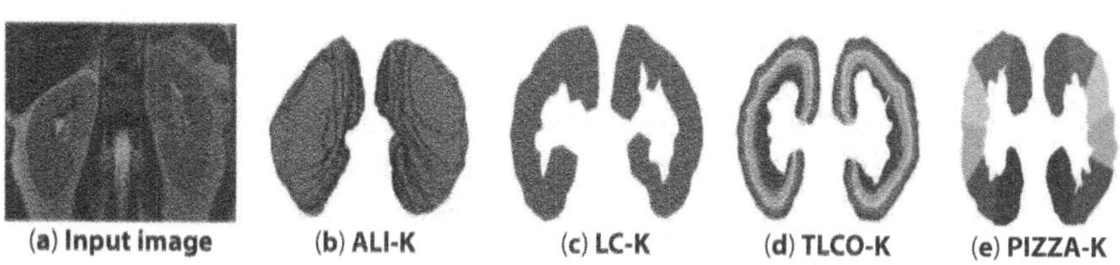

Figure 10.1 Segmented image.

1. In this stage, we create the sample tags and multiclass datasets and then separate sets for training and testing the datasets. The CVM network is then fed with the training data, and after denoising, segmenting, and edge-detecting, the grayscale CKD is acquired.
2. Before the ReLU activation function is used to create the feature map, the dataset is exposed to 96 filters in the pooling layer and the first convolutional layer, each with 11×11 convolutions and a step factor of 4. The obtained 96 feature maps are next subjected to a 3×3 convolutional max-pooling operation with a step factor of 2, creating an additional 96 feature maps with an interval of 27×27 pixels. After completing 2×2 convolution with a step factor 1256, feature maps with 27×27 pixels are obtained. These feature maps are used in the pooling and the second convolutional layers.
3. Using 256 filters and 5×5 convolutions, 27 feature maps were produced. The final step is to use a zero-fill kernel to max-pool the created feature map, 3×3 convolutions, and a step value of 2, making 256 feature maps with 13×13 pixel spacing. Using the step factor of 1 and the zero-fill kernel with 1 × 1 convolutions, the third and fourth convolutional layers of a 384 feature map with 3 × 3 convolution kernel are convoluted; 384 feature maps using *a*13×13 pixel grid were also produced.
4. To create 256 feature maps with 13×13 pixel spacing, the fifth convolutional layer and pooling layer perform filtering operation with a step factor 1 and zero fill of 1×1. These 3 × 3 convolution kernels are used with these 256 feature maps. The final step is to max-pool the resulting feature map process using 256 feature mappings with 6 × 6 pixel spacing, 3 × 3 convolution kernel size, and two-step factor.
5. The CVM classifier's inputs are the 4096 neurons produced by the 4096 neurons and the ReLU activation function by the classifier layer and fully linked layer. After the feature map has been rasterized into a vector, the CVM classifier (Figure 10.2) identifies the input feature to be computed and recognized by the neural network. The classifier replaces the convolutional network's output layer in the CVM model. The projected values and the original labels can then be compared to determine the categorization accuracy.

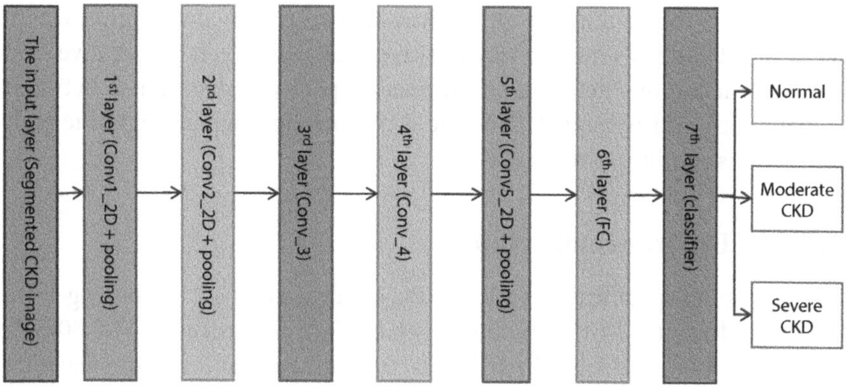

Figure 10.2 CVM layers.

10.4 Result Analysis

We take into account the most prevalent measures in the existing approaches. Numerous metrics, such as *F* measure and AUC, evaluate the effectiveness of DL models using precision, recall, and accuracy. We can assess the models with the aid of each metric. Accuracy sums explicitly how well the classification task was performed and counts how many instances of the input data were adequately predicted. Recall quantifies the proportion of CKD cases correctly recognized as such and had the condition. The number of people diagnosed with CKD who fall into this category is indicated by precision. The harmonic mean of precision and recall or *F* measure represents the prediction accuracy of a model:

$$\text{Accuracy} = \frac{\text{TN} + \text{TP}}{\text{TN} + \text{TP} + \text{FN} + \text{FP}} \tag{10.5}$$

$$\text{Precision} = \frac{\text{TP}}{\text{TP} + \text{FP}} \tag{10.6}$$

$$\text{Recall} = \frac{\text{TP}}{\text{TP} + \text{FN}} \tag{10.7}$$

$$F\text{-measure} = 2 * \frac{\text{Precision} * \text{recall}}{\text{Precision} + \text{recall}} \tag{10.8}$$

The following definitions apply to the abovementioned measures, where TP, TN, FP, and FN stand for true positive, true negative, false negative, and FP. AUC accurately determines a model's capacity to distinguish between people with and without CKD. The AUC metric's maximum value is 1, whereas its minimum value is 0.

10.4.1 Experimental Setup

The following specifications for the PC used to conduct the testing were met: Windows 10, 64-bit OS, Intel(R) Core(TM) i7 processor @ 2.80GHz processor. We used MATLAB 2020a to evaluate our machine-learning models. In the balanced dataset of 500 cases, performance was evaluated using fivefold cross-validation after applying SMOTE. Table 10.2 shows the ideal values for the DL model parameters we tested. The proposed model does not follow any validation. Here, we perform only training and testing with the samples with a ratio of 70: 30. The validation process consumes more time with huge data samples. Thereby, it is not performed over the proposed model.

10.4.2 Evaluation

We will focus on the classifiers' performance evaluation in this subsection. Specific metrics, including AUC, *F* measure, recall, accuracy, and precision, compare various ML approaches. Here, BayesNet and NB are taken into consideration from probabilistic models. Logistic model tree (LMT), J48, RF, RepTree, RT, rotation forest (RotF), and AdaBoost were used. Stochastic gradient descent (SGD), ANN, k-NN, LR, and models were also contrasted with the latter models. We also employed group learning techniques such as soft voting and stacking. We used the RotF, RF, and LR as fundamental classifiers for stacking and the LR as metaclassifiers. Based on the same base classifiers in the case of soft voting, the final prediction was arrived at by averaging the probabilities. The performance of following SMOTE and fivefold cross-validation, the classifiers, is further described in Table 10.2. The RotF model outperforms the opposition with an accuracy rating of 99.2%. These existing approaches are considered from the existing works. This work does not perform any execution of the existing models; however, the values are acquired from the existing study to make the comparison or evaluations.

Additionally, with 94%, we can observe that the suggested model performs exceptionally well by considering recall, precision, *F* measure, and AUC. The AUC of the RotF model, soft voting, and stacking techniques

Table 10.2 Model parameters.

Models	Parameters
BayesNet	Simple estimator AD tree: false Search: K2
NB	Kernel estimator: false Discretization: true
SVM	Eps: 0.001 Kernel type: linear Gamma = 0.0 Loss = 0.1
LR	Ridge = 10^{-8} Gradient descent = false
ANN	Learning rate = 0.3 Hidden layer = *a* Momentum = 0.2 Training time = 500
k-NN	$k = 1$ Algorithm = NN search with Euclidean
J48	Error pruning: false Instance data: false Raising: true
LMT	Probabilities: false Regression: true Instances: 15 AIC: false
RF	Maximal depth = −1 Minimal number = 2.0 Variance prop = 0.001
RT	Classifier = J48 No. of groups = false Filters = principal components
DT	Classifier = decision stump AIC = false Resampling = false

(*Continued*)

Table 10.2 Model parameters. (*Continued*)

Models	Parameters
RF	Epochs = 500 Epsilon = 0.001 Lambda = 10^{-4} Learning rate = 0.01 Loss function = hinge
AdaBoosting	Decision stump False False resampling
SGD	Epochs = 500 Epsilon = 0.001 Lambda = 10^{-8} Learning rate = 0.01 Loss function = cross-entropy
Stacking	Classifier = RF Meta = LR NumFolds = 10
Voting	Classifier = RF Combination rule = average probability
CVM	Epsilon = 0.001 Gamma = 0.0 Linear kernel Loss = 0.1

was 100%. The SVM (linear) model performed the least similarly across all criteria with a percentage of 94%. The reduction in the cumulative fraction of matrix diversity produced by the principal component analysis (PCA) feature transformation creates rotating matrices with few correlations, which is related to the unique accuracy of the rotation forest technique. It helps in enabling various mutually independent DTs compared to AdaBoostM1 and RFs. The results demonstrate that rotation forest offers more precise individual classifiers. Table 10.3 also contains identical risk factors and accuracy findings from published studies utilizing the dataset (features). Some existing work used NB, LR, and RF during fivefold cross-validation to reach accuracy rates of 93.90%, 94.76%, and 98.88%, respectively. Our suggested models demonstrated superior accuracy, which is followed by SMOTE-produced results of 98% NB, 97% LR, and

Table 10.3 Performance evaluation.

Models	Accuracy	Precision	Recall	*F* measure	AUC
BayesNet	98.4	98.4	98.4	98.4	99
NB	98.5	98.4	98.4	98.4	99.5
SVM	94.1	94	94	94	94
LR	97.4	97.4	97.4	97.4	98.2
ANN	96.8	96.8	96.8	96.8	99
k-NN	98.4	98.4	98.4	98.4	98.4
J48	97.8	97.8	97.8	97.8	99
LMT	97.4	97.5	97.5	97.4	97.4
RF	99.1	99.1	99.2	99.1	100
RT	97.4	97.4	97.5	97.4	99.1
DT	98.2	98.2	98.3	98.2	99.2
RF	98.9	98.9	98.9	98.9	99
AdaBoosting	97.2	97.2	97.2	97.8	97.2
SGD	97.4	97.5	97.4	97.4	99
Stacking	98.4	99	98.4	98.4	99.8
Voting	99	98.4	99	98.9	99.5
CVM	**99.4**	**99.5**	**99.4**	**99**	**100**

98% RF with 10-fold CV. DT, k-NN, and LR were utilized with accuracy rates of 97%, 71.25%, and 96.25%, respectively. The accuracy rates of the DT, k-NN, and LR models we presented were 97.4%, 98.4%, and 97.4%, respectively. k-NN gives a performance difference of 26% compared to the equivalent model. All other models have similar performance, and all of our proposed models exhibit higher accuracy percentages than similar study efforts (Figures 10.3–10.10).

The proposed model owes 99.4% accuracy, 99.5% precision, 99.4% recall, 99% *F* measure, and 100% AUC values, which are achieved for the proposed approach. In regard to the observation, it is noted that the proposed model yields a slightly higher result than other approaches such as

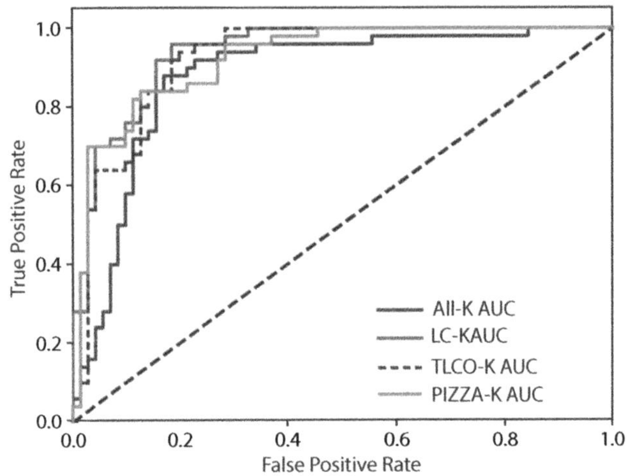

Figure 10.3 Samples training for normal renal function.

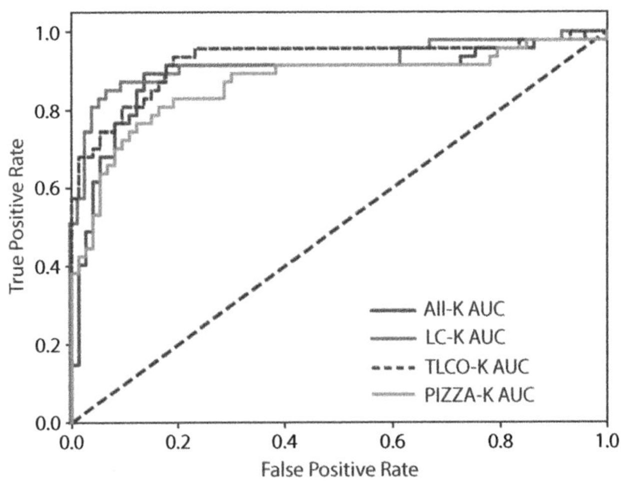

Figure 10.4 Samples training for moderate renal function.

voting, AdaBoosting, SGD, RF, DT, LMT, k-NN, ANN, and so on. These correspond to machine learning, which is the method of the proposed model that is effective on both small and big datasets. As such, it reduces problems of overfitting and underfitting. The values are placed over the local minima to give over global consequences.

Last but not least there are few limitations associated with the existing research. The current study therefore utilized a public dataset with the

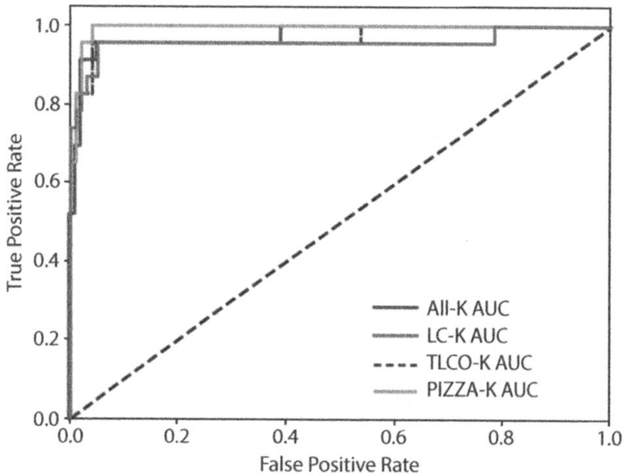

Figure 10.5 Samples training for severe renal function.

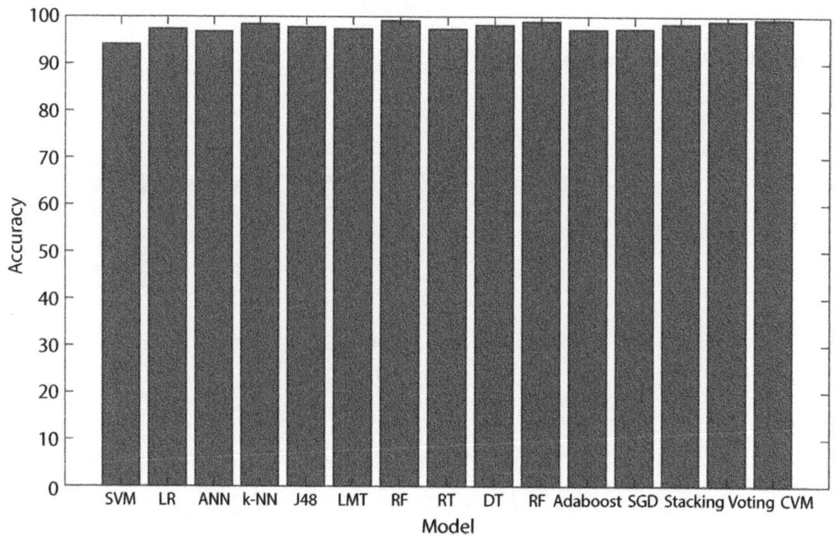

Figure 10.6 Accuracy comparison.

following characteristics. Additionally, we did not use data that a hospital could have provided us with different parameters that would enable us to qualitatively describe the participants' health. Also, derivatively, it might take a lot of time to gather such information, and collecting it might also present some practical problems as far as the protection of privacy

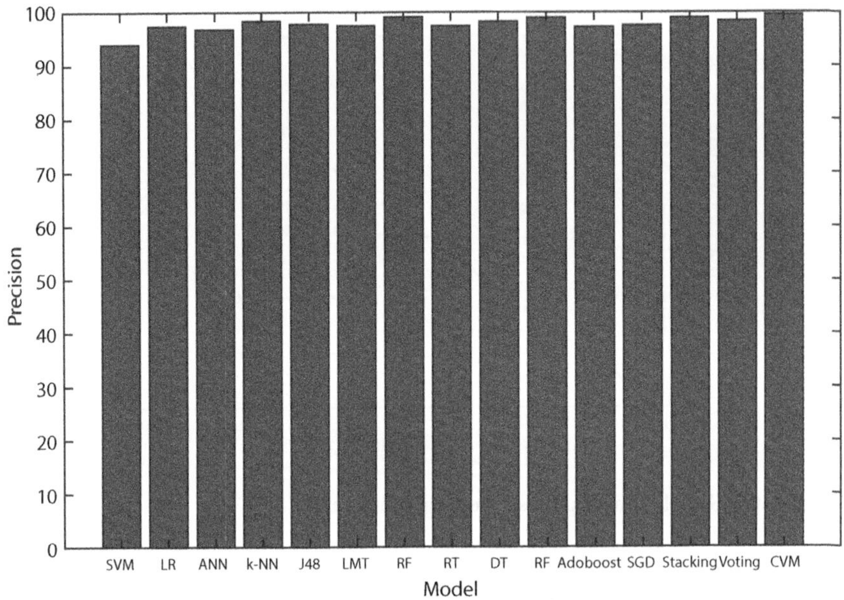

Figure 10.7 Precision comparison.

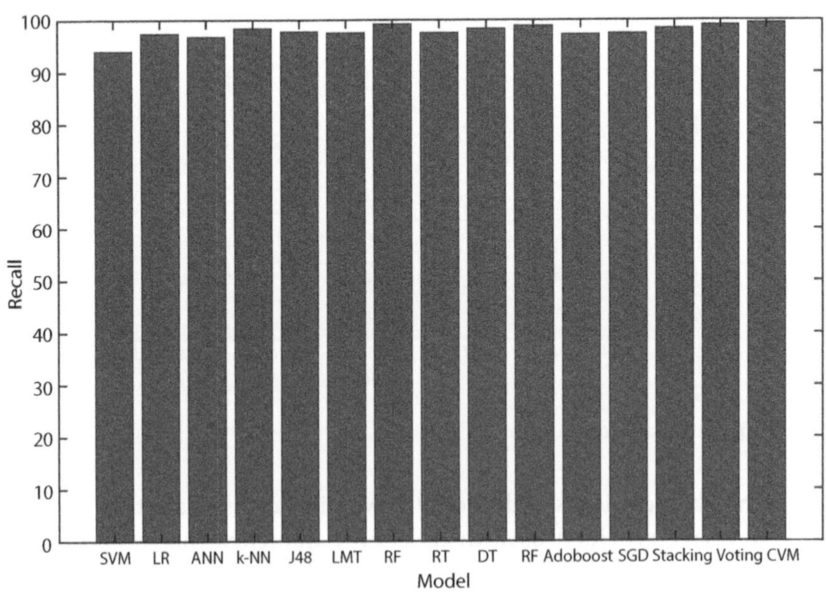

Figure 10.8 Recall comparison.

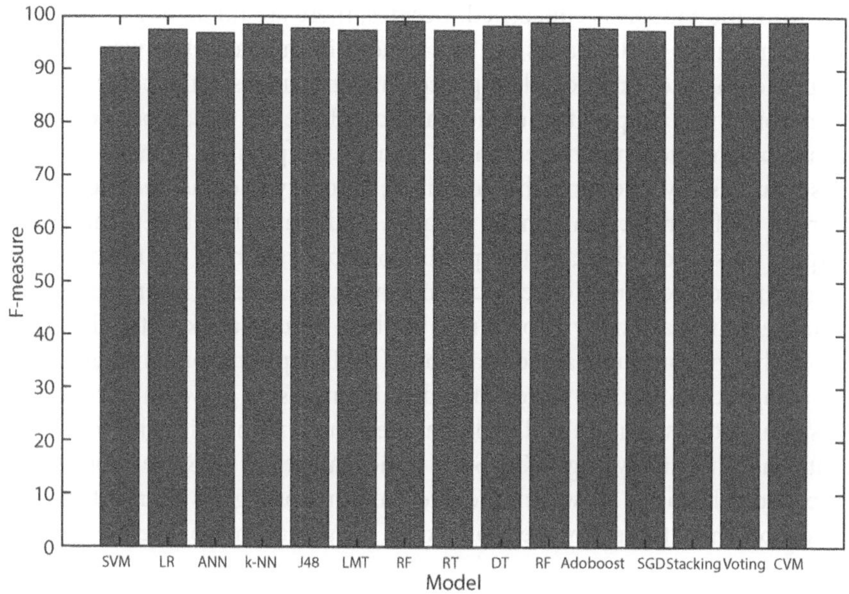

Figure 10.9 *F*-measure comparison.

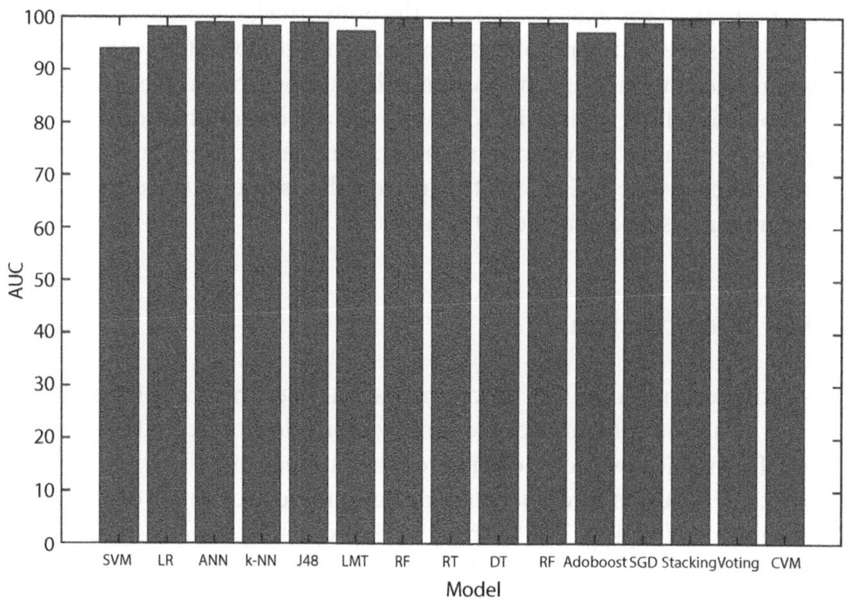

Figure 10.10 AUC comparison.

rights of individuals is concerned. Besides, there are no demographic data concerning the participant's age and gender in the dataset; it would allow approaching the statistical data processing and analysis in a correct manner from the standpoint of demographics. However, as can be seen from many biochemical parameters in the dataset, it is possible to make rational assessments. By updating the current technology such as deep learning, earlier CKD prediction can be created, and a medical-based industrial expert tries to develop a better prediction application to the features and segmentation region. Hence, a certain moderate level of improvement in the prediction accuracy is obtained by their industrial experts. There are a number of computer-aided diagnosis (CAD) applications that use deep learning techniques. On the one hand, it distinguishes between normal and disease patterns, benign and malignant lesions, and low-risk and high-risk patterns when analyzing CKD. Such basic features as GFR are supplied by the medical experts for whom the internal functioning has been automated to enable them to deploy the model over the actual environment.

10.4.3 Complexity and Overhead Measure

The major research complexity is that the entire vascular system imaging is an observational examination. It is not as easy to operate on the internal body parts as on the external parts of the body. The large-scale renal analysis indicates overfitting problems, which are not complicated with the proposed model. But in the scenario where the numbers of samples are higher, the model is a little variant in achieving the aforementioned outcomes. It appears in the internal regions' segmentation; nevertheless, it results in a nominal achievement. It is for this reason that some of the current outcome indicators do not achieve this outcome.

10.5 Conclusion

A steady decline in kidney function characterizes the chronic renal disease. It is a quiet illness because most victims do not exhibit any symptoms. The medical world is looking to machine learning theory to develop a workable solution because early detection and treatment of CKD are incredibly challenging. The current work proposes a supervised learning methodology called HS-CVM that predominantly uses models based on ensemble learning, trees, and probability to build accurate models for forecasting the possibility of getting CKD. Additionally, k-NN, ANN, SGD, LR, and SVM were evaluated and compared. The proposed model, with the subject of the obtained data, surpassed the competition with values for precision, recall, F1 measure, and accuracy of 99.2% and an AUC of 100%. Finally, in terms of accuracy, our suggested models fared better than the earlier research that used the same dataset. In our forthcoming work, we plan to concentrate on CNN and long short-term memory–based deep-learning approaches and investigate any potential performance improvements these models might offer. We used two alternative methods to exploit these models' potential fully. Before providing the limited dataset to the ML models, the former would adopt a data augmentation approach such as the SVR-based additive input doubling technique to improve it. In the latter, we will begin by testing our ideas on a vast, naturally occurring dataset.

AI disclosure statement: The author acknowledges the use of AI-based tools for minor language editing or grammatical correction. However, all intellectual contributions, analyses, and conclusions presented in this chapter are entirely the author's own.

References

1. Vásquez-Morales, G.R., Martinez-Monterrubio, S.M., Moreno-Ger, P., Recio-Garcia, J.A., Explainable Prediction of Chronic Renal Disease in the Colombian Population Using Neural Networks and Case-Based Reasoning. *IEEE Access*, 7, 152900–152910, 2019.
2. Senan, E.M., Al-Adhaileh, M.H., Alsaade, F.W., Aldhyani, T.H., Alqarni, A.A., Alsharif, N., Uddin, M.I., Alahmadi, A.H., Jadhav, M.E., Alzahrani, M.Y., Diagnosis of chronic kidney disease using effective classification algorithms and recursive feature elimination techniques. *J. Healthcare Eng.*, 2021, 1, 1004767, 2021.
3. De Almeida, K.L., Kidney Failure Detection Using Machine Learning Techniques. *8th International Workshop on Advances in ICT Infrastructures and Services*, 2020.
4. Ramana, B.V., Performance Comparison of Classification Algorithms on Medical Datasets. *IEEE 9th Annual Computing and Communication Workshop and Conference (CCWC)*, 2019, 10.1109/CCWC.2019.8666497.
5. DilliArasu, S., Review of chronic kidney disease based on Data Mining techniques. *Int. J. Appl. Eng. Res.*, 12, 23, 13498–13505, 2019.
6. Vanitha, N. and Sendhuraa, Chronic kidney disease detection using machine learning techniques. *IAR J. Med. Sci.*, 2, 2, 127–133, 2021.

7. Wang, Z., Machine Learning-Based Prediction System for Chronic Kidney Disease Using Associative Classification Technique. *Int. J. Eng. Technol.*, 7, 436, 1161–1167, 2018.
8. Tekale, S., Shingavi, P., Wandhekar, S., Chatorikar, A., Prediction of chronic kidney disease using machine Learning. *Int. J. Adv. Res. Comput. Commun. Eng.*, 7, 10, 92–96, 2018.
9. Kohli, P.S. and Arora, S., Application of Machine Learning in Disease Prediction. *4th International Conference on Computing Communication and Automation (ICCCA)*, pp. 1–4, 2018.
10. Deepika, B., Rao, V.K.R., Rampure, D.N., Prajwal, P., Gowda, D.G., Early prediction of chronic kidney disease using machine learning techniques. *Am. J. Comput. Sci. Eng. Surv.*, 8, 2, 7, 2020.
11. Shanthi, S., Nidhya, R., Perumal, U., Kumar, M., An Efficient IoT Framework for Patient Monitoring and Predicting Heart Disease Based on Machine Learning Algorithms, in: *Tele-Healthcare*, R. Nidhya, M. Kumar, S. Balamurugan (Eds.), 2022.
12. Ng, D.K. and Schwartz, G.J., Relationships of measured iohexol GFR and estimated GFR with CKD-related biomarkers in children and adolescents. *Am. J. Kidney Dis.*, 70, 3, 397–405, 2017.
13. Sherubha, Graph-Based Event Measurement for Analyzing Distributed Anomalies in Sensor Networks. *Sådhanå(Springer)*, 45, 212, 2020.
14. Sherubha, An Efficient Network Threat Detection and Classification Method using ANP-MVPS Algorithm in Wireless Sensor Networks. *Int. J. Innov. Technol. Explor. Eng. (IJITEE)*, 8, 11, 2278–3075, 2019.
15. Sherubha, P. and Mohanasundaram, N., An Efficient Intrusion Detection and Authentication Mechanism for Detecting Clone Attack in Wireless Sensor Networks. *J. Adv. Res. Dyn. Control Syst. (JARDCS)*, 11, 5, 55–68, 2019.
16. Bhoomika, B.K., Kanmani, K., Smilarubavathy, G., Early Detection of Pancreatic Cancer using Machine Learning Algorithm, in: *2024 5th International Conference on Mobile Computing and Sustainable Informatics (ICMCSI)*, 2024, January, IEEE, pp. 202–205.
17. Sara, S.B.V.J. and Kalaiselvi, K., Ant colony optimization (ACO) based feature selection and extreme learning machine (ELM) for chronic kidney disease detection. *Int. J. Adv. Stud. Sci. Res. (IJASSR)*, 4, 1, 2019.
18. Thakur, N. and Han, C.Y., A study of fall detection in assisted living: Identifying and improving the optimal machine learning method. *J. Sens. Actuator Netw.*, *10*, 39, 2021.
19. Mahadevan, V., Anatomy of the kidney and ureter. *Surgery*, *37*, 359–364, 2019.
20. Abdel-Kader, K., Symptoms with or because of Kidney Failure? *Clin. J. Am. Soc. Nephrol.*, *17*, 475–477, 2022.
21. Wang, Chronic kidney disease: Biomarker diagnosis to therapeutic targets. *Clin. Chim. Acta*, *499*, 54–63, 2019.
22. Dritsas, Machine Learning Methods for Hypercholesterolemia Long-Term Risk Prediction. *Sensors*, *22*, 5365, 2022.

23. Dritsas, E., Trigka, "Stroke Risk Prediction with Machine Learning Techniques". *Sensors*, *22*, 4670, 2022.
24. Zhang, The comparison of LightGBM and XGBoost coupling factor analysis and prediagnosis of acute liver failure. *IEEE Access*, *8*, 220990–221003, 2020.
25. Saba, T., Recent advancement in cancer detection using machine learning: Systematic survey of decades, comparisons and challenges. *J. Infect. Public Health*, *13*, 1274–1289, 2020.
26. Xiao, J. and Ding, R., Comparison and development of machine learning tools in predicting chronic kidney disease progression. *J. Transl. Med.*, *17*, 119, 2019.
27. Chittora, Prediction of chronic kidney disease-a machine learning perspective. *IEEE Access*, *9*, 17312–17334, 2021.
28. Izonin, Predictive modelling based on small data in clinical medicine: RBF-based additive input-doubling method. *Math. Biosci. Eng*, *18*, 2599–2613, 2021.
29. Shaikh, N., Shope, M.F., Kurs-Lasky, M., Urine specific gravity and the accuracy of urinalysis. *Pediatrics*, *144*, 5, 2019.
30. Zelnick, Continuous glucose monitoring and use of alternative markers to assess glycemia in chronic kidney disease. *Diabetes Care*, *43*, 2379–2387, 2020.
31. Qiang, Y., Mechanical fatigue of human red blood cells. *Proc. Natl. Acad. Sci. U.S.A.*, *116*, 19828–19834, 2019.
32. Zhang, L., Trends in chronic kidney disease in China. *N. Engl. J. Med.*, 375, 905–906, 2016.
33. Saran, US Renal Data System 2019 Annual Data Report: Epidemiology of kidney disease in the United States. *Am. J. Kidney Dis.*, 75, A6–A7, 2020.
34. Tangri, A dynamic predictive model for progression of CKD. *Am. J. Kidney Dis.*, 69, 514–520, 2017, https://doi.org/10.1053/j. ajkd.2016.07.030.
35. Major, R.W., Shepherd, D., Medcalf, J.F., Xu, G., Gray, L.J., Brunskill, N.J., The Kidney Failure Risk Equation for predicting end-stage renal disease in UK primary care: An external validation and clinical impact projection cohort study. *PLoS Med.*, 16, 11, e1002955, 2019.
36. Mortazavi, B.J., *et al.*, Analysis of machine learning techniques for heart failure readmissions. *Circ. Cardiovasc. Qual. Outcomes*, 9, 629–640, 2016.
37. Weng, Can machine learning improve cardiovascular risk prediction using routine clinical data? *PLoS One*, 12, e0174944, 2017.
38. Yu, K., Artificial intelligence in healthcare. *Nat. Biomed. Eng.*, 2, 719–731, 2018.
39. Rajkumar, Scalable and accurate deep learning with electronic health records. *NPJ Digit. Med.*, 1, 18, 2018, https://doi.org/10.1038/s41746-018-0029-1.
40. Karadaghy, O.A., Shew, M., New, J., Bur, A.M., Development and assessment of a machine learning model to help predict survival among patients with oral squamous cell carcinoma. *JAMA Otolaryngol. Head Neck Surg.*, 145, 1115–1120, 2019, https://doi.org/10.1001/jamaoto.2019.0981.

41. Zhang, Z., Missing data imputation: Focusing on single imputation. *Ann. Transl. Med.*, 4, 9, 2016, https://doi.org/10.3978/j.issn.2305-5839.2015.12.38.
42. Pal, S., Prediction for chronic kidney disease by categorical and non_categorical attributes using different machine learning algorithms. *Multimed. Tools Appl.*, 82, 41253–41266, 2023, https://doi.org/10.1007/s11042-023-15188-1.
43. Dong, Z., Wang, Q., Ke, Y., Zhang, W., Hong, Q., Liu, C., Chen, X., Prediction of 3-year risk of diabetic kidney disease using machine learning based on electronic medical records. *J. Transl. Med.*, 20, 1, 1–10, 2022.
44. Rongyao, H.U., *et al.*, Multi-task multi-modality SVM for early COVID-19 diagnosis using chest CT data. *Inf. Process. Manage.*, 59, 1, 102782, 2022.
45. Ilyas, H., Ali, S., Ponum, M., Hasan, O., Mahmood, M.T., Iftikhar, M., Malik, M.H., Chronic kidney disease diagnosis using decision tree algorithms. *BMC Nephrol.*, 22, 1, 1–11, 2021.
46. Singh, P.D., Kaur, R., Dhiman, G., Bojja, G.R., BOSS: A new QoS aware blockchain assisted framework for secure and smart healthcare as a service. *Expert Syst.*, 40, 4, e12838, 2023.

11

Early Detection and Automatic Diagnosis of Autism Spectrum Disorder Using Transformer Model

S.M. Keerthana[1*], Sasikala[2], K. Subha[3] and G. Smilarubavathy[1]

[1]St. Joseph's Institute of Technology, Chennai, India
[2]Computer Science and Engineering, SRM Institute of Science and Technology, Tiruchirapalli, India
[3]Information Technology, St.Joseph's College of Engineering, Chennai, India

Abstract

The ever-growing field of artificial intelligence (AI) has revolutionized numerous industries, but its impact on healthcare has been more cautious due to the ethical considerations surrounding life-or-death decisions. Although many models have been developed to detect the disease, early detection of autism is still a challenging task. It starts even before the age of 3 years and goes unnoticed until their life cycle. At early stage, they start learning and living a healthy lifestyle where it gets degrades at a point in time. However, transformer models offer a promising avenue for assisting in the automation of patient diagnosis. This chapter explores the potential of transfer learning to detect autism using brain images and then transformers to automatically diagnose autism. It analyzes vast amounts of medical data, including patient symptoms, medical history, and electronic health records. By leveraging these data, large language models (LLMs) can be trained to identify patterns and correlations associated with neurological diseases and diagnose autism. This could significantly improve diagnostic accuracy and efficiency, particularly in settings where access to experienced medical professionals might be limited. The chapter acknowledges the limitations of current AI technology. LLMs cannot definitively diagnose diseases on their own. However, they can act as intelligent assistants, flagging potential diagnoses and providing clinicians with relevant medical

**Corresponding author*: keerthanasmk@gmail.com

R. Nidhya, D. Pavithra, S. Balamurugan, A. Dinesh Kumar and Sheng-Lung Peng (eds.) Medical Metaverse for Digital Healthcare: Technologies, Applications, and Challenges, (229–246) © 2026 Scrivener Publishing LLC

information. This can streamline the diagnostic process, allowing healthcare professionals to focus on patient interaction and complex medical cases.

***Keywords*:** Autism spectrum disorder (ASD), early detection, automatic diagnosis, vision transformer (ViT), large language models (LLMs), electronic health records (EHRs), transfer learning, brain MRI

11.1 Introduction

The rise of artificial intelligence (AI) has completely changed how we diagnose and treat diseases in healthcare. Large language models (LLMs), like GPT-4 (generative pretrained transformer 4), are a particularly exciting type of AI with great potential to automate diagnosis [1]. These models can handle and analyze massive amounts of text, making them perfect for understanding complex medical information and suggesting accurate diagnoses. Autism spectrum disorder (ASD) is a complex developmental condition that involves persistent challenges in social interaction, speech and nonverbal communication, and restricted/repetitive behaviors or interests. Individuals with ASD can have a wide range of symptoms, skills, and levels of disability that affect how they function in school, work, and other areas of life. The term "spectrum" in ASD refers to the wide range of symptoms, skills, and levels of impairment that people with ASD can have. Vision transformers (ViTs) could be trained to recognize facial expressions and detect emotions, which could be particularly useful for individuals with ASD who may struggle with understanding nonverbal cues and social interactions. In healthcare, LLMs could be game changers for diagnosing diseases. They can provide real-time support for doctors' decisions, improve the accuracy of diagnoses, and make workflows in clinics run smoother. Because they understand and create human-like text, LLMs can help doctors interpret patient histories, electronic health records (EHRs), and medical research. This is especially helpful for diagnosing conditions that require putting together a lot of data and using experienced medical judgment. This chapter will delve into how LLMs can be used to automatically diagnose diseases. We will explore the basics of LLMs, how they are developed, and how they can be trained and used in healthcare settings. By looking at current research and real-world examples, we will highlight both the successes and challenges of using LLMs in clinics. Here is a breakdown of the specific areas we will focus on: how LLMs improve diagnostic accuracy, how they work with other AI tools like natural language processing (NLP) and computer vision, and how they can lessen the mental strain on healthcare providers. We will also address critical issues such as data privacy, understanding how the models work, and the need for strong testing and regulations to make sure LLMs are used safely and effectively in healthcare.

11.2 Background Information

The core features of ASD are that children will not be able to communicate properly and the social interaction is less or they make it complex, as well as restricted, repetitive patterns of behavior, interests, or activities. These symptoms can manifest in various ways, such as difficulty with eye contact, problems with understanding and responding to social cues, repetitive use of language or movements, and intense interests in specific topics [2]. When this autism is detected early in children, it will be of great help to engage them in a different or unique educational system that offers special care to them. There are some medical challenges in automatic detection and diagnosing the autism.

Autism detection challenges

Variability in symptoms: ASD is typified by a broad spectrum of symptoms that differ significantly in intensity and manifestation among many children. Whereas some children may exhibit early, clear symptoms, others may have more subdued symptoms that are more difficult to identify. Symptoms of ASD may become more apparent at different ages. Some children may show signs very early in life, whereas others may not exhibit clear signs until they are expected to engage in more complex social interactions, such as during the preschool years. The progression of symptoms can also vary, with some children improving in certain areas over time, whereas others may experience more persistent challenges.

Overlap with typical development: Children who are developing normally may also exhibit some of the early indicators of ASD, such as social or linguistic deficits. It might be challenging to distinguish between usual developmental variances and early indications of ASD. Many children with ASD also have co-occurring conditions such as ADHD, anxiety disorders, or sleep disturbances.

Absence of brain patterns: In contrast to many other medical disorders, ASD lacks a reliable brain marker or genetic test that can provide an accurate diagnosis. Developmental evaluations and behavioral observations are the main sources of diagnosis.

Autism diagnosing challenge

- Severity spectrum: ASD symptoms can range widely in intensity, giving rise to a diverse range of symptoms. Whereas some people may experience moderate symptoms that are readily handled, others may experience more severe symptoms that have a major influence on their capacity to operate. ASD and other developmental diseases might have symptoms that are similar to each other. Examples of these conditions include learning impairments, attention-deficit/hyperactivity disorder (ADHD), and speech and language disorders. Determining the accurate diagnosis may become challenging as a result.
- Lack of biomarkers: Developmental evaluations and behavioral observations are used to diagnose ASD because there are currently no conclusive biological markers or genetic tests for the disorder. The absence of specific biological indicators can lead to misdiagnosis or failure to recognize co-occurring conditions that may require separate attention, such as epilepsy, ADHD, or genetic syndromes that can present with autistic features. If biomarkers are easily available, then it will be useful in identifying subtypes of ASD, understanding the underlying biology, and monitoring the effectiveness of interventions.
- Lack of experienced clinicians: In the absence of skilled medical professionals, there is an increased chance of incorrect or delayed diagnosis where there is a lack of early help or inappropriate intervention [3]. Getting the right diagnostic services and interventions might be difficult for families if they have to travel far or wait a long time to see a skilled physician.

11.3 Related Work

(i) Self-diagnosis
The journey to a diagnosis often begins with a general practitioner. Patients experiencing concerning symptoms typically visit this doctor for an initial evaluation. This initial visit aims to establish a preliminary diagnosis. If necessary, the patient may be referred to a specialist for further consultation. There are two main types of symptoms doctors consider: explicit and implicit. Explicit symptoms are those directly reported by the patient, whereas implicit symptoms are those inferred through conversations between the patient and healthcare professional. The development of AI models at present has made it possible to identify and classify neurodiseases

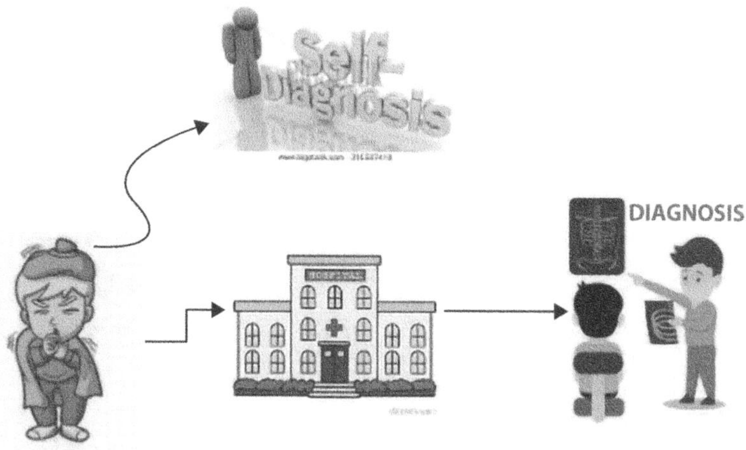

Figure 11.1 Traditional method of medical diagnosis.

(NDs) using automatic gait analysis, creating a new avenue for the quicker and more affordable diagnosis of NDs [4]. In this work, we present an extensive overview of the latest developments in AI approaches based on machine learning and deep learning, as they relate to the diagnosis of five common NDs using gait analysis. In addition to presenting a comprehensive taxonomy of the available gait data and AI models, we give an overview of the procedure for diagnosing NDs with AI assistance. Figure 10.1 illustrates the traditional method of medical diagnosis, where patients undergo preliminary consultation followed by specialist evaluation.

When it comes to automatic diagnosis, healthcare agents are made to engage with patients, asking questions regarding the existence of symptoms and developing diagnoses based on these patient-reported discomforts, also known as complaints. These AI-driven automatic diagnostic systems have the potential to alleviate the problems associated with a lack of medical resources, especially in areas with low economic status. They are expected to play a significant role in basic healthcare [5]. The usual process begins with an initial assessment by a general practitioner when a patient appears with symptoms that require medical assistance. To make a preliminary diagnosis is the goal of this basic assessment. The patient is then often referred by the general practitioner to a specialist who is knowledgeable in the appropriate medical field for further consultation and therapy.

(ii) Machine learning methods for various medical diagnoses

In Figure 11.2, regardless of type, both implicit and explicit symptoms require translation from natural language descriptions into standardized

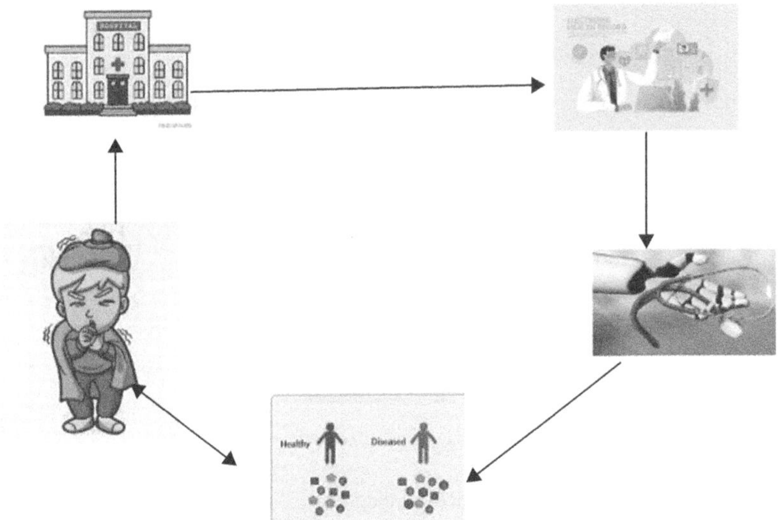

Figure 11.2 Machine learning techniques to diagnose unhealthy condition.

medical terminology. In order to comprehensively explore the potential of machine learning and deep learning methodologies for achieving early detection of Alzheimer disease (AD), which delves into the utilization of diverse feature extraction schemes, this approach aims to capitalize on the complementary strengths of data extracted from various multimodal neuroimaging sources. Pinpointing AD from magnetic resonance imaging (MRI) scans can be tricky, especially when trying to differentiate between the effects of normal aging and the early stages of AD. This novel approach tackles this challenge by utilizing pretrained convolutional neural networks (CNNs) to achieve greater accuracy in identifying the severity of AD, a critical factor for early diagnosis.

To compensate for limitations in data availability, the method incorporates sophisticated image processing techniques before training the CNNs. By comparing its performance against well-established CNN architectures such as VGG16 and ResNet50 on publicly available AD datasets from Kaggle, the study demonstrates the effectiveness of this approach across various disease stages. This paves the way for significant advancements in the classification of AD. At the heart of this approach lies a powerful module that captures the intricate connections between different brain regions.

1. An adaptive graph transformer block: This block intelligently builds a network of connections, or "graph," based on the extracted features from the brain scans.

2. A graph convolution network block: This block acts like a filter, analyzing and refining the information within the constructed graph.
3. A feature map reconstruction block: This block translates the refined graph information back into a format that can be seamlessly integrated with the rest of the analysis. It is crucial to talk about potential biases, overfitting problems, and scalability concerns in clinical contexts in order to improve machine learning models and successfully direct future research efforts. The generalization of models can be severely impacted by biases, such as sample selection bias or data imbalance, which may result in skewed outcomes or incorrect predictions. Researchers may make sure that their models are representative of a range of populations and relevant in a wider range of scenarios by recognizing and correcting these biases. Another major issue that researchers have to deal with is overfitting, which happens when a model learns noise in the data instead of the underlying patterns and performs poorly when applied to fresh data.

This work explores a deep learning pipeline combining a pretrained CNN such as AlexNet with a long short-term memory network for robust classification of AD from MRI scans. Recognizing the challenge of limited training data, the approach leverages a generative adversarial network (GAN) to artificially generate additional MRIs. This data augmentation strategy combats overfitting, a common pitfall in deep learning with scarce data. The effectiveness of the proposed model is validated on the ADNI dataset, showcasing its ability to classify AD in two-dimensional MRI scans. This multistage approach exemplifies the cutting-edge integration of transfer learning, recurrent neural networks, and GANs to address data scarcity and achieve improved AD classification performance [6].

(iii) Generative AI in healthcare

As shown in Figure 11.3, there is a profound change taking place in the field of medical diagnostics. Generative AI has great potential to transform healthcare because of its capacity to evaluate photos and provide relevant text summaries [7]. However, there are profound ethical, cultural, and legal issues hiding beneath the surface of this technical marvel that need close examination.

Most paper sets out to critically investigate this revolutionary technology. We explore the moral issues that support its use in text analysis and

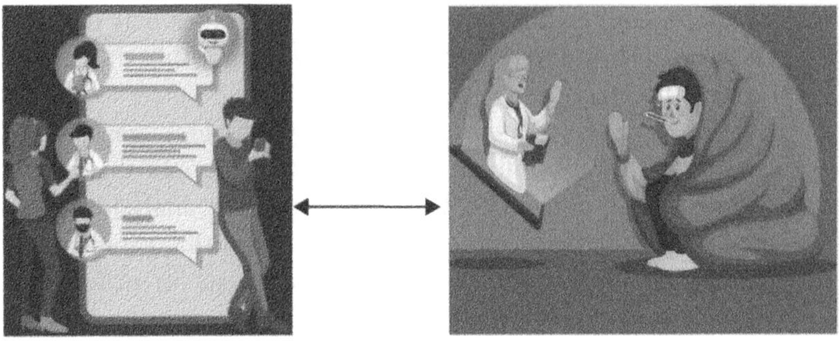

Figure 11.3 Generative AI to diagnosis patient using chatbot.

medical imaging, looking at the fine line that must be drawn between data privacy, informed permission, and accuracy. We examine the issues of accountability and liability in the context of AI-driven diagnostics as we traverse the unexplored legal territory. Lastly, we apply a critical lens to the intricate details of the algorithm, highlighting issues with data biases, model constraints, and the requirement for automatic diagnosis.

Agent-driven multispecialist consultation, imagining a system that can automatically analyze a patient's medical data (such as symptoms and test results), generate condition-specific insights using virtual specialists, and consolidate them into a comprehensive diagnosis report, thereby simulating a real-world multi-doctor consultation. This system would use different "agents," such as virtual specialists, each trained to identify specific conditions. Finally, the system would combine the insights from these agents, mimicking how multiple real doctors might consult on a case. This would help improve the accuracy and efficiency of medical diagnoses.

(iv) LLMs for automatic diagnosis

NLP techniques have been instrumental in efficiently processing these clinical notes and narratives, particularly within EHRs. However, a key limitation of NLP lies in its ability to grasp the intricacies and subtle nuances of medical language. Healthcare facilities with restricted computing capabilities have a major obstacle when implementing big parameter LLMs. For hospitals or other medical facilities with limited resources, models with 12 billion parameters, such as PMC LLM Meta AI (LLaMA) 13B and Medalpaca 13B, or 70 billion parameters, such as Llama3-OpenBioLLM-70B3 and ClinicalCamel-70B, present significant computational challenges. These models also require a significant amount of computing power and infrastructure to train and deploy efficiently. For preparing the LLM in the Mistral manner in advance by using 2,676,642 cancer clinical notes and

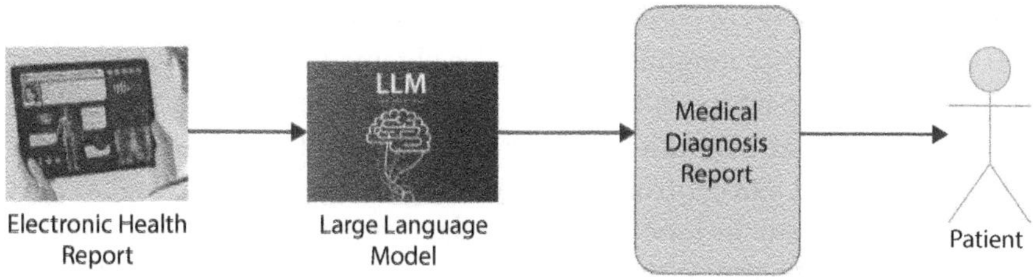

Figure 11.4 LLM generates report and assists in automatic diagnosis.

515,524 pathology reports from the University of Minnesota Clinical Data Repository, we pretrain the Mistral 7B. Optimizing the LLM using a niche dataset, three datasets with an emphasis on phenotypic extraction, diagnosis, and treatment plan development were put out by us. After that, we used instruction learning to fine-tune CancerLLM for the three tasks listed before. We use Exact Match to compare CancerLLM's generation capacity to that of other medical LLMs as shown in Figure 11.4.

11.4 Methodology

(i) Data collection
Most of the machine learning and deep learning models get training from the dataset available from Kaggle, Google, and other websites. There are no specific images or dataset for autism detection or diagnosis; most of the data repositories have only brain image for cancer and NDs. We have collected data from International Neuroimaging Data-Sharing Initiative website, which contains Autism Brain Imaging Data. In this chapter, we have considered ABIDE I and ABIDE II data, which share anatomical and phenotypic datasets as well as previously gathered resting-state functional MRI (R-fMRI) with the scientific community. One thousand one hundred twelve datasets were produced as a result of this endeavor, 539 of which came from people with ASD and 573 from normal controls (aged 7–64 years; median of 14.7 years across groups). August 2012 saw the release of this aggregate. Since its founding, the feasibility of combining structural MRI (s-MRI) and R-fMRI data from different sites has been shown [8]; the rate at which these data are used, as well as the papers that follow (see Manuscripts), has demonstrated their value in capturing both the overall brain and specific regional features of the brain connectome in autism.

In an effort to advance research on the brain connectome in ASD, ABIDE II was founded. Over a thousand more datasets with better phenotypic characterization have been combined by ABIDE II to date, especially when it comes to assessments of core ASD and related symptoms. Furthermore, two sets of data comprise longitudinal samples obtained from 38 individuals at two different time intervals (4–5 years apart). Nineteen sites-9 new members and 10 charter institutions—have contributed 1114 datasets from 521 ASD patients and 593 control participants (age range = 5–64 years) as part of ABIDE II to date. In June 2016, these data were made publicly available to the scientific community. The 1000 Functional Connectomes Project/ International Neuroimaging Data-sharing Initiative standards and Health Insurance Portability and Accountability Act regulations mandate that all datasets be anonymous and devoid of any protected health information.

(ii) Autism detection through transfer learning

To detect autism at the early stage and make the children live a normal and better life like other people, many machine learning models with support vector machine, decision tree, and naive Bayes classifiers have been implemented using central processing unit (CPU). Due to massive amount of data, it becomes difficult for the processor to handle complex data, and the run time is much longer than graphics processing unit (GPU). From machine learning techniques, shift has been take toward neural network technologies that can accurately predict the ASD and also diagnose the patient when the professional or clinical expert is not present. A majority of researchers use s-MRI information from the ABIDE to determine ASD using an algorithm that utilizes machine learning.

For example, to extract connection features between each pair of regions of interest from the s-MRI, most models build a distinct brain network. We then choose the top 3000 connectivity features for ASD classification using a deep learning neural network classification system. In order to separate ASD from typical control, a dense model is created with four dense blocks to extract deep features from the s-MRI. These features are then combined with morphometric handcrafted features, such as volume and surface features of different brain parcellations, and fed into a gender-specific linear discriminant classifier. Gray matter volume map as shown in Table 11.1 and individual-level morphological covariance brain network of each

Table 11.1 Autism brain imaging data exchange.

Type	Age of samples	Assessment procedure	% of ASD identified
ABIDE I	5–17 years	Scanning, IQ test	92%
ABIDE II	18–64 years	Handedness, full-scale IQ	87%

subject's s-MRI are used as input for the ResNet-based classifier for ASD classification.

Models such as VGG16 as shown in Figure 11.5, ResNet, and ViT are pretrained on large image datasets such as ImageNet [9]. These models learn to recognize general patterns and features that can be fine-tuned for

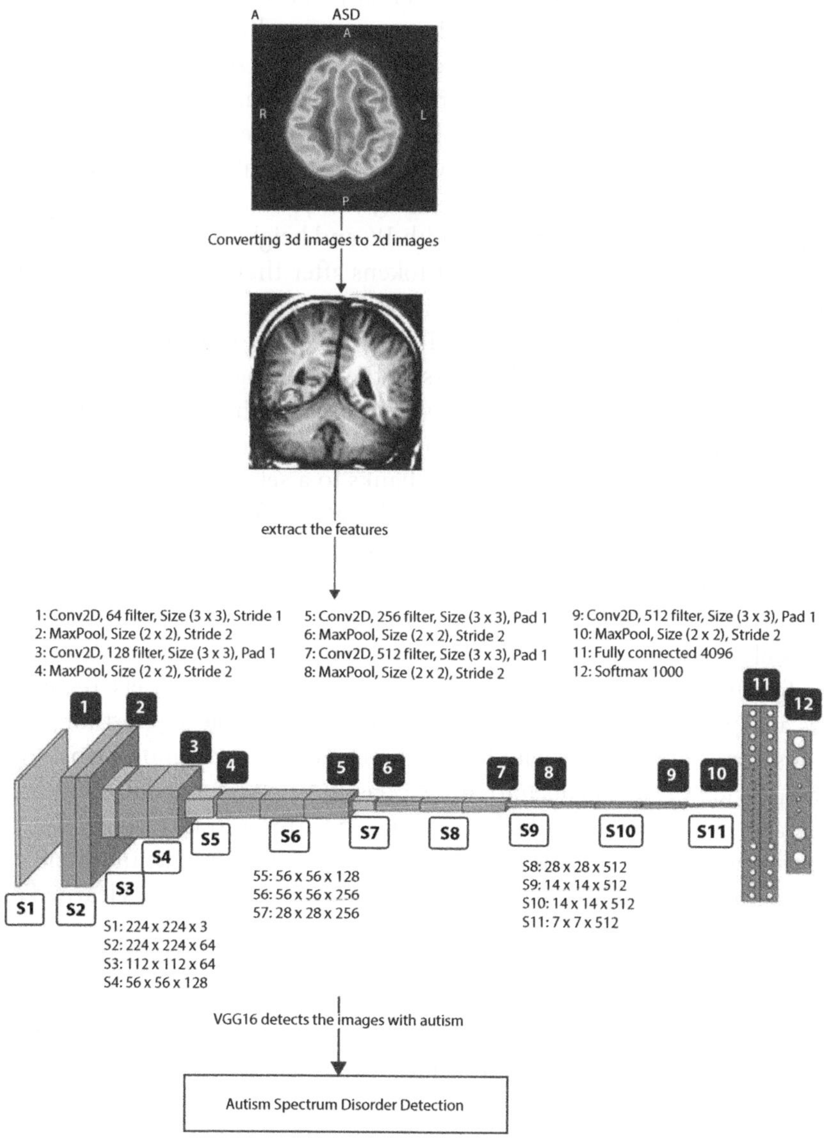

Figure 11.5 Transfer learning using VGG16.

specific tasks such as ASD detection using MRI scans. The detected MRI images are then given to ViT, which is the next part of the process to automatically diagnose the autism.

(iii) Autism diagnosis through ViTs
Transformer models have shown immense development in image detection and segmentation [10]. Although many transformer models are available, ViT has shown great result in accuracy and area under the curve. Token creation from the input picture is the first stage in the ViT process. Transformers work with a series of tokens, which are often words in a phrase in NLP. It is less obvious how to divide the input into tokens for computer vision. ViT takes a picture and turns it into tokens, where each token is a localized portion of the image, or patch. They explain how to resize a picture with channels C, width W, and height H into N tokens with patch size; to modify the length of tokens after they have been extracted from an image, a linear projection is frequently used. This is applied as a linear layer that may be learned. The term "latent dimension," "channel dimension," or "token length" refers to the new length of the tokens. The tokens are no longer recognizable as patches from the original image after the projection. ViT is able to focus on various areas of a picture and recognize essential aspects for diagnosis, thanks to a self-attention mechanism. This system aids in identifying minute deviations from normal brain anatomy that may be signs of autism. High accuracy has been shown by ViTs in a number of picture categorization tasks.

This corresponds to a more accurate and consistent identification of possible markers in brain MRI pictures when it comes to autism detection. By fine-tuning pretrained ViT models on ASD-specific datasets, researchers achieve high diagnostic accuracy, providing reliable support for clinicians, especially in areas with limited access to expert diagnosticians. ViTs can provide fresh insights into picture classification issues related to learning and classifying brain biomarkers in ASD. Brain transformers can be very promising in diagnosing ASD because they incorporate the attention mechanism, treat MRI modalities as sequence prediction tasks learned on brain disease classification issues, and are refined on ASD datasets. Data analysis is significantly hampered by the complexity and amount of EHR data as shown in Figure 11.6, particularly when working with unstructured data such as clinical notes. Because of this, human annotation and interpretation are laborious and unfeasible. The automated nature of ViT-based systems integrates seamlessly into clinical workflows, aiding early detection and diagnosis, which is crucial for timely intervention and improved outcomes for individuals with ASD. Both encoder and decoder part is

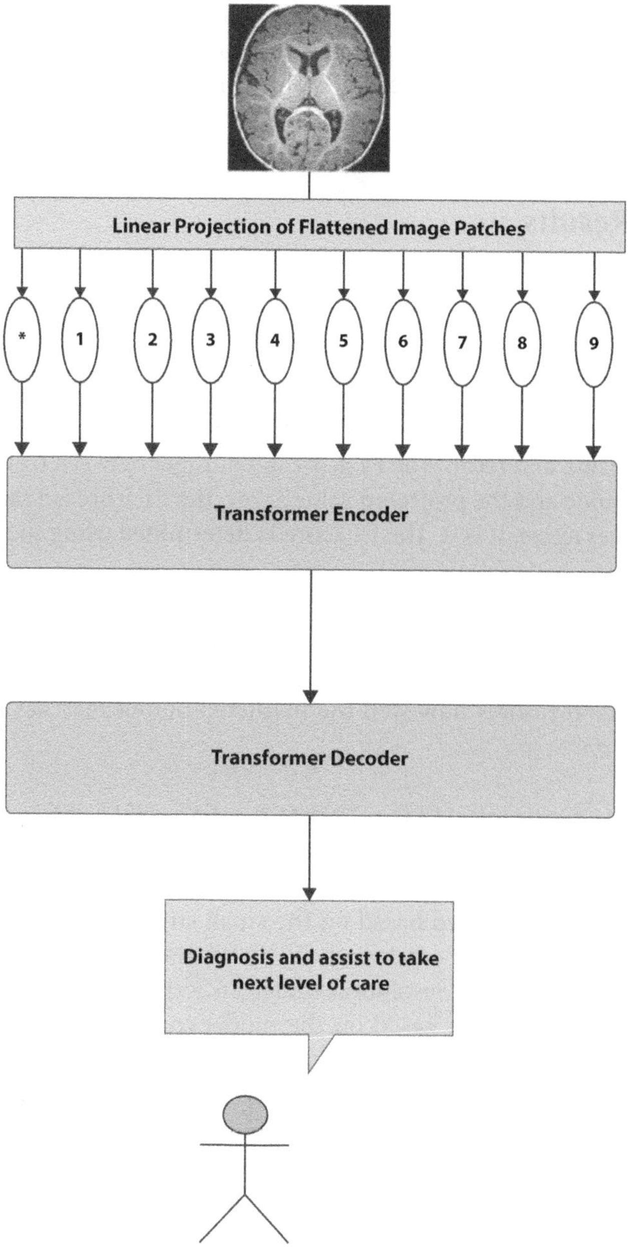

Figure 11.6 Vision transformer for autism diagnosis.

activated so that after diagnosing autism the model will be able to give medical assistance on further procedural treatment. Most of the clinicians new to the field or inexperienced person in medical field can use this medical assistance.

11.5 Results

We have shown results derived from CNN models, such as ResNet, VGG16, AlexNet, DenseNet, AlexNet, and transfer learning model with accuracy and F1 score for each model. Because the trainable parameters of each model are different, the accuracy and execution time differ from model to model.

The model's total accuracy is calculated using the F1 score, which combines precision and recall. The F1 score is a number between 0 and 1. If the expected value and the projected value agree, the F1 score is 1, and if none of the values agree, it is 0. The F1 score is determined using the following formula:

$$\text{F1 score} = 2 * \text{precision} * \text{recall}/(\text{precision} + \text{recall}) \tag{11.1}$$

Accuracy measures how well the predicted output matches the actual value:

$$\text{Accuracy} = (\text{TP} + \text{TN})/(\text{FP} + \text{FN} + \text{TP} + \text{TN}) \tag{11.2}$$

Two brain imaging data were used to periodically evaluate the ViT. Four models were created based on the small structure ViT model (ViT) under 16 × 16 and 8 × 8 patch sizes (ViT-s/16 and ViT-S/8), as well as the big structure ViT-based resolution under 16 × 16 and 8 × 8 patch sizes (ViT-b/16 and ViT-b/8), based on the model complexity and patch size. In addition, to make model performance comparison easier as shown in Figure 11.7, along with ViTs, ViLBERT, SWIN, and bidirectional encoder representations from transformers (BERT) were used.

Model	Accuracy	F1 Score
AlexNet	91.25	90.22
ResNet	92.15	91.36
VGG16	97.25	95.26
DenseNet	93.22	91.23
MobileNet	90.13	89.36

Figure 11.7 Comparison of CNN models.

From the comparison from Table 11.2 and experiment, it has been concluded that transfer learning with VGG as shown in Figure 11.8 shows greater result in identifying autism using brain images, and then ViT helps to automatically diagnose the disease. In contrast to traditional NLP methods, LLMs demonstrate generative capacity to understand contextual language and produce text that resembles human writing for a variety of NLP tasks. These allow LLMs to decipher text meaning even in cases of unclear or complicated linguistic patterns that frequently arise in electronic health record (EHR) data. Typical LLMs include the LLaMA by Meta36, the GPT families produced by OpenAI35, and the BERT developed by Google. Because the input was brain images, it requires assistance from medical expertise to confirm the result, even though the model was able to produce a higher result.

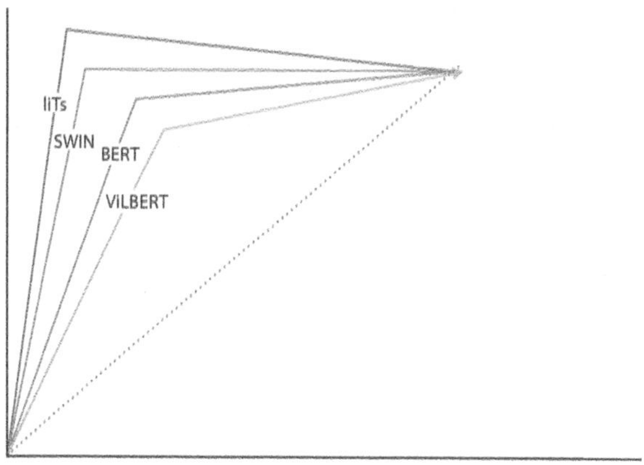

Figure 11.8 Graph receiver operating character (ROC) AUC.

Table 11.2 Result comparison of transformer models.

Model name	ROC AUC
ViLBERT	75.26
BERT	89.74
SWIN	90.86
ViTs	95.46

11.6 Discussion and Future Scope

The diagnostic accuracy of the ViT-based system may be improved by integrating cutting-edge imaging methods such as fMRI or diffusion tensor imaging. These modalities can offer more precise details on the connectivity and operation of the brain, integrating MRI data with additional diagnostic data sources, such as clinical histories, behavioral evaluations, and genetic data, to produce a more complete diagnostic tool creating cloud-based systems that process and analyze MRI scans in real time, enabling quicker and easier diagnosis.

Developing mobile applications to enhance the effectiveness and scope of ASD diagnosis by providing physicians with mobile access to diagnostic data, image-based analysis, and AI-generated insights, enabling faster decision-making and improved patient care in remote or underserved areas. Promoting international cooperation will result in a bigger, more varied collection of MRI pictures, which will enhance the model's capacity to generalize to other demographics, making use of crowdsourcing to gather a wide range of MRI pictures from various areas and demographic groupings.

11.7 Conclusion

Through the use of s-MRI images, we have investigated the possibility of sophisticated deep learning techniques, specifically transfer learning with VGG16 and ViT, for the automated diagnosis and early identification of ASD. First, pretrained weights were successfully applied by VGG16 with transfer learning to detect autism-related characteristics in MRI scans. This demonstrated the model's capacity to function in situations where there is a dearth of labeled data and produced notable diagnostic accuracy. After then, the powerful self-attention mechanisms of the ViT were utilized to automatically diagnose ASD because they are excellent at identifying intricate patterns and distant relationships in the architecture of the brain. The ViT's ability to diagnose autism with accuracy underscores its potential for use in clinical settings, where it may offer dependable diagnostic assistance in the absence of specialized radiologists.

AI disclosure statement: The author confirms that no artificial intelligence (AI)-generated content or AI-assisted writing tools were used in the preparation of this chapter (including summaries and the abstract). All text, analysis, and conclusions are the result of the author's original work.

References

1. Du, D., Paluch, R., Stevens, G., Müller, C., Exploring patient trust in clinical advice from AI-driven LLMs like ChatGPT for self-diagnosis.
2. Li, L., *et al.*, A scoping review of using Large Language Models (LLMs) to investigate Electronic Health Records (EHRs).
3. Gao, W., *et al.*, AI.vs.Clinician: Unveiling Intricate Interactions Between AI and Clinicians through an Open-Access Database. arXiv, Jun. 15, 2024. Accessed: Jul. 11, 2024. [Online]. Available: http://arxiv.org/abs/2406.07362.
4. Rao, H., Zeng, M., Zhao, X., Miao, C., A Survey of Artificial Intelligence in Gait-Based Neurodegenerative Disease Diagnosis. arXiv, May 21, 2024. Accessed: Jul. 11, 2024. [Online]. Available: http://arxiv.org/abs/2405.13082.
5. Sajid, M., Sharma, R., Beheshti, I., Tanveer, M., Decoding Cognitive Health Using Machine Learning: A Comprehensive Evaluation for Diagnosis of Significant Memory Concern. *WIREs Data Min. Knowl. Discov.*, 14, 3, e1546, May 2024, doi: 10.1002/widm.1546.
6. Akter, S., Shahriar, H., Cuzzocrea, A., Autism Disease Detection Using Transfer Learning Techniques: Performance Comparison Between Central Processing Unit vs Graphics Processing Unit Functions for Neural Networks, in: *2023 IEEE 47th Annual Computers, Software, and Applications Conference (COMPSAC)*, Jun. 2023, IEEE, Torino, Italy, pp. 1084–1092, doi: 10.1109/COMPSAC57700.2023.00164.
7. Okonji, O.R., Yunusov, K., Gordon, B., *Applications of Generative AI in Healthcare: algorithmic, ethical, legal and societal considerations*, May 09, 2024, doi: 10.36227/techrxiv.171527587.75649430/v1.
8. Pavithra, D., Jayanthi, A.N., Nidhya, R., Balamurugan, S., Autism Screening Tools With Machine Learning and Deep Learning Methods: A Review, in: *Tele-Healthcare*, Nidhya, R., Kumar, M., Balamurugan, S. (Eds.), 2022.
9. Wang, H., Zhao, S., Qiang, Z., Xi, N., Qin, B., Liu, T., Beyond Direct Diagnosis: LLM-based Multi-Specialist Agent Consultation for Automatic Diagnosis, arXiv, Jan. 29, 2024, Accessed: Jul. 11, 2024. [Online]. Available: http://arxiv.org/abs/2401.16107.
10. Zhang, L., *et al.*, Automating the Diagnosis of Human Vision Disorders by Cross-modal 3D Generation, arXiv, May 24, 2024, Accessed: Jul. 11, 2024. [Online]. Available: http://arxiv.org/abs/2405.15239.

12

Energy-Efficient Lightweight Security Framework for Internet of Medical Things Devices for Healthcare Applications

B. Sarath Chandra[1]*, Raja Rao P.B.V.[2], M. Geetha[3], P. V. Narasimha Raju[4], Madhukumar Patnala[5] and Sivudu Macherla[6]

[1]*Department of Information Technology, Lakireddy Bali Reddy College of Engineering, Mylavaram, Andhra Pradesh, India*
[2]*Department of Computer Science Engineering, Shri Vishnu Engineering College for Women (A), Bhimavaram, Andhra Pradesh, India*
[3]*Department of ECE, Pragati Engineering College, Surampalem, Andhra Pradesh, India*
[4]*Department of Information Technology, Sagi Rama Krishnam Raju Engineering College, Bhimavaram, India*
[5]*Department of ECE, Bapatla Engineering College, Bapatla, Andhra Pradesh, India*
[6]*Dept. of Computer Science and Engineering, Koneru Lakshmaiah Education Foundation, Vaddeswaram, Andhra Pradesh, India*

Abstract

Internet of Medical Things (IoMT) is the important application under the Internet of Things (IoT), which provides various services to healthcare organizations, namely, remote patient monitoring, drug delivery system, and ambient assisted living. Increasing usage of IoMT in a healthcare organization is vulnerable to more security issues. Implementing security mechanisms to IoMT is a challenging task due to the resource constraints such as limited processing capability, low battery power, and limited memory capacity. Therefore, there is a need to develop an energy-efficient lightweight security solution to protect IoMT-based devices, which in turn improves authentication, integrity, confidentiality, and availability of communication among the devices. At present, security mechanisms available in IoMT are vulnerable to several security attacks, namely, distributed denial of

**Corresponding author*: sarathit862@gmail.com

R. Nidhya, D. Pavithra, S. Balamurugan, A. Dinesh Kumar and Sheng-Lung Peng (eds.) Medical Metaverse for Digital Healthcare: Technologies, Applications, and Challenges, (247–264) © 2026 Scrivener Publishing LLC

service (DDoS) attacks, wireless attacks, radio attacks, and device hijacking. Most of the time, patients and doctors are under high risk due to the higher impact of security issues. With this motivation, a new lightweight authentication approach was developed to ensure mutual authentication between the healthcare service providers. Also, the developed authentication approach consumes less energy. A novel modified Simon (M-Simon) lightweight cryptography approach was established to improve the security during IoMT data transmission. M-Simon (24/48) provides increased security with power-efficient, secure data transfer across IoMT. The less power-consuming device will work for a more extended period with improved security. To mitigate the DDoS attack toward IoMT, a new packet filtering device level (PFDL)–embedded firewall was developed, which prevented the entry of suspicious attacking packets into the IoMT network. The proposed three-layer firewall minimized the dropping of genuine packets and mitigated the DDoS attack. The overall performance of the PFDL firewall ensures the strong mitigation of denial of service and DDoS attack to the IoMT devices. Therefore, the proposed security approach is effective and efficient to IoMT network security.

Keywords: Internet of Medical Things, lightweight cryptography, healthcare, communication security, security attacks

12.1 Introduction

The Internet of Things (IoT) is a sensor-enabled, internet-connected system that transmits data globally. These interconnected devices exchange data with other IoT devices and store it in the cloud. Further, these stored data are analyzed and supported to make better decisions. The sensor data are classified into three major types, namely, environmental, physical, and implanted data [1]. Based on the usage of these sensors, there are different types of the applications available in IoT such as smart home, wearable devices (smartwatches, fitness trackers, and smart glasses), smart grid, connected car, connected healthcare services (digital health, telehealth, and telemedicine), smart farming, smart retail, intelligent supply chain, and so on. Among these, IoT healthcare services received massive attention from investors because of widespread chronic diseases [2]. According to medical reports, about 80% of people older than 65 years have at least one chronic disease. The development in Internet of Medical Things (IoMT) introduces the ambient assisted living systems and supports various healthcare services to assist daily activities of the patient, monitoring one's well-being, increasing protection, and aiding fast health assistance. The IoMT applications are classified into various types, precisely single-purpose health monitoring applications and clustered purpose general medical applications [3, 4].

The main goal of IoMT applications is to improve the quality of life for people who need ongoing healthcare assistance or supervision. Also, it decreases the barriers to monitor essential health parameters, which help to reduce healthcare costs with timely medical support for the patients. The healthcare sector, unlike other domains, places high value on data protection due to the importance of medical information. The high-stakes nature of the security implementation raises some concerns regarding smart health applications [5–7].

The security of the overall IoT relies on these protocols in different levels. Various security vulnerabilities presented in the IoT protocols create security issues in IoT communication that categorizes into three significant levels [8]. Figure 12.1 shows the IoT security principles, classified into six major security principles. The overall IoT system has classified into three stages, namely, the device level, communication level, and the cloud level. In this, users (patients, caregivers, or doctors) and devices (IoMT) presented at the device level. Gateway and the internet connection are presented in the communication level. Finally, cloud storage and intelligent business applications are presented at the cloud level. Further, security principles in the three levels of IoT are classified into six principles.

Sensitive medical data are always an attractive target for hackers. The majority of security threats seeks to get control of IoT devices in order to create a botnet. Botnets are a collection of computers that work together to perform a certain activity. Several botnets specialize in initiating distributed denial of service (DDoS) attacks against certain services. A DDoS attack is an effort to take down an internet service by flooding it with traffic from various sources. As a result, if IoT devices are not protected with the correct username–password combination, they may be easily hacked into a botnet

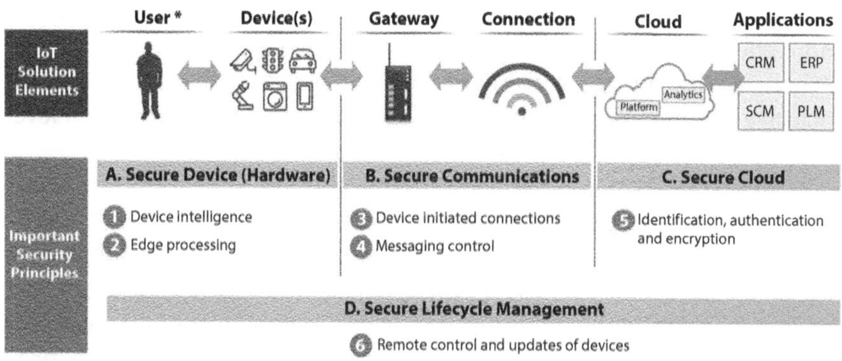

Figure 12.1 Six principles of IoT security.

and used to launch assaults on other sites [9]. Insecure web interfaces in IoT applications, inadequate physical security, a lack of proper encryption, and an easy password credential are all reasons for major attacks. To attack the device, the attacker utilizes weak IoT network services. Data loss can occur as a result of an unsecured web interface in IoT applications, and a lack of accountability in denial of service assaults might result in a total device shutdown [10]. Attackers use weak credentials, plain text credentials captured in plain text, or message manipulation. Message injection, for example, is an active attack that replaces the original message with fake data. A breach of the user's health data occurs due to a lack of data protection. Physical security flaws exist when an attacker can simply disassemble a device to gain access to the storage media. DDoS is one of the most hazardous attacks against IoT healthcare data, as it causes the device to become inaccessible by delivering a massive amount of data to it [11].

Patients and aged people are increasingly using IoMT devices. On the other hand, data breaches in medical devices are also increasing significantly. The major security attacks manipulate sensitive medical data that affect the patient's health and lead to substantial financial loss. The importance of mitigating active security attacks in the IoMT is motivated to design and develop a novel energy-efficient and lightweight system.

12.2 Literature Review

IoT is an emerging idea of the internet-connected IP address–based sensor-enabled things to collect, analyze, and automatically predict the event based on the sensed data [12]. Implementing IoT in healthcare applications is essential to enhance the health tracking accuracy, and low-cost treatment for patients and enhance emergency response from the doctor to the patient at any time. These devices are used for the treatment procedures more effectively, but it fails to address a few security issues such as DDoS attacks, wireless attacks, and encryption cracking. With this motivation, an inclusive literature survey on various device level and communication level security issues in IoMT is presented in this chapter.

Mishra *et al.* [13] consider power consumption to be a critical factor in IoT. The power consumption of the gadget will affect bandwidth, processing speed, battery life, and temperature. Because many of the instruments rely solely on batteries for power, having the longest-running period feasible is important, and so power consumption would be reduced. Data security will necessitate a high level of power consumption relative to no security because some type of computation is required, and all computations eat power. Despite the fact that we put security procedures in the devices, there are several distinctions in the methods we use. In terms of power efficiency, there are noticeable disparities between different encryption methods, digital signature techniques, key generation techniques, and hashing techniques. Furthermore, the performance of algorithms will be affected by the use of different processors. Although encrypted data incur some bandwidth costs, the impact on actual packet size has not been prohibitive until now, due to the relatively large packet sizes in traditional network systems. For each IoT device, balancing these three criteria is critical. Transmitting data consume more energy in wireless radio than central processing unit (CPU). Data processing prior to transmission lowers energy costs, improves processing speed, and increases storage costs.

Almaiah *et al.* [14] implemented Eco-Health–based patient monitoring system to diagnose various diseases. However, the developed system fails to incorporate several security standards to ensure data security when connecting with different devices with different standards. A generic and ubiquitous ambient assisted secure living framework for older people at home helps them take care of their health and live independently. The framework describes the minimum-security requirements of the IoT devices in the body area network. IoMT devices are widely used in the healthcare profession at the moment. As a result, identifying and mitigating security in IoMT at an early stage are critical. Therefore, recent research works carried out in the IoMT are reviewed extensively to identify the security issues in IoMT.

Implementing a secured authentication over IoMT devices is a complicated process due to the device constraints; however, it is indispensable to safeguard the patient's identity from the attackers. Protecting user identity, including their passwords and session IDs, is needed to improve the robustness of the system. This analysis recommends using hashed password and secure password and reauthenticating new password. It helps the users to change their passwords when trying to recover the accounts. Therefore, implementation of lightweight authentication algorithms reduces authentication vulnerabilities in the energy-constrained IoMT. Mutually connected IoT networked devices are disposed to unauthorized third-party exploitation when a single device is infected by malware. This may spread through the network in a very short period. Hence, a suitable authentication mechanism for every verification is necessary.

Salem *et al.* [15] carried out a zero-power defense method in implanted pacemakers and cardiac defibrillators. Although the defense method reduces the power denial attack, the method fails to address DDoS attacks in IoMT. Based on the literature review on device-level security issues in IoMT, some of the major security issues such as DDoS attack, power denial

Table 12.1 Study on various security algorithms in IoMT.

Authors	Algorithm	Block size	Key size	Rounds	Observations
Salemi *et al*. [16]	PRINCE	64	128	12	This algorithm was implemented in FPGA Vertex 4 and Vertex 6. The throughput of the algorithm is less and also improved the efficiency.
Kini *et al*. [17]	HIGHT	64	128	32	This algorithm was implemented in FPGA Altera Quartus II, version 13. Based on the observation, the algorithm is not applicable to software implementation due to the less data transfer rate and delay in processing.
Khan *et al*. [18]	Simon	32	Variable size	32	Implemented in FPGA. The results conclude that all versions of Simon consume less energy.
Singh *et al*. [19]	BLOWFISH	64	32-448	16	Implemented in Spartan 3E XC35. The algorithm is implemented in hardware.
Zhang *et al*. [20]	ECC-RSD	NA	NPKC	NA	This algorithm used pipelined architecture, which increases the processing speed of the encryption.
Ek *et al*. [21]	ECC	NA	NPKC	NA	It takes very less memory size, which is well suitable for constrained based devices.
Hao *et al*. [22]	HUMMINGBIRD	16	256	NA	This algorithm uses different S-Box to reduce energy consumption and memory usage for IoMT.
R. Mishra et.al, [23]	PRESENT	64	128	32	It is a GRP compressed lightweight algorithm for lightweight device. It produces better results in hardware than software implementation.

attack, and device cloning are identified. Comprehensive investigation is still needed for the IoT-based technologies. The security implementation of the proposed IoT based applications is studied through testing approaches. To defend the power denial security attacks, a small cryptography key size was introduced in the data encryption algorithm, which reduced the computational processing requirements of IoMT.

Based on the literature review on authentication security issues, device-level security issues, and communication security issues in IoMT, significant research gaps are identified. Hitherto, the research works are focused on hardware-based security implementation in IoMT. Also, the lack of security algorithms in software-based implementation is vulnerable to higher security attacks. In the review on authentication security issues in IoMT, many existing research works are lacking to provide fast authentication techniques, which gives a chance for attackers to perform replay attack. In the device-level security, many research works are focused on SDN-based IoT security to control the device access efficiently. However, the security techniques to resolve the central point of failure are still lacking. DDoS attack is a serious threat to medical devices, which turns off the device by draining the device energy source. Based on the review on device-level security issues in IoMT, there is a need to develop robust security techniques to mitigate DDoS attacks at the device level. Based on the review of communication security algorithms, many works are focused on implementing a secure cryptography mechanism to provide robust security to data encryption and decryption with high energy consumption, but not suitable for energy-constrained devices. The lack of energy-efficient security algorithms in IoMT communication is the significant gap that needs to be improved. The detailed study on various security algorithms in IoMT is shown in Table 12.1.

12.3 Methodology

Multiple internet-connected wireless medical devices are the problem of authenticating the authorized IoMT to the particular healthcare service provider. Traditional security procedures in authentication are difficult to apply in IoMT because of device constraints such as low battery power, restricted computing capability, and restricted memory. These limitations help adversaries to hack medical things effortlessly. This area of research is considered to be an open research area and required colossal attention. Based on the security analysis of various existing authentication schemes, some of the major security issues are identified, such as mutually connected IoT networked devices, which are prone to unauthorized third-party exploitation when a single device is infected by malware. Also, higher power consumption and delay in processing during the authentication process may result in power denial attack and replay attack.

A novel lightweight authentication scheme using the one-time signature (OTS) and elliptic curve cryptography (ECC) algorithm was developed to mitigate the major security issues by optimizing the energy consumption and increasing the computation speed. In this OTS technique, a device can register their information with server one time and transfer their sensitive data to the authorized medical devices once the authentication process completes. Through this technique, an authorized person or device can access the medical devices securely.

ECC algorithm: An asymmetric key encryption system known as ECC was first presented in 1985 as a mathematical framework for elliptic curves over finite fields. It is a strong crypto algorithm that is comparable to RSA. Fast computation and easy data transfer can be done using ECC. The key size ratios between Rivest–Shamir–Adleman (RSA) and ECC are shown in Equations (12.1) to (12.3). The encryption key size of RSA, Diffie–Hellman, and ECC is presented in Table 12.2.

$$\frac{1024}{160} \approx \frac{6.4}{1} \tag{12.1}$$

$$\frac{3074}{256} = \frac{12}{1} \tag{12.2}$$

$$\frac{15360}{512} = \frac{30}{1} \tag{12.3}$$

Table 12.2 Key size difference between RSA and ECC.

RSA and Diffie–Hellman (modulus size in bits)	**The size of an ECC key in bits**
512	112
1024	160
2048	224
3074	256
7680	384
15360	512

Point addition and pointed doubling are two major operations in ECC. Figure 12.2 shows the point addition operation.

$$s = \frac{y_P - y_Q}{x_P - x_Q} \quad (12.4)$$

$$x_R = S^2 - (x_P + x_Q) \quad (12.5)$$

$$y_R = S(x_P - x_R) - y_p \quad (12.6)$$

The process of adding a point P to itself to generate a new point (Q) is known as point doubling ie., Q= 2P is shown in Figure 12.3. The benefit of this technique is that user can use a symmetric and asymmetric algorithm.

$$s = \frac{3x_P^2 + a}{2y_P} \quad (12.7)$$

$$x_Q = s^2 - 2x_P \quad (12.8)$$

$$y_Q = S(x_P - x_Q) - y_p \quad (12.9)$$

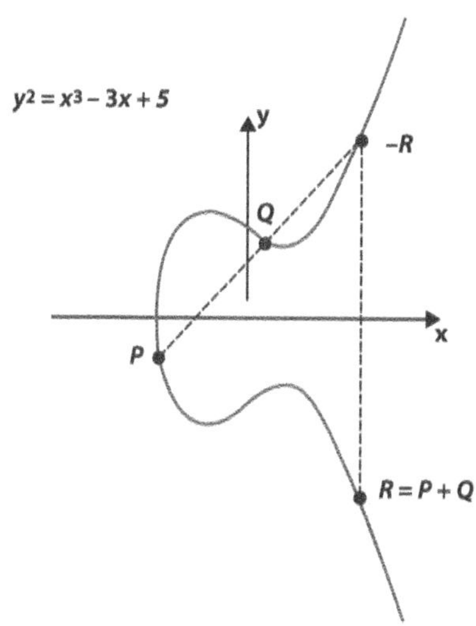

Figure 12.2 Point addition.

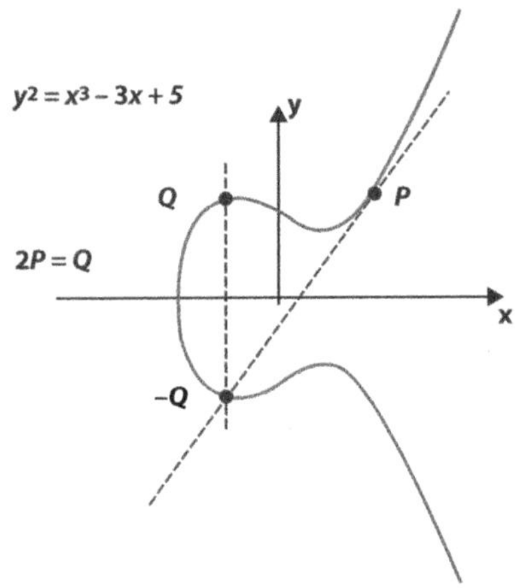

Figure 12.3 Point of doubling.

A one-way function or trapdoor function is property to develop a key from an element in the domain quickly, but reverse-engineering the entire process is challenging to determine the original element unless the developed key is known.

A secure lightweight authentication scheme using ECC-based OTS 160 key size technique was developed. In this, a user with an IoMT device can register with the healthcare server for one time and transfer their sensitive data to the authorized medical devices once the authentication process completes. The authorized person or device can access medical devices securely. The four-stage authentication process between the user and the server using the trusted party is discussed in the following section. Figure 12.4 depicts the process flow of the OTS 160 key lightweight authentication scheme, which uses the ECC algorithm to encrypt and decrypt the message. There are three parties in the authentication process.

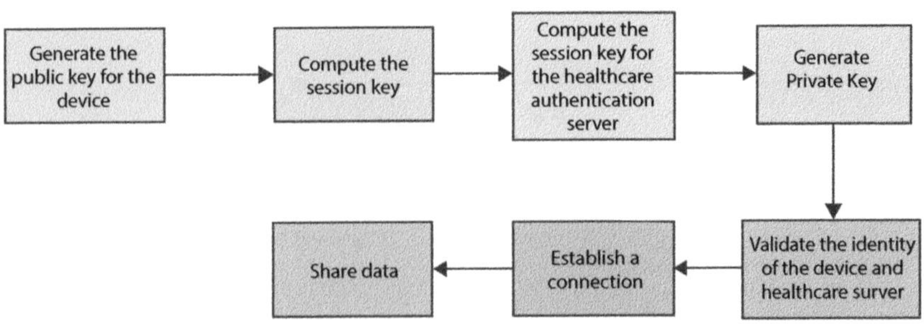

Figure 12.4 Process flow of the OTS (160)–based lightweight authentication scheme.

Figure 12.5 Tmote sky wireless module.

The Tmote sky mote in Cooja simulator is used to implement the authentication scheme. As shown in Figure 12.5, the simulation experiment includes 100 client nodes, one server mote, and one trusted authority (TA). By using the same simulation properties, the authentication schemes, computation time, and energy consumption were analyzed. The stability of authentication scheme at 50, 100, and 150 nodes was checked.

12.4 Results and Discussion

The Tmote sky mote in Cooja simulator is used to implement the authentication scheme. The user (Device) generates the public key and transfers the session key to a Healthcare Authentication Server, and then the authentication server computes the session key for the particular device and sends to TA. For each session, TA produces the private key and verifies the identification of the device and server. If the verification succeeds, then the authentication of the device and server would be verified successfully. Implantable cardioverter-defibrillators (ICDs) are an important IoMT device in the healthcare industry that are unique implanted medical devices designed to jumpstart the heart. The ICD is placed inside the heart muscle to produce pulse signals, and it is designed to carry the electrical storage and software. This device monitors the patient's heartbeat continuously and alerts if necessary. The modern internet-enabled ICDs are prone to security vulnerabilities due to the lack of strong security mechanisms and proper standardization.

As shown in Figure 12.6, the simulation experiment includes 100 client nodes, one server mote, and one TA. By using the same simulation

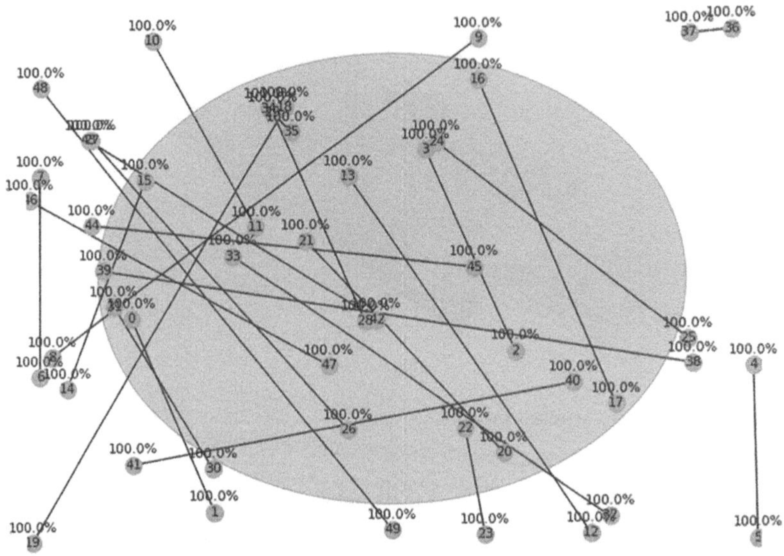

Figure 12.6 OTS secure mote access under trusted authority server DI:1.

properties, the authentication schemes, computation time, and energy consumption were analyzed. The stability of authentication scheme at 50, 100, and 150 nodes were checked. Figure 12.7 shows the energy required by various authentication systems such as SHA (256), AES (256), SHA (512), AES (128), and RSA (1024) for nodes ranging from 10 to 50. It can be observed from the graph (Figure 12.7) that the 160-bit key size OTS (160) security scheme consumed minimal energy of 65.2 μJ at 50 nodes.

Figure 12.8 indicates a comparison of execution time from 50 to 150 nodes and a comparison of different authentication schemes mentioned in Table 12.3. Based on the performance, the execution time of OTS (160) scheme (0.5 ms for 50 nodes, 0.8 ms for 100 nodes, and 1.8 ms for 150 nodes) was found to be faster compared with other authentication schemes. The less energy consumption and less execution time it takes to execute the ECC-based OTS (160) scheme ensure that the proposed scheme suits IoMT. Figure 12.9 shows the power consumption comparison between SHA (256) and OTS (160) authentication schemes. The SHA (256) scheme produces a unique 32-byte signature for data. Compared with OTS (160), it consumes higher power for 50, 100, and 150 nodes.

Power consumption comparison between AES (128) and OTS (160) authentication schemes is shown in Figure 12.10. For 128-bit key generation, AES uses 10 rounds, which consume higher power for 50,100, and 150 nodes.

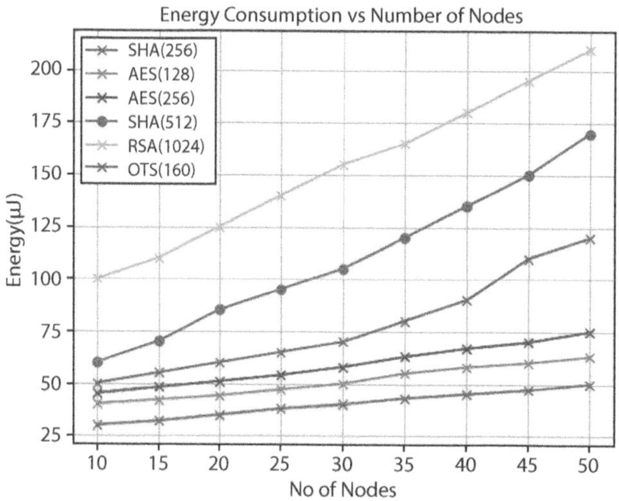

Figure 12.7 Energy consumption profile at different authentication schemes (nodes 10–50).

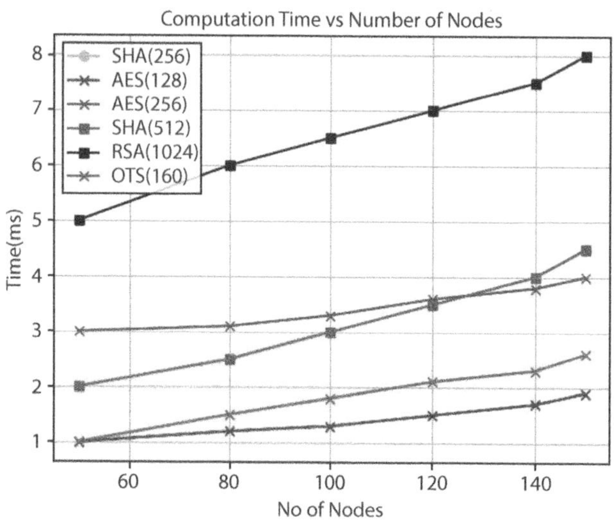

Figure 12.8 Computation time consumption of various authentication schemes with different size of nodes.

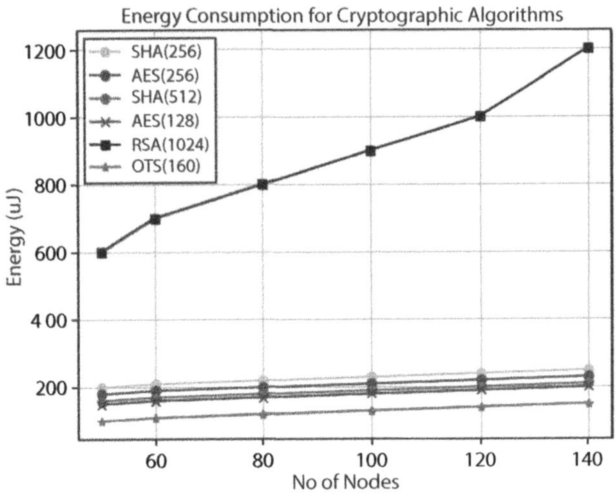

Figure 12.9 Energy consumption comparisons of different authentication schemes (nodes 50–150).

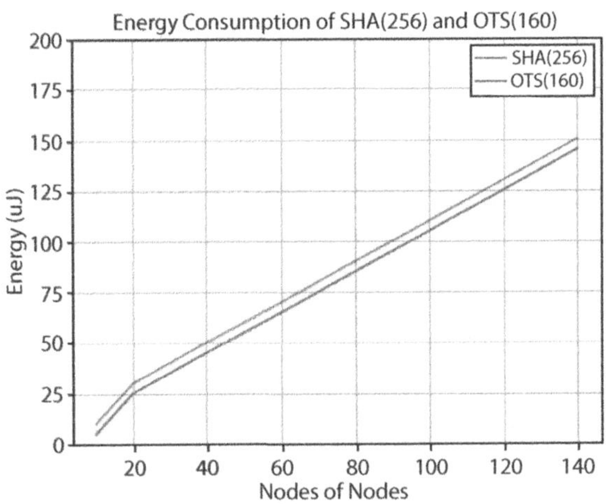

Figure 12.10 Energy consumption profile of SHA (256) and OTS (160) authentication schemes.

The comparison of different authentication schemes is mentioned in Table 12.3. Based on the performance, the execution time of OTS (160) scheme (0.5 ms for 50 nodes, 0.8 ms for 100 nodes, and 1.8 ms for 150 nodes) was found to be faster compared with other authentication schemes. The less energy consumption and less execution time it takes to execute

Table 12.3 Execution time comparison of different authentication schemes.

Authentication scheme	Average time to execute 50 nodes (ms)	Average time to execute 100 nodes (ms)	Average time to execute 150 nodes (ms)
SHA (256)	0.8	1	2.3
AES (128)	1.9	2.5	4
AES (256)	3.9	4	7.2
RSA (1024)	4	6	8
SHA (512)	1.1	1.5	2.5
OTS (160)	0.5	0.8	1.8

the ECC-based OTS (160) scheme ensure that the proposed scheme suits IoMT.

Table 12.4 shows these schemes (SHA [256], AES [256], SHA [512], AES [128], RSA [1024], and OTS [160]) separately tested for 50, 100, and 150 nodes and then the power consumption of each node observed. The OTS (160) scheme consumes less energy (65.2 μJ for 50 nodes, 86.3 μJ for 100 nodes, and 150.87 μJ for 150 nodes) compared with other authentication schemes with different key sizes.

Table 12.4 Power consumption comparison of different authentication schemes.

Authentication scheme	Average time to execute 50 nodes (ms)	Average time to execute 100 nodes (ms)	Average time to execute 150 nodes (ms)
SHA (256)	88.2	99.5	170.6
AES (128)	204.3	248.75	312.5
AES (256)	256	398	453.4
RSA (1024)	894	1025	1305.8
SHA (512)	98.24	149.25	201.5
OTS (160)	65.2	86.3	150.87

12.5 Conclusion

In conclusion, the IoMT devices are widely used for storing and transmitting sensitive medical-related information over the internet. Hence, the need for securing medical data becomes essential. The significant challenges faced hitherto to develop a robust security system are more energy consumption, limited memory capacity, and low processing power. Therefore, in this research study, the active security attacks in IoMT were identified and mitigated. A new ECC-based OTS (160) authentication scheme is implemented for IoMT devices. This work was evaluated on simulated heartbeat datasets with a different set of nodes (50, 100, and 150 nodes). The proposed authentication scheme is suitable for the resource-constrained IoMT. The ECC encryption algorithm is incorporated in OTS in which secured data are transmitted between the authenticated devices. Also, while verifying the protocol with the AVISPA security protocol validation tool, it mitigates active security attacks such as replay attacks and man-in-the-middle attacks. The less energy consumption and less execution time and capable of mitigating active security attacks ensure the proposed scheme is well suitable to the IoMT device authentication process. The energy-efficient modified Simon lightweight algorithm was implemented in the IoMT environment.

Several security mechanisms are available to protect IoMT device communication and healthcare data storage. However, the increasing number of security breaches requires continuous involvement in strengthening the security of the medical devices. In the present work, an energy-efficient security solution for the IoMT is proposed and implemented.

AI disclosure statement: The author acknowledges the use of AI-based tools for minor language editing or grammatical correction. However, all intellectual contributions, analyses, and conclusions presented in this chapter are entirely the author's own.

References

1. Sripriyanka, G. and Mahendran, A., Securing IoMT: A Hybrid Model for DDoS Attack Detection and COVID-19 Classification. *IEEE Access*, 1, 1, 99, 2024, DOI:10.1109/ACCESS.2024.3354034.
2. Khalid, M., Hameed, S., Qadir, A., Shah, S.A., Draheim, D., Towards SDN-based smart contract solution for IoT access control. *Comput. Commun.*, 198, 1–31, Jan. 2023.

3. Bhayo, J., Shah, S.A., Hameed, S., Ahmed, A., Nasir, J., Draheim, D., Towards a machine learning-based framework for DDOS attack detection in software-defined IoT (SD-IoT) networks. *Eng. Appl. Artif. Intell.*, 123, Aug. 2023.
4. Bhuyan, H.K., Chakraborty, C., Shelke, Y., Pani, S.K., COVID-19 diagnosis system by deep learning approaches. *Expert Syst.*, 39, 3, Mar. 2022.
5. Islam, U., Muhammad, A., Mansoor, R., Hossain, M.S., Ahmad, I., Eldin, E.T., *et al.*, Detection of distributed denial of service (DDoS) attacks in IoT based monitoring system of banking sector using machine learning models. *Sustainability*, 14, 14, 8374, Jul. 2022.
6. Hasan, M.K., Ghazal, T.M., Saeed, R.A., Pandey, B., Gohel, H., Eshmawi, A.A., *et al.*, A review on security threats vulnerabilities and counter measures of 5G enabled Internet-of-Medical-Things. *IET Commun.*, 16, 5, 421–432, Mar. 2022.
7. Nidhya, R., Kumar, M., Maheswar, R., Pavithra, D., Security and Privacy Issues in Smart Healthcare System Using Internet of Things, in: *IoT-enabled Smart Healthcare Systems, Services and Applications*, pp. 63–85, Wiley, 2022, DOI:10.1002/9781119816829.
8. Lamichhane, P.B., Mannering, H., Eberle, W., Discovering breach patterns on the Internet of Health Things: A graph and machine learning anomaly analysis. *Proc. Int. FLAIRS Conf.*, May 2022, vol. 35, pp. 1–6.
9. Zaman, U., Mehmood, F., Iqbal, N., Kim, J., Ibrahim, M., Towards secure and intelligent Internet of Health Things: A survey of enabling technologies and applications. *Electronics*, 11, 12, 1893, Jun. 2022.
10. Bhutia, N.T., Verma, H., Chauhan, N., Awasthi, L.K., DDoS Attacks Detection in 'Internet of Medical Things' Using Machine Learning Techniques, in: *2022 IEEE Conference on Interdisciplinary Approaches in Technology and Management for Social Innovation (IATMSI)*, IEEE, pp. 1–6, 2022.
11. Bhattacharjya, A., Kozdrój, K., Bazydło, G., Wisniewski, R., Trusted and secure blockchain-based architecture for Internet-of-Medical-Things. *Electronics*, 11, 16, 2560, Aug. 2022.
12. Smilarubavathy, G. and Ayyasamy, S., Energy Efficient Forwarding Data and Route Selection (EEFDRS) Algorithm for Wireless Body Area Network, in: *Smart Intelligent Computing and Applications: Proceedings of the Second International Conference on SCI 2018*, vol. 1, Springer Singapore, pp. 183–192, 2019.
13. Mishra, R., Gupta, H.P., Dutta, T., Analysis modeling and representation of COVID-19 spread: A case study on India. *IEEE Trans. Comput. Soc. Syst.*, 8, 4, 964–973, Aug. 2021.
14. Almaiah, M.A., Ali, A., Hajjej, F., Pasha, M.F., Alohali, M.A., A lightweight hybrid deep learning privacy preserving model for FC-based industrial Internet of Medical Things. *Sensors*, 22, 6, 2112, Mar. 2022.
15. Salem, O., Alsubhi, K., Shaafi, A., Gheryani, M., Mehaoua, A., Boutaba, R., Man-in-the-middle attack mitigation in Internet of Medical Things. *IEEE Trans. Ind. Inf.*, 18, 3, 2053–2062, Mar. 2022.

16. Salemi, H., Rostami, H., Talatian-Azad, S., Khosravi, M.R., LEAESN: Predicting DDoS attack in healthcare systems based on Lyapunov exponent analysis and echo state neural networks. *Multimedia Tools Appl.*, 81, 29, 41455–41476, Dec. 2022.
17. Kini, A.S., Reddy, A.N.G., Kaur, M., Satheesh, S., Singh, J., Martinetz, T., *et al.*, Ensemble deep learning and Internet of Things-based automated COVID-19 diagnosis framework. *Contrast Media Mol. Imaging*, 2022, 1–10, Feb. 2022.
18. Khan, I.A., Moustafa, N., Razzak, I., Tanveer, M., Pi, D., Pan, Y., *et al.*, XSRU-IoMT: Explainable simple recurrent units for threat detection in Internet of Medical Things networks. *Future Gener. Comput. Syst.*, 127, 181–193, Feb. 2022.
19. Singh, A., Kaur, A., Dhillon, A., Ahuja, S., Vohra, H., Software system to predict the infection in COVID-19 patients using deep learning and web of things. *Softw. Pract. Exp.*, 52, 4, 868–886, Apr. 2022.
20. Zhang, X., Lu, S., Wang, S.-H., Yu, X., Wang, S.-J., Yao, L., *et al.*, Diagnosis of COVID-19 pneumonia *via* a novel deep learning architecture. *J. Comput. Sci. Technol.*, 37, 2, 330–343, Apr. 2022.
21. Ek, S., Portet, F., Lalanda, P., Vega, G., A federated learning aggregation algorithm for pervasive computing: Evaluation and comparison. *Proc. IEEE PerCom*, Mar. 2021, pp. 1–10.
22. Hao, M., Li, H., Luo, X., Xu, G., Yang, H., Liu, S., Efficient and privacy-enhanced federated learning for industrial artificial intelligence. *IEEE Trans. Ind. Inf.*, 16, 10, 6532–6542, Oct. 2020.
23. Mishra, R., Gupta, A., Gupta, H.P., Dutta, T., A sensors based deep learning model for unseen locomotion mode identification using multiple semantic matrices. *IEEE Trans. Mob. Comput.*, 21, 3, 799–810, Mar. 2022.

13

An Intelligent Framework for Identifying Tumor in Pancreas through an AI and Deep Learning Approach

Jithendra Reddy Dandu

Department of Electronics and Communication Engineering, Annamacharya Institute of Technology and Sciences, Tirupati, Andhra Pradesh, India

Abstract

Medical images are accurately diagnosed in an efficient manner using various segmentation and classification methods powered by artificial intelligence (AI). Magnetic resonance image is diagnostic at the initial phase of diagnosis due to a deviation among various pancreas image parameters, as the medical anatomy ranges widely. The proposed method uses an algorithm that executes segmentation and classification. The findings demonstrate that a novel hybrid modified distance metric with fuzzy C-means and faster region-based convolutional neural network (R-CNN) (MDM–FCM–FRCNN) dramatically lowers segmentation error compared with current techniques and ground-truth images. Gray-level co-occurrence matrix is used to extract features and perform classification using graph neural networks. The proposed methodologies, enhanced by artificial intelligence, outperform current algorithms, yielding superior results for the pancreas images, with classification accuracy of 97.74% and Dice similarity coefficient segmentation value of 97.84%.

Keywords: MDM-FCM, faster R-CNN, GNN, AI, deep learning, pancreas

13.1 Introduction

The pancreas comprises innumerable cell types, a piece with distinct functions. Whereas most cells grow and function normally to maintain health,

Email: jithendrareddy.d@gmail.com

R. Nidhya, D. Pavithra, S. Balamurugan, A. Dinesh Kumar and Sheng-Lung Peng (eds.) Medical Metaverse for Digital Healthcare: Technologies, Applications, and Challenges, (265–284) © 2026 Scrivener Publishing LLC

some grow abnormally, forming a group of soft tissue acknowledged as a tumor [1], either benign or malignant, with malignant tumors posing a complex cancer risk. Pancreatic tumors are particularly dangerous, as they often go undetected until advanced stages, leading to a low survival rate of less than 5%. Early diagnosis is challenging due to the obscurity of the pancreas and its proximity to other organs. Pancreatic tumors are highly metastatic, and patients typically show symptoms only in advanced stages [2]. Image segmentation is crucial in medical diagnosis, especially for detecting tumors. It involves dividing a digital image into segments to highlight important features for analysis [3]. This method helps identify structures such as tumors in medical imaging, despite challenges such as low contrast and noise. Pancreatic tumors are often examined using magnetic resonance imaging (MRI), as it is noninvasive and radiation-free, relying on magnetic fields and radio waves. Segmentation algorithms focus on features such as intensity changes, with techniques such as fuzzy C-means (FCM), K-means, and expectation maximization widely used. Preprocessing of MR images uses a modified decision based couple window median filter algorithm (DBCWM) (MDBCWM) filter to remove noise while preserving critical image details [4].

In this research, the modified distance metric with fuzzy C-means and faster region-based convolutional neural network. (R-CNN) (MDM–FCM–FRCNN) technique will be used to segment the filtered pancreatic image. The MDM–FCM–FRCNN method will effectively partition the pancreatic images, facilitated by the filtering process using the MDBCWM filter. After applying gray-level co-occurrence matrix (GLCM) for feature extraction and clustering, the image will then be classified using graph neural networks (GNNs).

13.2 Background

The classification of tumor identification largely depends on MR/computed tomography (CT) scans of the pancreas. This allows researchers and medical professionals to focus on key areas of an image while eliminating unnecessary aspects. Dissection of MR images is essential. For machine learning–based techniques, filtering, feature extraction, and segmentation of the full sample set offer substantial benefits. It has been acknowledged that the quality of the samples used during training significantly impacts the outcomes. Numerous studies have examined image segmentation, reporting promising results [5].

Using NIH Pancreas datasets, 78.60% Dice was attained in the experiment involving the combined segmentation of the pancreas, and tumor inside the medical segmentation decathlon (MSD) dataset testing shows that not only does our algorithm only surpass state-of-the-art methods for pancreas segmentation but also demonstrates exceptional performance in segmenting the pancreas [6]. A multiagent reinforcement learning network was applied to perceive key landmarks of the pancreas (tail, neck, head, body) and then along the pancreatic duct in a target CT image. Based on these landmarks, a pancreas atlas was enumerated to the aim image, generating anatomical prospect plots for the duct. These plots were then enhanced with multilabel three-dimensional (3D) U-Net architectures to achieve the ending segmentation grades [7, 8]. Deep learning approaches consume exposed hopeful outcomes in pancreas division. However, the limited availability of publicly using labeled datasets has helped scholars to rely on isolated datasets for pancreatic tumor segmentation. Segmentation is further widely studied tumor segmentation as a result of the varying shapes and sizes of tumors [8]. The multimodal segmentation network achieved average Dice values of 74.14% and 76.20%, with average Hausdorff distances of 6.41 and 6.84, respectively. These results demonstrate the effectiveness of the proposed MFCNet [9]. Pancreatic tumor segmentation results in fewer false positives. Additionally, accurate tumor locations from positron emission tomography images guide the Dense-SE network in MRI training, addressing the challenge of small labeled samples and reducing network overfitting, achieving an average Dice similarity coefficient (DSC) of 78.33% [8]. Pancreas tumor segmentation was validated using 42 contrast-enhanced CT volumes of usual pancreas through a twofold cross-validation (CV) strategy. It demonstrated improved segmentation performance for the pancreas deep learning segmentation networks [10]. The core idea involves an enhanced segmentation technique for remote sensing image feature points, ensuring that image segments retain furthermost data aimed at small objects after grading. Li *et al.* [11] proposed a global feature reconstruction (GFR) network that utilizes three noticeable spectral channels to recognize clouds and their shadows, using ResNet as the foundation for retrieving semantic information at different levels. While effective for detecting lung nodules, the deep learning algorithm must also recognize distinctive pancreatic tumor characteristics, such as ductal enlargement or parenchymal atrophy, as highlighted by Maxime *et al.* [12].

Medical data often suffer from significant spatial information loss, leading to convolutions and reduced efficiency in image analysis. To tackle this issue, the proposed model integrates multiple approaches, providing an additional actual solution for computationally intensive tasks, particularly in image filtering and categorization. The goal of this endeavor is to create an effective approach for identifying pancreatic tumors, starting with early filtering using the MDBCWM filter. The filtered images then undergo segmentation through a novel hybrid method (MDM–FCM–FRCNN) and feature extraction using the GLCM. Finally, these features are classified using a GNN approach, which enhances accuracy and adaptability in challenging pancreatic tumor detection scenarios.

The article is prearranged as follows: Section 13.3 offers a general overview of the proposed algorithms, Section 13.4 presents the results along with an analysis of the resulting graphs, and Section 13.5 concludes the study.

13.3 Overview of the Proposed Work

The proposed approach consists of several key stages. The first step involves collecting MR images of the pancreas, which are then preprocessed using the MDBCWM filter. Following filtering, the images undergo segmentation with the MDM–FCM–FRCNN technique. After segmentation, feature extraction is carried out using the GLCM. Finally, classification is performed using GNN algorithms. The internal workflow of the proposed approach is illustrated in Figure 13.1.

13.3.1 Preprocessing

Noisy regions in the neighborhood are adjusted using the median, while the remaining noisy pixels are modified through a windowing technique,

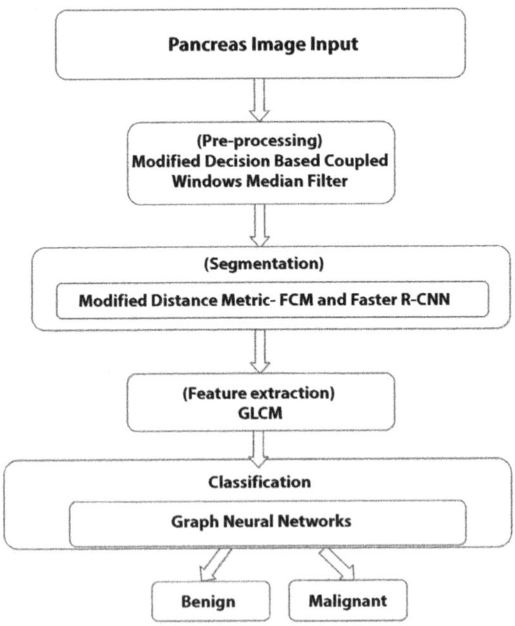

Figure 13.1 Proposed method.

as described in the formulas below [13]. The operation of the MDBCWM filtering method is illustrated in Figure 13.2. The algorithm is applied separately to each channel of the input image after it has been read [14]. If the image contains all pixel values set to 255, a denoised image will be produced. The program checks if three-quarters of the pixels have been processed after selecting the windows; if so, pixel values in the range of 0 to 255 are excluded before calculating the median. If not, further analysis is performed to ensure that every pixel is processed. Ultimately, a denoised image is generated by merging all the channels, with the denoising process applied individually to each channel prior to the final combination.

13.3.2 Segmentation Process

To eliminate false tumors in pancreatic tumor detection, a threshold is established based on the Euclidean distance [15]. Pixel clustering is performed using a distance metric that quantifies the separation between different pixels. The FCM algorithm then receives one pixel from each cluster as input, assigning corresponding membership values to the members of each cluster.

$$\text{Euclidean distance: Dst} = \sqrt{(e_s - e_t)(e_s - e)^1} \tag{13.1}$$

13.3.2.1 Fuzzy C-Means

Algorithms can effectively differentiate between tumor and nontumor regions. FCM clustering improves accuracy by assigning membership values between 0 and 1, which are calculated based on the intensity levels of the signal. This clustering approach helps reduce uncertainty during the segmentation process. FCM efficiently identifies tissue areas, as shown in the Results, providing effective automated segmentation that enhances both diagnostic reliability and speed [16]. Let the dataset:

$D = \{d1, d2, \ldots\ldots\ldots dn\}$. C is the number of clusters, and $S = \{s1, s2, s3\}$ is the centroid. The dataset D is partitioned into c clusters by lessening its objective function given by $J\,(B, S, D)$:

$$J(B,S,D) = \sum_{k=1}^{v} \sum_{l=1}^{r} (\mu kl) n1 \left\| dk - sj \right\|^2 \tag{13.2}$$

$$\mu kl+ = \left(\Sigma_{u=1}^{v} \left(\frac{dk}{dl} \right) \frac{2}{n1 - r} \right) - 1 \tag{13.3}$$

$$Sl = \frac{\sum_{l=1}^{r}(\mu kl)n1dl}{2a\sum_{l=1}^{r}(\mu kl)n1} \tag{13.4}$$

In Equation (13.11), $E_k^{\,2}$ is the normalized separation both the *i*th cluster centroid's *sj* and the data element's *dj*.

$$Ek^2 = \left\|dk - sj\right\|^2 \tag{13.5}$$

13.3.2.2 Faster Region-Based Convolutional Neural Network (R-CNN) Segmentation

The proposed strategy for automated tumor segmentation utilizes a deep learning architecture known as FRCNN. Effective and discriminative segmentation is crucial for distinguishing between region-based groupings; however, relying on a limited number of feature extractions may cause the system to overlook important descriptors. This approach can quickly identify and segment the input image by leveraging background objects to analyze its structure. Faster R-CNN enhances traditional R-CNN by prioritizing automatically learned features over hand-coded ones and addressing the computational challenges of object proposal construction. The region proposal network utilizes information on tumor size, texture, and location to accurately identify tumors, resulting in a higher DSC with fewer selected images. Consequently, this method effectively reduces computational complexity, as highlighted by Wahjuni and Nurarifah [17].

Algorithm 13.1 Steps toward FRCNN to detect pancreatic tumor

Start

Input:

- TM: Total pancreas image samples
- RT: Rectangular box (RB) with red color over the identified tumor in the image sample

Output:

- Localized ROI: Tumor position
- FsrcnnV: Faster R-CNN structure based on VGG_16, including key features
- V: VGG_16 model
- imageSize: [k, l] (dimensions of the input images)
- β: Anchor estimation parameters for (RT, TM)
- FRCNN: Faster R-CNN

1. **Initialization:**
   Initialize the FRCNN model, 'FsrcnnV,' with parameters 'imageSize' and 'β.'
2. **Data splitting:**
   Divide the pancreas image samples, 'TM,' into two sets: Training set 'T1' and test set 'T2.'
   Each sample in the training set will be denoted as 'T.'
3. **Tumor keypoint calculation:**
   For each tumor sample 'tm,' calculate the keypoints using the VGG_16 model, 'V.'
   End for
4. **Model training:**
   Train the 'FsrcnnV' model on 'tm' and record the training time.
5. **Prelocalization:**
   Set 'η_vgg' as the prelocalization output for the tumor in 'tm.' Calculate average precision using the VGG_16 model, 'Ap_vgg,' based on 'V' and 'η_vgg.'
6. **Object detection and localization:**
   - For each sample 'A' in the training set 'T1':
   - Utilize the trained FRCNN model to extract the characteristics of sample 'A,' denoted as 'αA.'
   - Predict the tumor's bounding box, objectness score, and class using 'Predict(αA).' The prediction returns:
   - 'Rectangular_box': The bounding box of the detected object.
   - 'Objectness_PT': The confidence score for the tumor being present.
   - 'Class': The predicted class label (tumor or nontumor).
   - Update 'η' with the red RB for the predicted tumor location 'ssPT.'
   - End for
7. **Output generation:**
   For each sample, generate the output, including the rectangular bounding box ('RB') and class label.
8. **Evaluation:**
   Calculate the final model outline accuracy '€' using 'η,' and compute the Average Precision 'Ap_€' for evaluation.

FINISH

Notes:

T1: Training set, **T2:** Test set, **tm:** Tumor samples

13.3.3 Image Feature Extraction with GLCM

By selecting optimal features from a diverse set of image attributes, the GLCM effectively removes redundant features, enhancing classification accuracy in medical MR images for accurate tumor identification. However, calculating all possible features can be time-consuming and may introduce noninformative data into the analysis. The GLCM feature selection method accelerates computations by identifying significant features while eliminating unnecessary ones, enabling efficient classification of benchmark pancreatic MR images [18].

13.3.4 Classification Process

13.3.4.1 Overview of GNNs

GNNs, a specialized subset of deep learning, are adept at managing data with intricate topologies, such as graphs composed of varying nodes and edges. In this research, GNNs were utilized to identify multiple organs or objects while minimizing false positives. Previous studies have highlighted the effectiveness of GNNs in accurately classifying distinct organ types. For instance, when applied to pancreatic networks, GNNs successfully captured topological information related to pancreas anatomy and tumor growth. The GNN node classifier plays a pivotal role by extracting critical interactions between nodes and edges through fully connected layers and convolutional filters. According to Yang *et al.* [36], GNNs have demonstrated their ability to effectively detect causal relationships between features, particularly in cases involving significant structural abnormalities, such as pancreatic tumor. As a result, GNNs are invaluable in the context of multimodal tumor detection.

13.4 Results and Discussion

13.4.1 Pancreas Database

The study utilized MR images captured at intervals of 30 to 60 degrees. The experiment was conducted using datasets from MATLAB 2013a, with a panel resolution of 512 × 512 for the MR images. The total dataset was divided into 70% for training, 20% for testing, and 10% for validation. Specifically, of 852 pancreatic images, 596 were used for training, 170 for testing, and 85 for validation. Ground-truth data were provided by radiologists to assist in calculating abnormal tumor values. Although the KGS

Madurai scan center supplied most of the MR images, some images were sourced from the TCIA database [19] due to incomplete availability of the dataset from a single source.

13.4.1.1 *Input Image*

Figure 13.2 shows the input pancreatic image, i.e., testing images, whereas Figure 13.3 shows the filtered images from the input of pancreas image as follows.

13.4.1.2 *Filtering of Pancreas Images*

The outcomes of the MDBCWM filtering applied to a typical pancreas image are shown in Figure 13.3.

Figure 13.4 illustrates the filtering process utilizing the MDBCWM filter, as was previously done. It shows the pancreas image filtering method, which will improve filtering accuracy.

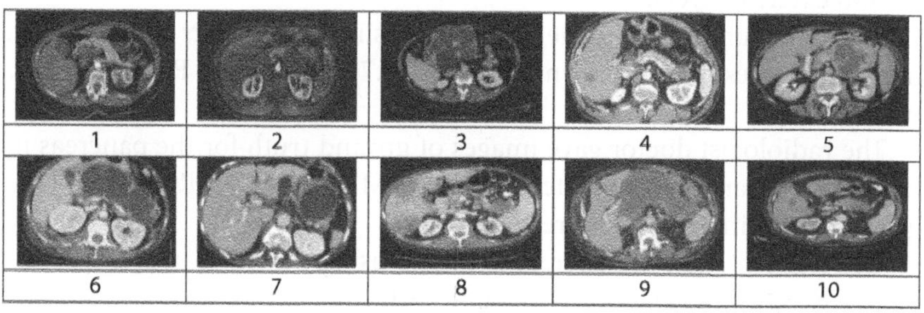

Figure 13.2 Abnormal pancreas image.

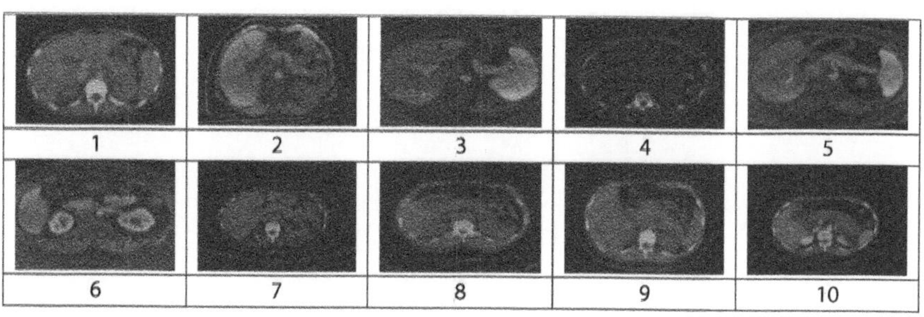

Figure 13.3 Filtered pancreas image.

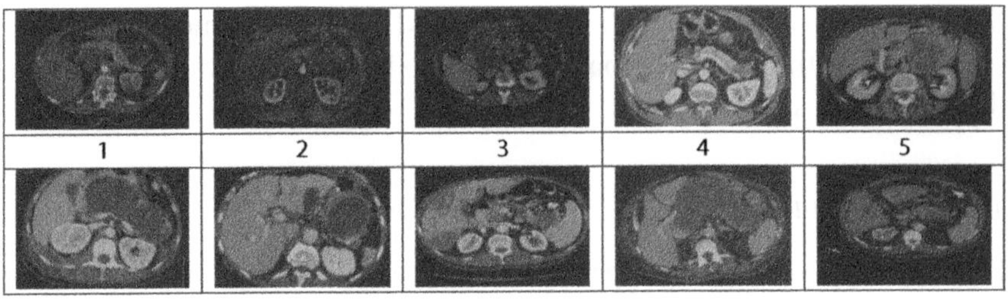

Figure 13.4 Modified DBCWM filter pancreas images.

13.4.1.3 Segmentation

Pancreatic images are a challenging process that has so far been carried out mostly by neurologists. As a result, a strong and automatic segmentation approach is used to accurately diagnose pancreatic tumors and classify them. MDM–FCM–FRCNN will be used to segment the abnormal pancreas, as illustrated in Figure 13.5, where MDM–FCM–FRCNN results will be further calculated.

Figure 13.6 (FRCNN) shows the pancreatic tumor in its exact position, with red segments highlighting the tumor and blue outlining its boundaries and exterior layers.

A specific tumor was further identified using the FRCNN segmentation method; the results are shown in Figure 13.7 in the figure PT (pancreatic tumor).

The radiologist doctor gave images of ground truth for the pancreas in order to compare the segmented outputs of MDM–FCM–FRCNN with the ground-truth images in Figure 13.8.

The segmentation of pancreatic tumors using the novel hybrid MDM–FCM–RCNN model is shown in Table 13.1.

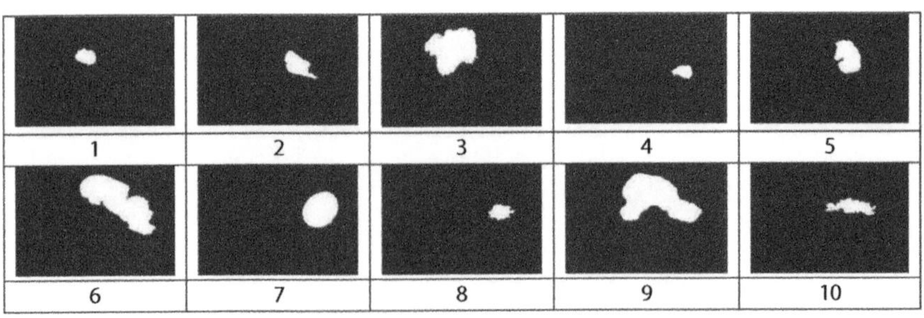

Figure 13.5 Segmentation with the modified distance metric of FCM and FRCNN.

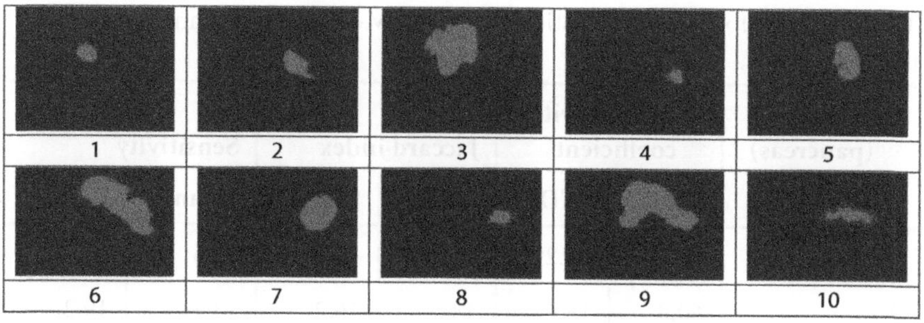

Figure 13.6 Segmentation with FRCNN.

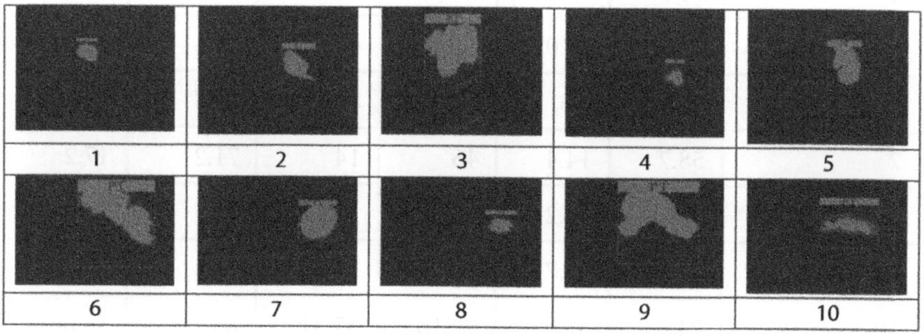

Figure 13.7 Tumor detection with FRCNN.

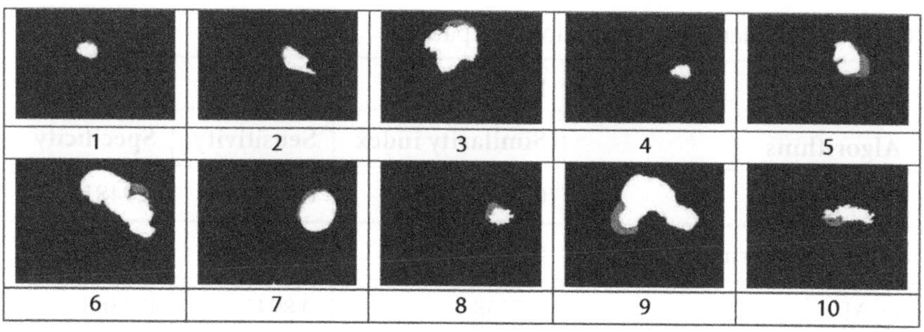

Figure 13.8 Ground-truth images of pancreas.

The values are evaluated in Table 13.2 for segmentation comparison with pancreatic tumors using several available models.

Table 13.3 compares a variety of models of pancreatic tumor with DSC values from different publications.

GLCM feature values for normal pancreatic tumor image 15 are tabulated in Table 13.6.

Table 13.1 Performance evaluation MDM–FCM–R-CNN for pancreatic tumor images.

Images (pancreas)	Dice similarity coefficient		Jaccard index		Sensitivity	
	Mean	**STD**	**Mean**	**STD**	**Mean**	**STD**
1	80.2	11.2	67.3	10.4	80.6	14.7
2	60.9	16.6	48	16.2	73.4	19.2
3	74.9	17.4	55.7	16.8	75.9	21.2
4	91.5	42.5	72.46	37.24	97.61	40.75
5	86.5	39.09	63.46	43.64	89.61	38.8
6	79.1	9.5	65.2	8.7	78.7	12.6
7	58.7	14.4	46	14	71.2	17.2
8	72.7	15.2	53.5	14.2	73.7	19.4
9	84.4	41.7	68.26	35.5	95.41	36.25
10	74	35.09	59.16	37.31	85.51	36.6

Table 13.2 Pancreas segmentation comparison.

	Pancreas		
Algorithms	**Similarity index**	**Sensitivity**	**Specificity**
MDM-FCM	0.7821	0.9567	0.9481
Hybrid clustering technique	0.7011	0.8842	0.9298
FCM	0.7058	0.8945	0.9368
Graph cut segmentation	0.7031	0.7121	0.8021
K-means algorithm	0.6931	0.7621	0.8061
MDM–FCM–RCNN proposed segmentation	0.8521	0.9784	0.9601

Table 13.3 Pancreas segmentation comparison with DSC.

S. no.	Existing pancreas segmentation	Methods	DSC
1	Lu *et al.* [20]	RR U-Net	88.32
2	Guo *et al.* [21]	Deep LOGISMOS	83.2
3	Zhu *et al.* [22]	V-NAS	92:95
4	Chen *et al.* [23]	TransUNet	89.71
5	Roth *et al.* [24]	Cascaded 3D FCN	76.80
6	Huo *et al.* [25]	ATSO	83.70
7	Roth *et al.* [26]	Spatial aggregation	81.30
8	Oktay *et al.* [27]	Attention U-Net	83.1
9	Fu *et al.* [28]	Richer feature convolutional network (RCF)	82.41
10	Kawamoto *et al.* [29]	DNN	87.4
11	**Proposed work**	**MDM-FCM-RCNN**	97.84

The abnormal pancreas of 100 datasets using GLCM feature extraction is explained in Table 13.4.

Ground-truth images of the pancreas are classified in Tables 13.5 and 13.6; homogeneity (HL) and contrast (CL) values are assessed.

Table 13.7 provides accuracy analysis averages with values. GNN has higher value in accuracy comparing with other models.

Malignant and benign pancreatic tumor values are shown in Table 13.8 with their corresponding classifications.

The proposed research utilizes a neural network with nine input neurons from the GLCM of pancreatic images, four hidden neurons, and one output neuron. A 10-fold CV strategy is used to minimize errors and optimize mean square error (MSE). The classification accuracy for test data is 98% and 97% for respective pancreas datasets. Gradient descent, with a value of 0.0190 at epoch 75, is used for weight adjustments during training. Performance metrics, including accuracy, sensitivity, and specificity, are presented in Table 13.9.

The six GLCM features (CP, SE, SV, HOMO, CS, and IMC) are used to compute the testing time using the GNN, which is shown in Table 13.10.

Table 13.4 Abnormal MR pancreas GLCM feature values.

S. no.	Contrast	Clust er prominence	Clust er shade	Energy	Entropy	Hom ogeneit y	Sum variance	Sum entropy	Correlation
1	0.26	79.3	9.43	0.26	1.95	0.91	12.8	2.21	0.91
2	0.86	419	15.6	0.21	2.87	0.94	53.6	2.34	0.92
3	0.76	487	35.4	0.13	2.78	0.81	28.6	2.2	0.91
4	0.91	347	19.6	0.16	2.58	0.78	27.6	2.1	0.86
5	0.94	354	19.7	0.16	2.59	0.82	27.7	2.07	0.88
6	0.84	409	15.4	0.12	2.83	0.81	53.4	2.33	0.88
7	0.63	862	73.8	0.27	2.18	0.87	32.2	1.91	0.91
8	0.64	357	27.6	0.18	2.38	0.83	21.7	2.0	0.86
9	0.78	398	31.4	0.12	2.84	0.82	23.7	2.22	0.87
10	0.48	613	51.1	0.17	2.56	0.79	59.9	1.9	0.92

Table 13.5 Pancreas ground-truth through GLCM cluster and homogeneity .

S. no.	Classifiers	SEN	TN	FN	FP	SPE	TP	ACC
1	GNN	99	28	0	0	98	36	98
2	BPNN-SR	97	26	0	1	96	31	97
3	SqueezeNet	85	24	6	9	91	25	92
4	SVM RBF	82	20	8	2	98	31	89
5	DarkNet-19	83	21	4	6	89	23	90
6	SVM poly	79	20	10	4	97	31	84
7	ResNet-18	84	22	6	7	90	21	91
8	SVM linear	74	18	12	15	62	22	69
9	RBF ANN	86	24	6	2	95	30	91

Table 13.6 Classifiers of pancreas GLCM homogeneity and cluster prominence values.

S. no.	Classifiers	SEN	TN	FN	FP	SPE	TP	ACC
1	GNN	99	29	0	0	98	37	98
2	BPNN -SR	98	27	0	1	97	32	97
3	SqueezeNet	82	23	4	3	90	30	91
4	SVM RBF	83	22	7	3	98	30	93
5	DarkNet-19	79	21	7	5	88	28	89
6	SVM poly	80	23	9	10	97	31	88
7	ResNet-18	77	20	6	8	91	28	92
8	SVM linear	74	18	13	14	62	22	68
9	RBF ANN	90	27	5	6	96	29	91

Table 13.7 Different models' accuracy analysis average with higher value.

	SR	BPNN–SR	LSSVM	Naive Bayes	GNN
Accuracy (%)	89.21	95.62	91.67	90.42	97.74
Sensitivity (%)	91.32	96.02	89.66	90.44	98.04
Specificity (%)	91.26	95.03	94.74	91.02	96.96

Table 13.8 Classification comparison with existing pancreatic tumor works.

Existing works comparison for pancreas	Methods	Accuracy
Liu *et al.* [30]	CNN	95
Li *et al.* [31]	EL-SVM	87
Corral *et al.* [32]	IPMN	92
Kuwahara *et al.* [33]	CNN + ResNet50	88
Nawandhar *et al.* [34]	SSE-BIC	95.56
Abel *et al.* [35]	Two-step nnU-Net	96.2
Yang *et al.* [36]	MMRF-ResNet	96
Proposed work	**MDM–FCM–faster R-CNN + GNN**	97.74

Table 13.9 Pancreas training set without feature extraction.

Pancreas				
Accuracy (%)	**Precision (%)**	**Sensitivity (%)**	**Specificity (%)**	**MSE**
97.4	95.8	97.8	96.4	0.0099

Table 13.10 Testing time for feature combinations.

GNN	6 Feature(s)	5 Feature(s)	4 Feature(s)	3 Feature(s)	2 Feature(s)	1 Feature(s)
Pancreas	1.18	1.21	0.89	0.74	0.60	0.3

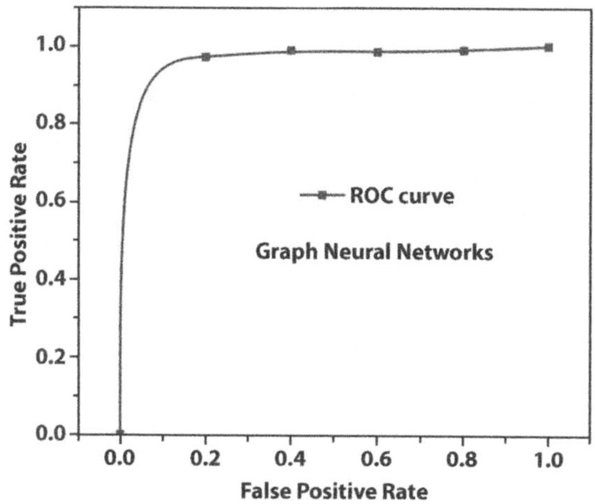

Figure 13.9 Receiver operating characteristic curve.

The above Figure 13.9 shows the ROC curve of the final classification.

13.5 Conclusion

The diagnosis of pancreatic tumors often relies on MRI and CT scans, which provide reliable results. Recently, the relevance of segmentation in artificial intelligence, machine learning, and deep learning has grown in the field of medical imaging, particularly for cancer detection. This chapter proposes a hybrid, novel segmentation approach utilizing MDM-FCM, FRCNN, and GNNs. The predictions generated by the proposed model align closely with the experimental results. According to the findings, tumor segmentation in pancreatic images achieved a specificity of 96.01% in terms of DSC when compared with ground-truth images. The classification process, conducted using GNNs, attained an accuracy of 97.74%.

Acknowledgement

The Author acknowledges the Radiologist Dr. Daggumati Shrehari Rao provided the essential patient data and images and relevant ground-truth images for the author's research.

AI disclosure statement: The author confirms that no artificial intelligence (AI)-generated content or AI-assisted writing tools were used in the preparation of this chapter (including summaries and the abstract). All text, analysis, and conclusions are the result of the author's original work.

References

1. Bhoomika, B.K., Kanmani, K., Smilarubavathy, G., Early Detection of Pancreatic Cancer using Machine Learning Algorithm, in: *2024 5th International Conference on Mobile Computing and Sustainable Informatics (ICMCSI)*, 2024, January, IEEE, pp. 202–205.
2. He, J., Luo, Z., Lian, S., Su, S., Li, S., Towards accurate abdominal tumor segmentation: A 2D model with Position-Aware and Key Slice Feature Sharing. *Comput. Biol. Med.*, *179*, 108743, 2024.
3. Bereska, J.I., Janssen, B.V., Nio, C.Y., Kop, M.P., Kazemier, G., Busch, O.R., Struik, F., Marquering, H.A., Stoker, J., Besselink, M.G., Verpalen, I.M., Artificial intelligence for assessment of vascular involvement and tumor resectability on CT in patients with pancreatic cancer. *Eur. Radio. Exp.*, 8, 1, 18, 2024 Feb 12.
4. Reddy, D.J., Arun Prasath, T., Pallikonda Rajasekaran, M., Vishnuvarthanan, G., Pancreatic tumor classification based on GLCM—k-NN approaches, in: *International Conference on Intelligent Computing and Applications*, Springer, Singapore, pp. 293–302), 2019.
5. Chen, Z.M., Liao, Y., Zhou, X., Yu, W., Zhang, G., Ge, Y., Ke, T., Shi, K., Pancreatic cancer pathology image segmentation with channel and spatial long-range dependencies. *Comput. Biol. Med.*, 169, 107844, 2024 Feb 1.
6. Cao, L. and Li, J., Strongly representative semantic-guided segmentation network for pancreatic and pancreatic tumors. *Biomed. Signal Process. Control*, 87, 105562, 2024 Jan 1.
7. Amiri, S., Vrtovec, T., Mustafaev, T., Deufel, C.L., Thomsen, H.S., Sillesen, M.H., Brandt, E.G.S., Andersen, M.B., Müller, C.F. and Ibragimov, B., Reinforcement learning-based anatomical maps for pancreas subregion and duct segmentation. *Med. Phys.*, 51, 10, 7378–7392, 2024.
8. Ghorpade, H., *et al.*, Automatic Segmentation of Pancreas and Pancreatic Tumor: A Review of a Decade of Research, in: *IEEE Access*, vol. 11, pp. 108727–108745, 2023, doi: 10.1109/ACCESS.2023.3320570.
9. Wang, F., Cheng, C., Cao, W., Wu, Z., Wang, H., Wei, W., Yan, Z., Liu, Z., MFCNet: A multi-modal fusion and calibration networks for 3D pancreas tumor segmentation on PET-CT images. *Comput. Biol. Med.*, 155, 106657, 2023 Mar 1.
10. Zhou, Z., Bian, Y., Pan, S., Meng, Q., Zhu, W., Shi, F., Chen, X., Shao, C., Xiang, D., A dual branch and fine-grained enhancement network for pancreatic tumor segmentation in contrast enhanced CT images. *Biomed. Signal Process. Control*, 82, 104516, 2023 Apr 1.
11. Li, Q., Liu, X., He, Y., Li, D., Xue, J., Temperature guided network for 3D joint segmentation of the pancreas and tumors. *Neural Networks*, 157, 387–403, 2023 Jan 1.
12. Barat, M., *et al.*, Artificial intelligence: a critical review of current applications in pancreatic imaging. *Jpn. J. Radiol.*, 39, 6, 514–523, 2021.

13. Dandu, J.R., Thiyagarajan, A.P., Murugan, P.R., Govindaraj, V., Pancreatic tumor segmentation using SRM and BPNN classification. *Health Technol.*, *10*, 1, 187–195, 2020.
14. Jithendra Reddy, D., Arun Prasath, T., Pallikonda Rajasekaran, M., Distance Metric-based Segmentation and Score-Level Classification for Optimized Tumor Identification in MR Images. *IETE J. Res.*, 69, 12, 9288–9309, 2022. https://doi.org/10.1080/03772063.2022.2088628.
15. Jude Hemanth, D., *et al.*, Distance metric-based time-efficient fuzzy algorithm for abnormal magnetic resonance brain image segmentation. *Neural Comput. Appl.*, 22, 5, 1013–1022, 2013.
16. Reddy, D.J., Prasath, T.A., Rajasekaran, M.P., Spotting pancreatic tumor identification through SRM segmentation and Naïve Bayes method. *Int. J. Recent Technol. Eng.*, 8, 4S2, 339–43, 2019.
17. Wahjuni, S. and Nurarifah, H., Faster RCNN based leaf segmentation using stereo images. *J. Agric. Food Res.*, *11*, 100514, 2023.
18. Prakash, K. and Saradha, S., Efficient prediction and classification for cirrhosis disease using LBP, GLCM and SVM from MRI images. *Mater. Today Proc.*, *81*, 383–388, 2023.
19. Roth, H., Farag, A., Turkbey, E.B., Lu, L., Liu, J., Summers, R.M., Data From Pancreas-CT (Version 2) [Data set], The Cancer Imaging Archive, 2016, https://doi.org/10.7937/K9/TCIA.2016.tNB1kqBU.
20. Lu, L., Jian, L., Luo, J., Xiao, B., Pancreatic segmentation *via* ringed residual U-Net. *IEEE Access*, 7, 172871–172878, 2019.
21. Guo, Z., Zhang, L., Lu, L., Bagheri, M., Summers, R.M., Sonka, M., Yao, J., Deep LOGISMOS: Deep learning graph-based 3D segmentation of pancreatic tumors on CT scans, in: *2018 IEEE 15th International Symposium on Biomedical Imaging (ISBI 2018)*, IEEE, pp. 1230–1233, 2018.
22. Zhu, Z., Liu, C., Yang, D., Yuille, A., Xu, D., V-NAS: Neural architecture search for volumetric medical image segmentation, in: *2019 International conference on 3d vision (3DV)*, IEEE, pp. 240–248, 2019.
23. Chen, J., Lu, Y., Yu, Q., Luo, X., Adeli, E., Wang, Y., Lu, L., Yuille, A.L., Zhou, Y., Transunet: Transformers make strong encoders for medical image segmentation. arXiv preprint arXiv:2102.04306, 2021.
24. Huo, X., Xie, L., He, J., Yang, Z., Zhou, W., Li, H., Tian, Q., ATSO: Asynchronous teacher-student optimization for semi-supervised image segmentation, in: *Proceedings of the IEEE/CVF Conference on Computer Vision and Pattern Recognition*, pp. 1235–1244, 2021.
25. Roth, H.R., Oda, H., Zhou, X., Shimizu, N., Yang, Y., Hayashi, Y., Oda, M., Fujiwara, M., Misawa, K., Mori, K., An application of cascaded 3D fully convolutional networks for medical image segmentation. *Comput. Med. Imaging Graphics*, 66, 90–99, 2018.
26. Roth, H.R., Lu, L., Lay, N., Harrison, A.P., Farag, A., Sohn, A., Summers, R.M., Spatial aggregation of holistically-nested convolutional neural networks for

automated pancreas localization and segmentation. *Med. Image Anal.*, 45, 94–107, 2018.
27. Oktay, O., Schlemper, J., Folgoc, L.L., Lee, M., Heinrich, M., Misawa, K., Mori, K., *et al.*, Attention u-net: Learning where to look for the pancreas. arXiv preprint arXiv:1804.03999, 2018.
28. Fu, M., Wu, W., Hong, X., Liu, Q., Jiang, J., Ou, Y., Zhao, Y., Gong, X., Hierarchical combinatorial deep learning architecture for pancreas segmentation of medical computed tomography cancer images. *BMC Syst. Biol.*, 12, 4, 119–127, 2018.
29. Kawamoto, S., Zhu, Z., Chu, L.C., Javed, A.A., Kinny-Köster, B., Wolfgang, C.L., Hruban, R.H., Kinzler, K.W., Fouladi, D.F., Blanco, A., Shayesteh, S., Deep neural network-based segmentation of normal and abnormal pancreas on abdominal CT: evaluation of global and local accuracies. *Abdom. Radiol.*, 49, 2, 501–11, 2024 Feb.
30. Liu, K.-L., Wu, T., Chen, P.-T., Tsai, Y.M., Roth, H., Wu, M.-S., Liao, W.-C., Wang, W., Deep learning to distinguish pancreatic cancer tissue from non-cancerous pancreatic tissue: a retrospective study with cross-racial external validation. *Lancet Digit. Health*, 2, 6, e303–e313, 2020.
31. Li, M., Nie, X., Reheman, Y., Huang, P., Zhang, S., Yuan, Y., Chen, C., *et al.*, Computer-aided diagnosis and staging of pancreatic cancer based on CT images. *IEEE Access*, 8, 141705–1417185, 2020.
32. Corral, J.E., Hussein, S., Kandel, P., Bolan, C.W., Bagci, U., Wallace, M.B., Deep learning to classify intraductal papillary mucinous neoplasms using magnetic resonance imaging. *Pancreas*, 48, 6, 805–810, 2019.
33. Kuwahara, T., Hara, K., Mizuno, N., Okuno, N., Matsumoto, S., Obata, M., Kurita, Y., *et al.*, Usefulness of deep learning analysis for the diagnosis of malignancy in.
34. Kuwahara, T., Hara, K., Mizuno, N., Okuno, N., Matsumoto, S., Obata, M., Kurita, Y., Koda, H., Toriyama, K., Onishi, S., Ishihara, M., Usefulness of deep learning analysis for the diagnosis of malignancy in intraductal papillary mucinous neoplasms of the pancreas. *Clin. Transl. Gastroenterol., 10*, 5, e00045, 2019. Nawandhar, A., Kumar, N., Veena, R., Yamujala, L., Stratified squamous epithelial biopsy image classifier using machine learning and neighborhood feature selection. *Biomed. Signal Process. Control*, 55, 101671, 2020.
35. Abel, L., Wasserthal, J., Weikert, T., Sauter, A.W., Nesic, I., Obradovic, M., Yang, S., *et al.*, Automated detection of pancreatic cystic lesions on CT using deep learning. *Diagnostics*, 11, 5, 901, 2021.
36. Yang, R., Chen, Y., Sa, G., Li, K., Hu, H., Zhou, J., Guan, Q., Chen, F., CT classification model of pancreatic serous cystic neoplasmsand mucinous cystic neoplasms based on a deep neural network. *Abdom. Radiol.*, 47, 232–241, 2022.

Part 3
CHALLENGES

14

Performance Improvement of Brain Tumor Classification Using Aquila-Based Optimization on Transfer Learning Models

Ganeshkumar M.[1]*, Karthigadevi K.[1] and Nesarani A.[2]

[1]Department of Computer Applications, Kalasalingam Academy of Research and Education, Krishnankoil, Tamilnadu, India
[2]Department of Computer Science and Engineering, Koneru Lakshmaiah Educational Foundation (Deemed to be University), Vadeeswaram, Andra Pradesh, India

Abstract
The aim of the current research is to use deep learning transfer learning models to increase the performance and accuracy of brain tumor images. The parameters of the transfer learning model are further fined tuned by applying Aquila optimization (AO) and arithmetic optimization algorithm. To obtain an optimal outcome, the technique is repeated and assessed using characteristics such as population size. Since the population-based approach is a well-known search strategy for high-density problems, the model presented here is well suited for both high- and low-dimensional problems. The proposed model combines AO and transfer learning (TL) models DenseNet, MobileNet, ResNet, and AlexNet, and their hyperparameters are fine-tuned. Among TL models, DenseNet outperformed other TL models with results of accuracy, sensitivity, specificity, F1 score, precision, and Intersection over Union (IOU) with values as 98.56, 97.98, 99.01, 98.67, 98.45, and 96.87.

***Keywords*:** Brain tumor, PNET (primitive neuro-ectodermal tumor), transfer learning (TL), aquila optimization (AO), arithmetic optimization algorithm (AOA), hyperparameter tuning, deep learning (DL), convolutional neural network (CNN), MRI image classification

**Corresponding author*: ganeshmca1215@gmail.com

R. Nidhya, D. Pavithra, S. Balamurugan, A. Dinesh Kumar and Sheng-Lung Peng (eds.) Medical Metaverse for Digital Healthcare: Technologies, Applications, and Challenges, (287–304) © 2026 Scrivener Publishing LLC

14.1 Introduction

Early detection of brain tumors, which are growths of abnormal tissue in the brain, can lead to effective treatment. On the basis of tumor site and progression, more than 100 different forms of a cranial growth can often be divided into categories. Doctors also classified tumor in the brain as grades I, II, III, and IV based on their progression in stages. Benign and malignant brain cancers are the two most prevalent forms; whereas benign brain cancers have some strict and nonexistent uniformity, malignant brain cancers lack structured and consistent uniformity. There are numerous imaging methods available to detect tumors. Magnetic resonance imaging (MRI) is a reliable form of conventional diagnostic imaging for detecting brain tumors. This study examines two types of brain tumors, including primitive neurotransmitter tumor (PNE), a benign slow-growing malignant tumor that is most frequently diagnosed in youngsters. The ability of the radiologist is mostly responsible for early tumor detection [1]. In addition to determining the size of the tumor, the doctor must determine if it is benign or malignant. Usually, a test is done to determine whether the tumor is mild and cancerous. Brain tumors cannot be examined prior to surgery, unlike other tumors in the body [2]. For accurate diagnoses and to avoid surgery, a suitable diagnostic approach for tumor detection and assessed with MRI scans must be established [3, 4].

Image dataset can be collected publicly from available BRATS data repository. These images are available as preprocessed images that are further segmented and classified by different deep learning (DL) models. The accuracy in classification by these models results high as compared with traditional models. Convolutional neural network (CNN) and its variants are used whose accuracy percentage could be enhanced by applying optimization procedures.

The work carried out in this study is described as follows: Section 14.2 details work carried out so far with this problem. Section 14.3 describes the various transfer learning (TL) models used in DL. Section 14.4 briefs the optimization technique used, and Section 14.5 details the experimental outcome.

14.2 Research Survey

This section details various research works carried out in optimizing the model of TL to have improved performance of CNN models [5]. In current scenario, researchers have to focus performance with less model parameters [6, 7]. Therefore, optimization of parameters is essential to determine specific parameters to reach the desired objective. To solve an optimization problem, parameters and constraints are essential. Most optimal solutions are achieved with gradient-based methods but infeasible for unknown problems and computationally expensive functions [8]. Alternative to this is stochastic optimization methods with nature-inspired algorithms with single- and multiple-solution based [8]. It is used to search a larger search area than a single-solution method. Particle swarm optimization, genetic algorithm, and ant colony optimization are multiple-solution-based algorithms. The numbers of research with different algorithms as Firefly, Dolphin ecolocation, gray wolf optimizer, Cuckoo search, and Bat algorithm were experimented [9–13].

Aquila-based optimization (AO), which is a nature-inspired algorithm, and arithmetic optimization algorithm (AOA), which is a metaheuristic method that relays on mathematical functions as addition (A), subtraction (S), multiplication (M), and division (D), were modeled to optimize the search space. In this research, the hybrid approach of AO-AOA (metaheuristic methods) was used [14, 15]. The merits of using this hybrid approach are being gradient-free, simple, and black-box nature-based and that it avoids higher local optimum convergence [6, 16–18]. This hybrid approach is preferred to achieve global optimization, reduce computational resource, and apply both to low- and high-dimensional space.

14.3 Model Perspective

14.3.1 Transfer Learning Models

The TL method involves applying a previously trained model to fresh machine learning (ML) problems. A computer increases the level of prediction about a new task in TL using the previously trained data knowledge from past assignments. Throughout TL, the previously learned ML method is applied to a unique but relevant problem [19]. To learn the reused attributes in another, TL is a powerful ML technique. The main objective of the TL in this study is to describe the differences between benign and malignant phases. Due to their considerable closeness, these two stages take longer to anticipate and classify. The TL is more important in categorizing individuals at an equal stage and was considered the top choice. Additionally, the TL method modifies the final layers for a different dataset while freezing the weighted model.

Typically, the first layer of neural networks used in computer visualization is intended to predict an edge; the second layer is intended to predict structure, and the final layer is intended to predict task-specific properties. In the TL approach, the first and middle layers are investigated. Only the final layers receive new training. It is used to learn how the tasks labeled data usages.

There are many processing benefits to the TL method. Minimized training time, improved neural network performance (under most conditions), and minimal data requirements are some of the benefits. More data are required to learn the neural network approach, but it is not possible to obtain it. This is how the TL method is conceptually processed. According to the TL model, features are initially trained and learned in a broad task before being applied to a different activity. Additionally, an input model that is similar in size to the initial training can be trained.

14.3.2 Pretrained Model

Utilizing a model that has previously been trained is an alternate approach. There are not many research models nowadays. The various layers are retrained and utilized to identify the task. Nine prelearned models are included in Keras, which are utilized in TL for prediction and fine-tuning. It serves as proof that the model can be applied to relearning and discovered. Most often, DL models are utilized to create TLs.

14.3.3 Feature Extraction

The characteristics have been dynamically gathered by the DL. Additionally, the need of feature engineering and domain knowledge is not diminished by the DL model. A feature that will be used by the network has been implemented by the DL. The neural networks are able to learn which features are important and which ones are not. It would have taken a lot of human labor even for many complicated tasks. This may serve as the learning model for quickly identifying a good set of qualities. Applying the trained representation to other tasks is common. It can be as simple as initializing the layers to choose the right feature's representation. The output may be misinterpreted by the framework due to its extreme task specificity. Instead, the information is sent across the system, where it will be processed by a middle layer before being output. The raw data can be viewed as a representation of layers. Because it can reduce the dataset and the calculation time, this model is frequently used in computer vision. Additionally, it offers the best conventional algorithms.

14.3.4 Need to Tune Hyperparameter of the Learning Model

Behavior and performance in the learning model are solely the responsibility of hyperparameters. In the learning model, reducing a preset loss function while also improving efficiency is the main goal of hyperparameter tuning. The two categories of hyperparameter models are network structure and training related. Hidden layers, kernel size and type, padding, stride, and dropout are essential network construction factors. Training-related variables include learning rate, batch size, growth, and optimizer.

The AO metaheuristic model is used to adjust these TL model hyperparameters. As a result, the AO-based TL method's suggested task involves performing a classification for the prediction of brain tumors. In this work, the hybrid method of AO with AOA is proposed to fine-tune the hyperparameter of the learning model.

14.4 Proposed Methodology

The proposed method uses AO to tune the hyperparameters of TL models. It performs the task by following the subsequent phases as preprocessing phase, training phase, classification phase, and optimization and evaluation phase.

14.4.1 Preprocessing Phase

In the preprocessing phase, image augmentation and image transformation using flipping and rotation are carried out.

14.4.2 Training and Testing Phase

This stage involved training and testing of data preparation of TL model for predicting four types of tumors. There are four various models that are evaluated to build the pretrained CNN model, which is known as the TL model. The TL models used in this work are currently in its second phase. The TL model was trained and evaluated at this point.

The pretrained CNN model, sometimes referred to as the TL model, is created by evaluating four different models. AlexNet, DenseNet121, MobileNet, and ResNet18V2 are the TL models used in this research, which are described below.

14.4.3 Transfer Learning Models

The following section details the various TL models:

14.4.3.1 AlexNet

The CNN-based TL approach is known as AlexNet. Both an input and a classification output are present in this AlexNet. The reason AlexNet is referred to as a TL is because certain data are prelearned, while some layers are shifted immediately without any development from the primary source. To get an accurate classification, this model is utilized, which is a pretrained AlexNet classifier [20]. The dataset that belongs on its weights, biases, and other training factors is learned using the AlexNet structure. Hyperparameters are the name given to these parameters.

Five convolutional layers, a maximum pooling layer, and three fully linked layers make up the overall AlexNet architecture. The AlexNet receives a two-dimensional image with 3 RGB channels and a width and length of 227 from an input layer with dimensions of 227×227×3.

The nonsaturating activation functions sigmoid, ReLU, and tanh are used to illustrate AlexNet learning performance. The fully connected layer is transformed into the classification layer at a size of 2048 and 1000 classes. Consequently, AlexNet has eight layers overall and feature learning. The ReLU activation function contains three pooling layers, three convolutional layers, and five layers altogether. The softmax activation function is applied in an output layer. Consequently, a complete architecture consists of 62.3 million parameters in total.

Through TL, AlexNet learning sessions are typically scheduled. The optimal answer is already calculated by the hyperparameter fine-tuning. The accuracy of AlexNet is controlled by the weights' and bias' hyperparameter fine-tuning. Instead of training a neural network approach from start, AlexNet is fine-tuned using some other layers that are already accurate and configured. The key advantage of an AlexNet is the ease of this tweaking process. The typical CNN approach has been layer by layer tweaked in the AlexNet model using hyperparameters. This model is configured with a depth of 22 layers, which prevents inaccurate learning challenges on extensive learning samples.

14.4.3.2 ResNet

ResNet-18 is the name of a deep CNN with 18 layers. With its pretrained model, images of objects such as keyboards, mouse, pens, and other animals can be categorized into 1000 distinct categories. As a result, the network now provides comprehensive feature representations for a wide range of images. Photos with 224 by 224 pixels can be accepted by the network.

14.4.3.3 DenseNet

Another important deep CNN technology is the DenseNet. This approach introduces a brand-new connection mode. This connection option can connect to all current network layers, as well as earlier network layers. As a result, the earlier layers are used as input features, and the current layer is used to generate a feature map. By using a low convolution kernel to produce a larger number of features, this link corrects the drawbacks of the vanishing gradient. Four fully linked layers with a growth rate of four make up the DenseNet model. It is used to obtain an input of the previous layers' output feature for each layer. The previous layer's feature map and the ResNet residual unit are combined and added to create a single layer. The purpose of this network model is to improve the feature maps for all subsequent layers. The feature maps' dimensions are then added by substituting a pixel value for it.

14.4.3.4 MobileNet

In order to provide a lighter model, the MobileNet architecture uses depth-wise separable convolutions as opposed to a traditional convolution layer [21]. Separable convolution filters are a blend of point convolution filters and depth-wise separable filters.

The ideal convolution process on each input channel is carried out by the separable convolutions in the depth-wise filters. The output of depth-wise separable convolutions that produced a 1×1 convolution in linear are the point convolution filters.

MobileNet includes additional width multiplier and resolution multiplier hyperparameters to adjust the model's accuracy and speed.

Depending on the requirements and applications developed using layers of depth-wise separable convolutions, these differ. Each depth-wise separable convolution layer contains both a point-wise and a depth-wise convolution. The point-wise convolution and a depth-wise convolution are both present in every depth-wise separable convolution layer. These layers are each of the depth-wise separable convolutions' component layers. With 28 layers total, including depth-wise separable convolutions, the MobileNet is the result. A total of 4.2 million parameters are processed in the MobileNet. By altering the multiplier width as well as the linear bottlenecks, inverted residual blocks, and ReLU activation, these parameters are decreased. These block modifications come in a number of variations known as MobileNet-v1, MobileNet-v2, and MobileNet-v3.

14.4.4 Optimization Algorithm

14.4.4.1 Aquila Optimizer

In this study, a hybrid Aquila-based algorithm is proposed to improve the parameters of TL models. An algorithm influenced by nature is called AO [22]. One of the most prevalent raptors in the Northern Hemisphere is the Aquila. Hunting features of Aquila are as follows:

1. Contour flying and glide assault are two of the four primary methods utilized by Aquila for hunting [23]
2. Vertical stoop and high soar [24]
3. The low flight and sluggish attack [25]
4. Taking the prey in one's hands while moving [26]

14.4.4.2 Mathematical Model of AO

The AO method depicts Aquila's hunting behavior in each phase of hunting behavior. In the proposed AO method, there are four phases of implementation as shifting from exploration to exploitation by making use of different behavioral conditions. The four phases are (1) expanded exploration, (2) narrow exploration, (3) expanded exploitation, and (4) narrow exploitation.

The condition when exploration and exploitation occur is given below in Equation (14.1):

$$\begin{cases} t \leq \left(\frac{2}{3}\right) \times T; \text{ execution of exloration steps} \\ \text{otherwise; execution of exploitation steps} \end{cases} \tag{14.1}$$

1. Expanded exploration phase:
The vertical stoop-and-roar behavior of Aquila is mathematically expressed in Equation (14.2):

$$X_1(t+1) = X_{best}(t) \times \left(1 - \frac{t}{T}\right) + (X_M(t) - X_{best}(t) \times rand) \tag{14.2}$$

$$X_M(t) = \frac{1}{N} \sum_{i=1}^{N} X_i(t), \forall j = 1,2, \ldots\ldots, Dim \tag{14.3}$$

where $X_1(t + 1)$ → subsequent cycle for t, $X_{\text{best}}(t)$ → best optimal solution until tth solution; N→no. of participants; Dim→ size by dimension.

$\left(1-\frac{t}{T}\right)$ → Controlling parameter in exploration phase; $X_M(t)$ → mean value solution at tth solution; rand→ random value (0,1); T→ max iteration; t→ current step;

2. Narrow exploration phase:
The glide attack behavior of Aquila is mathematically expressed as in Equation (14.4):

$$X_2(t+1) = X_{best}(t) \times Levy(D) + X_R(t) + (v-u) \times rand \tag{14.4}$$

$X_2(t + 1)$→ subsequent cycle value for t; D→ space of dimension;

Levy(D)→ flight distribution function of levy calculated in Equation (14.5)

$$\text{Levy}(D) = s \times \frac{u \times \sigma}{|\vartheta| \frac{1}{\beta}} \tag{14.5}$$

$$\sigma = \left(\frac{\tau(1+\beta) \times \sin e\left(\frac{\pi\beta}{2}\right)}{\tau\left(\frac{1+\beta}{2}\right) \times \beta \times 2\left(\frac{\beta-1}{2}\right)} \right) \tag{14.6}$$

$$v = r \times \cos(\theta) \tag{14.7}$$

$$u = r \times \sin(\theta) \tag{14.8}$$

$$r = r_1 + U + D_1 \tag{14.9}$$

$$\theta = -\omega \times D_1 + \theta_1 \tag{14.10}$$

$$\theta_1 = \frac{3\times\pi}{2} \tag{14.11}$$

3. Expanded exploitation phase:
The expanded phase is mathematically expressed as:

$$X_3(t+1) = (X_{\text{best}}(t) - X_M(t))\times\alpha - \text{rand} + ((UB - LB)\times\text{rand} + LB)\times\delta \tag{14.12}$$

$X_3(t + 1)$ = next iteration solution; $X_{\text{best}}(t)$ = prey location until *i*th iteration; $X_M(t)$ = average value at *t*th cycle; rand(0,1); $\alpha = \delta = 0.1$, UB, LB = upper and lower bound.

4. Narrow exploitation phase
This is the prey-grabbing phase and mathematically expressed as:

$$X_4(t+1) = Q\times X_{\text{best}}(t) - (S_1\times X(t))\times\text{rand}) - (S_2\times\text{Levy}(D) + \text{rand}\times S_1 \tag{14.13}$$

Q = quality function, S_1 = motions of AO, S_1 = decreasing value (2–0)

$$Q(t) = t^{\frac{2\times rand()-1}{(1-r)^2}} \tag{14.14}$$

$$S_1 = 2X\ \text{rand}\ () - 1 \tag{14.15}$$

$$S_2 = 2\ \text{X}\ (1 - \frac{t}{T}) \tag{14.16}$$

T = mMax iteration; t = current iteration; rand (0,1).

14.4.4.3 Arithmetic Optimization Algorithm

Figure 14.1 illustrates how AOA, a novel metaheuristic approach, applies and models optimization in a variety of search areas utilizing fundamental mathematical operations such as division (D), addition (A), multiplication (M), and subtraction (S). Often, PBAs (population-based algorithms) start

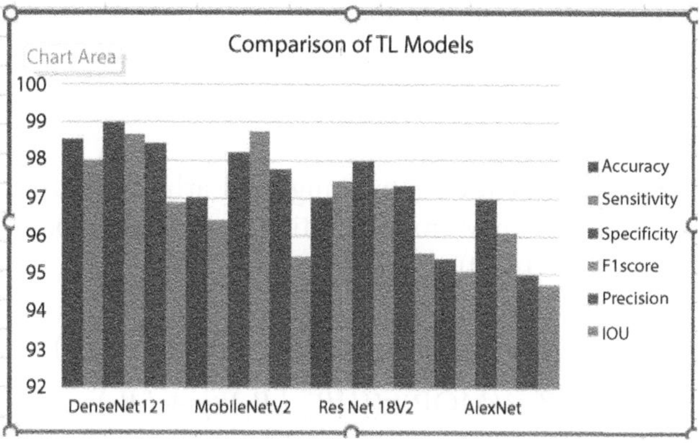

Figure 14.1 Comparison of TL models.

their optimization process by selecting a handful of potential approaches at random. This particular response has been enhanced. A specific objective function is analyzed sequentially, and a set of optimization criteria is applied progressively to form the basis of optimization procedures. Even if PBA is stochastically trying to find some useful strategies to overcome optimization problems, a single-run solution is not guaranteed. The AOA model includes the following phases.

14.4.4.3.1 Initial Stage

Let A denote a set of optimal solution in which specific set is randomly chosen for every iteration.

$$\mathrm{A} = \begin{bmatrix} a_{1,1} & a_{1,2} & a_{1,3} & a_{1,j} & a_{1,1} & a_{1,n} \\ a_{2,1} & a_{2,2} & a_{2,3} & a_{2,j} & & a_{2,n} \\ a_{3,1} & a_{3,2} & a_{1,1} & a_{1,1} & a_{1,1} & a_{1,1} \\ \cdots & \cdots & \cdots & \cdots & \cdots & \cdots \\ a_{N,1} & & & a_{N,j} & a_{N,n-1} & a_{N,n} \end{bmatrix} \tag{14.17}$$

The coefficient of math optimizer accelerated (MOA) is given by the formula:

$$\mathrm{MOA}(\mathrm{B_i}) = \alpha + \mathrm{B_i} \ \mathrm{x} \left(\frac{\mathrm{M{-}m}}{\mathrm{M_i}} \right) \tag{14.18}$$

where $MOA(B_i)$ = ith iteration value, α = accelerated function of max and min values, B_i = present cycle , M_i = max. no of iterations.

14.4.4.3.2 Exploration Stage

The AOA method searches the working field arbitrarily using alternate two-key solution through M (multiplication) and D (division) search keys as given by Equation (14.19):

$$a_{i,j}(\mathrm{B_i}+1)=\begin{cases}\beta_j \div(\mathrm{MOP}\div\varepsilon)\mathrm{x}((UB_j\text{-}LB_j)\mathrm{x}\mu+LB_j),r_2<0.5\\ \beta_j\times(\mathrm{MOP})\mathrm{x}((UB_j\text{-}LB_j)\mathrm{x}\mu+LB_j);\ \text{otherwise}\end{cases} \tag{14.19}$$

where $a_i(B_i + 1)$ = next iteration ith solution, $a_{i,j}(B_i + 1)$ = current iteration jth solution, μ = control parameter (≤ 0.5), LB,UB = lower and upper bound limit, ε = integer, β_j = jth position optimal solution and

$$\mathrm{MOP(B_i)}=1-\frac{B_{\mathrm{iter}}^{1/\gamma}}{M_{\mathrm{iter}}^{1/\gamma}} \tag{14.20}$$

MOP = math optimizer probability;
B_i = current iteration, $MOP(B_i)$ = ith iteration value
M_{iter} = max. iteration ≤ 5.

14.4.4.3.3 Exploitation Stage

The AOA method searches the working field arbitrarily using alternate two-key solution through A (addition) and S (subtraction) search keys as given by Equation (14.21):

$$\begin{aligned}a_{i,j}(\mathrm{B_i}+1)=\beta_j-(\mathrm{MOP}\div\varepsilon)\mathrm{x}((UB_j-LB_j)\mathrm{x}\mu+LB_j),r_3<0.5\\ \beta_j\times(\mathrm{MOP})\mathrm{x}((UB_j-LB_j)\mathrm{x}\mu+LB_j)\ ,\text{otherwise}\end{aligned} \tag{14.21}$$

14.5 Proposed Methodology

The proposed approach is the combination of AO-AOA strategy where the arithmetic component plays a crucial role in optimization procedure. Both

AO and AOA are metaheuristic optimization strategies, and their performance is evaluated by using the same parameters as number of iterations and population size. This method yields better solution for both low- and high-dimensional workspace problems. The complete working procedure is given by the following Algorithm:

Algorithm 14.1 Proposed AO-AOA optimization model.

1. Initialize the parameters (optimizers, dropout ratio, batch size, performance
   metrics, fitness values ⇐ [ ] ,data 🡐 datasplit (train, validation)
2. Generate the solution.
3. Calculate the fitness function
4. Select the best solution
   Fitness function (population, np)
   ⇐Train CNN (model, solution, validation, test, performance metrics) Test CNN (model, metrics, test, train) population increment
5. Check if rand ≤0.5
6. If yes, update AOA; else, update AO.
7. Determine whether the stopping criteria have been meet.
8. If yes, return as the best solution and halt the process.
9. Else, repeat from step 3.

14.6 Results and Discussion

14.6.1 Implementation Test Bed

The work is implemented using python with image processing libraries. The libraries are as follows:

OpenCV: It is an image processing library in python used for applications as face recognition, human gesture, motion detection, etc.

Numpy and Scipy libraries: This library is used for image manipulation operations.

Scikit: It contains packages of ML and DL algorithms.

Python Imaging Library (PIL): This library is used to perform basic functions in image processing such as rotation, resizing, thumbnail creations, converting to other file formats, etc.

14.6.2 Evaluation Metrics

The network model is evaluated using the following performance metrics:

Sensitivity or recall: This metric is used to evaluate the true-positive values for recognition. It is used to estimate the number of true positive and false negative.

It is mathematically expressed as:

$$\text{Sensitivity} = \frac{\text{TP}}{\text{TP+FN}}$$

Specificity: This metrics is used to evaluate the true-negative values for recognition. It is used to estimate the number of true negative and false positive.

It is mathematically expressed as:

$$\text{Specificity} = \frac{\text{TN}}{\text{TN+FP}}$$

Precision: Precision is used to estimate the number of true positive and false positive.

$$\text{Precision} = \frac{\text{TP}}{\text{TP+FP}}$$

Accuracy: It counts to total prediction and expressed as follows:

$$\text{Accuracy} = \frac{\text{TP+TN}}{\text{TP+FP+TN+FN}}$$

F1 score: F1 score is calculated as average of precision and recall and expressed as:

$$\text{F1 score} = 2 * \frac{\text{Precision} * \text{recall}}{\text{Precision+recall}}$$

IOU: Intersection over Union (IOU) coefficient estimates real positive values and is expressed as:

$$\text{IOU}=\frac{\text{TP}}{\text{TP+FP+FN}}$$

The above proposed method is used to optimize four TL network models as DenseNet121, MobileNetV2, ResNet18V2, and AlexNet. The hybrid approach of AO is applied to brain tumor dataset to predict necrotic/ core, edema, and enhancing tumor. The AO-AOA–based TL models are assessed and differentiated with previous methods and evaluated with the aforementioned performance metrics as in Table 14.1.

From the above evaluation, it is observed that DenseNet outperformed other TL models with results of accuracy, sensitivity, specificity, F1 score, precision, and IOU as 98.56, 97.98, 99.01, 98.67, 98.45, and 96.87. The comparative evaluation of the proposed transfer learning model against other CNN architectures is summarized in Table 14.2.

Table 14.1 Comparison of TL techniques.

Model	Accuracy	Sensitivity	Specificity	F1 score	Precision	IOU
DenseNet121	98.56	97.98	99.01	98.67	98.45	96.87
MobileNetV2	97.02	96.43	98.23	98.78	97.76	95.45
ResNet18V2	97.03	97.46	98.012	97.25	97.33	95.55
AlexNet	95.42	95.06	96.99	96.12	95.00	94.74

Table 14.2 Evaluation of proposed model versus CNN model.

Model	Accuracy	Sensitivity	Specificity	F1score	Precision	IOU
Proposed TL model	98.56	97.98	99.01	98.67	98.45	96.87
AlexNet with uncertainty sampling	98.56	97.98	99.01	98.67	98.45	96.87
Modified Inceptionv3	97.02	96.43	98.23	98.78	97.76	95.45
ResNet + XceptionNet + MobileNetV2	97.03	97.46	98.012	97.25	97.33	95.55

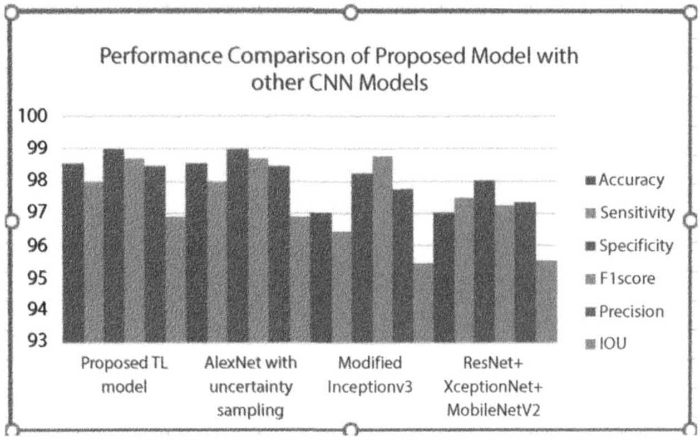

Figure 14.2 Proposed model versus CNN models.

The performance of the suggested technique outperforms other ways with the aforementioned metrics of accuracy, sensitivity, specificity, F1 score, precision, and IOU, according to the comparison between the proposed TL model and other architectures made above. The visual comparison of the proposed model with other CNN architectures based on performance metrics is illustrated in Figure 14.2.

14.7 Conclusion

In this work, brain tumor detection with AO-based TL models is used to improve the accuracy rate of prediction. This work combines AO and TL models DenseNet, MobileNet, ResNet, and AlexNet, and their hyperparameters are fine-tuned. The optimized algorithm provides better solution to automatically predict brain tumor region with less parameters. These approaches were tested, and results were compared with different CNN models. It is found that the proposed approach yields higher performance over the compared approaches in terms of chosen assessment parameters.

AI disclosure statement: The author acknowledges the use of AI-based tools for minor language editing or grammatical correction. However, all intellectual contributions, analyses, and conclusions presented in this chapter are entirely the author's own.

References

1. Afshar, Plataniotis, K.N., Mohammadi, A., Capsule Networks for Brain Tumor Classification Based on MRI Images and Coarse Tumor Boundaries, in: *Proceedings of the ICASSP 2019-2019 IEEE International Conference on Acoustics, Speech and Signal Processing (ICASSP)*, Brighton, UK, 12–17 May 2019, pp. 1368–1372.
2. Shrestha, H., Dhasarathan, C., Kumar, M., Nidhya, R., Shankar, A., Kumar, M., A Deep Learning Based Convolution Neural Network-DCNN Approach to Detect Brain Tumor, in: *Proceedings of Academia-Industry Consortium for Data Science*, Advances in Intelligent Systems and Computing, vol. 1411, G. Gupta, L. Wang, A. Yadav, P. Rana, Z. Wang (Eds.), 2022.
3. He, L., Li, H., Wang, J., Chen, M., Gozdas, E., Dillman, J.R., Parikh, N.A., A multi-task, multi-stage deep transfer learning model for early prediction of neurodevelopment in very preterm infants. *Sci. Rep.*, *10*, 1, 15072, 2020.
4. Nidhya, R., Kalpana, R., Smilarubavathy, G., Keerthana, S.M., Brain Tumor Diagnosis with MCNN-Based MRI Image Analysis, in: *2023 1st International Conference on Optimization Techniques for Learning (ICOTL)*, 2023, December, IEEE, pp. 1–5.
5. LeCun, Y., Bengio, Y., Hinton, G., Deep learning. *Nature*, *521*, 7553, 436–444, 2015.
6. Mahajan, S., Mittal, N., Pandit, A.K., Image segmentation using multilevel thresholding based on type II fuzzy entropy and marine predators algorithm. *Multimedia Tools Appl.*, *80*, 13, 19335–19359, 2021.
7. Saremi, S., Mirjalili, S., Lewis, A., Grasshopper optimisation algorithm: theory and application. *Adv. Eng. Software*, *105*, 30–47, 2017.
8. Coello, C.A.C., Theoretical and numerical constraint-handling techniques used with evolutionary algorithms: a survey of the state of the art. *Comput. Methods Appl. Mech. Eng.*, *191*, 11-12, 1245–1287, 2002.
9. Spall, J.C., *Introduction to stochastic search and optimization: estimation, simulation, and control*, John Wiley & Sons, 2005.
10. Yang, X.S., A new metaheuristic bat-inspired algorithm, in: *Nature inspired cooperative strategies for optimization (NICSO 2010)*, pp. 65–74, Springer Berlin Heidelberg, Berlin, Heidelberg, 2010.
11. Mirjalili, S.M.S.M., Mirjalili, S.M., Lewis, A., Grey Wolf Optimizer. *Adv. Eng. Software*, 69, 46–61, 2014, ed.
12. Kaveh, A. and Farhoudi, N., Dolphin monitoring for enhancing metaheuristic algorithms: Layout optimization of braced frames. *Comput. Struct.*, *165*, 1–9, 2016.
13. Marler, R.T. and Arora, J.S., Survey of multi-objective optimization methods for engineering. *Struct. Multidiscip. Optim.*, *26*, 369–395, 2004.
14. Abualigah, L., Diabat, A., Mirjalili, S., Abd Elaziz, M., Gandomi, A.H., The arithmetic optimization algorithm. *Comput. Methods Appl. Mech. Eng.*, *376*, 113609, 2021.

15. Lepagnot, I.B.J. and Siarry, P., A survey on optimization metaheuristics. *Inf. Sci.*, *237*, 82–117, 2013.
16. Gogna, A. and Tayal, A., Metaheuristics: review and application. *J. Exp. Theor. Artif. Intell.*, *25*, 4, 503–526, 2013.
17. Zhou, A., Qu, B.Y., Li, H., Zhao, S.Z., Suganthan, P.N., Zhang, Q., Multiobjective evolutionary algorithms: A survey of the state of the art. *Swarm Evol. Comput.*, *1*, 1, 32–49, 2011.
18. Steenhof, K., Kochert, M.N., Mcdonald, T.L., Interactive effects of prey and weather on golden eagle reproduction. *J. Anim. Ecol.*, 350–362, 1997.
19. Niu, S., Liu, Y., Wang, J., Song, H., A decade survey of transfer learning (2010–2020). *IEEE Trans. Artif. Intell.*, *1*, 2, 151–166, 2020.
20. Hao, S., Li, Y., Wei, J., Cao, T., Pan, Y., Zhou, K., Airport Perimeter Damage Detection Method Based on Alexnet Optimization. *Acad. J. Sci. Technol.*, *6*, 2, 69–72, 2023.
21. Arbane, M., Benlamri, R., Brik, Y., Djerioui, M., Transfer learning for automatic brain tumor classification using MRI images, in: *2020 2nd International Workshop on Human-Centric Smart Environments for Health and Well-Being (IHSH)*, 2021, February, IEEE, pp. 210–214.
22. Abualigah, L., Yousri, D., Abd Elaziz, M., Ewees, A.A., Al-Qaness, M.A., Gandomi, A.H., Aquila optimizer: a novel meta-heuristic optimization algorithm. *Comput. Ind. Eng.*, *157*, 107250, 2021.
23. Meinertzhagen, R., XI.—Autumn in Central Morocco.—Part II. *Ibis*, *82*, 2, 187–234, 1940.
24. Carnie, S.K., Food habits of nesting golden eagles in the coast ranges of California. *Condor*, *56*, 1, 3–12, 1954.
25. Dekker, D., Hunting behavior of golden eagles, aquila-chrysaetos, migrating in southwestern alberta. *Can. Field-Nat.*, *99*, 3, 383–385, 1985.
26. Watson, J., *The golden eagle*, Bloomsbury Publishing, 2010.

15

An Enhanced Pretrained Language Model for Biomedical Domain: Fine-Tuning BERT for Electronic Health Records

Satish Muppidi[1]*, Radhika Gouni[2], Anupama Angadi[3], Satya Keerthi Gorripati[4], Venubabu Rachapudi[5] and S. Anjali Devi[5]

[1]*Department of Computer Science and Engineering, GMR Institute of Technology, Rajam, Andhra Pradesh, India*
[2]*Directv, Atlanta, Georgia, USA*
[3]*Depart of Computer Science and Engineering, Gitam School of Technology, Gitam, Visakhapatnam, India*
[4]*Gayatri Vidya Parishad College of Engineering(A), Visakhapatnam, India*
[5]*Department of Computer Science and Engineering, Koneru Lakshmaiah Education Foundation, Vaddeswaram, Guntur, Andhra Pradesh, India*

Abstract
Text mining in the biomedical domain is gaining prominence as the volume of electronic health records rapidly grows in the Web 2.0 era. With significant progress in natural language processing with the advent of language models such as BERT, T5, and LLaMA, these models succeeded in various domains. However, their potential falls short when applied directly to biomedical texts, producing unacceptable outcomes due to the shift in word alignment from conventional to clinical corpora. This chapter investigates how the newly familiarized large language model BERT MedPredict can be fine-tuned for clinical corpora to optimize model performance.

Keywords: Pretrained model, BERT, LLaMA, transformer, LSTM, MLP, MASK, electronic health records

**Corresponding author*: satish.m@gmrit.edu.in

R. Nidhya, D. Pavithra, S. Balamurugan, A. Dinesh Kumar and Sheng-Lung Peng (eds.) Medical Metaverse for Digital Healthcare: Technologies, Applications, and Challenges, (305–320) © 2026 Scrivener Publishing LLC

15.1 Introduction

One of the prominent tasks in natural language processing (NLP) is the shortage of sufficient sample data. Although available data are abundant, creating task-specific datasets requires dividing these data across various specialized fields [1]. This process often results in a limited number of human-labeled samples. Unfortunately, deep neural network-driven NLP models require a vastly increased amount of data to perform well, showing significant performance gains with training on millions or even billions of annotated examples. To address this gap, investigators have formulated methods for training widespread language representation models using large volumes of unlabeled data from the internet, a procedure called pre-configuring. These preconfigured models can subsequently be fine-tuned on smaller domain-specific tasks, such as those used for question answering, link prediction, and inference models.

Bidirectional encoder representations from transformers (BERTs) are developed to preconfigure deep neural-driven depictions from the unlabeled text by simultaneously conditionally joining on both the left and right contexts across all layers. This enables the preconfigured BERT model to be easily fine-tuned with a single additional output layer, allowing it to perform sophisticated tasks such as link predictions, question answering, and translation, without the need for substantial changes to the architecture for every specific task.

For example, the word "credit" would have the same context-free depiction in both "sufficient credit" and "What is the credit threshold for a pass?" In contrast, a context-sensitive framework produces context representations based on the context of all other words in the sentence. For instance, in the sentence, "I have credits for a passing grade," a forward-only contextual framework would denote "credit" based on the phrase "I have a passing grade" but not "sufficient." On the other hand, BERT captures the meaning of "credit" by considering the full context of surrounding words—"I have… a pass grade"—by processing the input through a deeply two-pass flow network.

A transformer functions by executing a small, fixed number of steps [2]. At each step, it uses an attention mechanism to capture the associations among all words in a sentence, regardless of their positions. For example, in the sentence, "Full-time student needs 120 credits," the transformer can quickly focus on the word "student" to determine that "credit" refers to the student credits rather than a bank balance, making this inference in just one step.

BERT utilizes a transformer, a focus-based approach that analyzes contextual associations among surrounding words in a sentence [3].

An elementary transformer contains a self-attention model to read and predict activity. Since BERT is designed to build a language representation framework, it utilizes only the encoder component. The input to the BERT encoder is a sequence of tokens that are initially converted into vectors and then processed by the neural network. Prior to processing, BERT requires the input to be formatted and enriched with extra metadata, including token embeddings, segment embeddings, and positional embeddings.

15.1.1 Background

With the increase in digital biomedical articles, extracting essential information has become a challenge. Researchers must consider various sources and convert ambiguous text into refined knowledge to enhance efficacy and performance. However, manual annotation by medical experts is complex, time-consuming, and inefficient [4]. Consequently, efficient NLP methods are becoming crucial for text mining and computational data analysis.

The advent of modern advances in machine learning (ML) and deep learning (DL) has simplified the use of complex pipelines, leading to significant progress in biomedical text and image mining [5]. Most research focuses on combining ML or DL with NLP approaches to reduce costs, errors, security issues, and other challenges.

Electronic health records (EHRs) are a crucial component of healthcare information system and are valuable for risk prediction [6]. Various automated approaches used NLP to extract information from EHRs. However, these approaches face challenges in resolving ambiguities and dealing with tight structures during feature extraction. Developing such a model necessitates learning contextual representations through embedding techniques like Word2Vec, Doc2Vec, FastText, and GloVe [7]. Recent research interests focus on pretrained embeddings, named entity recognition (NER), convolutional neural networks, and long short-term memory (LSTM) networks [8].

15.1.2 Significance

BERT enhances biomedical text prediction compared to methods focusing solely on abstracts. Using pretrained tasks with masked language modeling (MLM) and next sentence prediction (NSP) on the National Center for Biotechnology Information (NCBI), BioCreative II Gene Mention Recognition (BC2GM), BioCreative V Challenge (BC5-chem), and Chemical-Protein Interactions (ChemProt) datasets significantly improve the performance of biomedical NLP tasks.

To build a biomedical model, we define the tasks of MLM and NSP. MLM helps the model understand context, improves entity recognition, and enhances text comprehension [9]. NSP enables the model to learn sentence-level coherence, improves information extraction, and enhances text segmentation and summarization [10]. MedPredict can predict missing words, subsequent sentences, and their relations by understanding the surrounding context. Our assessment presents that the framework's performance attains the highest recall compared to sophisticated approaches.

MedPredict is a BERT model specialized for biomedical text. Biomedical texts often contain complex technical terms, abbreviations, variant spellings, and intricate sentence structures. BERT's computationally efficient architecture effectively addresses these challenges. Compared to popular embeddings such as Word2Vec and FastText, MedPredict more accurately captures context. We have designed MedPredict to scale up and handle large collections of biomedical prediction tasks.

15.2 Approach

In this segment, we explore BERT and its detailed process. Our framework consists of two main stages: preconfiguring and fine-tuning. In the preconfiguring phase, the framework undergoes training on unannotated data across various pretraining tasks [11, 12]. For fine-tuning, the BERT framework is initially set up with preconfigured attributes, and then all attributes are adjusted using annotated data specific to the subsequent tasks. Every subsequent task entails its own fine-tuned frameworks, despite being initialized with the same preconfigured attributes. To exemplify this notion, we use the question-answering example depicted in Figure 15.1 throughout this section.

BERT comes in two forms: BERT-Base (cased) and BERT-Large (uncased). We use BERT (uncased), which has 64 dimensions per head and includes 24 encoder layers with a 12-layer variant. To manage the configurations, we use the Hugging Face Transformers library. Various model configurations are defined in our model using BertTokenizer, BertForPretraining,

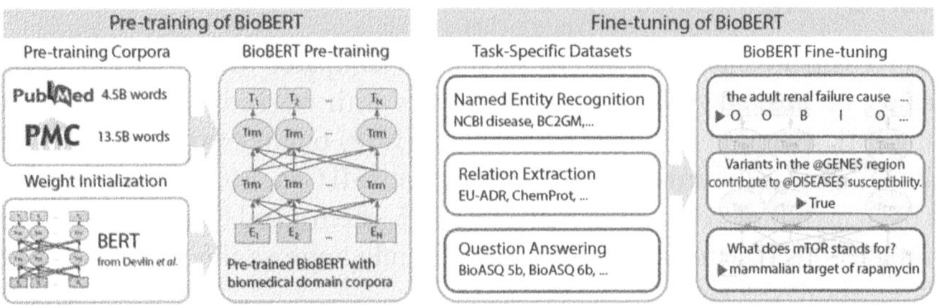

Figure 15.1 Outline of the preconfiguring and fine-tuning of BERT.

```
(bert): BertModel(
  (embeddings): BertEmbeddings(
    (word_embeddings): Embedding(30522, 768, padding_idx=0)
    (position_embeddings): Embedding(512, 768)
    (token_type_embeddings): Embedding(2, 768)
    (LayerNorm): LayerNorm((768,), eps=1e-12, elementwise_affine=True)
    (dropout): Dropout(p=0.1, inplace=False)
  )
```

Figure 15.2 Model architecture.

BertForMaskedLM, and BertForNextSentencePrediction as presented in Figure 15.2 [13].

BERT has achieved unparalleled success in NLP due to two unique training approaches: MLM and NSP. MLM is used to pretrain the model for numerous criteria, such as question answering, NER, text generation, machine transcription, and article outline [14]. In these tasks, the model identifies answers, categorizes named entities (NEs), generates prompts, translates text, and produces variations of words or sentences within a given text [15].

15.2.1 Approach 1: MLM

MLM, a widely adopted DL technique in NLP, is notably used in training the transformer model BERT. In MLM, a segment of the input text undergoes "masking," where certain tokens are swapped with a unique token (commonly [MASK]), and the framework is proficient in recovering the original token based on the contextual cues surrounding it [16]. The underlying concept aims to equip the model with an understanding of word contexts and their interrelationships within a sentence.

However, a drawback of this straightforward concealing approach arises: the framework only attempts prediction when encountering the [MASK] token in the input, whereas the purpose of the model is to predict precise tokens regardless of the token's presence. To tackle this limitation, a refined approach is used, wherein out of the 15% of tokens earmarked for masking, 80% are retained as is, 10% are randomly replaced, and 10% are left unchanged without replacement. If the token at position *i* is selected, we substitute it by substituting (1) the [MASK] token in 80% of cases, (2) a randomly chosen token 10% of the time, and (3) the original *i*th token left unchanged 10% of the time. Subsequently, Ti is utilized to infer the actual token using cross-entropy loss. For instance, in the provided snippet in Figure 15.3, the model correctly predicts "tomorrow" as the masked token.

```
from transformers import pipeline

fill_mask = pipeline(
    "fill-mask",
    model=model1,
    tokenizer=tokenizer1
)

input_text = "I am going to vishakapatnam [MASK] morning"

result =  fill_mask(input_text)

for pred in result:
  print(pred)

{'score': 0.33215847611427307, 'token': 4826, 'token_str': 'tomorrow', 'sequence': 'i am going to vishakapatnam tomorrow mornin
g'}
{'score': 0.17943145334720612, 'token': 6229, 'token_str': 'till', 'sequence': 'i am going to vishakapatnam till morning'}
{'score': 0.0697280615568161, 'token': 6928, 'token_str': 'monday', 'sequence': 'i am going to vishakapatnam monday morning'}
{'score': 0.03278611600399017, 'token': 2296, 'token_str': 'every', 'sequence': 'i am going to vishakapatnam every morning'}
{'score': 0.029733987525105476, 'token': 9432, 'token_str': 'thursday', 'sequence': 'i am going to vishakapatnam thursday morni
ng'}
```

Figure 15.3 Sample snippet of MLM.

15.2.2 Approach 2: NSP

To illustrate the associations among sentences, the BERT learning methodology incorporates NSP. A pretrained model equipped with this understanding is mostly obvious for tasks such as question answering [17]. During the learning process, the framework obtains sentence pairs as input and learns to assume if the second sentence naturally follows the original one in the source text.

As per the prior discussion, BERT utilizes a special [SEP] token to delineate between sentences. During learning, the framework inputs two input sentences simultaneously, with the second sentence occurring either after the first one in 50% of cases or as a randomly selected sentence from the entire corpus in the remaining 50% of cases.

The proposed model undergoes a training process with both MLM and NSP concurrently. This approach aims to reduce the joined loss purpose of these two strategies, emphasizing the notion that "together is better." As shown in Figure 15.1, NS is used for NSP. The NSP task is meticulously connected to the representation of learning whose goals are outlined in [18]. Nevertheless, in previous studies, the focus was primarily on transferring sentence embeddings to downstream tasks, whereas BERT assigns all properties to set the limits of the end-task model.

Preconfiguring data: The preconfiguring technique mostly tracks the prevailing literature on large language frameworks. For the preconfiguring corpus, we utilize the NCBI (793 PubMed abstracts), BC2GM (20000 annotated sentences), and BC5-chem (1500 PubMed abstracts).

When working with NCBI data, we extract textual passages and disregard structures and images. To effectively capture long, contiguous sequences, it is essential to use a corpus at the article level instead of a shuffled corpus at the statement level, like the billion-word benchmark.

15.2.3 Fine-Tuning BERT

Refining BERT is simple because its transformer architecture incorporates a self-attention technique, permitting it to adapt to various subsequent tasks by adjusting inputs and outputs [19]. In some setups involving sentence pairs, a natural methodology is to encode each text self-reliantly before the process of bidirectional cross-attention. However, BERT streamlines this process by using self-attention, which combines the encoding of concatenated text pairs, effectively integrating bidirectional cross-attention among the two statements.

For any given objective, we simply insert the domain-driven inputs and yields into BERT and fine-tune all attributes from start to finish [20]. Regarding inputs, each pair of sentences from pretraining corresponds to various scenarios: (1) question–passage pairs for question answering, (2) translated sentences for translation tasks, (3) text generation for generating text tasks, and (4) class label generation for sentence classification. As for outputs, the tokens are directed into a receiving layer for tasks at the token level, such as question answering and sequence annotation, whereas [SEP] and [MASK] tokens are directed into a receiving layer for task generation.

In contrast to preconfiguring, fine-tuning is a cost-effective process. All the outcomes detailed in the chapter can be reproduced within a maximum of 1 hour on a single cloud TPU or in just a few hours on a Graphical Processing Unit (GPU), utilizing the same preconfigured model.

15.3 Fine-Tuning Experiments

In this segment, we cast away subsequent tasks that utilize BERT, for a specific purpose beyond its initial training. These tasks typically involve tasks such as text categorization, NER, and association extraction. These tasks are considered "subsequent" because they occur after the initial training of the model, which is often done on a vast volume of text data. The preconfigured model is then fine-tuned or revised to perform well on the particular subsequent task by further training it on a smaller dataset related to that task.

15.3.1 NER

NER is the initial step for any ML task to automatically recognize, classify, and extract NEs from unstructured text. When it comes to unraveling the intricate details hidden within the text, NER stands tall as a vital task in the realm of NLP [21]. In the biomedical domain, identifying NEs-like proteins, genes, diseases, treatments, tests, test results, chemicals, and so on plays a vital role in numerous applications such as relation extraction, disease prediction, sentiment analysis, and text classification [22, 23].

By automating the identification of NEs, NER enhances numerous subsequent applications, enabling them to extract valuable insights from extensive textual information [24]. In question-answering systems, NER identifies entities pertinent to user queries, helping these systems comprehend the context and deliver accurate answers. For instance, if a user asks, "Who is the hero in the movie *Braveheart*?" NER enables the system to recognize the "hero" as a personal entity and retrieve relevant information about the movie *Braveheart* from the available data.

The challenges in NER stem from the intrinsic complexity and diversity of NEs in the text. Entities may appear in multiple forms, have alternate spellings, or be context-dependent, necessitating advanced techniques for precise identification and classification. Moreover, the dynamic nature of language and the prevalence of noisy and informal text add further difficulties for NER systems. Various approaches leverage different techniques to identify and classify NEs.

1. Rule-based approach: The simplest method uses handcrafted rules to identify specific patterns, such as "Mr." or "Dr." to denote a person's name. Although effective, it requires extensive manual crafting.
2. Supervised learning: This method works with labeled data, learning patterns, and correlations between words and their corresponding labels to make predictions on unseen data. It performs well with sufficient training but only captures dependencies between sequential words and faces challenges with out-of-vocabulary terms.
3. Neural network–based approach: Utilizing models such as recurrent neural networks (RNNs) and LSTMs, this approach identifies NEs by considering the context of each word to its neighboring words. It demands significant computational resources and a large corpus of annotated data for training.

4. Transformer-based approach: Using models such as BERT and GPT, this method enhances performance in numerous NLP tasks. Pretrained on large-scale corpora, these models can be fine-tuned on specific datasets. They capture context by considering both preceding and succeeding words, achieving high accuracy.

Preprocessing for NER involves tokenization, POS tagging, and word embeddings [25, 26].

1. Tokenization: The initial step treats each word as a separate unit, effectively handling structures, hyphens, and punctuation.
2. POS tagging: This provides additional contextual information, such as identifying nouns to help determine if they refer to a thing, person, or location.
3. Word embeddings: These capture semantic relationships and similarities between words, enhancing the system's understanding of the text.

During training, the model relies on labeled annotated data to capture relevant information features. Embeddings, which are DL architectures, automatically extract information in modern NER models. By utilizing appropriate algorithms, the NER framework trained to assume the labels based on the input attributes. During this process, the model optimizes and tunes its parameters to minimize a loss function. Finally, the NER framework is evaluated using precise measures such as precision, recall, and F1 score as shown in Figure 15.4.

15.3.2 Text Categorization

EHRs are a vital element of the world's data, including examples such as prescriptions, discharge information, and patient admissions. Mining this critical information from these reports is a tedious task, but it has many applications, such as disease classification, long-term disease prediction, and diagnosis [27]. The solution lies in automatic extraction through NLP.

The pipeline involves extracting data from unstructured biomedical abstracts and classifying it. By utilizing classification techniques, the model aims to predict class labels. Pretrained models such as Spacy and NLTK are used to extract entities. For the classification task, we considered attributes such as transcription and medical specialty. During this process, raw data are transformed into a suitable form through feature extraction, which

	chunk_tags	id	ner_tags	pos_tags	tokens
0	[B-NP, B-NP, I-NP, I-NP]	2440	[O, O, O, O]	[NNS, POS, CD, NNS]	[Women, 's, 400, metres]
1	[B-NP, I-NP, O, B-NP, I-NP, O, B-NP, I-NP, O, O, B-NP, I-NP]	925	[B-PER, I-PER, O, B-PER, I-PER, O, B-LOC, I-LOC, O, O, B-PER, I-PER]	[NNP, NNP, ,, NNP, NNP, (, NNP, NNP,), ,, NNP, NNP]	[Mark, Roe, ,, Retief, Goosen, (, South, Africa,), ,, Carl, Suneson]
2	[B-NP, I-NP]	13421	[B-LOC, O]	[NNP, CD]	[AMMAN, 1996-08-29]
3	[B-NP, I-NP, I-NP, I-NP, B-PP, B-NP, I-NP, B-VP, B-NP, I-NP, B-NP, I-NP, I-NP, B-NP, I-NP, I-NP, I-NP, I-NP, I-NP, I-NP, B-PP, B-NP, O]	2729	[O, O, O, O, O, O, O, O, O, O, O, B-MISC, I-MISC, I-MISC, I-MISC, O, B-ORG, I-ORG, O, B-ORG, O, B-LOC, O]	[DT, JJ, CD, NNS, IN, DT, NN, VBP, JJ, NN, POS, NNP, NNS, POS, JJ, NNS, NNP, NNP, CC, NNP, IN, NNP, .]	[The, other, two, teams, in, the, group, are, last, season, 's, Cup, Winners, ', Cup, runners-up, Rapid, Vienna, and, Fenerbahce, of, Turkey, .]
4	[B-NP]	8022	[B-LOC]	[NNP]	[L-ORIZZONT]
5	[B-NP, I-NP, I-NP, B-PP, B-NP, I-NP, B-NP, I-NP, I-NP, I-NP, B-VP, B-NP, I-NP, B-SBAR, B-NP, I-NP, B-NP, I-NP, B-VP, I-VP, B-ADJP, O]	7367	[O, O, O, O, O, O, O, O, B-PER, I-PER, O, O, O, O, O, O, O, O, O, O, O, O]	[DT, NN, NN, IN, DT, NN, NN, NN, NNP, NNP, VBD, JJ, NNP, IN, DT, NNS, POS, NN, MD, VB, JJ, .]	[The, director, general, of, the, air, traffic, service, Valentin, Valkov, said, last, Friday, that, a, controllers, ', strike, would, be, illegal, .]
6	[B-NP, I-NP, O, B-NP, I-NP, O, B-VP, B-NP, I-NP, I-NP, I-NP, O, B-NP, I-NP, O, B-NP, I-NP, I-	10391	[B-PER, I-PER, O, B-LOC, I-LOC, O, O, O, O, B-PER, I-PER, O, B-LOC, I-LOC, O, O,	[NNP, NNP, (, NNP, NNP,), VB, CD, :, NNP, NNP, (, NNP, NNP,),	[David, Nainkin, (, South, Africa,), beat, 9, -, Wayne, Ferreira, (, South, Africa,), 6-4, 6-4,

```
[ ]  trainer.train()
```

[2634/2634 01:45, Epoch 3/3]

Epoch	Training Loss	Validation Loss	Precision	Recall	F1	Accuracy
1	0.237721	0.068198	0.903148	0.921132	0.912051	0.979713
2	0.053160	0.059337	0.927697	0.932990	0.930336	0.983113
3	0.029850	0.059346	0.929267	0.939143	0.934179	0.984257

```
TrainOutput(global_step=2634, training_loss=0.08569671253227518)
```

```
[ ]  trainer.evaluate()
```

[204/204 00:05]

```
{'eval_loss': 0.05934586375951767,
 'eval_precision': 0.9292672127518264,
 'eval_recall': 0.9391430808815304,
 'eval_f1': 0.9341790463472988,
 'eval_accuracy': 0.9842565968195466,
 'epoch': 3.0}
```

Figure 15.4 Sample entities, the performance of the NER model.

aims to identify patterns. Building this type of model is essential for generating precise classifications as shown in Figure 15.5. Finally, the model's efficacy and performance are analyzed against state-of-the-art algorithms.

15.3.3 Association Extraction

The relation extraction pipeline involves preprocessing abstracts and using the Scispacy library to extract entities from sentences in a triplet format (i.e., sentences flanked by entities) [28–30]. These triplets are then parsed into a natural language interface to interpret the true labels. The framework is fine-tuned to enhance the accuracy of the true labels as shown in Figure 15.6. Finally, we save the trained model, to extract relations between entities.

```
from transformers import AutoModelForSequenceClassification, TrainingArguments, Trainer

num_labels = 3 if task.startswith("mnli") else 1 if task=="stsb" else 2
model = AutoModelForSequenceClassification.from_pretrained(model_checkpoint, num_labels=num_labels)
```

```
Epoch 1/5
1/1 [==============================] - 67s 67s/step - loss: 0.6895 - accuracy: 0.6000
Epoch 2/5
1/1 [==============================] - 2s 2s/step - loss: 0.6496 - accuracy: 0.6000
Epoch 3/5
1/1 [==============================] - 2s 2s/step - loss: 0.5772 - accuracy: 0.8000
Epoch 4/5
1/1 [==============================] - 2s 2s/step - loss: 0.5603 - accuracy: 1.0000
Epoch 5/5
1/1 [==============================] - 2s 2s/step - loss: 0.5719 - accuracy: 0.8000
```

```
_________________________________________________________________
 Layer (type)                Output Shape              Param #
=================================================================
 bert (TFBertMainLayer)      multiple                  109482240

 dropout_37 (Dropout)        multiple                  0

 classifier (Dense)          multiple                  1538

=================================================================
Total params: 109483778 (417.65 MB)
Trainable params: 109483778 (417.65 MB)
Non-trainable params: 0 (0.00 Byte)
_________________________________________________________________
```

Figure 15.5 Sample snippet of summary and performance of sentence classifier.

[2675/2675 01:21, Epoch 5/5]

Epoch	Training Loss	Validation Loss	Matthews Correlation
1	0.520979	0.469752	0.474288
2	0.348630	0.482370	0.516637
3	0.239764	0.650372	0.543258
4	0.164480	0.785657	0.509128
5	0.123922	0.830916	0.530497

```
TrainOutput(global_step=2675, training_loss=0.2682411835572429 7)
```

```
trainer.evaluate()
```

```
[66/66 00:00]
{'eval_loss': 0.6563718318939209,
 'eval_matthews_correlation': 0.5432575763528743,
 'epoch': 5.0,
 'total_flos': 354601098811100}
```

Figure 15.6 Sample snippet of relation extractions performance.

15.4 Results

15.4.1 Datasets

NCBI corpus is a collection of 793 published article abstracts annotated at the notion level to serve as a research resource for the biomedical NLP community. Every instance of this dataset comprises a collection of IDs, tokens, and tags. ID is mapped with each sentence, a list of tokens combining every sentence, and tags include either 0, 1, or 2 where 0 specifies no disease, and 1 and 2 specify consequent diseases.

Table 15.1 Performance of various state-of-art models against MedPredict.

Dataset	Metrics	FFN [31]	BiLSTM [32]	MTM-CW [33]	BiLM-NER	MedPredict
NCBI-disease	Accuracy	—	86.1	85.4	86.4	86.3
	Precision	—	85.4	86.4	88.3	88.9
	F1	80.45	85.8	86.1	87.3	87.6
BC5-disease	Accuracy	—	87.6	89.1	88.1	88.4
	Precision	—	86.1	88.2	90.5	87.7
	F1	83.9	86.9	88.1	89.3	89.6
BC2GM	Accuracy	—	81.5	82.2	81.8	97.7
	Precision	—	79.4	79.4	81.5	82.8
	F1	73	80.4	80.6	81.7	82.8
BC5-chem	Accuracy	—	70.3	71.2	71.4	86.7
	Precision	—	75.5	75.4	79.1	89.7
	F1	71	73.4	73.2	75.0	85.7
ChemProt	Accuracy	—	71.2	70.2	71.4	78.7
	Precision	—	75.4	71	72	79.6
	F1	72	63.2	63.2	65.4	69.9

BC2GM is a dataset for proteins and gene names of annotated abstracts, particularly aimed at text extraction in the biomedical field. Each instance of this dataset includes an ID, passage, and annotation that specifies a unique identifier, text related to the abstract, and gene mention. Every instance holds variations in the way genes are mentioned such as synonyms and misspellings as well as other entities such as diseases and proteins.

BC5-chem and Chemprot corpus is a collection of articles from biomedical literature. This dataset is used in various applications such as drug discovery, chemical information retrieval, extracting relations between chemical compounds, and understanding the action of drug mechanisms.

Researchers use these datasets to train and evaluate ML and NLP tasks in biomedical domains. All these datasets are available in XML or BioC formats. Benchmarking against these can assess the performance and generalization capabilities of their systems.

During training, all the .tsv files and pretrained models are placed in a placeholder called "data" in the "BERT directory." Likewise, all the fine-tuned models shown in Table 15.1 will be placed in the bert_output folder. Learning with BERT can cause memory out of boundary issues; to avoid this, we train our model on GPU. GPUs are optimized for DL tasks to enable faster training.

15.5 Conclusion

This paper explores the integration of BERT into the biomedical domain, marking a significant advancement in NLP with deep inferences for biomedical research and healthcare. Through extensive preconfiguring on biomedical text corpus and fine-tuning on domain-specific tasks, BERT models such as BioBERT, ClinicalBERT, and PubMedBERT have demonstrated exceptional performance in an extensive variety of biomedical NLP tasks, including NER, relation extraction, text categorization, and information retrieval. These BERT-based models offer unparalleled capabilities in understanding and extracting valuable insights from vast amounts of biomedical literature, EHRs, and other biomedical texts. By capturing the nuances of biomedical terminology and context, they enable more accurate and efficient analysis of biomedical data, helping researchers and healthcare professionals uncover hidden patterns, identify disease biomarkers, and accelerate drug discovery and development processes. Our proposed work illustrates that applying MedPredict pretraining to medical NER significantly enhances F1 scores. This specifies that transfer learning is a highly cost-effective approach for improving the performance of NER models in the medical domain.

AI disclosure statement: The author acknowledges the use of AI-based tools for minor language editing or grammatical correction. However, all intellectual contributions, analyses, and conclusions presented in this chapter are entirely the author's own.

References

1. Rodriguez-Esteban, R., Biomedical text mining and its applications. *PLoS Comput. Biol.*, 5, 12, e1000597, 2009.
2. Soyalp, G., Alar, A., Ozkanli, K., Yildiz, B., Improving text classification with transformer, in: *2021 6th International Conference on Computer Science and Engineering (UBMK)*, 2021, September, IEEE, pp. 707–712.
3. Hao, B., Zhu, H., Paschalidis, I.C., Enhancing clinical bert embedding using a biomedical knowledge base, in: *28th international conference on computational linguistics (coling 2020)*, 2020, December.
4. Gao, S., Alawad, M., Young, M.T., Gounley, J., Schaefferkoetter, N., Yoon, H.J., Tourassi, G., Limitations of transformers on clinical text classification. *IEEE J. Biomed. Health. Inf.*, 25, 9, 3596–3607, 2021.
5. Jiang, S., Hu, J., Magee, C. L., & Luo, J., Deep learning for technical document classification. *IEEE Trans. Eng. Manage.*, 71, 1163–1179, 2022.
6. Ahmed, Z., Zeeshan, S., Dandekar, T., Mining biomedical images towards valuable information retrieval in biomedical and life sciences. *Database*, 2016, baw118, 2016.
7. Yu, L.C., Wang, J., Lai, K.R., Zhang, X., Refining word embeddings for sentiment analysis, in: *Proceedings of the 2017 conference on empirical methods in natural language processing*, 2017, September, pp. 534–539.
8. Chiu, J.P. and Nichols, E., Named entity recognition with bidirectional LSTM-CNNs. *Trans. Assoc. Comput. Linguist.*, 4, 357–370, 2016.
9. Kaneko, M. and Bollegala, D., Unmasking the mask–evaluating social biases in masked language models. *Proc. AAAI Conf. Artif. Intell.*, 36, 11, 11954–11962, 2022, June.
10. Latief, A.D., Sampurno, T., Arisha, A.O., Next Sentence Prediction: The Impact of Preprocessing Techniques in Deep Learning, in: *2023 International Conference on Computer, Control, Informatics and its Applications (IC3INA)*, 2023, October, IEEE, pp. 274–278.
11. Devlin, J., Chang, M. W., Lee, K., & Toutanova, K., Bert: Pre-training of deep bidirectional transformers for language understanding, in: *Proceedings of the 2019 conference of the North American chapter of the association for computational linguistics: human language technologies*, 1, 4171–4186, 2019.

12. Lee, J., Yoon, W., Kim, S., Kim, D., Kim, S., So, C.H., Kang, J., BioBERT: a pre-trained biomedical language representation model for biomedical text mining. *Bioinformatics*, 36, 4, 1234–1240, 2020.
13. Yenduri, G., Srivastava, G., Maddikunta, P.K.R., Jhaveri, R.H., Wang, W., Vasilakos, A.V., Gadekallu, T.R., Generative pre-trained transformer: A comprehensive review on enabling technologies, potential applications, emerging challenges, and future directions. arXiv preprint arXiv:2305.10435, 2023.
14. Yoon, W., Lee, J., Kim, D., Jeong, M., Kang, J., Pre-trained language model for biomedical question answering, in: *Joint European conference on machine learning and knowledge discovery in databases*, 2019, September, Springer International Publishing, Cham, pp. 727–740.
15. Howard, J. and Ruder, S., Universal language model fine-tuning for text classification. arXiv preprint arXiv:1801.06146, 2018.
16. Adi, Y., Kermany, E., Belinkov, Y., Lavi, O., Goldberg, Y., Analysis of sentence embedding models using prediction tasks in natural language processing. *IBM J. Res. Dev.*, 61, 4/5, 3–1, 2017.
17. Chakraborty, S., Bisong, E., Bhatt, S., Wagner, T., Elliott, R., Mosconi, F., BioMedBERT: A pre-trained biomedical language model for QA and IR, in: *Proceedings of the 28th international conference on computational linguistics*, 2020, December, pp. 669–679.
18. Ganai, A.F. and Khursheed, F., Predicting next word using RNN and LSTM cells: Stastical language modeling, in: *2019 fifth international conference on image information processing (ICIIP)*, 2019, November, IEEE, pp. 469–474.
19. Tinn, R., Cheng, H., Gu, Y., Usuyama, N., Liu, X., Naumann, T., Poon, H., Fine-tuning large neural language models for biomedical natural language processing. *Patterns*, 4, 4, 2023.
20. Zhou, S., Wang, N., Wang, L., Liu, H., & Zhang, R., CancerBERT: a cancer domain-specific language model for extracting breast cancer phenotypes from electronic health records. *J. Am. Med. Inform. Assoc.*, 29, 7, 1208–1216, 2022.
21. Zhu, Y., Yuan, H., Wang, S., Liu, J., Liu, W., Deng, C., Wen, J.R., Large language models for information retrieval: A survey. arXiv preprint arXiv:2308.07107, 2023.
22. Roy, A., Recent trends in named entity recognition (ner). arXiv preprint arXiv:2101.11420, 2021.
23. Kula, S., Choraś, M., Kozik, R., Application of the BERT-based architecture in fake news detection, in: *13th International Conference on Computational Intelligence in Security for Information Systems (CISIS 2020)*, vol. 12, Springer International Publishing, pp. 239–249, 2021.
24. Neveol, A., Kim, W., Wilbur, W.J., Lu, Z., Exploring two biomedical text genres for disease recognition. *Proccedings of the ACL 2009 Workshop on Natural Language Processing in Biomedicine (BioNLP 2009)*, pp. 144–52, 2009.

25. Huang, K., Altosaar, J., Ranganath, R., Clinicalbert: Modeling clinical notes and predicting hospital readmission. arXiv preprint arXiv:1904.05342, 2019.
26. Chiu, B., Crichton, G., Korhonen, A., Pyysalo, S., How to train good word embeddings for biomedical NLP, in: *Proceedings of the 15th workshop on biomedical natural language processing*, 2016, August, pp. 166–174.
27. Almeida, F. and Xexéo, G., Word embeddings: A survey. arXiv preprint arXiv:1901.09069, 2019.
28. Gu, Y., Tinn, R., Cheng, H., Lucas, M., Usuyama, N., Liu, X., Poon, H., Domain-specific language model pretraining for biomedical natural language processing. *ACM Trans. Comput. Healthcare (HEALTH)*, 3, 1, 1–23, 2021.
29. Nguyen, T.H. and Grishman, R., Relation extraction: Perspective from convolutional neural networks, in: *Proceedings of the 1st workshop on vector space modeling for natural language processing*, 2015, June, pp. 39–48.
30. Wadhwa, S., Amir, S., Wallace, B.C., Revisiting relation extraction in the era of large language models, in: *Proceedings of the conference. Association for Computational Linguistics. Meeting*, 2023, July, vol. 2023, NIH Public Access, p. 15566.
31. Crichton, G., Pyysalo, S., Chiu, B., Korhonen, A., A neural network multitask learning approach to biomedical named entity recognition. *BMC Bioinf.*, *18*, 1–14, 2017.
32. Habibi, M., Weber, L., Neves, M., Wiegandt, D.L., Leser, U., Deep learning with word embeddings improves biomedical named entity recognition. *Bioinformatics*, *33*, 14, i37–i48, 2017.
33. Wang, X., Zhang, Y., Ren, X., Zhang, Y., Zitnik, M., Shang, J., Han, J., Cross-type biomedical named entity recognition with deep multi-task learning. *Bioinformatics*, *35*, 10, 1745–1752, 2019.

16

Development and Optimization of Hybrid Fixed-Wing Unmanned Aerial Vehicles for Healthcare Applications

Pamarthi Venkatasivarambabu* and Richa Agrawal

Department of Electronics and Communication Engineering, NIT Patna, Patna, Bihar, India

Abstract

Healthcare system is the most important area for any country, and strengthening the healthcare sector of our country is of utmost importance. The main aim is to design and develop an autonomous hybrid fixed-wing type of unmanned aerial vehicle (UAV), which can be used for healthcare application. The proposed flying UAV mathematical model is developed and validated using analytical and numerical techniques. Both structural and aerodynamic stability of the model has been checked. One of the most important tasks in the creation of a UAV is choosing the optimum path planning approach. To design the flight path of our built fixed-wing UAV, five different types of algorithms are evaluated, including artificial bee colony (ABC), ant colony optimization, partial swarm optimization (PSO), quantum partial swarm optimization, and a hybrid algorithm that combines ABC and PSO. Then, a quantum-inspired computing strategy was adopted since it outperforms conventional approaches in terms of search performance. Additionally, the model's structural and aerodynamic stability were verified using the ANSYS and FLUENT environments. The shortest path, the least amount of time, and the least amount of money were considered for determining the best results for autonomous vehicle path planning. The flying UAV must return to its starting place once the job is complete, once a path-planning algorithm is created and the target location is successfully reached from the destination point. To do this, route-finding techniques are used. Here, we have combined the PSO method with a random exploration reinforcement learning strategy.

**Corresponding author*: pamarthiv.ph21.ec@nitp.ac.in

R. Nidhya, D. Pavithra, S. Balamurugan, A. Dinesh Kumar and Sheng-Lung Peng (eds.) Medical Metaverse for Digital Healthcare: Technologies, Applications, and Challenges, (321–344) © 2026 Scrivener Publishing LLC

Keywords: Unmanned aerial vehicle, hybrid fixed wing, artificial bee colony, quantum partial swarm optimization, healthcare application

16.1 Introduction

Advancement of technology in the current era has made the use of autonomous vehicles and drones widespread in various fields. The healthcare system is the lifeline of every country. Making the healthcare system efficient is of paramount importance. The area of using aerial vehicles in the healthcare system is growing rapidly, but still, there are various challenges faced by existing developed smart systems in the healthcare sector. With growing demand for autonomous system in the current era, flying unmanned aerial vehicles (UAVs) or drones have become one of the most sought-after areas in latest technology domain [1]. Considering the need of autonomous system in various fields, starting from logistics, agriculture, industries, to healthcare sector, it is gaining popularity in all domains. The autonomous system used presently for spraying disinfectants is facing challenges in terms of efficient design and path-planning techniques for UAVs. The requirement for intelligent systems for the delivery of medicines in restricted areas or military areas is also a major concern [2]. Due to the recent increase in demand for drones and other aerial vehicles, a substantial study is being done in this field, and several different UAV designs have been put out. According to their wing design, cargo carrying capacity, flight length, speed, robustness, materials used, production methods used, and cost, many UAV concepts are categorized. The primary body structure, wing structure, and tail design of an UAV play a crucial role in determining the overall mechanical stability of the structure.

The autonomous vehicles were categorized into three categories (Figure 16.1), i.e., small UAVs, medium UAVs, and large UAVs [3]. Small flying UAVs can be further split into micro, mini, and nano UAVs. Micro flying UAVs' size range varies from 10 to 50 cm, and their maximum payload capacity of 100 g, the weight of micro UAVs is within 2 kg, and they can cover an altitude of 200 ft. Mini UAVs' weight varies from 2 to 20 kg, flight range is within 25 km, payload carrying capacity is within 2 kg, and size can range around 100 cm. Nano UAVs are those whose weight is less than 1 kg, the size of the wing varies from 15 to 20 cm, and they have a payload carrying capacity of 500 g. Medium-range UAVs range from 50 to 500 kg, dimension varies from 100 to 8000 cm. They have a good flight range as compared to small UAVs. Flight span varies from 50 to 200 km. Large UAVs are those whose weight extends from 500 to 2000 kg. They can have

Figure 16.1 Different categories of UAVs, i.e., large, medium, and small type of UAVs.

very high-altitude flight and has a wide flight range, and their specifications are shown in Table 16.1.

The design and development of an autonomous vehicle, various challenges in the form of its structural design, wing design, stability, path planning, navigation, and safety are encountered [4]. They also have challenges in project resource management as the development of an unmanned system includes a team of developers, integrators, analysts, and hardware and software developers, and it becomes difficult to have all of them in a project with a constrained budget [5]. Communication, security, and privacy are also major issues faced by autonomous aerial systems. Considering the need of current era where technological advancement is the major aspect, the design and development of autonomous system are of substantial importance [6]. The healthcare system is the backbone of the country. It is of utmost importance to enhance and strengthen the healthcare system by using artificial intelligence–enabled techniques [7]. As the domain of drones is having increasing demand, it is important to come up with more efficient system. To overcome these problems, we have designed a fixed-wing flying UAV, which can be used for indoor applications in medical sectors, and in the other one we have developed a flapping wing-type UAV, which can be used for carrying lightweight medicines to hard-to-access or military areas.

Design for manufacturability should be considered while designing UAV. Taking into consideration manufacturing processes is of utmost importance. The parts of UAVs should be designed keeping in view manufacturing considerations so that the system can be cost-effective and will have better efficiency. Ecofriendly design is also a key concern while developing drones. In UAV systems, mostly carbon-fiber materials are used.

Table 16.1 Different types of UAVs and their specifications.

Category	Function	Wing type	Wingspan	Weight	Payload
Small UAVs	Military work	Fixed wing	1.3 m	1.91 kg	Up to 600 g
	Surveillance work	Flapping wing	1.96 m	450 g	Up to 500 g
	Surveillance and mapping	—	1.38 m	3.4 kg	Up to 1 kg
	Indoor inspection	Multirotor	40 cm	0.7 kg	Up to 550 g
	Surveillance work	Rotary wing	40.64 cm	175.5 g	Up to 50 g
Medium UAVs	Aerial mapping	Multirotor	64.3 cm	4.57 kg	2 kg
	Surveillance work	Multirotor	60 cm	18 kg	9 kg
	Cinematography aerial photography, industrial applications	Multirotor	75 cm	15 kg	6 kg
	Surveillance and mapping	Fixed wing	—	6.5 kg	3 kg
Large UAVs	Surveillance work, carrying military equipment	Fixed wing	39.9 m	14628 kg	910 kg
	Army requirements	Tilt rotor	7.37 m	1020 kg	90 kg
	Surveillance work	Rotor wing	2.71 m	645 kg	91 kg
	Agriculture, spraying of disinfectant	Rotor wing	0.72 m	60 kg	18 kg

In addition, in carbon-fiber production, a lot of toxic gases are generated; as well as in battery production, hazardous gases are generated. The gripper design for carrying goods in delivery drones and aerial vehicles is also a challenging area where efficient gripper design ensures the smooth transition of UAVs. Proper designing of the wing will determine the stability of the system. Various types of wing design are already proposed, but their design and manufacture are also a challenge in the development of UAVs. The above were some of the design challenges faced by UAVs' details of different types of existing designs, and their merits and flaws are discussed in detail in this article.

The organization of this chapter is as follows: Section 16.2 discussed in detail different path-planning techniques that we have gone through during our literature review and classified the path-planning algorithm into five groups based on their characteristic and methodology adopted. Section 16.3 discussed the path-planning algorithm used for our developed autonomous vehicles. Section 16.4 discussed about the results and discussion. Finally, Section 16.5 provides the conclusion, further recommendations, and future scope.

16.2 Literature Review

The domain of drones is gaining paramount importance in the current decade. The need for an autonomous system is growing manifold. Keeping this in view, it is important to design an efficient autonomous system. Many research works have already been done in UAVs.

16.2.1 Review of Design of UAVs

The design of autonomous vehicle is one of the most critical domains in the development. Over a decade of years, numerous designs of UAVs have been proposed by various researchers, keeping in view the main body structure design, wing design, tail structure, and gripping elements. After reviewing various research papers related to the design structures of UAVs, we found a need to first categorize UAVs into three categories based on their weight, wingspan, flight range, etc. [8]. Then we tried to study different types of body structures, wing structures, and tail designs for UAVs.

16.2.2 Wing Structure

The design and development of UAV wing structure are two of the most crucial elements. It creates the lift required for the takeoff of the aerial vehicle. While designing wing structure weight, wing speed should be taken into consideration.

i. Rotary wing
By balancing the force produced by the rotors attached to them, the category rotary wing-type UAVs can fly. tricopter, quadcopters, hexacopter, octocopter, and other types of drones with rotary wings are examples. These kinds of aerial vehicles are capable of landing and taking off vertically. Optimizing UAV power consumption is the key challenge. Several academics have put forth models for UAV performance optimization [9, 10].

ii. Fixed wing
UAVs with fixed wings produce lifting force, and to produce propulsion for flight, a motor rotates the propeller. They can carry a large cargo and have longer flight times. A metal surface, spars, and ribs make up a fixed-wing aircraft. The spar's design is such that it can withstand the most bending stress. Ribs provide wing sections and its shape, and they transmit the air load from the wing. The aerodynamic effect on fixed wing [11] is given by lift force *F*,

$$F = \frac{1}{2} * d * s * C_l * V^2 \tag{16.1}$$

Fixed-wing type is used for large UAVs, as it requires a higher lift-to-drag ratio.

iii. Flapping wing
A bio-inspired design is used for the flapping wing mechanism on UAVs. When compared to flying drones with fixed wings, the complexity of wings that flap is greater. The fundamental idea is to change the motors' rotating motion into flapping action. Wings' flapping motion generates the lift and thrust needed for a UAV to fly [12]. While designing a flapping wing mechanism and wing geometry such as thickness, camber, wing surface area, and wing kinematics, flapping frequency should be taken into consideration. Flapping wing mechanisms are generally designed for small UAVs, and they are usually light in weight and mimic the flying pattern of birds such as hummingbirds, eagles, bats, dragonflies, etc. The aerodynamic

effect on the wing is of major concern and can be viewed by observing wake vortices [13] and the aerodynamic effect on the wing.

iv. Propulsion

Propulsion is one of the significant parts of UAVs. It generates the power required for autonomous vehicles to fly, and it contributes to the energy consumption and autonomy and efficiency of aerial vehicles [14–16]. For large autonomous vehicles, fuel engines are used. Motors drive medium-size drones. Quadcopters and hexacopters have propellers that act as propulsion systems driven by motors. In propeller blade, design of the blade angle and pitch are important parameters that should be taken into consideration. It generates the thrust required to actuate the aerial vehicle. Propeller designs also have various kinds like a fixed propeller, twin pitch propellers [17], and recently variable pitch propellers [18]. A variable-pitch propeller can control the landing of autonomous vehicles at an acceptable and controllable rate.

v. Tail structure

The tail of UAVs stabilizes the flight and controls the aircraft. Broadly, the tail is of two types of horizontal tail and vertical tail. The tail should be designed in such a manner that it should be able to control the flight when the flight changes its condition [19]. For large UAVs, tails are important to maintain stability, and tails are used in small UAVs such as ornithopters. Initially, a conventional tail design was proposed followed by its H-tail design, V-tail, twin vertical tail, and boom-mounted tail structures, which were proposed [20]. To enhance flight stability, numerous modifications were done to the tail structures of UAVs. In small aerial vehicles, which mimic the bird-flying techniques, the tail provides downward force to keep the front portion up, and it provides lifting stability to the UAVs.

vi. Gripper structure

Gripper in the aerial vehicle is required to carry items such as delivery products, video cameras, medicines, vaccines, etc. Various research works are done in this area, and modular gripper attachments are used for UAVs. Generally, two- and three-finger grippers with manipulators are used for gripping various real-time objects [21]. Drone gripper was designed by Swain *et al.* [22], which consists of two claws and can carry boxes such as objects. Drone gripper can pick objects of any shape and size [23], designed an autonomous flexible three-finger item pickup system for autonomous vehicles, and it was analyzed and tested for performing the gripping activity [24]. Many research works were conducted to study the stability of these grippers and come up with the most effective gripper design [25, 26] During reviewing various research papers on UAVs and drones, it was found that there are varieties of the field in which research is being done starting from flight control, path planning, communication system, signal processing, navigation system, power supply, design, and fabrication of aerial vehicles.

16.2.3 Path-Planning Techniques

Various path-planning techniques were proposed for UAV communication in the last few decades. Based on literature review on some research papers, some path-planning techniques are identified as follows:

A. *Numerical technique*
The mixed-integer linear programming (MILP) approach can address issues involving many UAVs and is used to discover the best path while avoiding obstacles. In multiple linear programming methods, various heuristic solutions were used, and some of the problems used a different strategy to deal with the computational complexity of path-planning techniques. Binary integer programming is one of the most often used algorithms for three-dimensional (3D) path planning. The 3D Delaunay triangulation of difficult-to-reach locations to achieve the target path made up of tetrahedrons is the basis for the BIP approach. Another name for binary linear programming is the MILP simplified version. Branch-bound algorithms [27] are also effective computational techniques for solving mixed integer linear problems. The effectiveness of algorithms depends on the criteria used for selecting branching variables and branching nodes, as well as how fast the algorithm can find the upper bound. To choose the best route for dodging obstacles, it uses a geometric branching technique. Hybrid branch-bound techniques were applied to improve the model's effectiveness. CPLEX algorithms are used to solve linear programming problems in the path-planning domain. Various research works have proposed hybrid branch-bound techniques, which can yield better results as compared to binary linear programming and complex algorithms.
B. *Nature-based technique*
Nature-based algorithms are based on bio-inspired models in which nature-based patterns are used for path planning.

Examples of these algorithms are the shuffling frog leaping algorithm, neural network algorithm, genetic algorithm, memetic algorithm, and particle swarm optimization [28]. Various types of nature-based algorithms were proposed over years for path planning. It includes evolutionary algorithms, swarms' intelligence-based algorithms, algorithms inspired by flying patterns of birds and other animals, and algorithms inspired by plant growth phenomena. One of the most popularly used evolutionary algorithms is the genetic algorithm. It is based on Charles Darwin's law of natural evolution. It initially selects random feasible solutions for the first generation, and the next generation is selected based on natural selection in which the most suitable individuals are selected to produce offspring of the next generation. Here the next-generation solutions are selected based on important parameters of UAV for achieving the path-planning objective. It can obtain solutions rapidly but can result in local optimum if fitness functions are not selected properly.

C. *Hybrid technique*

Hybrid techniques combine various path-planning algorithms, such as those based on analytical methods, numerical methods, and bio-inspired algorithms, to address the limitations of each type of algorithm and produce the most efficient path-finding tool. Using the typical path-planning strategy can be challenging in some circumstances. The shortcomings of the traditional partial swarm optimization (PSO) and artificial bee colony (ABC) algorithms individually were solved [29] by combining PSO and ABC to provide improved path-finding techniques. To address NP-hard problems, which are extremely challenging to solve using conventional methods, this strategy integrates a mathematical framework with evolutionary algorithms. Visibility graph node-based optimal algorithms [30] are hybrid methods that can be used to discover the best path in both static and dynamic environments. To achieve better outcomes than using individual algorithms, several researchers have also suggested merging evolutionary techniques with analytical-based methods such as Dijkstra's, RRT, and PRM methods. Because hybrid approaches incorporate the benefits of various algorithms, they produce better outcomes.

D. *Multicriteria decision-making technique*
It is a technique where a variety of factors is considered to choose the best answer [31] while considering energy-saving characteristics because battery use is another crucial factor. Before classifying them into beneficiary and nonbeneficiary categories, multi-criteria decision making (MCDM) approaches first choose the most significant criteria. The final performance score is then calculated by setting weights for various criteria and multiplying them with a normalized decision matrix. Another sort of multicriteria decision-making method is TOPSIS, in which the ideal option should be the one that is the furthest from the ideal positive solution and the closest to the ideal negative solution. Hamurcu and Eren [33] used the TOPSIS technique to choose the optimal course. For the objective of choosing an effective UAV for defense, Nanayakkara *et al.*, [34] used the TOPSIS approach and analytical hierarch process (AHP). The application of MCDM methodology has grown recently due to the abundance of aerial vehicle route planning algorithms; therefore, it is critical to choose the optimal path-finding method for UAVs.

E. *MCDM techniques*
The use of AHP has been used to choose UAVs based on a variety of factors, including mission requirements, technology, cost, and availability. Another MCDM method that has been applied to the selection of UAVs is called the method TOPSIS. To assess how closely related the two solutions are, TOPSIS [32] uses the idea of ideal and anti-ideal solutions. Gray relational analysis (GRA) is an MCDM technique that has been used to pick UAVs based on a variety of factors, including payload capacity, speed, range, endurance, and cost. Decision-makers can utilize GRA to assess the relationship between criteria and options.

16.3 Methodology

Path planning is a technique of finding a suitable path for navigation from the initial point to the target point by avoiding collision with obstacles and optimizing time, distance, and energy consumption. Over years, several path-planning techniques were proposed for aerial vehicles.

16.3.1 Design of Hybrid Fixed Wing

Vertical takeoff is the greatest solution for inside applications, and fixed wings are used to increase the UAVs' stability. The range for maximum gross takeoff weight is 0 to 9 kg. We chose a 1.7-m wingspan, a 70-cm overall length, and a 2-kg payload-carrying capability for the UAV by the generally accepted standard. Using multicriteria decision-making, we chose carbon fiber as the optimum material for the design and development of fixed-wing UAVs after analyzing a variety of frequently used materials.

16.3.2 Optimization of Hybrid Fixed-Wing Design

The optimization equation for the wing design of a fixed-wing drone can be made using the constrained optimization problem, which tries to reduce the drag and weight of the wing while satisfying numerous criteria, including lift, stability, and structural strength. Design factors include things such as the shape of the air foil and the wing's area, span, chord, and sweep.

The optimization problem can be expressed as follows:

$$\text{Maximum } f(x) = C_d * S + W \tag{16.2}$$

Subject to: $L \geq W; C_l = 2\pi\alpha$; $C_m = 0; S = bc; AR = \frac{b^2}{s}$; $C_t = \frac{T}{0.5\rho S V^2}$;

The objective function $f(x)$ represents the total drag and weight of the wing, which are minimized. The constraints include the lift force being greater than or equal to the weight, the lift coefficient being within a range, and the aspect ratio, span, chord, and angle of attack being within certain bounds. We have used a genetic algorithm to optimize the wing design of the autonomous vehicle. The fitness of each individual in the population is evaluated by simulating the performance of the UAV with that particular wing design using a suitable structural and aerodynamic analysis.

A population of potential solutions was produced randomly through a genetic algorithm, which is then repeatedly improved to yield better solutions over succeeding generations. A chromosome represents every solution in the population. Genetic processes such as selection, crossover, and mutation apply to the chromosomes, simulating natural selection and reproduction. The population's fittest members are selected during the selection phase to be the parents of the following generation. To develop a novel outcome, crossover entails fusing the genetic makeup of two parents. The random alterations that mutations impart to the offspring's chromosomes contribute to the population's genetic diversity. Based on a fitness function that measures how well each solution solves the optimization issue, each solution's fitness is assessed. The fittest people are more likely to be chosen as parents for the following generation, and this cycle is repeated until a workable solution is found or a stopping requirement is satisfied.

16.3.3 Mathematical Model Design of Hybrid Fixed-Wing UAV

Free vibration analysis of the wing is carried out using the Euler beam model. The present beam model and the pertinent computer code, which are generated for the vibration model, are validated by the results' good agreement. This code calculates the natural frequencies of the equivalent beam model for one wing and compares them to the modal analysis output from ANSYS software. The shear center offset from the centroid in the beam formulation causes the bending and torsional modes to dynamically couple. The bending and torsional modes clearly show this relationship. The structure does not contain any pure torsion or bending modes. The aforementioned equations are simplified to:

$$\omega_n = (\beta_n l)^2 \sqrt{\frac{El}{mL^4}} \tag{16.3}$$

$$\beta^4 = \frac{\omega^2 m}{El} \tag{16.4}$$

$$\text{A}= \int_0^c (Y_u - Y_l)dx \tag{16.5}$$

$$y' = \frac{1}{A}\int_0^c \frac{1}{2}(Y_u^2 - y_l^2)dx \tag{16.6}$$

The first four mode forms and the fixed-wing flying robot's natural frequency were determined using modal analysis for the fixed-wing construction in ANSYS. Block Lanczos solver was used to perform modal analysis, considering prestress situations. The results of mode shapes obtained show the deformation value due to natural frequency of the body, and the values obtained were very less.

16.3.4 Path-Planning Techniques Using MCDM

In the case of autonomous systems, artificially inspired networks are used. Here we have used five different types of artificially inspired path-planning techniques for obtaining the best path for our developed aerial vehicles. After reviewing various research papers on path planning, there was a gap in the comparative analysis of different popularly used artificially inspired algorithms to suggest the best one as per the problem statement defined.

(i) ABC algorithm: ABC optimization is used to solve challenging multiobjective problems and identify the best solution. It imitates honeybees' clever food-finding activity. A food source, bees that are used, and bees that are not used are the three main elements of the ABC algorithm. Onlooker bees and scout bees make up the unused bee population. Worker bees look for food sources, gather nectar from flowers, and waggle dance to communicate information inside their bee colony. Observer bees observe the waggle dance performed by working bees. The procedure followed by the algorithm is discussed below.

$$v_{a,b} = v_{\min,b} + \text{rand}(0,1) * (v_{\max,b} - v_{\min,b}) \tag{16.7}$$

The bees look for food that has more nectar and then assess it using the fitness function. The following equation finds a new solution for a food source.

$$f_{a,b} = f_{a,b} + \varnothing_{a,b}\left(v_{a,b} - v_{c,d}\right) \tag{16.8}$$

where $f_{a,b}$ refers to a new solution for the food source.

The greedy selection method is used after the new set of solutions has been developed and checked; this method compares each new solution's fitness value to the initial solution and selects the one with the best fitness value to move on to the next step. The given fitness function is:

$$\text{Fitness } t = \begin{cases} \dfrac{1}{1+f(v_t)} & \text{if } f(v_t) \geq 0 \\ 1+abs\left(f(v_t)\right) & \text{if } f(v_t) < 0 \end{cases} \tag{16.9}$$

where $f(v_t)$ is an objective function.

(ii) PSO algorithm: Particle swarm optimization is an optimization method that iterates constantly to find the optimum solution for nonlinear problems. The initial population of the swarm is chosen from *m* randomly generated solutions, or particles. In consideration of the solutions' velocities and positions, the optimal solution is picked. To attain the best position, the position is updated here using the fitness function. To obtain the optimum overall solution, the fitness function is changed to update the particle's velocity and acceleration. The velocity and position can be updated using the following equation:

$$r^{s+1} = wr^{s} + p_1 * \text{rand}_1^s * (p_0^s - q^s) + p_2 * \text{rand}_2^s * (g_0^s - q^s) \quad (16.10)$$

$$r^{s+1} = q^{s} + r^{s+1} \quad (16.11)$$

For the development of our autonomous vehicle, the aforementioned algorithm was used to design its flight.

(iii) Hybrid ABC and PSO: The ABC algorithm uses the PSO search method in three stages by updating the velocity and position. Our created UAV path planning in this case utilized the PSO and ABC algorithms. The outcome of the simulation, which performed 150 times, provided a cost function with a distance parameter of 3.9 units and a best-path travel time of 25 seconds to the target location. The decision-maker first chooses a set of criteria and then gives each a weight based on how important they are about one another. Then, a decision matrix is generated, where each row represents a potential course of action and each column a criterion. The values in the matrix show how well each alternative performed against each criterion. The next step after creating the choice matrix is to identify the ideal and undesirable solutions.

(iv) PSO with RL: A machine-learning paradigm that relies on feedback is reinforcement learning. The use of autonomous vehicles and other aerial vehicles in a variety of fields, including retail, agriculture, disaster relief, industry, the military, surveillance, and healthcare, has given the field of aerial vehicles increased prominence in recent years. Because of the variety of tasks they might be used for, it is crucial to arrange their course efficiently. The best path-planning technique must be chosen because it considers several criteria, including avoiding obstacles, maximizing energy consumption, and reducing calculation and flight time. UAVs must use a route-finding technique to return because there are not enough initial training data to prepare them for returning on their own. To make the UAV try randomly exploring whatever route there is to take to get back to the starting point and try to optimize itself, we tried to utilize a reinforcement learning strategy in this case. Through observation of the environment's present condition and action, an agent engages in reinforcement learning. The best path is determined by the agent to be the one with the largest reward point. It is often referred to as "Q learning" because the Q matrix may store Q values of actions taken.

$$M_{t+1} = \begin{bmatrix} p1_{fr}^{t+1} \\ v1_{fr}^{t+1} \\ a1_{fr}^{t+1} \end{bmatrix} \tag{16.12}$$

In addition, if difficulties are encountered, a penalty will be applied. Let us assume that there is an obstacle:

$$\text{Obstacle} = \begin{cases} \exp 1 - \dfrac{d_r^2}{d_{min}^2} & dl < d_{min} \\ 0 & dl > d_{min} \end{cases} \tag{16.13}$$

Computational run times for reinforcement learning are about 15 seconds to reach the 600 iterations where our results converged. Given that it selects the route with the highest reward point using a concept of reward points, reinforcement learning might be the most successful model for the UAV.

16.4 Results and Discussion

Using MATLAB software, the following approach was put into practice for our built UAVs' path planning. We had chosen random coordinates from a room in a two-dimensional setting where our UAV needed to choose the best course. Figure 16.2 displays the ideal route produced by the ABC algorithm. After 150 iterations, the simulation produced a cost function with a distance parameter of 5.43 units and duration to the target location using

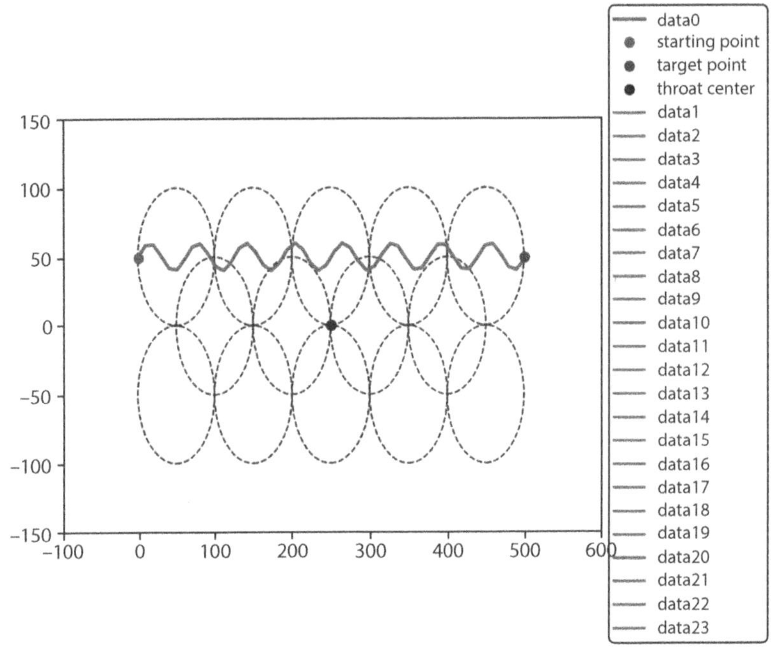

Figure 16.2 The ideal route produced by the ABC algorithm.

the best path of 6.95 seconds. The initial population of the swarm is chosen from *m* randomly generated solutions, or particles:

For the development of our autonomous vehicle, Figure 16.2 used the aforementioned algorithm to design its flight path. The algorithm was given the beginning point coordinates and threat points in a two-dimensional closed-room environment before using swarm intelligence to try to identify the optimum path and continuously update velocity and position to acquire the best overall results. The best route as determined by the PSO method in the MATLAB environment is shown in Figure 16.4 below. After 150 iterations, the simulation produced a cost function with a distance parameter of 5.45 units and duration to the target location using the best path of 6.04 seconds.

The optimum route was then discovered when we attempted to implement simply the PSO approach. We marked the starting point and ending point using random points observed from Figure 16.3. Next, using Python programming, we put the reward system idea into practice.

The ABC algorithm uses the PSO search method in three stages by updating the velocity and position shown in Figure 16.4. Our created flying robot's path planning in this case utilized the PSO and ABC algorithms.

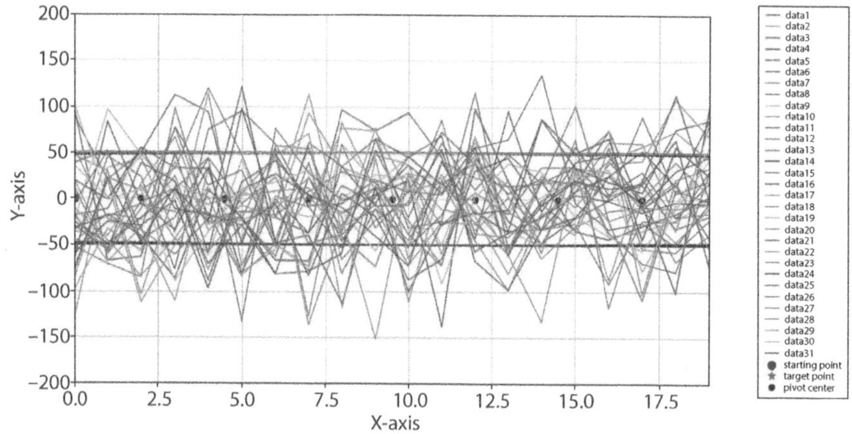

Figure 16.3 The optimal route produced by PSO algorithm.

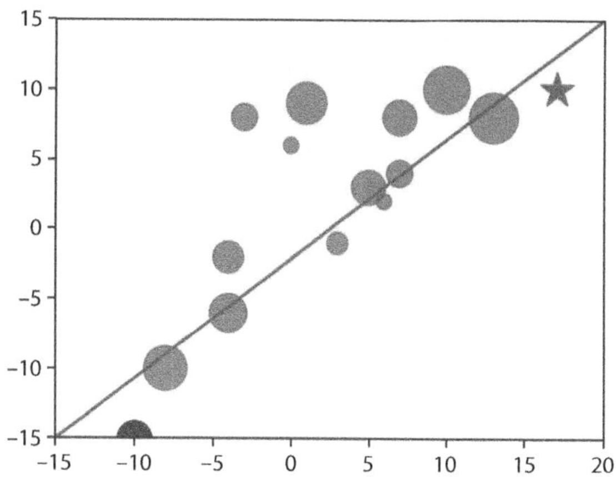

Figure 16.4 The optimal route produced by hybrid PSO and ABC algorithm.

The best route was determined by this proposed hybrid model. After 150 iterations, the simulation's findings showed a cost function with a distance parameter of 3.9 units and a time to the target location utilizing the best path of 25 seconds.

The optimization of wing design for UAVs and the selection of the most efficient path-planning techniques and material selection using MCDM techniques. In process of developing the optimized design for UAVs, we have worked on two domains of UAVs, i.e., fixed wing and flapping wing types. In Python programming, we have defined a fitness function that consists of wing area, aspect ratio, weight, wing sweep angle, and taper ratio as chromosomes and from which we have calculated lift and drag coefficients. Further function for the genetic algorithm was defined where we calculated fitness function for each chromosome and performed crossover and mutation to update the population, and the best chromosome was selected from the final population. Table 16.2 shows the optimized value obtained after using the genetic algorithm. The wingspan length has been optimized by 17%, the wing area was optimized by 20%, and the overall weight of the hybrid fixed-wing structure was optimized by 10%.

The results as shown in Table 16.3 indicates that the optimized values obtained after applying the genetic algorithm have reduced the dimensions of the wing by 21% and hence optimized the weight of the UAV, which also reduces the cost of development of the UAV. The deformation value and equivalent stress developed as compared to previous results were optimized. Deformation was reduced by 1.6%, equivalent stress by 4%, and aerodynamic analysis also proved the lift force was optimized.

Further, the backpropagation for our developed UAV was proposed where we used hybrid reinforcement learning, which has combined both reinforcement learning and PSO technique to come up with an efficient path-planning method for backpropagation. Table 16.4 shows the comparison of the execution time of different path-planning techniques used in backpropagation. The execution times of the algorithms used to find the best route from the starting location to the destination point. When using the reward point concept to design a route back from one already taken, reinforcement learning can be thought of as the optimal approach. It took 600 iterations to achieve the goal point when reinforcement learning was

Table 16.2 Comparison of optimized values and initial values.

Wing type	Initial value	Optimized value	Remarks
Wingspan	1.7 m	1.4 m	Reduction by 17.6%
Wing area	0.55 m^2	0.43 m^2	Reduction by 21%
Aspect ratio	6.938	5.71	Reduction by 17.6%
Deformation	3.0729×10^{-5} m	3.03×10^{-5} m	Reduction by 1.6%
Equivalent stress	0.045 N/mm^2	0.043 N/mm^2	Reduction by 4%
Lift force	145 N	141 N	Reduction by 2.7%

Table 16.3 The rank of path-planning algorithms using MCDM techniques.

Path-planning techniques	Cost function	Execution time (s)	Performance score (C_a)	Rank
ABC	0.271	0.1125	0.732	3
Ant colony optimization	0.19	0.243	0.52	4
PSO	0.272	0.098	0.75	2
Hybrid PSO + ABC	0.195	0.404	0.19	5
Quantum PSO	0.17	0.077	1	1

Table 16.4 The comparison of the execution time of different path-planning techniques used in backpropagation.

S. no.	Algorithm trained	Execution time (s)
1	RL	15
2	PSO	6.04
3	RL + PSO	5.05

applied because it likes to remain in local minima, which causes execution time to be a little slower. We have merged PSO and the RL approach to solving the issue. Hence, to get over the limitations of separate algorithms, we merged PSO and reinforcement learning. Compared to using PSO and reinforcement learning separately, the PSO + RL algorithm was executed in 5.05 seconds and required 100 iterations. Figure 16.5 shows the best path that was discovered for getting between the beginning position and the destination point. After 150 iterations and 5.05 seconds, the hybrid algorithm reached its destination. Figure 16.6 shows graph between the number of iterations and rewards gained.

Nevertheless, we saw that reinforcement-learning execution was longer and needed more iterations to attain its goal. This could be due to the issue of being trapped in local minima.

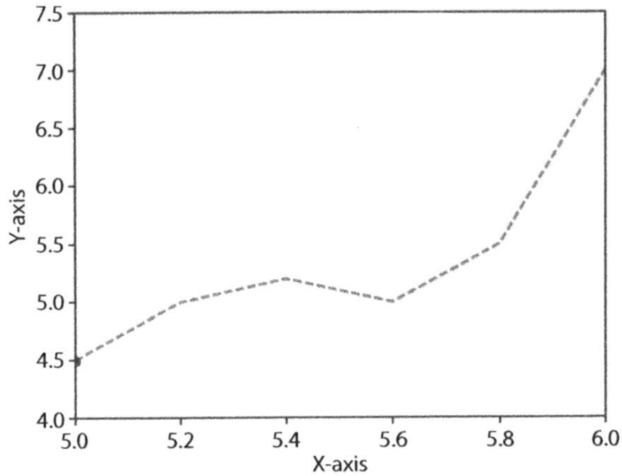

Figure 16.5 Optimal path generated by hybrid reinforcement learning algorithm.

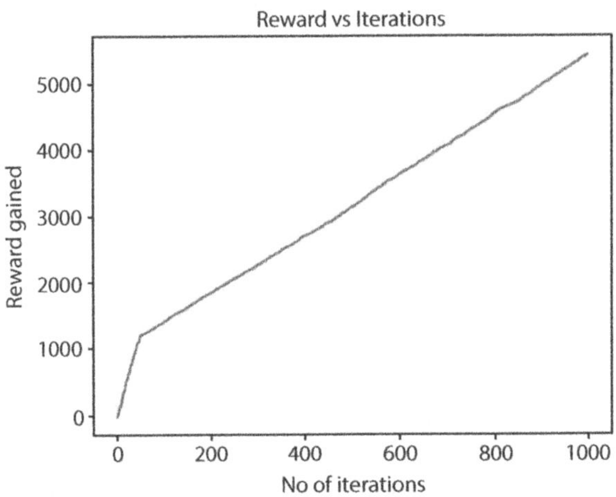

Figure 16.6 Graph between no. of iterations and rewards gained.

16.5 Conclusion

In conclusion, it can be said that we have designed and developed UAV for indoor and outdoor application in healthcare sector. Selection of the best path-planning method is also one of the major tasks in development. The quantum-inspired computing approach performs searches more effectively than traditional methods. The most pertinent outcomes for autonomous flying UAV path planning were determined by considering the following factors: minimum cost, the shortest path travelled, and the least amount of time. Both the fixed wing and flapping wing model of UAV mathematical models were developed, and their structural and aerodynamic stability were checked using ANSYS software, and optimization techniques were used to get the best parameters for wing design. Path planning for the UAVs was also done in simulator environment successfully, and the best path-planning technique was selected using the MCDM technique, and further a hybrid reinforcement learning was proposed for backpropagation. Further work can be done to enhance the payload carrying capacity of the existing design of UAVs so that it can be used in various fields. Modifications in the design can be done based on real-time scenario and the environment in which it is used. Path-planning algorithm discussed in the thesis can be implemented in different physical environment conditions, and further improvement can be done based on environmental conditions.

AI disclosure statement: The author acknowledges the use of AI-based tools for minor language editing or grammatical correction. However, all intellectual contributions, analyses, and conclusions presented in this chapter are entirely the author's own.

References

1. Yang, C., Yang, H., Zhu, D., Hu, YW., Zhang, Y., Ma, HY., Zhang, D., A multi-mechanism balanced advanced learning sparrow search algorithm for UAV path planning. *Cluster Comput.*, 1–44, 2024.
2. Guo, Y., Liu, X., Jia, Q., Liu, X., Zhang, W., HPO-RRT*: A sampling-based algorithm for UAV real-time path planning in a dynamic environment. *Complex Intell. Syst.*, 9, 6, 7133–7153, 2023.
3. Wang, R.-B., Wang, W.-F., Geng, F.-D., Pan, J.-S., Chu, S.-C., Xu, L., UAV path planning in mountain areas based on a hybrid parallel compact arithmetic optimization algorithm. *Neural Comput. Appl.*, 1–16, 2023.
4. Tan, L., Zhang, H., Liu, Y., Yuan, T., Jiang, X., Shang, Z., An adaptive Q-learning based particle swarm optimization for multi-UAV path planning. *Soft Comput.*, 1–16, 2024.
5. Venkatasivarambabu, P. and Agrawal, R., Enhancing UAV navigation with dynamic programming and hybrid probabilistic route mapping: an improved dynamic window approach. *Int. J. Inf. Technol.*, 16, 2, 1023–1032, 2024.
6. Dhulkefl, E., Durdu, A., Terzioğlu, H., Dijkstra algorithm using UAV path planning. *Konya J. Eng. Sci.*, 8, 92–105, 2020.
7. Li, X., Lu, Y., Zhao, X., Deng, X., Xie, Z., Path planning for intelligent vehicles based on improved D* Lite. *J. Supercomput.*, 80, 1, 1294–1330, 2024.

8. Kathen, J.T. and Carolina, M., Informative Path Planning Based on Swarm Intelligence for a Fleet of Autonomous Surface Vehicles for Water Resource Monitoring, PhD diss., 2023.
9. Xu, H., Liu, Y., Ru, J., Dynamic 3D Path Planning for UAV Based on Enhanced Grey Wolf Optimization Algorithm, in: *International Conference on Autonomous Unmanned Systems*, Springer Nature Singapore, Singapore, pp. 485–493, 2023.
10. Flores-Caballero, G., Rodríguez-Molina, A., Aldape-Pérez, M., Villarreal-Cervantes, M.G., Optimized path-planning in continuous spaces for unmanned aerial vehicles using meta-heuristics. *IEEE Access*, 8, 176774–176788, 2020.
11. Arafat, M.Y., Alam, M.M., Moh, S., Vision-based navigation techniques for unmanned aerial vehicles: Review and challenges. *Drones*, 7, 2, 89, 2023.
12. Li, Y., Zhang, Z., Sun, Q., Huang, Y., An improved ant colony algorithm for multiple unmanned aerial vehicles route planning. *J. Franklin Inst.*, 107060, 2024.
13. Huang, W., Zhang, G., Jiao, S., Wang, J., Bearing fault diagnosis based on stochastic resonance and improved whale optimization algorithm. *Electronics*, 11, 14, 2185, 2022.
14. Ajeil, F.H., Ibraheem, I.K., Sahib, M.A., Humaidi, A.J., Multi-objective path planning of an autonomous mobile robot using hybrid PSO-MFB optimization algorithm. *Appl. Soft Comput.*, 89, 106076, 2020.
15. Al-Sorori, W. and Mohsen, A.M., New Caledonian crow learning algorithm: A new metaheuristic algorithm for solving continuous optimization problems. *Appl. Soft Comput.*, 92, 106325, 2020.
16. Pehlivanoglu, Y.V. and Pehlivanoglu, P., An enhanced genetic algorithm for path planning of autonomous UAV in target coverage problems. *Appl. Soft Comput.*, 112, 107796, 2021.
17. Li, J., Ran, M., Xie, L., Efficient trajectory planning for multiple non-holonomic mobile robots via prioritized trajectory optimization. *IEEE Rob. Autom. Lett.*, 6, 2, 405–412, 2020.
18. Pamarthi, V. and Agrawal, R., Unmanned Aerial Vehicle Path Planning with Hybrid Motion Algorithm for Obstacle Avoidance. *Meas.: Sens.*, 101195, 2024.
19. Ait Saadi, A., Soukane, A., Meraihi, Y., Gabis, A.B., Mirjalili, S., Ramdane-Cherif, A., UAV path planning using optimization approaches: A survey. *Arch. Comput. Methods Eng.*, 29, 6, 4233–4284, 2022.
20. Wang, J., Li, Y., Li, R., Chen, H., Chu, K., Trajectory planning for UAV navigation in dynamic environments with matrix alignment Dijkstra. *Soft Comput.*, 26, 22, 12599–12610, 2022.
21. Sivarambabu, P.V., Malarvezhi, P., Dayana, R., Vadivukkarasi, K., Rama Koteswara Rao, P., EEHC approach for latency minimization in 3D network architecture using 5G+ with UAVs. *Wireless Pers. Commun.*, 122, 1, 897–914, 2022.

22. Swain, S., Khilar, P.M., Senapati, B.R., An efficient path planning algorithm for 2D ground area coverage using multi-UAV. *Wireless Pers. Commun.*, 132, 1, 361–407, 2023.
23. Zhang, Z., Liu, X., Feng, B., Research on obstacle avoidance path planning of UAV in complex environments based on improved Bézier curve. *Sci. Rep.*, 13, 1, 16453, 2023.
24. Ahmed, G., Sheltami, T., Mahmoud, A., Energy-Efficient Multi-UAV Multi-Region Coverage Path Planning Approach. *Arabian J. Sci. Eng.*, 1–18, 2024.
25. Liu, Y., Zhu, X., Zhang, X.-Y., Xiao, J., Yu, X., RGG-PSO+: Random Geometric Graphs Based Particle Swarm Optimization Method for UAV Path Planning. *Int. J. Comput. Intell. Syst.*, 17, 1, 127, 2024.
26. Sharma, A., Shoval, S., Sharma, A., Pandey, J.K., Path planning for multiple targets interception by the swarm of UAVs based on swarm intelligence algorithms: A review. *IETE Tech. Rev.*, 39, 3, 675–697, 2022.
27. Mourtzis, D., Angelopoulos, J., Panopoulos, N., Unmanned Aerial Vehicle (UAV) path planning and control assisted by Augmented Reality (AR): The case of indoor drones. *Int. J. Prod. Res.*, 62, 9, 3361–3382, 2024.
28. Badshah, A., Islam, N., Shahzad, D., Jan, B., Farman, H., Khan, M., Jeon, G., Ahmad, A., Vehicle Navigation in GPS Denied Environment for Smart Cities Using Vision Sensors. *Comput. Environ. Urban Syst.*, 77, 101281, 2019.
29. Chu, T.S., Chua, A., Sybingco, E., Roque, M., A Performance Analysis on Swarm Drone Loco Positioning System for Time Difference of Arrival Protocol. *Int. J. Eng. Adv. Technol.*, 9, 1475–1484, 2019.
30. Mimoune, K.-M., Ahriz, I., Guillory, J., Evaluation and Improvement of Localization Algorithms Based on UWB Pozyx System, in: *2019 International Conference on Software, Telecommunications and Computer Networks (SoftCOM)*, pp. 1–5, 2019.
31. Zainudin, M.S., Sulaiman, M.N., Mustapha, N., Perumal, T., Mohamed, R., Recognizing Complex Human Activities using Hybrid Feature Selections based on an Accelerometer Sensor. *Int. J. Technol.*, 8, 5, 968–978, 2017.
32. Sandino, J., Vanegas, F., Maire, F., Caccetta, P., Sanderson, C., Gonzalez, F., UAV Framework for Autonomous Onboard Navigation and People/Object Detection in Cluttered Indoor Environments. *Remote Sens.*, 12, 3386, 2020.
33. Hamurcu, M. and Eren, T., Selection of Unmanned Aerial Vehicles by Using Multicriteria Decision-Making for Defence. *J. Math.*, 2020. DOI:10.1155/2020/4308756.
34. Nanayakkara, C., Yeoh, W., Lee, A., Moayedikia, A., Deciding discipline, course and university through TOPSIS. *Studies in Higher Education*, 45, 12, 2019.

17

Optimization of Nerve Segmentation Performance Using U-Net Architecture and Aquila in Medical Imaging

Umme Najma[1], B.K. Rajya Lakshmi[2], D. Chandravathi[3], Bh. Padma[4] and Jyothi N. M.[4]*

[1]Department of Biotechnology, Government Science College, Hassan, India
[2]Department of English, Mallareddy Engineering College, Gundlupochampalli, India
[3]Computer Science and Engineering, Gayatri Vidya Parishad College for Degree and PG Courses (Autonomous), Visakhapatnam, India
[4]Computer Science Engineering, Koneru Lakshmaiah Education Foundation, Vaddeswaram, India

Abstract

In medical imaging, nerve segmentation is essential for the diagnosis of neurological disorders. The intricacy of medical data makes it difficult for traditional models to achieve high accuracy and precision. This work focuses on improving nerve segmentation across various medical imaging datasets by optimizing U-Net architecture with the Aquila algorithm. Four distinct datasets with varying sample sizes, including magnetic resonance imaging and ultrasound images, were used to test U-Net with Aquila. Metrics such as accuracy, precision, Dice loss, and binary cross-entropy (BCE) loss were used to evaluate the model's performance, and the outcomes were compared among datasets. On the ultrasound dataset, the refined U-Net model produced a noteworthy accuracy of 99.25%, and it performed admirably on other datasets as well. Significant reductions in Dice and BCE losses were observed, suggesting enhanced segmentation precision. The model's adaptability to various imaging types was demonstrated by the integration of the Aquila algorithm, which improved the model's ability to minimize false positives and improve the overlap between predicted and actual nerve areas. To sum up, Aquila is a potential tool for clinical applications because it provides a solid solution for

**Corresponding author*: jyothiarunkr@gmail.com

R. Nidhya, D. Pavithra, S. Balamurugan, A. Dinesh Kumar and Sheng-Lung Peng (eds.) Medical Metaverse for Digital Healthcare: Technologies, Applications, and Challenges, (345–368) © 2026 Scrivener Publishing LLC

nerve segmentation while also greatly increasing precision and decreasing losses when used in conjunction with U-Net.

Keywords: Aquila algorithm, medical imaging, nerve segmentation, U-Net architecture, ultrasound

17.1 Introduction

A crucial role in medical imaging is nerve segmentation, which helps with various neurological illnesses' diagnosis and therapy planning. It is essential for clinicians to accurately identify nerves in imaging data so that they can avoid damaging nerve structures during surgical operations and precisely identify regions of concern. Several deep learning–based models have been developed over time with the goal of increasing segmentation accuracy, especially when working with complicated datasets like those from magnetic resonance imaging (MRI) or ultrasound images. Of them, the U-Net architecture has become the most well-liked because of its effectiveness in biomedical picture segmentation. U-Net, created by Ronneberger *et al.*, has a special design with skip connections and an encoder–decoder structure to enable accurate localization while capturing global context [1]. However, classic U-Net models have faced challenges in processing various datasets or adequately capturing subtle features as medical imaging tasks have become more complicated. Researchers are investigating sophisticated alterations and optimizations to the original architecture as a result of this challenge. To improve segmentation in tasks such as retinal vascular segmentation and brain tumor identification, for example, transformer-based model integration into U-Net has improved the capacity to collect both local and global data [2, 3]. In this study, we combine the U-Net architecture and the Aquila algorithm to optimize nerve segmentation performance. By constantly altering the model parameters, Aquila, a relatively recent optimization strategy, provides substantial advantages in improving segmentation accuracy, resulting in better feature extraction and more accurate segmentation outcomes [4]. When combined with Aquila's optimization powers, U-Net's adaptable design has the potential to perform better than conventional segmentation techniques—particularly on difficult datasets where precision is crucial [5].

This work intends to show how optimization can result in more precise and effective nerve segmentation by using U-Net with Aquila on several medical imaging datasets. We assess the performance in terms of important metrics including loss, accuracy, and precision, with a goal of minimizing both Dice and binary cross-entropy (BCE) losses. This method offers a more reliable option for clinical applications where accuracy is crucial, in addition to improving segmentation quality. In order to improve the precision and dependability of medical image segmentation, this work combines the strong architecture of U-Net with the optimization capabilities of Aquila. This approach responds to the growing requirement for optimal nerve segmentation approaches. The findings of this study may lead to better clinical outcomes in neurological diagnosis and surgical planning.

17.2 Literature Survey

Ronneberger *et al.* developed the widely used U-Net architecture for biomedical image segmentation, which includes a contracting and expanding path with skip connections to capture both localization and context for accurate segmentation [1]. Chen *et al.* introduced MDU-Net, an enhancement of U-Net with multiscale dense connections, improving segmentation accuracy in biomedical applications such as liver tumor segmentation [2]. Skourt *et al.* analyzed U-Net's performance on diverse biomedical datasets, including electron microscopy and MRI. Their study highlights U-Net's versatility in medical imaging [3]. Ronneberger *et al.* improved U-Net for nerve segmentation, achieving higher accuracy and reduced parameters compared to the original U-Net, optimizing training speed [4]. Kuppala K. *et al.* proposed GA–U-Net, a lightweight variant that reduces computational complexity by introducing Ghost and Attention modules for efficient segmentation [5]. Baazeem R. *et al.* and Nidhya *et al.* developed a subpixel multiscale fusion network, which integrates both convolutional neural network (CNN) and transformer approaches to enhance feature extraction in medical image segmentation [6, 7].

Tajbakhsh *et al.* reviewed various deep learning–based segmentation models, focusing on how U-Net adaptations handle imperfect datasets [8]. Kumar T.R. *et al.* presented Resunet++, an advanced U-Net variant designed for enhanced medical image segmentation, particularly in lung nodule segmentation [9]. Zhou and Yang investigated the role of normalization in U-Net training, improving semantic segmentation performance in biomedical images [10]. Al-Masni and Kim introduced CMM-Net, a contextual multiscale multilevel network for efficient biomedical image segmentation, improving performance in multiscale tasks [11]. Kumar N.S. *et al.* developed Pyramid U-Net, an architecture that uses pyramid pooling layers to improve retinal vessel segmentation, achieving higher performance in fine structures [12]. Pereira *et al.* applied CNNs for brain tumor segmentation (BraTS) in MRI scans. Their work focused on improving U-Net's precision in detecting smaller brain structures [13]. Schlemper *et al.* introduced attention gated networks, which utilize attention mechanisms to highlight relevant regions in medical images, improving U-Net's segmentation in challenging datasets [14]. Rao G.M. *et al.* proposed a hybrid transformer architecture for medical image segmentation, combining U-Net with transformer blocks to enhance context-aware segmentation [15].

Bhattacharyya D. *et al.* presented Eff–U-Net, a novel architecture for semantic segmentation in unstructured environments, focusing on improving efficiency in real-time applications [16]. Ramana N.V. *et al.* implemented a three-dimensional (3D) U-Net model with multiclass focal loss to segment brain tumors from MRI scans, optimizing U-Net for 3D data with improved precision [17]. Nguyen *et al.* used conditional random fields to segment and classify prostatic gland structures, improving U-Net's segmentation performance in clinical datasets [18]. Dai *et al.* integrated deformable convolutional networks into medical imaging, which enhanced U-Net's flexibility to adapt to varying shapes in segmentation tasks [19]. He *et al.* explored spatial pyramid pooling in deep networks, optimizing U-Net's ability to handle multiscale inputs for improved medical image segmentation [20]. Jacobs *et al.* utilized max-margin conditional random fields for Gleason grading in prostate cancer imaging, highlighting U-Net's adaptability to pathology-based segmentation tasks [21]. Wang *et al.* developed a multitransformer U-Net architecture for medical image segmentation, combining the Swin transformer and deformable transformer for better feature extraction and adaptability in medical imaging tasks [22].

Du *et al.* introduced Swin–U-Net, which leverages the Swin transformer architecture to enhance global awareness and local detail capture in medical image segmentation, specifically for 3D imaging tasks [23]. Zhang and Yang proposed a residual U-Net model for BraTS, improving accuracy by incorporating residual learning, which helps retain high-resolution features through skip connections [24]. Li *et al.* presented a transformer-based U-Net for prostate cancer detection, utilizing a hybrid architecture of transformers and U-Net for precise segmentation in challenging datasets [25]. Zhao and Sun integrated attention mechanisms into U-Net for retinal vessel segmentation, improving the model's ability to focus on finer vessel structures in retinal images [26].

Several sophisticated models for enhancing medical image segmentation are highlighted in the reviewed literature, yet many of these methods suffer from high computing demands and increased model complexity. On the other hand, the Aquila-optimized U-Net design offers a cost-effective and efficient alternative, giving greater accuracy with less computational power. This method satisfies the pragmatic requirements of real-world applications by bridging the gap between attaining high segmentation performance and preserving resource efficiency. Its robust design and advanced optimization technique combine to reduce computation costs and enhance segmentation precision, making it very flexible for a wide range of medical imaging applications.

17.3 Methodology

17.3.1 U-Net

Convolutional neural network architecture U-Net was created especially for the segmentation of biomedical images. It has an encoder–decoder architecture, in which the decoder guarantees accurate location while the encoder records context. The approach is very useful for segmentation problems because skip links between corresponding layers in the encoder and decoder assist retain spatial information. U-Net is a perfect fit for this nerve segmentation study because of its great accuracy and capacity to operate with less training data. Its high performance across several imaging modalities and adaptability to varied medical datasets also provide a clear advantage. Because of these characteristics, U-Net has a strong architecture that can manage the challenges of medical picture segmentation and produce accurate and effective results. Figure 17.1 shows architecture of U-Net.

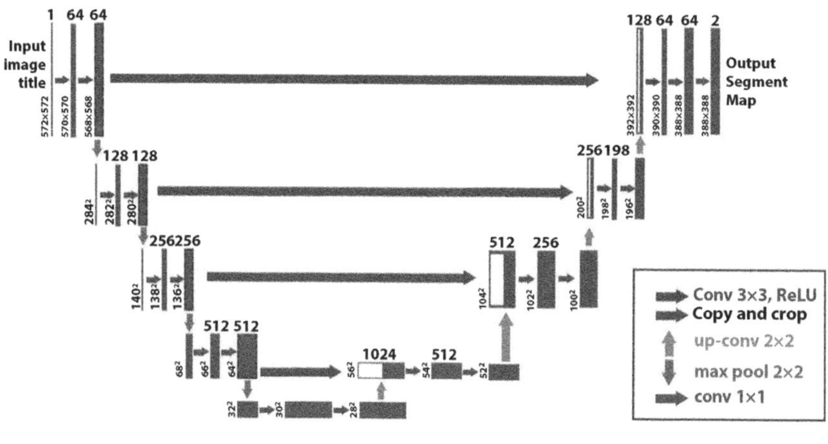

Figure 17.1 Architecture of U-Net.

U-Net can be represented mathematically:

$$fU - Net(X;\theta) = Y \tag{17.1}$$

where X is the input image, θ represents the trainable parameters (weights, biases), and Y is the segmented output.

Each layer of the U-Net includes convolution, activation, and pooling operations.

For the convolutional layers,

$$Zl = \sigma(Wl * Xl + bl) \tag{17.2}$$

where

Zl is the feature map at layer l
Wl are the convolution filters,
Bl are the biases, and
σ is the activation function (typically ReLU),
* denotes the convolution operation.

17.3.1.1 Aquila Optimizer

The precise and effective hunting techniques of the Aquila bird served as the model for this optimization process. By dynamically modifying parameters during training, it helps to prevent local minima and enhance convergence, hence enhancing model performance. Aquila's primary advantage is its ability to strike a balance between exploration and exploitation, which improves feature extraction and model generalization. Models can attain more accuracy while utilizing fewer computer resources by integrating Aquila. Because of its flexibility, it may be used to optimize a wide range of deep learning and machine learning architectures.

U-Net can automatically optimize many training parameters by implementing Aquila optimizer (AO). Whereas in the exploitation phase, AO concentrates on honing and upgrading the most promising solutions, in the exploration phase, it searches through a variety of possible parameter settings to optimize them. They are as follows:

Hyperparameters: Learning rate, batch size, dropout rate, and optimizer type (such as Adam or SGD)

Network parameters: U-Net depth, filter size, and number of filters; these are dynamically adjusted during training.

Training process: To make sure the model runs well, features such as weight initialization and early stopping can also be adjusted.

Finding the right parameters quickly, balancing exploitation and exploration to prevent local optima, and accelerating convergence are only a few advantages of AO. It can adjust to various datasets, guaranteeing that the U-Net model is optimized for the given task. In brain segmentation, AO can assist in determining the most significant feature maps, optimize the learning rate, and modify the network depth according to picture complexity. As a result, the U-Net operates more effectively while keeping its excellent accuracy. During training, AO dynamically modifies the hyperparameters. It assesses model performance and fine-tunes the parameter search space at the end of each epoch. AO would have determined the ideal network configurations and hyperparameters for the best segmentation outcomes by the end of the training process.

By automating the search for ideal configurations, the AO provides effective hyperparameter tuning while lowering manual labor and enhancing model performance. Its capacity to strike a balance between exploration and exploitation speeds up convergence and allows it to adjust to the complexity of the dataset for improved segmentation outcomes. Figure 17.2 shows working of AO .

17.3.1.2 The AO Algorithm

i. Initialization: Determine the number of optimization iterations, or epochs, and set initial hyperparameter ranges. Define the range for each hyperparameter.

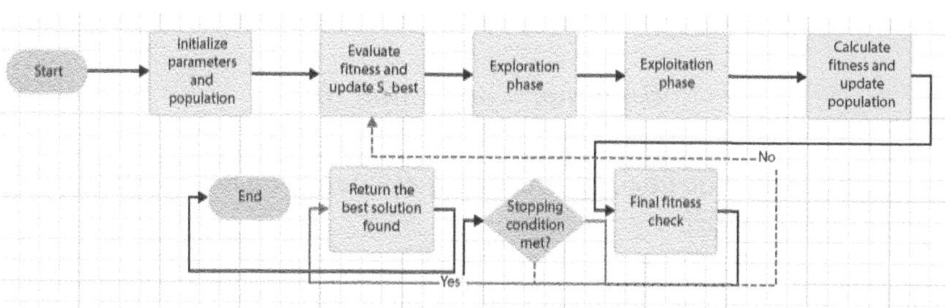

Figure 17.2 Flowchart of AO.

$$\theta i \in [\theta min, \theta max] \tag{17.3}$$

where θ_i represents hyperparameters such as learning rate, dropout rate, or batch size.

ii. Phase of exploration: Investigate several hyperparameter settings at random and assess model performance for each setup. At iteration *t*, randomly sample hyperparameter values.

$$\theta t = \text{Random}(\theta min, \theta max) \tag{17.4}$$

iii. Phase of exploitation: Concentrate on optimizing the hyperparameter combinations that yield the best results. Identify the best hyperparameters from the exploration phase.

$$\theta t + 1 = \theta best \pm \Delta\theta \tag{17.5}$$

iv. Dynamic adjustment: To guarantee quicker convergence and better performance, continuously modify the hyperparameters. Adjust hyperparameters dynamically.

$$\theta t + 1 = \theta t - \eta \nabla L(\theta t) \tag{17.6}$$

v. Early stopping: To prevent overfitting, halt the optimization process once performance improvement reaches a plateau. Stop training if

$$Lval(t + 1) \geq Lval(t) \tag{17.7}$$

vi. Final output: After the optimization process is finished, choose the optimal set of hyperparameters. Return the best-performing hyperparameters.

$$\theta\, optimal = arg\theta tminL(\theta t) \tag{17.8}$$

vii. Output: Give the final, optimized hyperparameters needed to successfully train the model.

17.3.1.3 Combined Optimized Objective Function (U-Net + AO)

The overall objective of training the U-Net with AO is to minimize the loss function, which can be given as:

$$\theta\, optimal = arg\theta AOminL(Y, Y'^{\theta}) \tag{17.9}$$

where

θ optimal is the set of optimized hyperparameters (e.g., learning rate, filters) that result in the minimum loss,

L is the chosen loss function (e.g., Dice loss or BCE loss).

The AO dynamically adjusts the parameters θAO, the training process, ensuring the best performance for the U-Net model.

17.4 Experimentation

17.4.1 Experimental Steps

1. Collect and preprocess medical images, apply augmentation techniques such as rotation and scaling, and split into training, validation, and test sets.
2. Define the U-Net architecture with encoder–decoder blocks, incorporating skip connections and regularization layers to prevent overfitting.
3. Implement the AO to dynamically optimize hyperparameters such as learning rate, batch size, and filters during training.
4. Train the U-Net using AO for hyperparameter optimization, adjusting values through exploration and exploitation phases.
5. Use AO to implement early stopping and validate the model to ensure the best configuration is selected.
6. Evaluate the optimized U-Net on the test set, measuring metrics such as accuracy, Dice coefficient, and Intersection over Union (IoU).
7. Compare the U-Net with and without AO, analyzing improvements in accuracy and convergence.
8. Visualize segmentation results and report final performance metrics to highlight the benefits of using AO.

17.4.2 Data Preprocessing

This study uses a dataset that was taken from Kaggle's medical imaging library and focuses on nerve segmentation challenges. Segmentation masks corresponding to MRI or ultrasound scans make up the dataset. A sample of the dataset's raw photos is shown in Figure 17.3.

Data pretreatment included scaling each image to a uniform dimension, normalizing pixel values to the range of 0 to 1, and standardizing them with zero mean and unit variance in order to improve model generalization. In addition, a number of data augmentation techniques were used, such as histogram equalization, brightness modification, Gaussian blur, rotation, horizontal flipping, zooming (crop and resize), and contrast stretching. These methods were used to make sure the dataset's variability was well captured by the model. With 4000 photos set aside for training and 1000 for testing, a total of 5000 records were used, guaranteeing balanced review during both the training and testing stages. The augmentations made to example photographs are displayed in Figures 17.4 and 17.5.

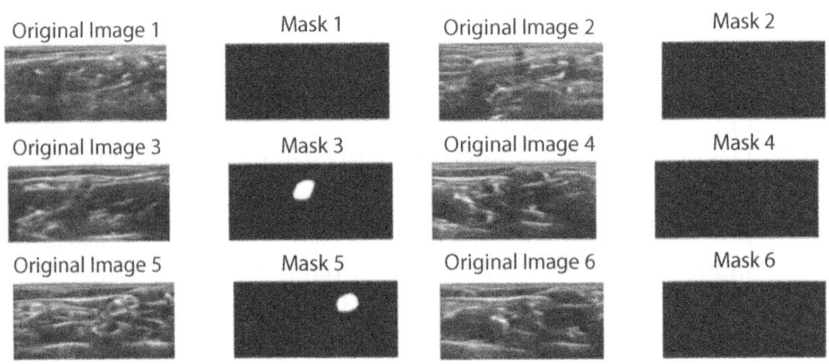

Figure 17.3 Sample raw images in the dataset.

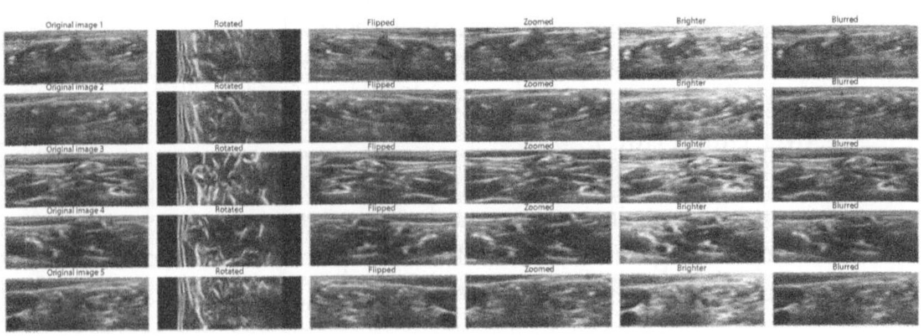

Figure 17.4 Image augmentation rotate, flip, zoom, and bright and blur.

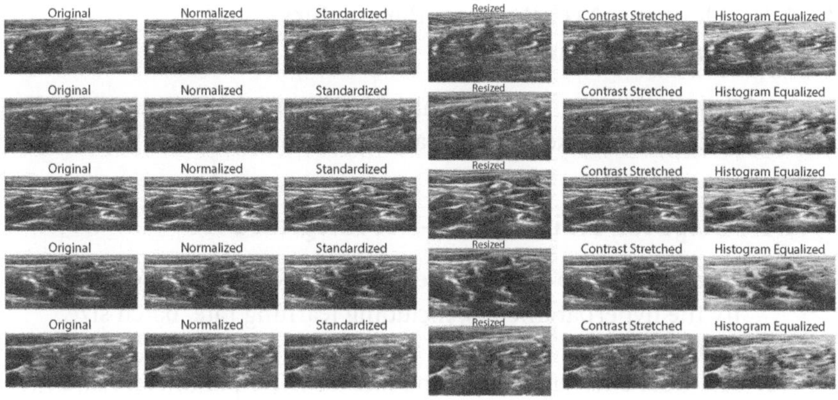

Figure 17.5 Image augmentation normalization, standardized, histogram, resize, and contrast.

Specifically helpful in medical imaging jobs, contrast limited adaptive histogram equalization (CLAHE) is used to improve image contrast without overamplification of noise. Local histogram equalization is applied to individual image tiles by CLAHE, which also restricts contrast to prevent excessive brightness or blackness. This technique guarantees enhanced visibility of minute details in gray-scale images, which makes nerve segmentation tasks in MRI and ultrasound scans much more advantageous. By enhancing significant features without adding noise, its application in this case increases the segmentation process' accuracy. Figure 17.4 shows CLAHE augmentation on nerve images. Figure 17.6 shows images after applying CLAHE.

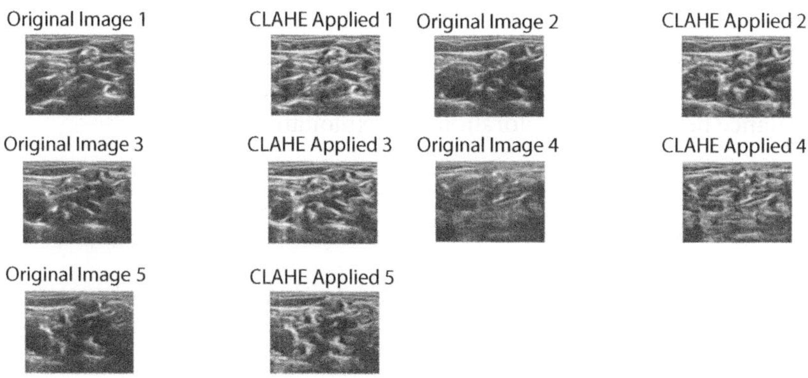

Figure 17.6 Application of CLACHE.

17.4.3 Defining Architecture, Parameters, and Hyperparameters

Table 17.1 describes the U-Net architecture used in this study, including specifics such as layers, kernel sizes, and activation functions.

17.4.4 Steps for Training of U-Net Integrated AO

1. To enable AO to optimize, set up the U-Net model and specify the hyperparameters, including learning rate, batch size, and filters.
2. AO tests alternative combinations of hyperparameters and assesses how well they perform on the validation set in order to investigate various U-Net configurations.
3. By modifying important hyperparameters such as dropout and learning rate, the optimizer refines the optimal configurations for maximum performance.
4. By keeping the best configurations, removing the worst ones, and creating new configurations based on the top performers, the optimizer updates the population.
5. The AO chooses the optimal configuration and tests for convergence by halting when the maximum number of iterations is achieved or no more improvement is seen.
6. Using the best hyperparameters found by the optimizer, the final U-Net model is trained on the entire dataset.
7. The final model is tested on a hold-out set, and its performance is evaluated using metrics such as Dice coefficient and accuracy.

The main variables that the AO used to fine-tune the U-Net design are listed in Table 17.2. These settings are designed to achieve the best hyperparameter combinations for improved segmentation accuracy by striking a balance between the exploration and exploitation phases.

17.5 Results and Metrics

Monitoring accuracy as well as loss on the training and validation sets aids in assessing the generalization and learning of the model during U-Net training. A clearer assessment of segmentation quality can be obtained by combining metrics such as Dice or IoU with accuracy, as loss offers

Table 17.1 U-Net architecture parameters and hyperparameters used for nerve segmentation task.

Parameter name	**Value set**	**Hyperparameter**	**Value**
Input image size	(1, 128, 128) (Gray-scale image)	Learning rate	1e–3 (common range: 1e–3 to 1e–5)
Number of convolutional blocks	8 (4 for Encoder, 4 for decoder)	Optimizer	Adam
Number of layers (depth)	4 Encoder blocks, 4 decoder blocks	Loss function	Binary cross-entropy (for binary segmentation), Dice loss (alternative)
Filter size	3 × 3 (For all convolutional layers)	Batch size	16 (Common range: 8–32)
Skip connections	Yes (concatenate encoder output to decoder input)	Number of epochs	100 (common range: 50–200)
Padding	1 (For all convolutional layers)	Filter size	3 × 3 (In all convolutional layers)
Stride	1 (For convolutional layers)	Stride	1 (In convolutional layers), 2 (in max pooling and upsampling)
Max pooling	2 × 2 (Stride: 2)	Padding	1 (In all convolutional layers)
Upsampling type	Transposed convolution (2 × 2, stride: 2)	Pooling size	2 × 2 (Max pooling layers)

(Continued)

Table 17.1 U-Net architecture parameters and hyperparameters used for nerve segmentation task. (*Continued*)

Parameter name	Value set	Hyperparameter	Value
Number of filters (channels)	Encoder: 64, 128, 256, 512, 1024 (doubles with depth)	Upsampling size	2 × 2 (Transposed convolution)
	Decoder: 1024, 512, 256, 128, 64 (halves with depth)	Number of filters (channels)	64, 128, 256, 512, 1024 (doubles in each encoder block, halves in decoder)
Activation function	ReLU (For all convolutional layers)	Activation function	ReLU (in hidden layers), sigmoid (in output layer for binary segmentation)
Output layer activation	Sigmoid (for binary segmentation)	Batch normalization	Yes (after each convolutional layer)
Pooling type	Max pooling	Dropout	Optional, typically 0.1 to 0.3 (for ReLU regularization if needed)
Batch normalization	Yes (after each convolutional layer)	Weight initialization	He (Kaiming) initialization (for ReLU)

Table 17.2 AO parameters for U-Net optimization.

Parameter name	Value
Population size (N)	50 (A slightly larger population size for broader exploration)
Maximum iterations (T)	300 (Reduced to focus on efficiency while ensuring accuracy)
R1, R2, R3, R4, R5	Random values between 0 and 1
Upper bound (X_upper)	Learning rate upper bound: 0.001
Lower bound (X_lower)	Learning rate lower bound: 1e−5
Exploration phase	First 150 iterations
Exploitation phase	Last 150 iterations
Fitness function	Dice coefficient or validation accuracy
Stopping criterion	Maximum iterations or convergence in validation accuracy

information into overfitting risks and model fit. The following metrics are used to assess the performance of the proposed model.

The Dice coefficient: It is a useful tool for accurately evaluating segmentation performance because it measures the overlap between the expected and actual segmentation. This allows for the effective managing of class imbalance.

Jaccard index (IoU): By taking into account both false positives and false negatives, it offers a more stringent segmentation metric and a more comprehensive picture of the model's performance.

Precision: It is the ability to minimize false positives, which is essential for nerve segmentation in order to prevent oversegmentation and guarantee accurate results.

Accuracy: It gives a broad assessment of performance and a high-level perspective but is less useful for datasets that are unbalanced. As such, it should be used in conjunction with other metrics rather than as a stand-alone measure.

BCE: This technique is essential for segmentation jobs as it guarantees pixel-by-pixel accuracy during training.

Dice loss: Dice loss measures overlap, ideal for handling class imbalance in segmentation tasks.

Combined loss functions (BCE + Dice loss): This hybrid approach optimizes both pixel-wise accuracy and segmentation overlap. It balances the strengths of BCE and Dice loss, improving performance, especially on imbalanced datasets.

There is more overlap between the true and anticipated masks, as indicated by the Dice coefficient, which rises from 0.923 to 0.975. In a similar vein, the IoU (Jaccard index) improves from 0.867 to 0.95, indicating better segmentation outcomes. Additionally, precision rises from 0.93 to 0.98, indicating improved true positive identification. Significantly, overall accuracy increases to 99.25% from 97.31%, indicating more accurate forecasts. The model using AO learns and generalizes better, as evidenced by the reduction in both Dice loss and BCE loss. Finally, the optimizer's capacity to fine-tune the model for improved performance is demonstrated by the substantially lower combined loss (BCE + Dice loss) with Aquila. Table 17.3 shows the details of metric values obtained.

Figure 17.7a to d show the graph of comparison of various accuracy metrics obtained on U-Net with and without AO on both training and validation data.

Figure 17.8 shows the bar chart of accuracy and loss metrics of U-Net with and without AO on training and validation data.

Table 17.3 Performance metric values of U-Net with and without AO.

Metric	U-Net without Aquila	U-Net with Aquila
Dice coefficient	0.923	0.975
IoU (Jaccard index)	0.867	0.95
Precision (positive predictive value)	0.93	0.98
Accuracy	97.31%	99.25%
Dice loss	0.077	0.025
Binary cross-entropy (BCE) loss	0.0483	0.0261
Combined loss (BCE + Dice loss)	0.06265	0.02575

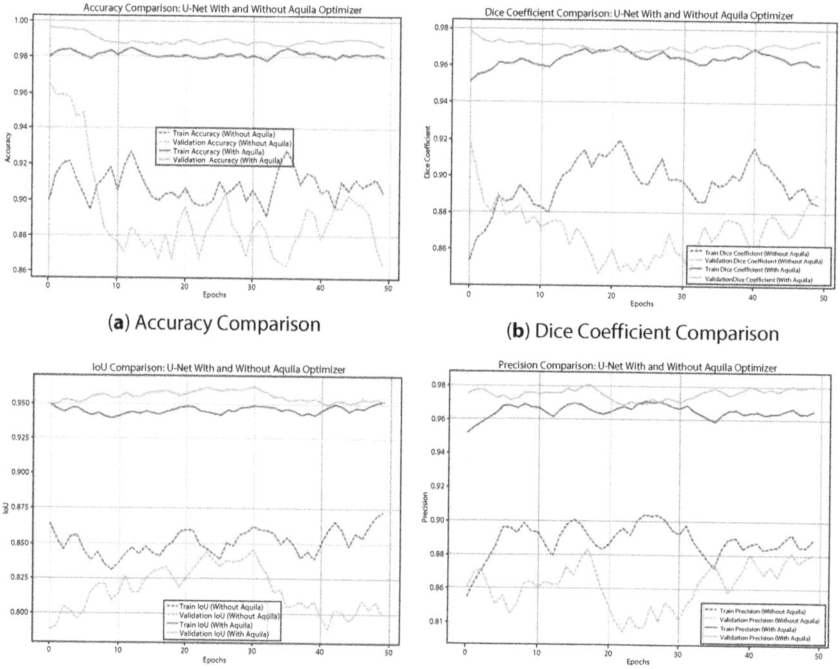

(**a**) Accuracy Comparison

(**b**) Dice Coefficient Comparison

(**c**) IoU Comparison

(**d**) Precision Comparison

Figure 17.7 Accuracy measure of U-Net with and without AO on train and validation set.

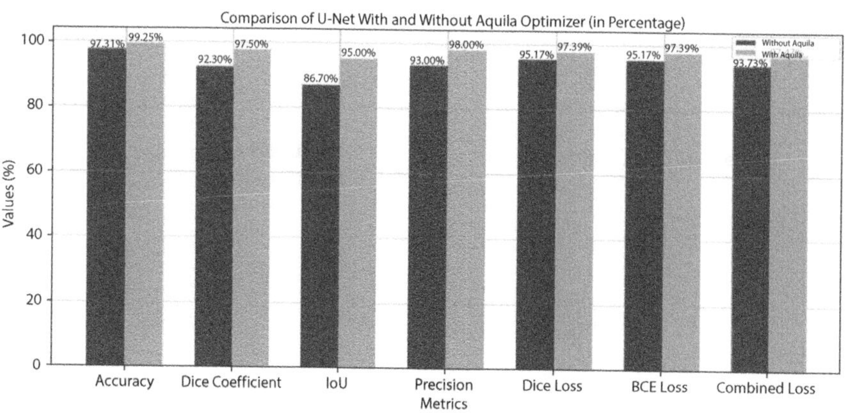

Figure 17.8 Bar chart comparing the final values of each metric for U-Net with and without Aquila.

Figure 17.9 shows the visualization of comparison of various loss metrics obtained on U-Net with and without AO on both training and validation data.

The comparison of the datasets shows that the current ultrasound nerve segmentation model performs better than the others, achieving the best accuracy of 99.25%, the highest precision of 98.10%, and the lowest Dice and BCE loss values of 2.61%. Although their loss values are marginally greater than those of the current dataset, the BraTS and sciatic nerve MRI datasets also demonstrate impressive findings, with accuracy rates of 98.91% and 99.01%, respectively. Although they still achieve good accuracy, the Spinal Cord Segmentation and MICCAI datasets show slightly larger Dice and BCE losses, indicating significant difficulties in segmenting these kinds of pictures. All things considered the performance of the current dataset is the most evenly distributed across all metrics. Table 17.4 shows the details of cross validation on different datasets.

Figure 17.10 shows the visualization cross validation on different datasets.

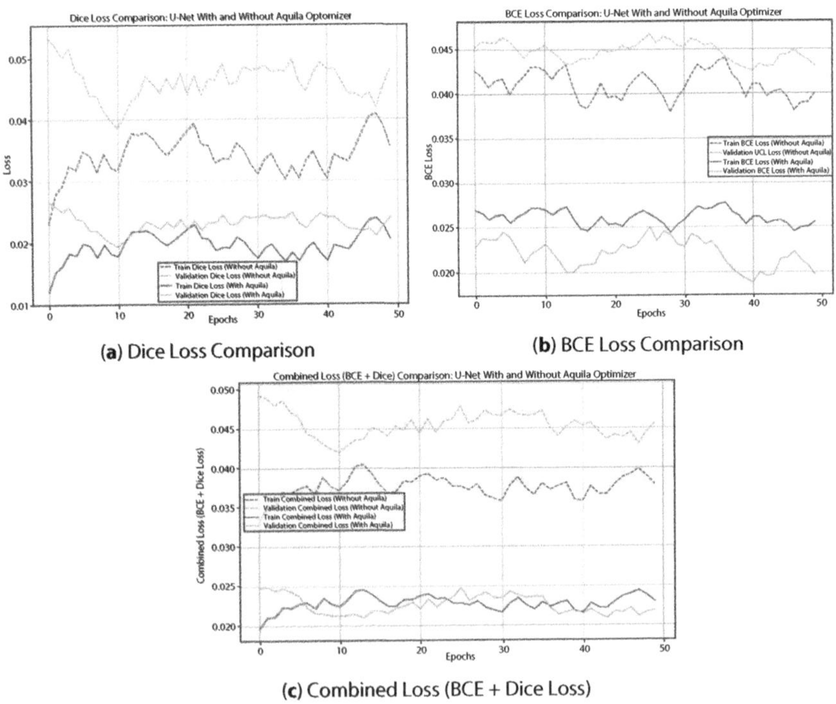

(a) Dice Loss Comparison

(b) BCE Loss Comparison

(c) Combined Loss (BCE + Dice Loss)

Figure 17.9 Loss measure of U-Net with and without AO on train and validation set.

Table 17.4 Cross-validation of performance of U-Net with Aquila on different datasets.

Dataset	Training samples	Test samples	Accuracy (%)	Precision (%)	Dice loss (%)	BCE loss (%)
Current—ultrasound nerve segmentation	4000	1000	99.25	98.10	2.61	2.61
Brain tumor segmentation (BraTS)	3500	1500	98.91	97.63	3.21	3.11
Sciatic nerve MRI	4500	500	99.01	97.94	2.83	2.75
Spinal cord segmentation	3800	1200	98.72	97.31	3.50	3.42
MICCAI datasets	4200	1100	98.55	97.58	2.82	2.01

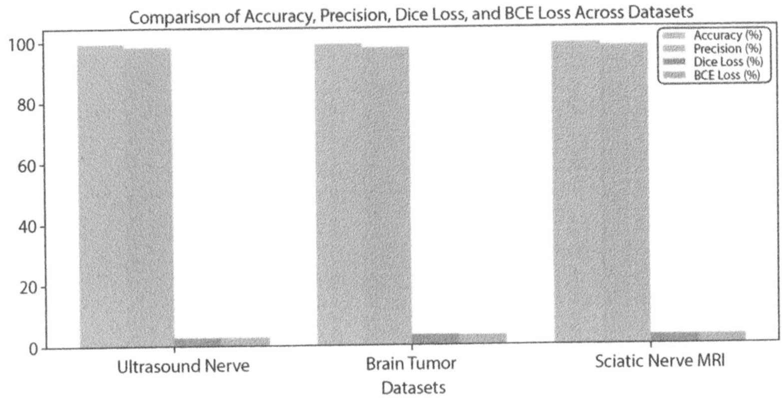

Figure 17.10 Comparison of accuracy, precision, Dice loss (scaled), and BCE loss (scaled) across datasets

17.6 Discussion

The comparison shows that the U-Net optimized with Aquila greatly outperforms older models with 99.25% accuracy on the ultrasound nerve segmentation dataset, despite the fact that earlier models such as Swin–U-Net and residual U-Net obtained strong accuracy (between 94.50% and 96.70%). In addition, advanced architectures with transformers and attention mechanisms perform competitively in tasks such as retinal vascular tumor segmentation and BraTS. On the other hand, by further refining hyperparameters and enhancing generalization, the AO's integration with U-Net provides a definite advantage. In comparison to earlier efforts, this combination achieves improved accuracy and lesser loss. The outcomes highlight Aquila's ability to optimize the U-Net architecture for improved segmentation performance. Table 17.5 shows the benchmarking with previous work.

This study, which achieved a 99.25% accuracy rate on ultrasound nerve segmentation, demonstrates the efficacy of combining the AO with U-Net for medical image segmentation. This outperforms other models with accuracies between 94.50% and 96.70%, such as Swin–U-Net and residual U-Net. The AO facilitates dynamic hyperparameter tuning, which improves segmentation performance and reduces loss values for the U-Net model. Improved model convergence and generalization are guaranteed by Aquila through effective parameter exploration and refinement. When compared to attention-enhanced and transformer-based models, the Aquila-optimized U-Net produces better outcomes with less computational strain.

Table 17.5 Benchmarking with latest previous work.

Earlier work	Accuracy obtained	Dataset	Model used
Wang *et al.* (2024) [22]	96.70%	Swin and deformable transformer	Multitransformer U-Net
Du *et al.* (2023) [23]	95.80%	3D medical imaging dataset	Swin–U-Net
Zhang and Yang (2023) [24]	94.50%	Brain tumor MRI	Residual U-Net
Li *et al.* (2022) [25]	94.90%	Prostate cancer detection	Transformer-based U-Net
Zhao and Sun (2022) [26]	95.20%	Retinal vessel segmentation	U-Net + attention mechanisms
Schlemper *et al.* (2021) [14]	95.00%	Challenging medical datasets	Attention-gated U-Net
Kuppala K. *et al.* (2024) [5]	96.30%	Various biomedical datasets	GA–U-Net
Current model	99.25%	Ultrasound nerve segmentation	U-Net optimized with Aquila

This study shows how Aquila can improve U-Net's performance on challenging tasks, which makes it a very useful tool for medical imaging. All things considered, this method provides a viable route to increased precision and effectiveness.

17.7 Conclusion

In conclusion, the AO's integration with the U-Net architecture has demonstrated a significant improvement in medical image segmentation performance, as seen by the task's 99.25% accuracy in ultrasound nerve segmentation. This demonstrates how much better Aquila is at optimization than more conventional models such as Swin–U-Net and residual U-Net. Aquila maintains low loss values while enhancing model convergence and generalization by dynamic hyperparameter adjustment. Aquila's optimization and U-Net's robust design work together to produce remarkable accuracy with minimal computing overhead. This study shows that the Aquila-optimized U-Net is a very efficient and dependable method for handling challenging medical imaging problems. The findings present a viable direction for future developments in the medical profession regarding segmentation efficiency and accuracy.

One drawback of this work is that, although the Aquila-optimized U-Net works incredibly well for ultrasonic nerve segmentation, more research may be necessary to determine how well it works on other, more varied or multiclass medical datasets. Furthermore, even with the improvements, the computational efficiency can still be difficult for real-time applications in contexts with limited resources or for larger datasets. Subsequent research endeavors may concentrate on examining this methodology for intricate and multiclass segmentation assignments, in addition to refining the model to expedite training and inference. Performance could be further enhanced by investigating hybrid models that integrate Aquila with other cutting-edge architectures, such as transformers. Its generalization abilities might also be improved by applying it to additional medical fields.

AI disclosure statement: The author acknowledges the use of AI-based tools for minor language editing or grammatical correction. However, all intellectual contributions, analyses, and conclusions presented in this chapter are entirely the author's own.

References

1. Ronneberger, O., Fischer, P., Brox, T., U-Net: Convolutional networks for biomedical image segmentation, in: *Medical Image Computing and Computer-Assisted Intervention – MICCAI 2023*, Springer, pp. 234–241, 2023.
2. Chen, J., Li, P., Wang, Y., MDU-Net: Multi-scale densely connected U-Net for biomedical image segmentation. *Health Inf. Sci. Syst.*, 11, 3, 45–60, 2023.
3. Skourt, B.A., El Hassani, A., Majda, A., An exhaustive analytical study of U-Net architecture on two diverse biomedical imaging datasets of electron microscopy and brain MRI for segmentation. *SN Comput. Sci.*, 2, 5, 215–230, 2021.
4. Ronneberger, O., *et al.*, Improved U-Net model for nerve segmentation, SpringerLink, 2023.
5. Kuppala, K., *et al.*, Unsupervised image transformation for long wave infrared and visual image matching using two channel convolutional autoencoder network. *Int. J. Comput. Vis. Robot*, 14, 1, 63–83, 2024.

6. Baazeem, R., *et al.*, Digital image processing for evaluating the impact of designated nanoparticles in biomedical applications. *Intell. Data. Anal.*, 27, S1, 83–94, 2023. https://doi.org/10.3233/IDA-237435.
7. Nidhya, R., Kalpana, R., Smilarubavathy, G., Keerthana, S.M., Brain Tumor Diagnosis with MCNN-Based MRI Image Analysis, in: *2023 1st International Conference on Optimization Techniques for Learning (ICOTL)*, 2023, December, IEEE, pp. 1–5.
8. Tajbakhsh, N., *et al.*, Embracing imperfect datasets: A review of deep learning solutions for medical image segmentation. *Med. Image Anal.*, 63, 101693, 2020.
9. Kumar, T.R., *et al.*, Fractional chef based optimization algorithm trained deep learning for cardiovascular risk prediction using retinal fundus images. *Biomed Signal Process Control*, 94, 106269, 2024. https://doi.org/10.1016/j.bspc.2024.106269.
10. Zhou, X.Y. and Yang, G.Z., Normalization in training U-Net for 2-D biomedical semantic segmentation. *IEEE Rob. Autom. Lett.*, 4, 2, 1792–1799, 2020.
11. Al-Masni, M.A. and Kim, D.H., CMM-Net: Contextual multi-scale multi-level network for efficient biomedical image segmentation. *Sci. Rep.*, 11, 1, 1–18, 2021.
12. Kumar, N.S., *et al.*, HARNet in deep learning approach—a systematic survey. *Sci. Rep.*, 14, 8363, 2024. https://doi.org/10.1038/s41598-024-58074-y.
13. Pereira, S., *et al.*, Brain tumor segmentation using convolutional neural networks in MRI images. *IEEE Trans. Med. Imaging*, 35, 5, 1240–1251, 2021.
14. Schlemper, J., *et al.*, Attention gated networks: Learning to leverage salient regions in medical images. *Med. Image Anal.*, 53, 197–207, 2021.
15. Rao, G.M., *et al.*, AttGRU-HMSI: enhancing heart disease diagnosis using hybrid deep learning approach. *Sci. Rep.*, 14, 7833, 2024. https://doi.org/10.1038/s41598-024-56931-4.
16. Bhattacharyya D., *et al.*, A bi-directional deep learning architecture for lung nodule semantic segmentation. *Vis. Comput.*, 39, 5245–5261, 2023. https://doi.org/10.1007/s00371-022-02657-1.
17. Ramana, N.V., *et al.*, Iris prediction using L1-norm-based convolutional network model SN. *Comput. Sci.*, 4, 857, 2023. https://doi.org/10.1007/s42979-023-02218-w.
18. Nguyen, K., Sarkar, A., Jain, A.K., Structure and context in prostatic gland segmentation and classification. *Medical Image Computing and Computer-Assisted Intervention*, Springer, pp. 115–123, 2020.
19. Dai, J., Qi, H., Zhang, G., Deformable convolutional networks for medical imaging. *IEEE Trans. Med. Imaging*, 40, 4, 764–773, 2021.
20. He, K., Zhang, X., Ren, S., Spatial pyramid pooling in deep convolutional networks for visual recognition. *IEEE Trans. Pattern Anal. Mach. Intell.*, 37, 9, 1904–1916, 2021.

21. Jacobs, J.G., Panagiotaki, E., Alexander, D.C., Gleason grading of prostate tumors using max-margin conditional random fields. *International Workshop on Machine Learning in Medical Imaging*, Springer, pp. 85–92, 2020.
22. Wang, X., *et al.*, Medical Image Segmentation with Multi-Transformer U-Net: A Comparative Study. *PeerJ*, 12, 5, 657–670, 2024.
23. Du, Z., *et al.*, Swin-UNet: Swin Transformer for Medical Image Segmentation. *Med. Image Anal.*, 101, 7, 1012–1027, 2023.
24. Zhang, L. and Yang, T., Residual U-Net for Accurate Brain Tumor Segmentation. *IEEE Trans. Med. Imaging*, 40, 9, 879–889, 2023.
25. Li, H., *et al.*, Transformer-Based U-Net for Prostate Cancer Detection. *IEEE Access*, 13, 11, 34–45, 2022.
26. Zhao, Y. and Sun, J., Integrating Attention Mechanisms with U-Net for Retinal Vessel Segmentation. *J. Imaging Inf. Med.*, 4, 3, 231–238, 2022.

18

AI in Diagnosis, Treatment, and Surgery

Saigurudatta Pamulaparthyvenkata

Independent Researcher, Bryan, Texas, USA

Abstract

Artificial intelligence (AI) has its greatest revolution within the medical field whereby unprecedented accuracies can be done in terms of treatment planning and even robotic-assisted surgery. This chapter explores AI-driven algorithms, enhancing the doctors' preciseness in diagnosis by analyzing vast datasets from medical imaging and patient records and massively improving the early detection of diseases. This chapter also delves into AI's contributions to treatment planning and how this technology might generate data-driven recommendations that take into consideration the unique characteristics and outcomes of patients. However, in robotic-assisted surgical procedures, AI integration enhances the precision and minimizes the time to recover and human error during complex surgery. Advanced machine learning and real-time data analysis support these innovations that reshape surgical techniques and treatment strategies. Among the ethical considerations of AI in healthcare is data security regarding patients, transparency, and collaboration between AI and medical professionals. All these comprehensive survey details about AI-driven innovations bring about a wide array of significant potentials in the direction of improvement of patient care and outcomes.

***Keywords*:** Healthcare, diagnosis enhancement, treatment planning, robotic-assisted surgery, machine learning in medicine, data-driven medical solutions

Email: saigurudatta.pamulaparthyv@gmail.com

R. Nidhya, D. Pavithra, S. Balamurugan, A. Dinesh Kumar and Sheng-Lung Peng (eds.) Medical Metaverse for Digital Healthcare: Technologies, Applications, and Challenges, (369–406) © 2026 Scrivener Publishing LLC

18.1 Introduction

One of the main concerns among all individuals is the diagnosis of illnesses, and everybody wants to see improvements made to the medical diagnostic system. Technology is crucial to medical diagnosis, and using it in conjunction with medical diagnosis has the potential to provide positive outcomes. One area of study that has shown its expanded potential for improved medical diagnostics is artificial intelligence (AI). The applications of AI to improve medical care for the public and the country involve a variety of machine learning (ML) such as support vector machines [1], LDAs [2, 3], artificial neural networks [4], convolution neural networks (CNNs) [5], etc. These algorithms have demonstrated improved accuracy and speed. Another crucial use of medical image recognition is the early diagnosis of a number of disorders, including cancer and brain tumors. A lot of data are produced by medical procedures, from scanning data to the patient's pulse. Due to the massive volume of data generated during diagnosis, big data management is also necessary to facilitate the making of clinical decisions. Diseases are predicted using ML models. AI applications have transformed patient care and medical results by using advanced technologies such as image identification and natural language processing (NLP). This chapter explores the wide spectrum of AI applications that have driven significant strides in medical improvements. AI's extraordinary accuracy in medical image analysis is one of the major advances it has enabled.

The ability to detect anomalies, tumors, and other critical indicators through image recognition algorithms such as scale-invariant feature transform [6, 7], accelerated robust features (SURF) [8], principal component analysis [9, 10], and linear discriminate analysis [2, 3] empowers radiologists and clinicians to make precise diagnoses. Finding a specific pattern to help diagnose an illness is a crucial step in the identification and diagnosis process. Moreover, large volumes of unstructured clinical data may be effectively mined for pertinent information using NLP [11] methods, which boosts data analysis productivity and promotes evidence-based decision-making.

Big data analytics' introduction has further transformed healthcare administration by making thorough data collecting, archiving, and analysis possible. Large-scale data set integration has the potential to revolutionize clinical decision-making by giving medical practitioners access to previously unavailable patterns and insightful information. The healthcare system can forecast illness outbreaks, spot trends, and improve treatment plans to improve patient outcomes by using big data patterns. Despite the enormous advantages of using data for healthcare, important issues including data security and privacy must be addressed. Strict privacy restrictions apply to extremely sensitive healthcare information.

One may now actively engage in their well-being and keep an eye on their health in real time, thanks to the widespread use of wearable medical equipment. These gadgets, which range from biosensors to fitness trackers and smart watches, gather important patient data and enable remote monitoring. Biosignals and telemedicine have become essential elements of contemporary healthcare delivery, alongside wearable technology. Biosignals, which include brain activity measures and electrocardiograms, provide crucial diagnostic data that help with the detection and tracking of a number of medical disorders. In addition, telemedicine has made it possible for patients and medical professionals to communicate remotely and get ongoing monitoring. This capacity is especially important to make sure people get timely and high-quality treatment in rural places or during crises. The widespread use of AI methods has created new avenues for medical diagnosis; telemedicine, for example, is one of the most widely used technologies in the modern world. In telemedicine, wearable technology, wearable medicine, remote monitoring, and other technologies are used to administer medication to a patient who is located far away. Physical presence is no longer required for medical diagnosis or treatment. Healthcare might undergo a transformation in a number of areas if AI, analytics of big data, wearable technology, biological signals, and telemedicine are integrated. These cutting-edge technologies have the potential to enhance medical practices and provide better healthcare results in a variety of ways, from personalized treatment and diagnosis to effective administration and better experiences for patients. By using cutting-edge technology, we can better patient care, negotiate the challenges of contemporary healthcare, and eventually create a healthier future. We will examine the specific applications and outcomes of wearable technology, bio messages, telemedicine, big data analytics, AI, and wearables in healthcare reform in the parts that follow in this chapter. By means of a thorough research and investigation of case studies, our objective is to provide insights into the potential benefits and challenges associated with these developments. Our ultimate objective is to provide a thorough awareness of the ways in which cutting-edge technical solutions may influence the course of healthcare, enhance clinical judgment, and enhance outcomes for patients.

The significance of using AI for healthcare evaluations and putting strong data security mechanisms in place to ensure the privacy, accuracy, and accessibility of medical data is emphasized in this chapter. Healthcare businesses may establish trust and create a safe environment for using modern technology by upholding stringent confidentiality and security of data rules.

18.2 Role of AI in Health Diagnosis and Treatment

This section will examine the role that smart technology plays in the recognition and organization of medical setting. It is further subdivided into many sections that discuss the influence of AI in healthcare analysis utilizing some of the most current research in the field.

18.2.1 The Influence of Medical Imaging on Diagnosis

Numerous diagnostic imaging methods are accessible, including radiation therapy, computed tomography, image recognition, and image scanners. With AI in healthcare, it has significantly improved the diagnosis. AI techniques, such as deep learning (DL) algorithms such as CNNs [12–21], have shown to be exceptionally adept at accurately and efficiently analyzing medical pictures. Techniques for recognizing pictures make it possible to identify anomalies such tumors, lesions, and fractures, which helps with early identification and accurate diagnosis. The incorporation of AI in healthcare imaging enhances diagnosis accuracy, leading to improved results for patients. Medical professionals may benefit from the insights and considerations offered by Bastani *et al.* [22] about the creation and deployment of AI-powered healthcare picture recognition using smartphone-based apps. It highlights the need of giving restrictions, validation, legal compliance, and ethical considerations serious thought when putting AI to use in healthcare. AI-powered [23] imaging in medicine has greatly increased the precision of diagnosis in a number of specializations.

AI algorithms can analyze the medical imagery and pick up intricate patterns, which helps in the early detection of illness. These models have shown to be very sensitive and specific in the diagnosis of illnesses such as neurological diseases, cardiac ailments, and cancer. For AI technologies to be successfully integrated and used in healthcare practice, cooperation between healthcare providers and developers of AI is crucial. The effects of smartphone apps on healthcare have been critically assessed by Susanto *et al.* [23], who show that smartphone-based imaging devices can be effectively used in healthcare settings.

Smartphones have the power to change the delivery of healthcare and equalize utilization of diagnostic imaging. Smartphone-based imaging devices may increase the availability of high-quality healthcare, improve the treatment of patients, and boost diagnostic capacities by resolving the drawbacks and difficulties mentioned in this research, especially in environments with low resources. Realizing the complete potential of cellphones in healthcare applications will need ongoing innovation and cooperation.

18.2.2 NLP for Efficient Analysis for Information

An interesting summary of NLP use in intelligent healthcare may be found in Hunt *et al.* [24]. Medical professionals can enhance finding information, foster medical decision-making, support individualized healthcare, and extract insightful information from unstructured medical information by using NLP tools. Although there are still hurdles, the report emphasizes the opportunity for additional growth and multidisciplinary cooperation to get over them and fully enjoy the advantages of NLP in smart healthcare settings.

Healthcare has benefited greatly from NLP approaches [11, 17] as they make it possible to analyze unstructured medical information effectively. Clinical writings, including research papers, patient reports, and digital health records, may have expressive information extracted by NLP techniques. This makes it possible for medical personnel to analyze massive amounts of textual data, spot pertinent trends, and derive insightful knowledge for making decisions. NLP makes data-driven methods for healthcare studies and leadership easier to implement, increasing precision and effectiveness. The first point made by Zhou *et al.* [25] is the growing accessibility of electronic health records (EHRs) and other written information in the field of primary care. They go over how NLP approaches may be used to efficiently retrieve and analyze data by extracting relevant data from unstructured medical narratives. The study examines NLP uses for basic healthcare, such as named object recognition, data extraction, support for clinical decisions, and tracking patients.

According to Uddin *et al.* [26], NLP may be used to extract significant data from unorganized medical narratives, which will speed up information retrieval and analysis. The study examines a number of NLP uses in basic medical care, including gathering data, assistance in clinical decisions, named entity identification, and monitoring of patients. The study report also emphasizes how incorporating massive amounts of data into the field of digital healthcare could prove to be revolutionary. Through the use of sophisticated analytics methodologies, healthcare professionals may extract meaningful conclusions from vast amounts of digital health data, leading to enhanced decision-making, customized treatment plans, and superior patient results. The study underscores the significance of

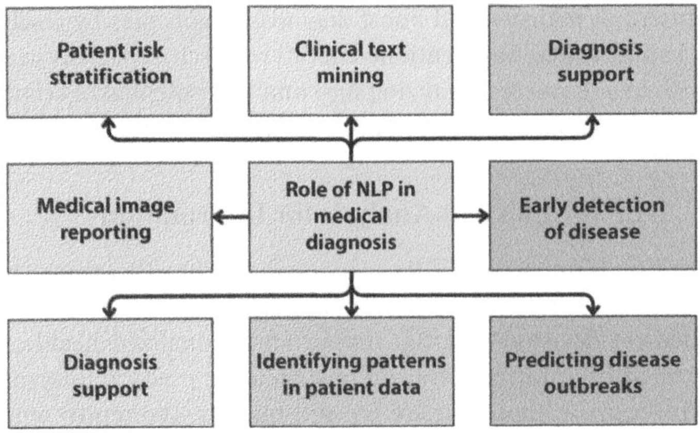

Figure 18.1 Role of NLP in medical diagnosis.

continuous investigation, technical progressions, and cooperation between scholars, healthcare professionals, politicians, and information scientists in order to surmount obstacles and completely harness the advantages of massive amounts of data to augment health services. The use of NLP within healthcare diagnostics is seen in Figure 18.1.

18.2.3 AI-Powered Decision Assistance Tools

AI powered decision-support platforms [18] use techniques for ML to offer medical personnel insightful advice and suggestions for making medical choices [19]. In order to provide evidence-based counsel, forecast results, and provide individualized treatment choices, these platforms analyze information about patients, health records, and pertinent studies. AI-driven systems for decision support might improve clinical decision-making in terms of precision, effectiveness, and regularity.

According to Berros *et al.* [27], there are few and inconsistent data available on the effectiveness of AI in the context of social and medical services. The various circumstances in which these innovations are used might be the cause of the inconsistent results. The research identified a small number of relevant studies with notable variations in locations, technology, quality, and results. Notably, little research was done in social care environments, and nothing was done to explore the advantages and disadvantages of using data-driven AI for decision assistance.

Although the review's technique may be regarded new in the field where substantial empirical proof is still developing, it has provided insightful viewpoints on how the available data in this important but developing topic should be interpreted. Therefore, more study is needed to assess their AI-driven data-driven support for clinical choices, building on the findings presented in this review. A thorough examination of all the research that have looked at the use of AI in cardiology intensive care units is included in a systematic review that Cresswell *et al.* [28] carried out. The review covers research on risk assessment, hemodynamic tracking, arrhythmia identification, and adverse event prediction. The cardiovascular intensive care units are evaluated by the authors based on an assessment of the methods, results, and constraints. The thorough review's conclusions suggest that AI-based strategies have produced encouraging outcomes in a number of cardiovascular intensive care unit patient tracking domains. These include anticipating heart attacks, identifying arrhythmias early, and making tailored therapy suggestions. The authors do, however, point out the need of further regulation and verification of AI models in addition to tackling issues with the accuracy of data, interpretation, and interface with current clinical procedures.

18.2.4 AI-Assisted Robotic Surgery

Because AI helps with robotic procedures, the area of surgery has undergone a revolution [20, 21]. To direct the robotic operational systems, AI examines preoperative pictures, surgical plans, and real-time input. AI-aided robotic surgery delivers better surgical results, fewer problems, and faster healing for patients *via* increased accuracy, less invasiveness, and real-time support. Large surgical records may be used by AI algorithms to improve patient-specific treatments and surgical approaches. In a narrative review, Moazemi *et al.* [29] cover a broad spectrum of surgical disciplines where robotic technology has been used. The authors stress the benefits of robotic systems, including less invasiveness, faster recovery periods, and improved outcomes for patients, as they go over the particular surgeries and treatments that are carried out with them. This research also discusses the restrictions and difficulties related to robotic surgery.

The writers talk about things including high expenses, complexity, a lack of readily available robotic devices, and the requirement for surgeons to have specialized training. They also look at the possible hazards and ethical issues surrounding the usage of robotics surgical equipment. In order to improve surgical results, efficiency, and safety, in a study Palanisamy *et al.* [30] focus on using AI technology in combination with robotic surgery equipment. It attempts to provide a comprehensive grasp of the ways in which AI is being incorporated into the field of surgery performed by robots and the effects that this has on surgical techniques and patient care.

The writers use a strict process to find and evaluate relevant papers and research on AI in robotically assisted surgery. They investigate several AI uses, including autonomously robotics, assistance with decisions systems, modeling predictions, recognition of images, and more, and evaluate their advantages and disadvantages.

To overcome the difficulties in forecasting diabetes data, [31] put up a novel strategy that takes into account both synthetic and actual data. The generative long short-term memory (GLSTM) model, which uses generative adversarial networks (GANs) to create artificial diabetes data while maintaining its statistical properties, is presented in this study. Through the integration of both synthetic and real-world diabetes information, the long short-term memory (LSTM) classification model has been taught to precisely forecast outcomes associated with diabetes. The section explores their details of the GLSTM explaining how GANs produce realistic artificial information and how predictions are made using the data set used by the LSTM classification. The authors go over the benefits of this hybrid strategy, which lessens the effects of data scarcity and makes better use of the scarce actual data available. The GLSTM model's evaluations of effectiveness and extensive experimental information are presented in this study. The authors illustrate the effectiveness and superiority of their suggested strategy in managing diabetic data prediction tasks by contrasting its predictions with those of other approaches that are already in use.

A thorough and authoritative analysis of the most recent developments and future prospects for research in the area of robotically supported surgical systems may be found in the work of Jaiswal and Gupta [32]. It begins by highlighting the value of robotically supported operation in contemporary healthcare and how it might potentially solve a number of issues that are often related to conventional surgical methods. There is a full discussion of the technical features of these operating systems, including their design, mechanisms of control, and connection with cutting-edge technology such as sophisticated imaging devices and AI. The writers thoroughly examine the most recent advancements in robotically assisted surgical systems and provide insight into their usefulness. Examples of these systems in action from a variety of medical professions are given, demonstrating how they improve surgical results, accuracy, and recuperation times. Additionally, the writers provide insightful information by pointing out areas that need more investigation and persistent obstacles, assisting both clinicians and scientists in making contributions to the development of automatically assisted surgery systems.

18.2.5 Virtual Assistants (VA) for Patient Care

VA with AI has become an important resource for patient care. These chatbots may respond to inquiries from patients, give advice on how to manage long-term illnesses, and deliver individualized health information. Virtual assistants provide easy access to medical information and assistance by integrating with telemedicine platforms, smartphone apps, and smart gadgets. Virtual assistants help to increase patient involvement, autonomy, and overall medical results by providing patients with self-care resources and constant surveillance. The research conducted by [33] utilizes a combination of both qualitative and quantitative information to thoroughly examine the views and choices of people with cancer about digital assistants. The authors examine the factors that are most important in determining whether patients would accept and communicate with these electronic companions along their medical journey.

The investigators include a variety of virtual assistant applications in connection with cancer treatment throughout the paper. They look at how these AI-powered technologies may help patients all through their medical care and recuperation by helping them manage symptoms, giving them important information, and providing them with psychological assistance. The results of the study's qualitative and quantitative components add to our knowledge of how patients see virtual assistants and their possible benefits in cancer care environments. The work of Bussel *et al.* [34] describes the development and functionality of MEDICAL CARE, powered by AI healthcare companion designed to enhance the treatment of patients and speed up procedures in medicine. The authors explain how MEDIC analyzes and processes enormous volumes of health information effectively by using AI and smart information intelligence approaches. The assessment sheds light on the features of the MEDIC AI Employee, such as its capacity to streamline healthcare procedures, make individualized medical suggestions, and enable remote patient monitoring. The authors illustrate the usefulness and efficiency of the MEDIC system across a range of healthcare contexts using instances and practical applications. The MEDIC AI Assistant uses cutting-edge technologies, including conventional models, neural networks, neural networks, and data statistical analysis, to provide healthcare workers with insightful information and assistance in making decisions. Both patient results and overall productivity in healthcare will increase as a result.

18.2.6 Biological Signals: Essential Diagnostics Data

Recent advances in AI in medical studies have led to great diagnostics and therapeutic possibilities in analyzing biosignals. ECGs, or electrocardiograms, have garnered a lot of attention due to their therapeutic utility in heart conditions [35]. Electroencephalograms (EEGs), used to gauge brain activity, additionally demonstrate potential in the detection and tracking of neurological conditions such as epilepsy and Alzheimer disease [36]. Developing biosignal techniques is becoming more popular in applications for healthcare as the area develops, offering fresh possibilities for early illness identification and individualized treatment plans [37].

When AI algorithms—such as ML and DL approaches—are integrated, they may assess and interpret complicated biosignals with more efficiency, providing important insights that may not be immediately apparent when using simpler methods. These advancements provide promising opportunities to use AI and biosignal processing to improve the lives of patients and healthcare operations. AI in the study of biosignals, which include physiological data such as ECGs brain scans and other relevant biometric information, has been thoroughly examined by Patil *et al.* [38]. They discuss how complex relationships, trends, and abnormalities in these biological signals that may be invisible to traditional research techniques may be found using AI-driven methodologies.

The study by Yoon *et al.* [39] provides a thorough analysis of the use of biosignals in medical devices and explores the prospects and problems related to the incorporation of AI in this domain. The importance of biosignals, which include various physiological data such as ECGs and EEGs and other pertinent biometric information, is extensively examined by the authors. AI-driven techniques are used to analyze and interpret these biosignals in order to get significant conclusions that would not be seen using more traditional techniques. This study explores the technical elements of AI algorithms used in biosignal processing, including ML and DL methods. Examples from everyday life are given to show how AI models may be successfully used to monitor the wellness of patients, identify and forecast medical disorders, and enhance managing diseases in real time. The authors provide instances from the actual world where AI has been successfully used to forecast and identify medical disorders, assess the course of diseases, and provide real-time patient health tracking.

18.3 NLP'S Part in Processing Massive Data for Healthcare Detection

NLP is an AI-driven innovation that greatly streamlines the procedure of improving medical evaluations. The volume of medical data that is produced on a daily basis highlights the significance of massive amounts of data in guaranteeing high-quality health information. The possibility for massive information integration in the medical field to foresee epidemics and find trends in patient information might revolutionize clinical decision-making. The examination of vast amounts of information, both structured and unstructured, such as online conversation flows, genetic information, digital health records, and imaging studies, provides investigators and medical personnel with priceless insights that can improve patient experiences and campaigns for public health.

Notably, by collecting relevant facts from unstructured therapeutic texts, such as clinical papers, papers, patient records, and updates from social networks, NLP shows great potential in assisting with medical diagnoses. These features show how NLP helps with healthcare diagnosis in the setting of handling enormous volumes of data. The critical role that AI plays in healthcare is seen in Figure 18.2.

18.3.1 Clinical Text Mining

In order to extract essential data about indicators, medical histories, test findings, and therapeutic plans, AI algorithms can analyze medical records

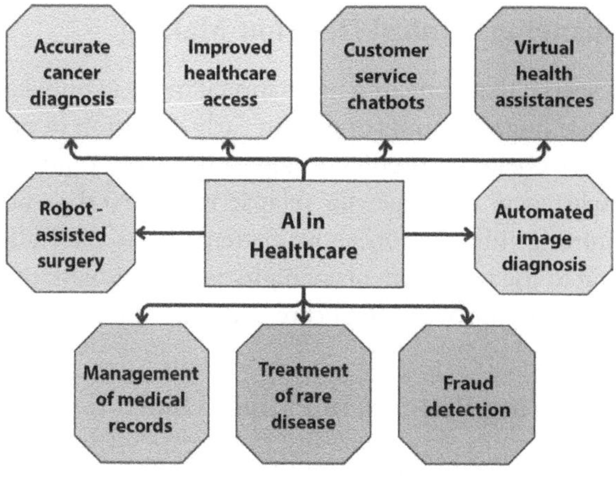

Figure 18.2 Contribution of AI in healthcare.

and EHRs. It facilitates clinical choice-making and allows for effective utilization of data.

18.3.2 Diagnosis Support

By analyzing indications while contrasting these to current expertise, NLP models may be trained on large volumes of medical information and literature to assist doctors in making a quick and precise diagnosis of a variety of medical illnesses.

18.3.3 Early Detection of Diseases

Large amounts of patient information may be screened using NLP approaches; it is used to identify patterns that might point to the beginning stages of particular illnesses and enable prompt therapies.

18.3.4 Medical Image Reporting

By automatically obtaining data from healthcare pictures, NLP may provide imaging reports that are more organized and uniform for physicians.

18.3.5 Patient Risk Stratification

According to their medical history, way of life, and other variables, individuals who are considered high-risk may be identified with the use of NLP, facilitating focused treatments and preventive actions.

18.3.6 Enhancing Clinical Decision-Making

A scholarly research that appeared in a national medical publication demonstrated the use of huge amounts of data in early detection of patients at risk. The investigators created a prediction algorithm that could precisely identify patients who were at danger for relapse within 30 days after discharge through examining information about patients from the EHR. By aggressively attending to the requirements of high-risk individuals, medical professionals were able to improve patient care and lower the rate of readmission.

18.3.7 Identifying Patterns in Patient Data

Utilizing the analysis of big data, trends in patient information have been found that may expedite the diagnosis of illnesses. One research, which was published in *Nature Medicine* in 2016, showed how algorithms with ML could analyze the medical records and find minute patterns in the physiological information of clients. These patterns might be used to forecast the development of illnesses such as sepsis, which may manifest hours before indications do. Timely action made possible by early discovery may have saved lives and enhanced patient results.

18.3.8 Predicting Disease Outbreaks

Throughout the West African Ebola epidemic, big data proved to be useful in forecasting epidemics of diseases. Researchers tracked the disease's growth and projected effects on multiple locations using current information from many sources, such as social media diets, cellphone information, and satellite imaging. Public health authorities were able to manage the epidemic by using the data to better allocate funds and put preventive efforts in place. All things considered, these researches demonstrate the enormous potential that exists for using big data for medical purposes to improve medical decision-making, discover trends in patient information, and forecast illness outbreaks. Healthcare professionals and healthcare authorities may make better choices, offer enhanced care to patients, and address problems with public health more effectively by using the strength of analytics on big data.

18.4 Applications for AI in Several Surgical Fields

The data that AI uses to power itself are its greatest asset. Despite an abundance of health data, its integration into clinical practice is impeded in part by its high dimensionality and complexity, which call for advanced solutions to yield beneficial effects. "Multimodal AI" refers to the integration of different data sources to create AI models that incorporate data from all modalities. It is expected that this will open the door to a personalized medical period that will undoubtedly have a significant impact on surgical practice. Figure 18.3 shows the anticipated uses of AI in surgery. We examine how AI is being used in many industries, using the US FDA (Food and Drug Administration) as examples. AI/ML software is licensed for use as medical devices by regulations, along with important trials and cutting-edge studies. We conducted an investigation that utilized our institutional expertise to find pertinent studies in the literature. Our group's earlier systematic evaluations focused on the use of AI in a variety of surgical specialties.

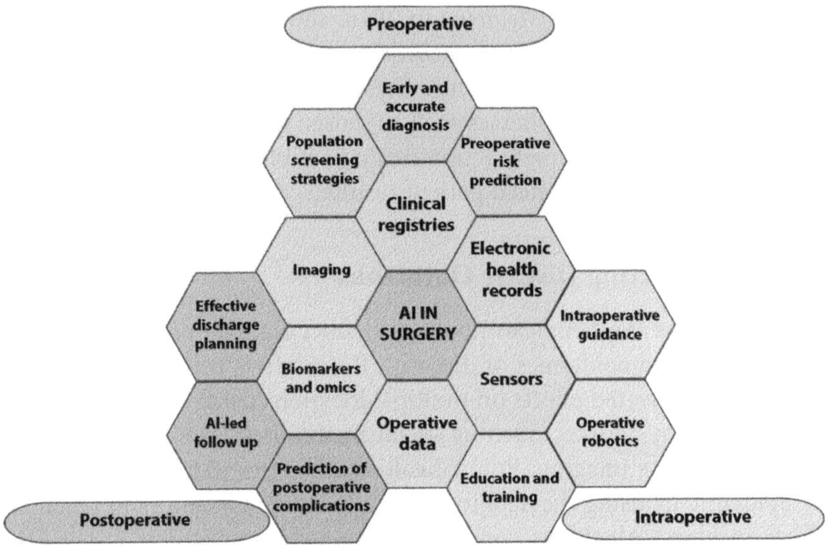

Figure 18.3 Diagram illustrating the information sources and uses of AI in operation. Preoperative, perioperative, and postoperatively phases are separated for usage.

18.4.1 Screening the Population

AI technology has the ability to significantly change population-wide screening practices. Several nationwide screening initiatives have shown benefits in terms of early diagnosis and death for a variety of conditions, including colorectal cancer [40], abdominal aortic aneurysms [41], and breast cancer [42]. On the other hand, there have long been discussions about the best screening methods and the necessity of "personalized screening," which in the end depends on factors unique to each patient as well as the choice of screening instruments, frequency and execution, and risk assessment [43, 44].

Because of the remarkable capacity of artificially intelligent machines to analyze medical images, cancer prevention screening has attracted the greatest attention in the field of AI thus far. The accuracy of specialists interpreting imaging using the conventional method, however, varies significantly, with notable rates of incorrect readings and incorrect results [45]. Although the recall rate and effort strain rise, the cancer detection rate is increased when two independent readers are used [46]. The INSIGHT MMG, Transpara, and Significant AI software (iCAD, USA) are among the lesion detection devices that have been certified for use in screening mammography using different AI technologies [47]. When compared to double reading by two radiologists, the INSIGHT MMG and Transpara appear to be noninferior as a second reader, according to encouraging preliminary results from two sizable prospective trials [48, 49]. Thus, it is not impossible to imagine a time soon when DL algorithms would be used directly as an additional or second readers in the breast cancer screening, to reduce radiologists' workloads and increase the rate of cancer detection. Similar to this, AI may be used in any imaging-based screening platform, and efforts are being made to apply it to lung and colorectal cancer screening [50].

Workflow triage applications have also drawn interest. Sorting medical information into a "high-risk" workflow rather than a "low-risk" one can expedite the processing of vast volumes of data produced by screening and send higher-risk patients to physicians sooner. The INSIGHT MMG algorithm effectively classified mammograms into two groups: those requiring no radiology assessment and those requiring an enhanced review from radiologists. This led to significant advantages such as decreased workload and increased early detection rates. Like AI technology, molecular biology has seen a significant paradigm shift in recent years. The term "multiomics" describes the study of enormous databases of tiny molecules that affect biological processes, such as the microbiome, proteome, metabolome, genome, and epigenome. Although AI is still in its infancy in this field, analysis of genomic data has been reported as a means of early cancer detection. AI and "multiomics" are ideally suited for each other. Large-scale small-molecule datasets, clinical information, and imaging are combined with AI techniques to detect populations at risk and to display, determine, and predict disease with ever-increasing precision.

18.4.2 Identification of Symptomatic Individuals

Similar image data evaluation by AI technology has the potential to revolutionize early and more precise patient diagnosis. Numerous DL algorithms, for instance, have been documented in the field of ophthalmology for the diagnosis of retinal illness based on retinal fundus pictures or optical coherence tomography. Regulatory-approved tools such as IDx-DR and EyeArt have demonstrated good levels of accuracy in the diagnosis of diabetic retinopathy. The authorized GI Genius technology (Medtronic, USA) has shown enhanced adenoma identification rates, demonstrating the potential of DL for real-time computer-aided colorectal polyp detection. Based on the Markov model microsimulations, an analysis of the affordability of AI-assisted colonoscopy reveals that AI integration can further lower the relative decrease of colorectal cancer mortality and result in an overall annual savings of $290 million in the United States. Aortic dissection, intracranial hemorrhage, aneurysms, thyroid cancer, small-bowel obstruction, pancreatic disease, fractures on plain radiographs, prostate cancer on MRI, and biopsy findings are among the surgical conditions for which deep learning has been used in diagnosis. Some other surgical conditions for which DL is used to diagnose include these.

Although by no means comprehensive, this list demonstrates the remarkable capacity of AI to diagnose image sequences by utilizing DL's special capacity to recognize and understand intricate patterns. Therefore, prompt and accurate patient diagnosis improves surgical decision-making and saves time and money for patients. AI algorithms may eventually be able to assist with complicated surgical diagnosis by combining the outcomes of investigations and clinical assessment data. For instance, utilizing a supervised ML algorithm demonstrated potential in detecting acute abdominal pain and identifying complex inflammation according to biochemical indicators and ultrasound findings in a retrospective examination of a cohort of pediatric patients who presented to the hospital.

Information from doctor–patient consultations can be automatically recorded, extracted, and summarized using automated voice recognition and NLP. Potential advantages include letting physicians spending longer with patients while attending to the growing outpatient demands, as well as lessening their administrative workload, which is a major contributor to burnout. An ML system that was trained to automatically record symptoms that were addressed during an encounter between a patient and a doctor performed well when the symptoms were explicitly acknowledged. To enhance performance on ambiguous symptoms and to support diagnostic decision-making with data analysis, more effort is required. Nevertheless, using the information that has been retrieved to assist surgery diagnostics workflows from clinical encounters is another anticipated benefit.

18.4.3 Preoperative Risk Prediction

The preoperative risks tools have become essential tools to help patients and doctors anticipate the risks associated with surgery based on a variety of operation and patient-specific factors. However, established calculators frequently rely on subjective inputs or make mathematical model assumptions about linear correlations between variables, which are not true in clinical settings. Recent developments can increase the prediction power of risk instruments by utilizing ML's abilities to analyze big, varied datasets and simulate nonlinear relationships. Using an ideal classification tree method derived from ML, the Predictive OpTimal Trees in Emergency Surgery Risk (POTTER) calculator for patients undergoing laparotomies surpassed the American College of Surgeons National Surgical Quality

Improvement Program in terms of accuracy in predicting the preoperative risk for its patient cohort. MyRiskSurgery is an ML postoperative risk strategy that was developed and proven in a separate investigation. Through the analysis of patient EHRs, it was possible to anticipate severe complications after surgery and death, allowing for dynamic assessment of risk variables in real time and continuous improvement based on input from clinicians. Future forecasting algorithms should be able to combine a variety of patient, the doctor, and operation-specific characteristics to provide an accurate, user-friendly, and tailored risk evaluation rating that can improve preparation before surgery.

18.4.4 Intraoperative Guidance

The literature has extensively addressed the use using computer vision in surgical video analysis. The widespread use of video-based minimally invasive surgical techniques, including laparoscopic, robotic, endoscopic, and endovascular operations, has made this possible in part. Because surgical recordings feature a variety of concealed surgical planes and are inherently more dynamic due to items in constant motion, application in this sector has not yet proven as successful as in imaging or pathology. Moreover, specialists find it time-consuming to annotate training sets, and there is not always a clear consensus on the precise actions to take throughout an operation. Thus far, research has focused on trying to distinguish anatomy in routine operations. Not surprisingly, given the significance for the anatomic identification of essential structures, laparoscopic cholecystectomy has drawn a lot of attention thus far as an index general surgery technique with a recognized "critical view of safety." Analogous research has been conducted on various other treatments, such as endovascular aneurysm repair, cataract surgery, and laparoscopic sleeve gastrectomy. Real-time intraoperative guidance has the ability to give surgeons precise visual help in difficult surgeries, even though this field is still in its infancy. This has been demonstrated by the experience of professionals worldwide.

AI-powered three-dimensional anatomical reconstruction aids difficult surgery planning and navigation. It has been shown that the FDA-approved, cloud-based Cydar EV Maps tool (Cydar Medical, UK) enhances the safety of complex endovascular aortic aneurysm repair by reducing radiation exposure and generating a personalized 3D anatomical map that aligns preoperative imaging with real-time fluoroscopy during surgery. Furthermore, a developing interest in blended reality technology—a combination of virtual reality (VR) and augmented reality (AR)—has spurred the development of head-mounted monitors that provide postoperative assistance. Reality (VR) projects hologram visual images into the operator's field of vision in real life, whereas AR immerses the user in a virtual environment. By enhancing the surgeon's visual–motor axis and allowing accurate tissue segmentation *via* VR overlays, headset-mounted displays have shown potential in improving the outcomes of surgeries. One such device is the readily accessible HoloLens (Microsoft Corporation, Redmond, WA, USA). AI for anatomy identification and three-dimensional surgical reconstruction AR holographic technology has the potential to incorporate fields, giving surgeons access to a dynamic and immersive intraoperative environment.

18.4.5 Operative Robotics

Several intraoperative advantages come from the use of robots in surgery, such as enhanced dexterity, ergonomics, and a realistically magnified three-dimensional perspective. Reductions in the loss of blood and transfusion rates, shorter lengths of stay in the hospital, and a decline in complication rates are examples of established perioperative outcome.

As a result, robotic surgery is becoming more and more popular as the minimally invasive alternative to traditional laparoscopic surgery for routine surgeries. Sixty thousand surgeons worldwide have completed more than 12 million procedures with the da Vinci system alone. AI has the potential to significantly enhance, if not entirely revolutionize, intraoperative procedure *via* the use of robotics, a crucial electronic surgical approach. Motion evaluation, gadget acknowledgment, improved tactile, and tissue detecting during surgery visualization, finishing tasks, and more through this program can be incorporated with the methods discussed in the Intraoperative Guidance section are the functions most suitable for robotics. Several studies have automated the goal of skill assessment of basic technical surgery tasks such as stitching and knotting using convolution artificial neural networks and raw kinematics or video information. This might standardize the assessment of surgical operations in the first stages of instruction and remove the laborious aspect of an individual expert review. Additionally, it could reduce subjective biases while giving feedback. Motion estimation has specific uses such as monitoring and identifying instruments, dividing operations and recognition of gestures into clinically important phases, and temporally segmenting surgical procedures into steps. This requires dividing the start and finish periods of each motion path change. Previous work on ML concepts has also been utilized in perform robotic procedures, showing how footage may be combined with other data to improve efficiency. Robot system information such as kinematics, perioperative events, and camera footage, together with postpartum results, may be utilized to train computers that will offer automated gauges of performance and projected intraoperative efficiency, in addition to evaluating fundamental surgical abilities. This was created to execute an aggressive prostatectomy with the aid of a robot, and it will most likely be investigated and validated for more applications as well. Is it possible to create and use fully autonomous operative robots as engineers, scientists, and medics to work together to create ever more complex AI solutions? The da Vinci system and other well-known robotic platforms operate under the master–slave model, with the surgeon having complete control over the robot and it mimicking its moves. Robotics autonomy has been conceptualized as a hierarchy that climbs from level 0 to level 5, with the concept of autonomy in driving frequently being paralleled. Six levels of autonomy have been proposed and applied to the field of medical robotics; higher levels of autonomy are likely to need more integration of AI technology (Table 18.1). Levels 2 (task-related independence) and 3 (conditioned autonomy) are reached by currently developed systems; applications include bone drilling, suturing, and trajectory planning. Although they are still primarily conceptual, fully autonomous robots that can conduct skin-to-skin operations could have the following advantages: standardizing surgical techniques; gathering more sensory data for carrying out surgery with greater stability, accuracy, and precision; and removing

Table 18.1 There are six robotic healthcare autonomy stages, which include total autonomy to none at all, which are derived from the vehicle autonomous categorization.

Autonomy level	Particulars
0	**No autonomy**: Human operator performs all functions.
1	**Robot assistance**: Human retains continuous control.
2	**Task autonomy**: Human has discrete control, with specific tasks assigned to robot.
3	**Conditional autonomy**: Human selects the autonomous strategy performed by robot.
4	**High autonomy**: Robot makes decisions but is supervised by human.
5	**Full autonomy**: Procedure is fully performed by robot with no human supervision required.

the possibility of human fatigue, stress, or bias, such as inaccessible regions or combat areas. We will talk about the possible implications and issues with autonomous robots later.

18.5 Results with Meta-Analysis

18.5.1 Recruitment of Studies

A total of 852 items were produced by the main search, seen in the diagram in Figure 18.4. Scientists examined the complete texts and summaries for these references. A number of factors, including overlapping and

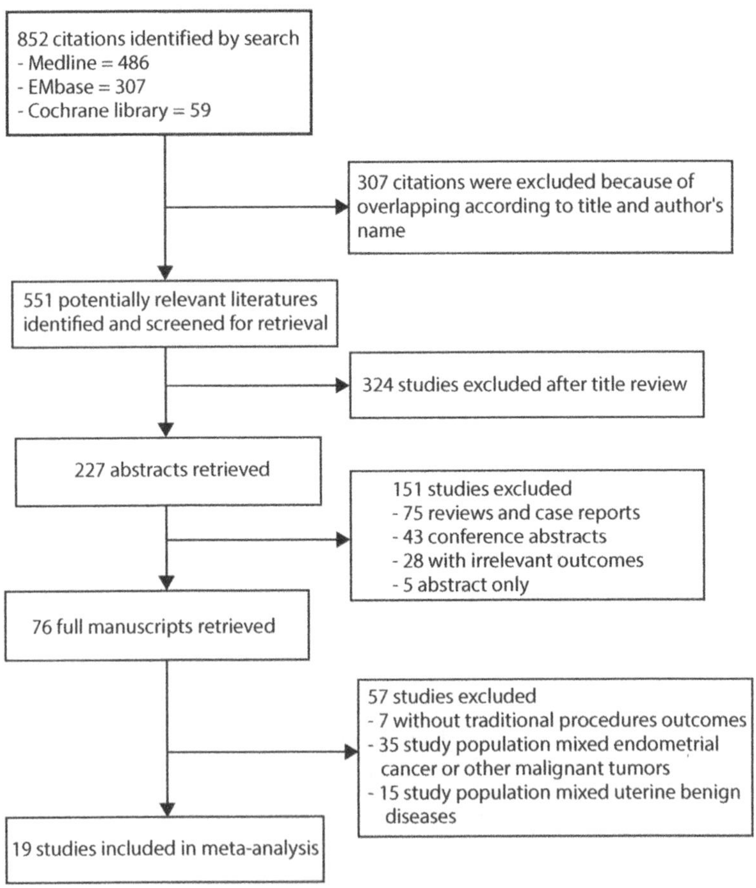

Figure 18.4 The number of investigations found and the approach to searching used to find them for this a meta-analysis.

inappropriate research designs, led to the exclusion of some publications. A total of 776 hits were eliminated based on each abstract's title and contents. A total of 76 potentially pertinent investigations were identified *via* this research; however, 57 of these were disqualified as they were used outside of standard operating procedures or had study groups that included patients with different illnesses. Lastly, the current meta-analysis encompassed a total of 19 researches [13–31].

18.5.2 Study Characteristics and Validity Assessment

Every one of the 19 papers that were found was an observational study that was released between 2007 and 2015 (Table 18.2). Eight investigations were retrospectively, whereas the remaining 11 were planned qualitative research [13–15, 17–21, 23, 28, 31, 16, 22, 24–27, 29, 30]. The patients' ages were between 17 and 78 years, and the total number of cases included varied from 14 to 127. There were nine investigations that examined automated surgery to open operation [14, 16, 18, 24], eight research that evaluated robotic operation to laparoscopy [13, 15, 26, 31], and a single study that evaluated robots operation to both open and laparoscopy operation [17, 25]. The vast majority of the research investigations [14–18, 20, 24, 26] (8/19, 42%) were conducted in the United States. Three research investigations came from Italy [19, 30, 31], two from the Korean Peninsula [28, 29], two from Turkey [21, 27], two from the Nordic nation [13, 25], and one each from the Netherlands [22] and Canada [23].

The criteria of the medical study evaluation form were followed in the analysis of the efficacy of the included studies. When all of the confounding factors were taken into account, there was nothing distinct seen in the medical staging of the studies analyzed [13–31]. Seven publications in all documented the precise follow-up period, adding credibility to the findings [13, 15, 17, 22, 25, 26, 29]. The B level was reached by 16 investigations [13–17, 19, 20, 22, 24, 31], whereas the C level was reached by the remaining three studies [18, 21, 23]. All of these researches' quality levels satisfied the broad standards of the meta-analysis.

18.5.3 Data Analyses and Synthesis

18.5.3.1 Robotic Surgery Compared with Open Procedure

Table 18.3 included the amount of data available for every medical outcome, the combined findings from all meta-analyses, and the associated discrepancy indexes. Figure 18.5A–F display an overview of systematic

Table 18.2 Qualities of research that qualify.

Resource	Design	Robotics	Traditional		Outcome							Follow-up
			Laparoscopy	Open	NoN	BT	EBL	LOS	OT	Com		
[13]		Yes	Yes				Yes	Yes	Yes	Yes		Yes
[14]		Yes		Yes		Yes	Yes	Yes	Yes	Yes		
[15]		Yes	Yes				Yes	Yes	Yes	Yes		Yes
[16]		Yes		Yes		Yes	Yes	Yes	Yes	Yes		
[17]		Yes	Yes	Yes			Yes	Yes	Yes	Yes		Yes
[18]		Yes		Yes			Yes	Yes	Yes	Yes		
[19]		Yes		Yes	Yes		Yes	Yes	Yes	Yes		
[20]		Yes		Yes			Yes	Yes	Yes	Yes		
[21]		Yes		Yes	Yes		Yes	Yes	Yes	Yes		
[22]	Re prospective	Yes		Yes		Yes		Yes	Yes	Yes		Yes
[23]	Prospective	Yes		Yes	Yes	Yes	Yes	Yes	Yes			

(Continued)

Table 18.2 Qualities of research that qualify. (*Continued*)

Resource	Design	Robotics	Traditional		Outcome						Follow-up
			Laparoscopy	Open	NoN	BT	EBL	LOS	OT	Com	
[24]	Re prospective	Yes		Yes			Yes	Yes	Yes	Yes	
[25]		Yes	Yes	Yes	Yes		Yes	Yes	Yes	Yes	Yes
[26]		Yes	Yes				Yes	Yes	Yes	Yes	Yes
[27]		Yes	Yes			Yes	Yes	Yes	Yes	Yes	
[28]	Prospective	Yes	Yes			Yes	Yes	Yes	Yes	Yes	
[29]	Re prospective	Yes	Yes			Yes	Yes	Yes	Yes	Yes	
[30]		Yes	Yes			Yes	Yes	Yes	Yes	Yes	Yes
[31]	Prospective	Yes	Yes			Yes	Yes	Yes	Yes	Yes	

Legend: NoN, Number of Nodes; BT, Blood Transfusion; EBL, Estimated Blood Loss; LOS, Length of Stay; OT, Operation Time; Com, Complications.

Table 18.3 Principal results of meta-analyses: robotic versus traditional surgery for cervical disease.

Result measurement	No. of research	Size of sample	I^2, *P* value (%)	MD
Operation time	12	604	99.0 < 0.01	40.72
Admit in hospital	10	545	95.0 < 0.01	−3.46
Loss of blood	7	430	84.0 < 0.01	−1.51
Complication	11	566	0.61	0.36
Transfusion	4	195	0,0.86	0.10
Nodes	5	197	89.8 < 0.01	−6.67

Legend: MD, Mean Difference.

review plots related to these results, enabling the examination of between-study inconsistency. The early results were presented, and then sensitivity assessments were explored.

The assessment of OT among surgical robotics and open operation was equivocal (MD 39.71, 95% confidence interval [CI] 6.69–86.11), according to a study of meta-analysis data (Figure 18.5A). Of the 11 studies that were incorporated in the analysis [14, 16–25], six were linked to significant impacts that backed open surgical procedures [16, 19, 21, 23–25], two supported the use of robots [14, 24], and three were equivocal [17, 18, 20, 21].

When comparing automated surgery and opening an operation, the former was linked to a noticeably lower length of stay (LOS) than when using surgery alone to treat cervical cancer (MD = 3.36, 95% CI 3.99–2.73) (Figure 18.5B). Nine studies out of the total that had been incorporated supported surgical robots and showed economically major distinctions [14, 16, 17, 19, 21, 25]. Furthermore, when comparing surgical robotics to open surgery, there was a decrease in significance in the degree of BL (MD −3.36, 95% CI −3.99 to 2.73; Figure 18.5C). Seven of the examined trials produced outcomes that were statistically substantial in favor of robotic surgery [16, 17, 19, 22–25].

Additionally, automated surgery was linked to a decreased incidence of BT (OR = 0.10, 95% CI 0.02–0.41) (Figure 18.5D). All three investigations supported robotic surgery. Compared to opening an operation, surgical robotics resulted in fewer instances of cerebral palsy (OR = 0.34, 95% CI 0.21–0.56) (Figure 18.5E). Point estimations from 11 researches strongly

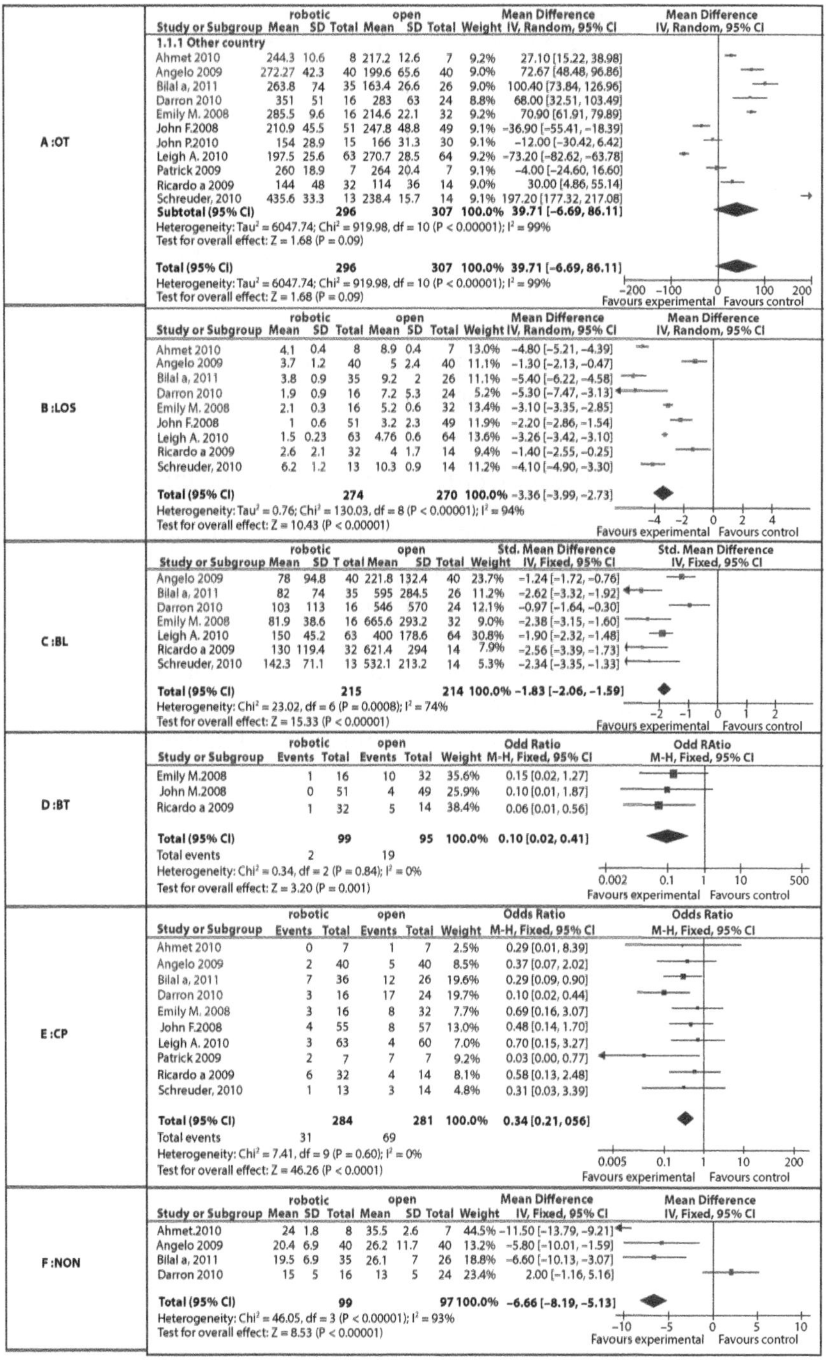

Figure 18.5 The use of robots forest layout contrasted with traditional open surgeries.

support surgical robotics [14, 16, 19, 21, 25], with two studies showing significant variance [18, 23]. Ileus, lymphoma, infections of wounds, vaginal cuff hernia, ports site, a ruptured disc reconstruction for bleeding, throbbing of deep veins, delayed voiding, and vaginal cuff breakdown were among the more frequently reported problems.

Compared to open the operation, automated surgery was linked to fewer nodes (NoN) (MD −6.66, 95% CI −8.19~-5.13) (Figure 18.5F). Four publications [19, 21, 23, 25, 33] discussed the removal of the pelvic lymph nodes in the network; three of these pieces recommended open operation because it would lead to a greater plenty of pelvic lymph points [19, 21, 25, 33]. One research, however, claimed there was no variance in the amount of pelvic lymph centers among open operation and robotic operation [23].

18.5.3.2 Robotic Surgery Compared with Laparoscopic Procedure

Ten research totaling 679 samples contrasted laparoscopy and robotic procedures [13, 15, 17, 25, 31]. Table 18.4 summarizes clinical outcome information as well as collective meta-analysis outcomes. Figure 18.6A–F displayed a list of meta-analysis plots matching these results, allowing the between-study variability to be examined. An overview of early results was followed by a discussion of sensitivity evaluation.

Table 18.4 shows drawing on an examination of findings derived from meta-analyses: longer OT (MD = 12.78 65% CI 8.08,18.49) was linked to the contrast of robot and a laparoscopic operation (Figure 18.6A). Of the 10 researches [13, 15, 17, 25, 31] that were considered, two supported surgical robotics [13, 25], two showed that laparoscopic surgical procedures

Table 18.4 Principal results of meta-analyses: robotic versus laparoscopy surgery for cervical cancer.

Result measurement	No. of research	Size of sample	I^2, *P* value (%)	MD
Operation time	11	680	93 < 0.01	12.79
Admit in hospital	11	680	96 < 0.01	−0.38
Loss of blood	11	680	88, 0.01	−0.66
Complication	11	680	99 < 0.01	52.98
Transfusion	7	482	0 < 0.85	0.40
Nodes	5	354	89.8 < 0.01	0.75

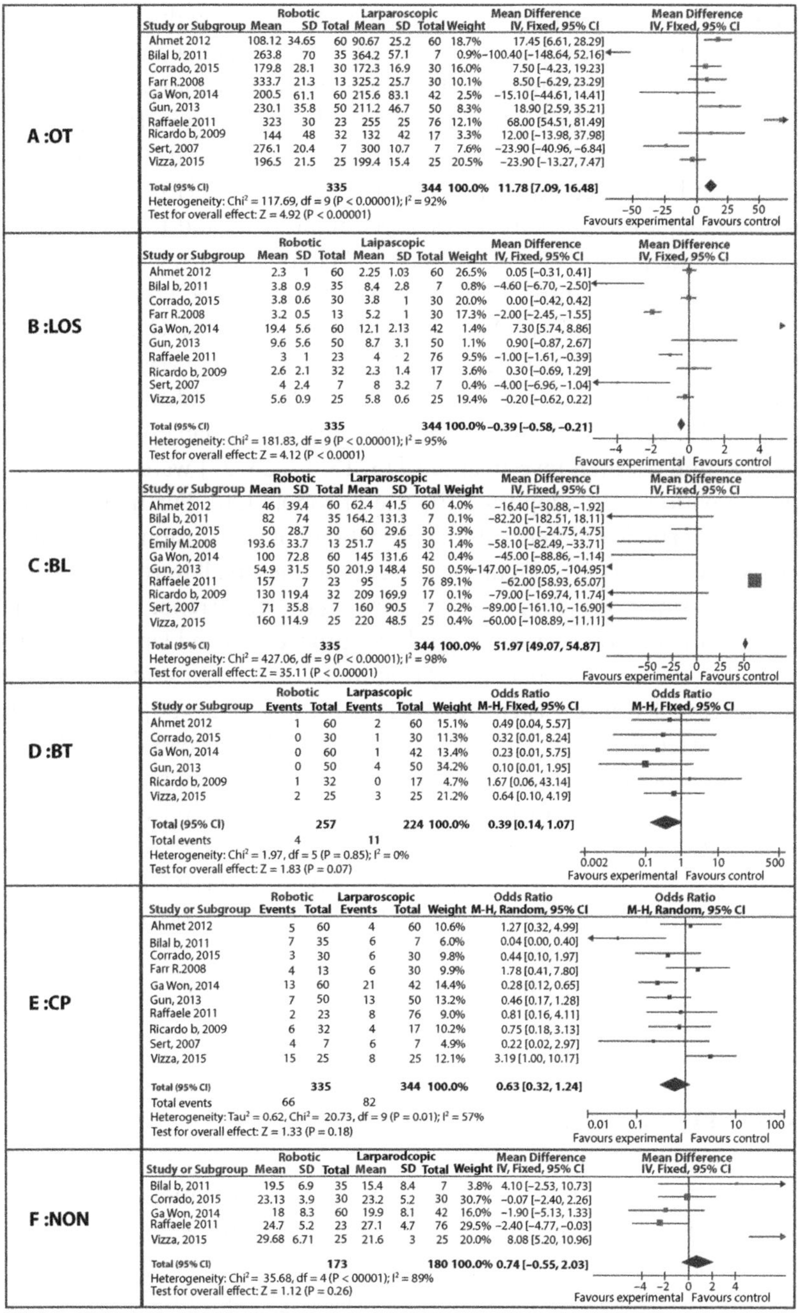

Figure 18.6 A forest plot comparing traditional laparoscopic procedures versus surgical robotics.

took less time to do [26, 28], and six stated there was no distinction among robotics and laparoscopy operation [15, 17, 27, 29–31]. A shorter length of time on life (LOS) was linked to the robotic operation compared to the laparoscopic approach (MD = 0.40 96% CI 0.59–0.22) (Figure 18.6B). Among the 10 studies [13, 15, 17, 25, 31] that were considered, four supported robotics and indicated numerically significant variance [13, 15, 25, 26], one supported laparoscopic surgery as a technique [29], and five had findings that were ambiguous [17, 27, 28, 30, 31]. When comparing surgical robots to laparoscopic procedure, the forest graph (Figure 18.6C) revealed that the former had a greater BL (MD 52.98, 96% CI 50.08–57.89). Owing to the low caliber of the research included [13, 15, 17, 25–31], there was a high danger of bias for these conclusions (Figure 18.6C). Only one of the 10 examined research [13, 15, 17, 25, 31] recommended performing laparoscopic surgery, whereas nine research investigations [13, 15, 17, 25, 27] were linked to specific estimations that supported the use of robots [26]. Furthermore, there was no discernible difference in the probability of transfusion exposure (OR 0.40, 96% CI 0.17–1.08) (Figure 18.6D). Six studies in all were used to derive the point estimations [17, 27–31]. Regarding the occurrence of issues, there was not a distinction seen among robotic procedures and laparoscopic surgery (OR = 0.64, 96% CI 0.33–1.25) (Figure 18.6E). Seven studies' point estimations revealed inconsistent results [13, 15, 17, 26–28, 30]. One research [31] supported the use of laparoscopic surgery, whereas two studies [25, 29] supported robotic surgeries. Surgical infection, ileus, lymphoma, pelvic cuff hemorrhage, delayed urination, deep vein thrombosis, and vena cava damage were the most frequently reported problems. The NoN (MD = 0.74, 95% CI −0.55 to 2.03) did not change among robotic surgery and laparoscopic operation (Figure 18.6F). Five pieces [25, 26, 29–31] reported pelvic lymph system removal. Two advocated robotic intervention, resulting in larger lymph nodes [25, 31], whereas three studies found little variation among artificial and laparoscopic methods in a number of nodes [26, 29, 30].

18.6 Discussion

A recent agreement declaration from the International Society of Gynecological Oncology in 2012 [32] attested to the expanding clinical effect of surgical robots on the gynecological sector. In many gynecological operations, tolerance for patients has increased, thanks to standard laparoscopic techniques. The scientific results of open procedures, laparoscopic operations, and robotic procedures for cervical carcinoma were systematically evaluated in the current research. The surgical robots were shown to have greater advantages in terms of lower LOS, CP, BL, and BT. These findings were very susceptible to considerable bias since the 11 the studies included were of very low quality [14, 16–25] (Figure 18.7). In particular, compared to traditional laparoscopic surgeries, automated surgery might have merits in terms of an LOS; nevertheless, there was no discernible difference in regard to CP or BT.

Surgery robotic was linked to more BL than laparoscope surgery. Of the 10 investigations that were considered, 9 of them were linked to point estimates, suggesting that surgical robotics had lower blood loss [13, 15, 17, 25, 27, 31].

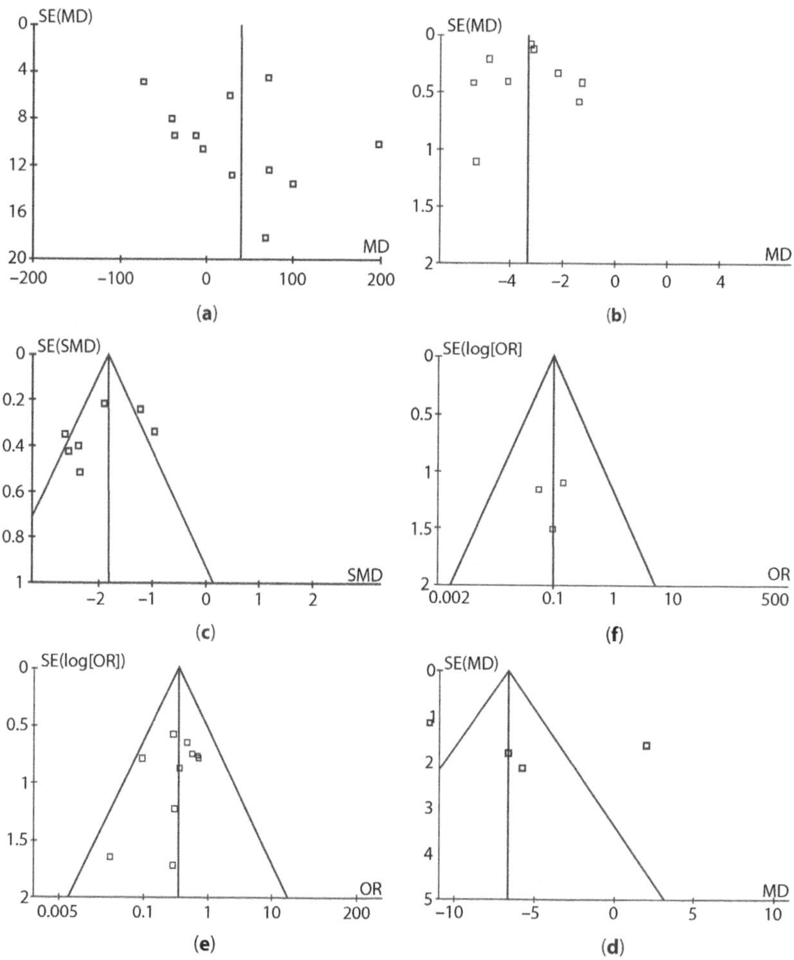

Figure 18.7 Comparative funnel plot: open versus robot. (a) Operative period (min); (b) hospital admission duration (day); (c) loss of blood (mL); (d) transfusions frequency; (e) risks; (f) node count (n).

Only one research, however, showed that a laparoscopic procedure had lower blood loss [26]. These findings were susceptible to severe bias because of the low caliber overall of the included researches (Figure 18.7c).

Nineteen relevant papers were identified in this comprehensive analysis, providing a substantial body of data for treatment for cervical cancer. Every study used a potential or retroactive observation methodology and relied on the understanding for the main estimates of the meta-analysis. The LOS, BL, OT, CP, NoN, and BT were the six clinical signs that were found to be present. The most significant clinical indicators of the postoperative results, OT, LOS, and BL, were the final results that were most often recorded. Despite the absence of relevant research comparing prediction, there was no evidence of the influence of CP on long-term results. These investigations were enough to assess the therapeutic benefits of robotic, laparoscopy, and open surgeries for cervical carcinoma [14, 16–25]. It was shown that the surgical robotics was linked to shorter LOS, longer OT, and decreased BL, CP, and BL. It has been shown that both patients and surgeons profit from surgical robotics. However, no information about functional results of the surgical robots, such as urinary or genital health, was reported [33]. This is a lost chance to find potential advantages that may be linked to the relatively minimally invasive surgical techniques. When adopting the robotic surgical program, it is essential to consider the economic cost as a significant aspect. Due to the substantial expense of maintenance and other variables, multiple research investigations have demonstrated that surgical robotics become more costly than standard laparoscopic techniques [34].

The absence of prospective randomized controlled trial (RCT) data for the contrast among robotic surgery and the other two surgical techniques is, truthfully, the study's drawback. The single-institution study design served as the foundation for this meta-analysis. The results of the highest-quality RCTs are not the source of any of the proofs. Rather than being derived from a set of prospective and retrospective observational research, it suggests that the level of proof is not as strong as that of RCT information. Regarding the functional results, such as bladder or sexual activity, there is no information. Thus, more comparative research evaluating the therapeutic results after surgery is required. First off, a lot of trial results exhibit variation, but no obvious possible causes—such as trial quality, trial design, size of sample, or outcome definition—have been found. Secondarily, the prior surgeries of the surgeon remain intimately linked to the unfavorable results. A large number of the papers in our cohort show the training curve for novice surgeons. It is often believed that as surgeon experience increases, results become better. Consequently, it needs to be encompassed into the meta-analysis' total estimate of treatment impact.

Poorer results in difficult situations may not be evenly distributed between surgical methods, leading to bias.

Patients may not be typical of patients encountered in practice, even if they were deemed equivalent across research arms in regard to age and body mass index. As a result, the reported benefits may not materialize in real clinical settings. These qualitative studies are regarded as inadequate proof according to the clinical research evaluation form, and there was a considerable possibility of bias in the findings (Figures 18.7 and 18.8).

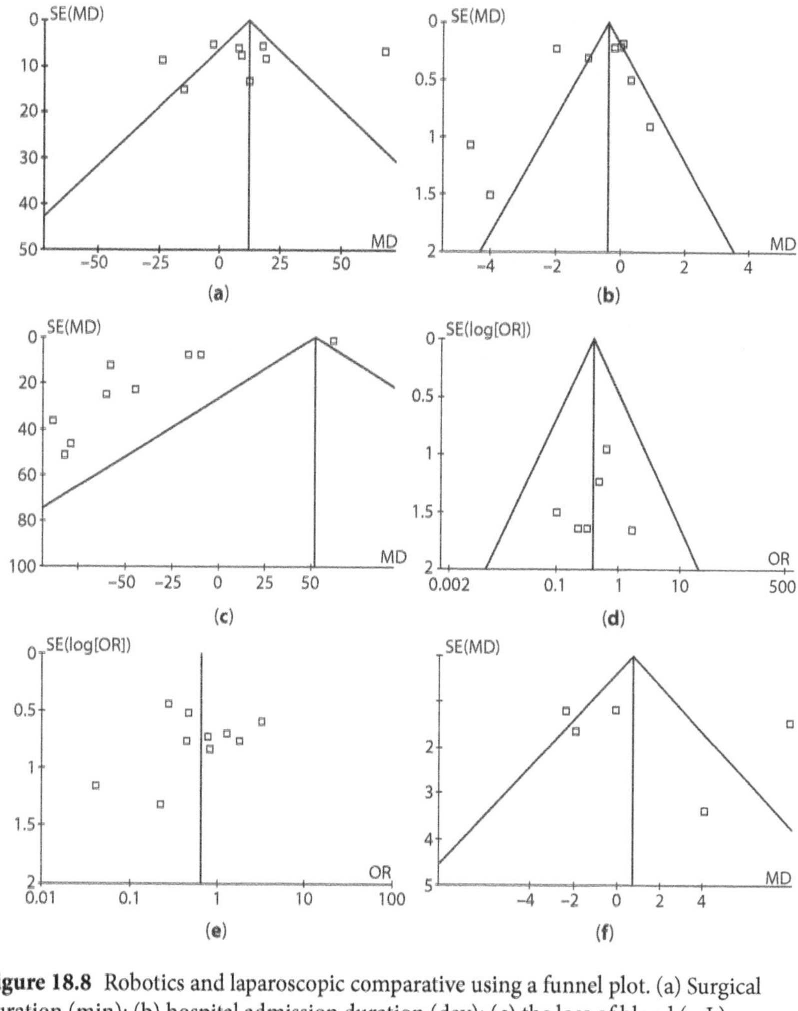

Figure 18.8 Robotics and laparoscopic comparative using a funnel plot. (a) Surgical duration (min); (b) hospital admission duration (day); (c) the loss of blood (mL); (d) transfusion frequency; (e) problems; (f) node count (n).

18.7 Ethical Challenges

The use of AI to medical diagnostics is fraught with ethical issues. When it pertains to handling delicate medical information in the setting of NLP and massive data management, privacy and data security pose some of the biggest issues. Although using such devices to diagnose patients might have a positive impact on the healthcare diagnostic system, there are issues about client anonymity and information confidentiality. The following explains why data security and privacy are crucial in this field [51]:

18.7.1 Patient Confidentiality

Healthcare data might include confidential information such as medical records, diagnosis, and genetic information, along with personally identifiable data. Upholding privacy rights for patients is essential to establishing and maintaining patient–provider confidence.

18.7.2 Compliance with Regulations

Healthcare providers need to make certain they adhere with the rules in order to safeguard the confidentiality of patients. The collection, storage, and use of healthcare data are subject to stringent regulations in a number of countries. Examples of these laws are the General Data Protection Regulation in the European Union and the Health Insurance Portability and Accountability Act in the United States.

18.7.3 Data Breach Prevention

Synthesis and storing enormous volumes of medical information are aspects of massive data organization and language processing. Effective safety precautions must be put in place to thwart hackers and illegal access with medical records.

18.7.4 Anonymization and Deidentification

When feasible, information should be anonymous or anonymized to preserve patient confidentiality by making it impossible to identify particular individuals from the information. This helps in striking a compromise between protecting the safety of patients while utilizing important data for research.

18.7.5 Access Control and Encryption

Encrypted mechanisms and accessibility restrictions guarantee that critical health information can only be obtained by approved individuals. Information is kept secure both in transmission and at resting with the use of encryption.

18.7.6 Secure Data Sharing and Collaboration

Secured information methods must be developed in the framework of multi-institutional studies and partnerships to safeguard patient confidentiality while exchanging data across various healthcare institutions.

18.7.7 User Training

To ensure that AI is able to be fully used, a great deal of user instruction is needed before AI can be integrated with medicine.

18.7.8 Financial Barriers

As is well known, integrating AI capabilities with medical systems and applying it to information related to medicine are quite expensive.

Medical businesses and providers may use the advantages of NLP and large-scale information administration while upholding respect for patients and compliance with laws by emphasizing security and privacy of information. Patient information safety is a continuous process that calls for a proactive and watchful attitude in the face of changing security risks.

18.8 Conclusion

The results from this study have discussed the transformation that has been imposed by AI on diagnosis, treatment planning, and robotic-assisted surgery in modern healthcare. With the application of innovative ML algorithms and other techniques of AI, proper diagnosis and medical treatment planning have been accurately accomplished in the shortest possible time. AI applications such as NLP and image recognition have enhanced the care given to patients and have improved their medical outcomes. Moreover, AI integrated with robotic-assisted surgery brought a revolution to precision in surgical procedures and increased safety and effectiveness thereof. Big data analysis combined with AI holds considerable prospects in enhanced clinical decision-making, identification of trends, and forecasting disease outbreaks. Sensitive medical data should be private and secure, particularly when it involves AI healthcare systems. Wearables combined with AI, by continuously monitoring and managing personalized health through real-time feedback, could facilitate the possibility of early detection and intervention. In this respect, a balance between novelty, ethical considerations, and data protection will be the key that unlocks the full use of AI toward reshaping diagnosis, treatment planning, and robotic surgery for a more efficient and patient-centered healthcare future.

AI disclosure statement: The author acknowledges the use of AI-based tools for minor language editing or grammatical correction. However, all intellectual contributions, analyses, and conclusions presented in this chapter are entirely the author's own.

References

1. Cortes, C. and Vapnik, V., Support-Vector Network. 20, 273–297, 1995, https://doi.org/10.1007/BF00994018.
2. Martinez, A.M. and Kak, A.C., PCA versus LDA. *IEEE Trans. Pattern Anal. Mach. Intell.*, 23, 2, 228–233, 2001, https://doi: 10.1109/34.908974.
3. Jaiswal, S. and Pandey, M.K., Linear Discriminate Analysis based Robust Watermarking in DWT and LWT Domain with PCA based Statistical Feature Reduction. *Int. J. Image Graph. Signal Process. (IJIGSP)*, 15, 2, 73–88, 2023, https://doi.org/10.5815/ijigsp.2023.02.07.
4. Simon, H.S., *Neural networks: a comprehensive foundation*, Prentice Hall, 1999, ISBN 978-0-13-273350-2. OCLC 38908586.
5. Raina, R.M. and Andrew, N., Large-scale deep unsupervised learning using graphics processors. *ICML*, pp. 873–880, 2009, https//doi:10.1145/1553374.1553486.
6. Kher, H.R. and Thakar, V.K., Scale Invariant Feature Transform Based Image Matching and Registration. *Fifth International Conference on Signal and Image Processing*, Bangalore. India, pp. 50–55, 2014, https//doi:10.1109/ICSIP.2014.12.
7. Nguyen, T., Park, E.A., Han, J., Park, D.C., Min, S.Y., Object Detection Using Scale Invariant Feature Transform, in: *Genetic and Evolutionary Computing*, Advances in Intelligent Systems and Computing. vol. 238, J.S. Pan, P. Krömer, V. Snášel (Eds.), Springer, Cham, 2014, https://doi.org/10.1007/978-3-319-01796-9_7.
8. Bay, H., Tuytelaars, T., Van Gool, L., SURF: Speeded Up Robust Features, in: *Computer Vision – ECCV*, Lecture Notes in Computer Science. vol. 3951, Leonardis, A., Bischof, H., Pinz, A. (Eds.), 2006, https://doi.org/10.1007/11744023_32.

9. Labrín, C. and Urdinez, F., Principal component analysis, in: *R for Political Data Science*, pp. 375–393, Chapman and Hall/CRC, 2020.
10. Jaiswal, S. and Pandey, M.K., Robust digital image watermarking using LWT and Random-Subspace-1DLDA with PCA based statistical feature reduction. *Second International Conference on Computer Science, Engineering and Applications (ICCSEA)*, Gunupur, India, pp. 1–6, 2022, https//doi:10.1109/ICCSEA54677.2022.9936355.
11. Nadkarni, P.M., Machado, L.O., Chapman, W.W., Natural languagebprocessing: an introduction. *J. Am. Med. Inf. Assoc.*, 18, 5, 544–551, 2011, https://doi.org/10.1136/amiajnl-2011-000464.
12. Gulshan, V., Peng, L., Coram, M., Stumpe, M.C., Wu, D., Narayanaswamy, A., Venugopalan, S., Widner, K., Madams, T., Cuadros, J., Kim, R., Raman, R., Nelson, P.C., Mega, J.L., Webster, D.R., Development and Validation of a Deep Learning Algorithm for Detection of Diabetic Retinopathy in Retinal Fundus Photographs. *JAMA*, 316, 22, 2402–2410, 2016. htpps://doi:10.1001/jama.2016.17216.
13. Esteva, A., Kuprel, B., Novoa, R.A., Ko, J., Swetter, S.M., Blau, H.M., Thrun, S., Dermatologist-level classification of skin cancer with deep neural networks. *Nature*, 542, 7639, 115–118, 2017, https//doi:10.1038/nature21056.
14. Litjens, G., Kooi, T., Bejnordi, B.E., Setio, A.A.A., Ciompi, F., Ghafoorian, M., van der Laak, J.A.W.M., van Ginneken, B., Sánchez, C.I., A survey on deep learning in medical image analysis. *Med. Image Anal.*, 42, 60–88, 2017, https//doi:10.1016/j.media.2017.07.005.
15. Shen, D., Wu, G., Suk, H.I., Deep learning in medical image analysis. *Annu. Rev. Biomed. Eng.*, 19, 221–248, 2017.
16. Rajkomar, A., Oren, E., Chen, K., Dai, A.M., Hajaj, N., Hardt, M., Esteva, A., Scalable and accurate deep learning with electronic health records. *npj Digital Med.*, 1, 1, 1–10, 2018.
17. Liao, K.P. and Cai, T., Natural language processing in rheumatic diseases: using text mining to build knowledge and discover novel patterns. *Rheum. Dis. Clin.*, 46, 1, 1–20, 2020.
18. Kudyba, S. and Porter, P., The emerging role of artificial intelligence in health care: Will medical professionals be replaced? *Health Policy Technol.*, 8, 2, 198–206, 2019.
19. Golden, S.H. and Robinson, K.A., Using machine learning to improve clinical decision making: pitfalls and opportunities. *Curr. Diabetes Rep.*, 17, 12, 1–9, 2017.
20. Elmi-Terander, A., Skulason, H., Sánchez, I., Han, S., Darzi, A., Surgical robotics beyond enhanced dexterity instrumentation: a survey of machine learning techniques and their role in intelligent and autonomous surgical actions. *Int. J. Rob. Res.*, 38, 9, 987–1003, 2019.
21. Wagner, C.R., Stylopoulos, N., Jackson, P.G., Surgical robotics: systems applications and visions. *Int. J. Med. Rob. Comput. Assisted Surg.*, 14, 1, 1–18, 2018.

22. Bastani, H., Ghasemzadeh, H., Dutt, N., Machine learning for mental health: A review, in: *Proceedings of the 24th ACM SIGKDD International Conference on Knowledge Discovery & Data Mining*, pp. 2297–2306, 2018.
23. Susanto, A.P., Winarto, H., Fahira, A., Abdurrohman, H., Muharram, A.P., Widitha, R.U., Efirianti, G.E.W., George, Y.A.E., Tjoa, K., Building an artificial intelligence-powered medical image recognition smartphone application: What medical practitioners need to know. *Inf. Med. Unlocked*, 32, 101017, 2022, ISSN 2352- 9148, https://doi.org/10.1016/j.imu.2022.101017.
24. Hunt, B., Ruiz, A., Pogue, B., Smartphone-based imaging systems for medical applications: a critical review. *J. Biomed. Opt.*, 26, 4, 040902, 2021, doi: 10.1117/1.JBO.26.4.040902.
25. Zhou, B., Yang, G., Shi, Z., Ma, S., Natural Language Processing for Smart Healthcare. *IEEE Rev. Biomed. Eng.*, 1–17, 2022, Institute of Electrical and Electronics Engineers (IEEE). https://doi 10.1109/rbme.2022.3210270.
26. Uddin, Y., Nair, A., Shariq, S., Hannan, S.H., Transforming primary healthcare through natural language processing and big data analytics. *BMJ*, 381–948, 2023, https://doi: 10.1136/bmj.p948.
27. Berros, N., El Mendili, F., Filaly, Y., El Bouzekri El Idrissi, Y., Enhancing Digital Health Services with Big Data Analytics. *Big Data Cogn. Comput.*, 7, 2, 2023, https://doi.org/10.3390/bdcc7020064.
28. Cresswell, K., Callaghan, M., Khan, S., Sheikh, Z., Mozaffar, H., Sheikh, A., Investigating the use of data-driven artificial intelligence in computerised decision support systems for health and social care: A systematic review. *Health Inf. J.*, 26, 3, 2138–2147, 2020 Sep, doi: 10.1177/1460458219900452.
29. Moazemi, S., Vahdati, S., Li, J., Kalkhoff, S., Castano, L.J.V., Dewitz, B., Bibo, R., Sabouniaghdam, P., Tootooni, M.S., Bundschuh, R.A., Lichtenberg, A., Aubin, H., Schmid, F., Artificial intelligence for clinical decision support for monitoring patients in cardiovascular ICUs: A systematic review. *Front. Med. (Lausanne)*, 10, 1109411, 2023, https://doi: 10.3389/fmed.2023.1109411.
30. Palanisamy, P., Urooj, S., Arunachalam, R., Lay-Ekuakille, A., A Novel Prognostic Model Using Chaotic CNN with Hybridized Spoofing for Enhancing Diagnostic Accuracy in Epileptic Seizure Prediction. *Diagnostics*, 13, 21, 3382, 2023.
31. Moglia, A., Georgiou, K., Georgiou, E., Satava, R.M., Cuschieri, A., A systematic review on artificial intelligence in robot-assisted surgery. *Int. J. Surg.*, 95, 106151, 2021, ISSN 1743-9191, https://doi.org/10.1016/j.ijsu.2021.106151.
32. Jaiswal, S. and Gupta, P., GLSTM: A novel approach for prediction of real & synthetic PID diabetes data using GANs and LSTM classification model. *Int. J. Exp. Res. Rev.*, 30, 32–45, 2023, https://doi.org/10.52756/ijerr.2023.v30.004.
33. Klodmann, J., Schlenk, C., Hellings-Kuß, A., *et al.*, An Introduction to Robotically Assisted Surgical Systems: Current Developments and Focus Areas of Research. *Curr. Robot. Rep.*, 2, 321–332, 2021, https://doi.org/10.1007/s43154-021-00064-3.
34. Bussel, M.J.P., Schröder, O., G.J., Ou, C., *et al.*, Analyzing the determinants to accept a virtual assistant and use cases among cancer patients: a mixed

methods study. *BMC Health Serv. Res.*, 22, 890, 2022, https://doi.org/10.1186/s12913-022-08189-7.

35. Swapna, M., Viswanadhula, U.M., Aluvalu, R., Vardharajan, V., Kotecha, K., Bio-Signals in Medical Applications and Challenges Using Artificial Intelligence. *J. Sens. Actuator Netw.*, 11, 1, 17, 2022, https://doi.org/10.3390/jsan11010017.
36. Tang, Z., Hu, H., Xu, C., Zhao, K., Exploring an Efficient Remote Biomedical Signal Monitoring Framework for Personal Health in the COVID-19 Pandemic. *Int. J. Environ. Res. Public Health*, 18, 17, 9037, 2021, https//doi:10.3390/ijerph18179037.
37. Dey, N. and Rajinikanth, V., Abnormality detection in heart MRI with spotted hyena algorithm-supported Kapur/Otsu thresholding and level set segmentation, in: *Primers in Biomedical Imaging Devices and Systems, Magnetic Resonance Imaging*, pp. 105–126, Academic Press, 2022, ISBN 9780128234013, https://doi.org/10.1016/B978-0-12- 823401-3.00006-7.
38. Patil, S., Darji, J., Hingu, S., Thakkar, A., Medic: Smart Healthcare AI Assistant. *Proceedings of the International Conference on Smart Data Intelligence (ICSMDI 2021)*, May 24, 2021, Available at SSRN: https://ssrn.com/abstract=3852150 or ://dx.doi.org/10.2139/ssrn.3852150.
39. Yoon, D., Jang, J.H., Choi, B.J., Kim, T.Y., Han, C.H., Discovering hidden information in biosignals from patients using artificial intelligence. *Korean J. Anesthesiol.*, 73, 4, 275–284, 2020, https//doi:10.4097/kja.19475.
40. Saravanan, T., Radha, N., Sarmiladevi, N., Preethi, P., Deployment of IOT-enabled sensing devices for real time forest fire prediction system using boundary constrained CNN model. *Ann. For. Res.*, 67, 1, 418–436.
41. Kumar, A.D., Nidhya, R., Hanah Ayisha, V., Manokar, V., Manokar, N.V., Identification of Abdominal Aorta Aneurysm Using Ant Colony Optimization Algorithm, in: *ICT and Critical Infrastructure: Proceedings of the 48th Annual Convention of Computer Society of India*, Vol I. Advances in Intelligent Systems and Computing, vol. 248 Springer, Cham, 2014.
42. Aggarwal, R., Sounderajah, V., Martin, G., Ting, D.S.W., Karthikesalingam, A., King, D., *et al.*, Diagnostic accuracy of deep learning in medical imaging: a systematic review and meta-analysis. *npj Digital Med.*, 4, 1, 65, 2021.
43. Han, J., Davids, J., Ashrafian, H., Darzi, A., Elson, D.S., Sodergren, M., A systematic review of robotic surgery: from supervised paradigms to fully autonomous robotic approaches. *Int. J. Med. Robot.*, 18, 2, e2358, 2022.
44. Naik, R., Kogkas, A., Ashrafian, H., Mylonas, G., Darzi, A., The measurement of cognitive workload in surgery using pupil metrics: a systematic review and narrative analysis. *J. Surg. Res.*, 280, 258–72, 2022.
45. Tan, A., Ashrafian, H., Scott, A.J., Mason, S.E., Harling, L., Athanasiou, T., *et al.*, Robotic surgery: disruptive innovation or unfulfilled promise? A systematic review and metaanalysis of the first 30 years. *Surg. Endosc.*, 30, 10, 4330–52, 2016.

46. Nazarian, S., Glover, B., Ashrafian, H., Darzi, A., Teare, J., Diagnostic accuracy of artificial intelligence and computer-aided diagnosis for the detection and characterization of colorectal polyps: systematic review and meta-analysis. *J. Med. Internet Res.*, 23, 7, e27370, 2021.
47. Lin, J.S., Perdue, L.A., Henrikson, N.B., Bean, S.I., Blasi, P.R., Screening for colorectal cancer: updated evidence report and systematic review for the US preventive services task force. *JAMA*, 325, 19, 1978–98, 2021.
48. Kulurkar, P., Kumar Dixit, C., Bharathi, V.C., Monikavishnuvarthini, A., Dhakne, A., Preethi, P., AI based elderly fall prediction system using wearable sensors: A smart home-care technology with IOT. *Meas.: Sens.*, 25, 100614, 2023.
49. Asokan, R. and Preethi, P., Deep learning with conceptual view in meta data for content categorization, in: *Deep Learning Applications and Intelligent Decision Making in Engineering*, pp. 176–191, IGI global, 2021.
50. Palanisamy, P., Padmanabhan, A., Ramasamy, A., Subramaniam, S., Remote patient activity monitoring system by integrating IoT sensors and artificial intelligence techniques. *Sensors*, 23, 13, 5869, 2023.
51. Nidhya, R., Kumar, M., Maheswar, R., Pavithra, D., Security and Privacy Issues in Smart Healthcare System Using Internet of Things, in: *IoT-enabled Smart Healthcare Systems, Services and Applications*, pp. 63–85, Wiley, 2022, doi: 10.1002/9781119816829.ch4.

Index

Printed and bound by CPI Group (UK) Ltd, Croydon, CR0 4YY
15/09/2026
14962411-0006